ANTHROPOLOGICAL CONSIDERATIONS OF PRODUCTION, EXCHANGE, VENDING AND TOURISM

RESEARCH IN ECONOMIC ANTHROPOLOGY

Series Editor: Donald C. Wood

Recent Volumes:

Volume 26: The Economics of Health and Wellness: Anthropological Perspectives – Edited by D. Wood

Volume 27: Dimension of Ritual Economy – Edited by P. McAnany & E. C. Wells

Volume 28: Hidden Hands in the Market: Ethnographies of Fair Trade, Ethical Consumption and Corporate Social Responsibility – Edited by Donald Wood, Jeffrey Pratt, Peter Luetchford, Geert De Neve

Volume 29: Economic Development, Integration, and Morality in Asia and the Americas – Edited by Donald C. Wood

Volume 30: Economic Action in Theory and Practice: Anthropological Investigations – Edited by Donald C. Wood

Volume 31: The Economics of Religion: Anthropological Approaches – Edited by Lionel Obadia & Donald C. Wood

Volume 32: Political Economy, Neoliberalism, and the Prehistoric Economies of Latin America – Edited by Donald C. Wood and Ty Matejowsky

Volume 33: Engaging with Capitalism: Cases from Oceania – Edited by Fiona McCormack and Kate Barclay

Volume 34: Production, consumption, business and the economy: Structural ideals and moral realities – Edited by Donald C. Wood

Volume 35: Climate change, culture, and economics – Edited by Donald C. Wood

Volume 36: The Economics of Ecology, Exchange, and Adaptation: Anthropological Explorations – Edited by Donald C. Wood

RESEARCH IN ECONOMIC ANTHROPOLOGY VOLUME 37

ANTHROPOLOGICAL CONSIDERATIONS OF PRODUCTION, EXCHANGE, VENDING AND TOURISM

EDITED BY

DONALD C. WOOD

Department of Medical Education,
Akita University Graduate School of Medicine,
Akita, Japan

emerald PUBLISHING

United Kingdom – North America – Japan
India – Malaysia – China

Emerald Publishing Limited
Howard House, Wagon Lane, Bingley BD16 1WA, UK

First edition 2017

British Library Cataloguing in Publication Data
A catalogue record for this book is available from the British Library

ISBN: 978-1-78743-195-9 (Print)
ISBN: 978-1-78743-194-2 (Online)
ISBN: 978-1-78743-240-6 (Epub)

ISSN: 0190-1281 (Series)

Printed and bound by CPI Group (UK) Ltd, Croydon, CR0 4YY

ISOQAR certified Management System, awarded to Emerald for adherence to Environmental standard ISO 14001:2004.

ISOQAR REGISTERED
Certificate Number 1985
ISO 14001

INVESTOR IN PEOPLE

CONTENTS

LIST OF CONTRIBUTORS

Lisa Marie Beiswenger	Department of Anthropology, The Ohio State University, Columbus, OH, USA
Riddhi Bhandari	Department of Anthropology, The American University, Washington DC, USA
Jeffrey H. Cohen	Department of Anthropology, The Ohio State University, Columbus, OH, USA
Hongyang Di	Department of Agricultural Economics, Texas A&M University, College Station, TX, USA
Edwins Laban Moogi Gwako	Department of Sociology and Anthropology, Guilford College, Greensboro, NC, USA
John S. Henderson	Department of Anthropology, Cornell University, Ithaca, NY, USA
Kathryn M. Hudson	Department of Anthropology and Department of Linguistics, University at Buffalo, Buffalo, NY, USA
Lauren C. Johnson	College of Education, University of North Georgia, Dahlonega, GA, USA
Rodolfo Maggio	Department of Psychiatry, The Warneford Hospital, University of Oxford, UK
Deborah Sick	School of Sociological & Anthropological Studies, University of Ottawa, Ottawa, ON, Canada
Serge Svizzero	Faculté de Droit et d'Economie, Université de La Réunion, Reunion Island, France
Tamar Diana Wilson	Independent Researcher, Los Cabos, Mexico

Donald C. Wood Department of Medical Education, Akita University Graduate School of Medicine, Akita, Japan

Shuru Zhong Department of Anthropology, Texas A&M University, College Station, TX, USA

Laurel Zwissler Philosophy and Religion Department, Central Michigan University, Mt. Pleasant, MI, USA

EDITORIAL ADVISORY BOARD

INTRODUCTION: PRODUCTION, EXCHANGE, VENDING, AND TOURISM

Volume 37 of *Research in Economic Anthropology* consists of four different sections, each reflecting one thematic element of the volume's title: production, exchange, vending, and tourism. Eleven original articles, each of which passed a rigorous peer review, fill the pages of the volume. Indeed, without the generous assistance of many anonymous referees (busy researchers themselves) *REA* would not have been able to reach the age of 39. Nor would it have the reputation for quality articles in (and relating to) economic anthropology that it has today. Therefore, before introducing this volume I would like to thank the 81 researchers who kindly served as referees for volumes 34, 35, and 36.

In alphabetical order, they are: Dave Abler, Galit Ailon, Maria De Lourdes Alcantara, Stephen Aldrich, Aaron Ansell, Greg Bankoff, Peggy Barlett, Jessica Barnes, Christine Beitl, Lucas Bessire, Caroline Brettell, Jorge Carrillo, Janice Chernela, Andrew Chesnut, Joon Nak Choi, Edward Chuma, Martha Angeles Constantino, Erin Coughlan, Michael Cusumano, Geert De Neve, Cheryl Doss, Malcolm Dow, Rohan D'Souza, Thomas Dunk, Gary Feinman, Edward Fischer, James Fisher, Wiebke Foerch, William Garriott, Kathryn Goldfarb, Andres Gramajo, David Groenfeldt, Michelle Hegmon, Stefanie Herrmann, Lee Hoffer, Carter Hunt, Jerry Jacka, Ulrich Jürgens, Alice Kehoe, Henry Kinnucan, Gina Koczberski, Peter Konijn, Rena Lederman, Carolyn Lesorogol, Jerome Levi, Claire Loussouarn, Sarah Mars, Robert Marzec, Hirokazu Miyazaki, Brian Moeran, Kim Møller, Daniel Murphy, Benjamin Orlove, Tommaso Pardi, Kyeyoung Park, Angus Phillips, Aaron Pitluck, Christine Quittkat, Annika Rabo, Anthony Rausch, Maureen Reed, John Renshaw, Susan Russell, Beken Saatçioğlu, Ikuya Sato, Bettina Schmidt, Mallika Shakya, Robert Shepherd, Brian Silverstein, Patricia Sloan-White, Alex Stewart, David Stoll, Amy Todd, Dan van der Horst, Soumhya Venkatesan, Casey Walsh, Travis Wendel, Bruce Whitehouse, Tanja Winther, Emily Yeh, and Christian Zlolniski.

Part I of this volume, which focuses on production, is comprised of three chapters. In the first, Edwins Gwako examines the (illegal) culture of home-brewing, and selling, of beer among Maragoli women (and its consumption by men) in western Kenya. Importantly, through a quantitative survey approach backed by ethnographic data, he looks beyond the many obvious negative facets of this deeply embedded practice in an attempt to better understand women's incentives for engaging in the production of such homemade beverages (which often contain highly questionable ingredients). Although it might seem that women brewers are perpetuating their own persecution by creating substances that tend to promote acts of violence against them, they appear as rational actors who are actively working to escape from poverty while seeking empowerment and protection from persecution and violence for themselves and their children. Gwako's findings call for increased social and legal protection for the women of the society.

Next, Deborah Sick reports on some discoveries from her own long-term ethnographic research on smallholder farmers in a rural part of Costa Rica. She finds that, although such small-scale producers have often been considered "problematic" by planners and "destined for extinction" by many others, producers in her research area have demonstrated a surprising degree of resilience, achieved partly through diversification strategies. The main crop of concern here is coffee, which, like the homemade alcohol churned out by the women subjects of the previous chapter, has had a variety of effects on the producers' lives. Interestingly, the recent income diversification that Sick finds is marked not by an increase in migration but by a decrease. Overall, regional pull factors emerge as the primary forces behind the changes that Sick identifies here. Rounding out the first part of this volume is Serge Svizzero's analysis of the prehistoric transitions to agriculture that ultimately gave rise to the smallholder production (indeed, all farm production) that was the focus of the preceding chapter. Like Sick's chapter, the focus here is on pull factors – those that compelled people to start to settle down and grow their own food. Notably, Svizzero argues against a push–pull model dichotomy, and for his hypothesis that the transitions to agriculture that marked the Neolithic Revolution are most likely to have occurred among complex hunter–gatherer societies occupying fertile, plentiful terrains.

The second part of this volume concentrates on exchange – a theme that actually applies in one way or another to most of the chapters in the collection. However, exchange is at the center of consideration for the authors of the four chapters here. Like the chapter that served to close Part I, the first chapter is an archaeological study. In it, Kathryn Hudson and John Henderson examine relationships between long-distance trade and centralized political organization in pre-Columbian American societies, arguing that the former was able to thrive in the absence of the latter in multiple instances over a very large span of time and distance. Theirs is, in part, an effort to move research on ancient American societies further away from lingering influences of Karl Polanyi and his associates on the field – specifically, from a focus on states and related institutions and toward greater illumination of the peculiar features of individual economies.

The next two chapters of this part of the volume share a concern with the elucidation of a specific market. The first, authored by Laurel Zwissler and grounded in ethnographic fieldwork conducted in Toronto and Pennsylvania, takes a critical look at fair-trade retailer Ten Thousand Villages and seeks to understand a clash of value systems which would seem to be inherent in any business that is built upon concepts of benevolence, assistance, and mutual aid. The chapter brings to mind volume 28 of *REA*, which was very much concerned with fair trade. Here, Zwissler explores a "middle ground" between producers and buyers – the shop floor, where employees struggle to sell goods in a "fair" manner. Dilemmas (i.e., fairness vs. profits) abound, and call for constant negotiation (and re-negotiation). Next, Lisa Beiswenger and Jeff Cohen take a close look at a more bounded, more easily-defined market – one that occupies a specific physical space: North Market in Columbus, Ohio. Combining qualitative and quantitative analysis, they explore the functions of this marketplace, which of course include provisioning. However, there is so much more. Beiswenger and Cohen's chapter shows one example of how public markets in the United States are adapting to suit the times and survive amidst the expansion of national chains by going far beyond the limitations of their original purpose.

In the final chapter of Part II, Rodolfo Maggio explores balancing acts in a suburb of Honiara, Solomon Islands – not circus tricks or street performances, but individual navigations between social relations and market transactions amidst conditions of scarcity. These transactions, as Maggio shows, are not only capable of damaging social (including kin) ties, but also can create new ties and relationships. What happens in Honiara household trade stores, especially regarding *kaon*, seems worthy of much greater attention.

Part III focuses on vendors and their activities – a topic that has been taken up in the pages of *REA* a number of times in the past. First, Shuru Zhong and Hongyang Di take a close look at street vendors in the city of Sanya, southern China (on Hainan Island). Despite Sanya's geographic distance from China's capital, the impacts of government policy are unmistakable here – vendors were unwelcome during the socialist era because of the capitalist undertones of their activities, and they are still persecuted today because of social stigmas and the idea that they are not "modern." Yet, they persist for a variety of reasons. Zhong and Di's research helps us to understand why this is true. Policymakers would be wise to pay more attention to their findings if they truly want to improve life for all residents of Sanya and so many other such cities of the world. The second chapter here, by Tamar Wilson, focuses on different vendors in a very different environment – Cabo San Lucas, Mexico, at the southern tip of Baja California. Once again, we meet vendors who have been very much at the mercy of state policy; many of the actors in Wilson's study were pushed out of agriculture due to Mexico's involvement in international trade agreements such as NAFTA, environmental degradation (that might have been prevented by better regulation), and a general lack of public support for peasants. The resilience of these vendors, most of whom apparently wanted to return to farming if possible, is another common theme between this and the preceding chapter. Again, policymakers are advised to pay more attention to Wilson's research, and to others like it.

Part IV wraps up this volume with two investigations of tourism situations. First, Riddhi Bhandari looks at tourism in Agra, India, which feeds voraciously on cash brought in by millions of people who flock there annually to view the Taj Mahal. She traces commercial relationships between capitalists and tour guides which also envelop tourists and which are full of risk but loaded with opportunity at the same time. Debt is managed in ways that are designed to keep the guides under control, but this is hard to achieve. A fine line – one between securing tourists' business and angering them – must be walked in this complicated network of relationships. Next, Lauren Johnson investigates the impacts of female sex tourism in Jamaica, a country marked by high levels of economic dependence on tourism and of unemployment. This, added to Jamaica's proximity to the United States and several other wealthy countries, makes for a situation loaded with opportunities but also with considerable risk. Men involved in this relatively un-stigmatized trade can earn much through their resilience, but they take the chance of viral (and other) infections – including HIV. It goes without saying that the state has tried to address these problems, but at the same time Jamaica needs tourism, and so it cannot risk hampering the industry. It is hoped that Johnson's ethnographic exploration of the situation will at least help guide local initiatives to improve the situation.

In sum, volume 37 of *REA* continues the series' nearly four-decade-long quest to shed light on the intersections of culture/society and economy – simply put, to better understand, anthropologically, human economic behavior – through investigations of the four key themes of production, exchange, vending, and tourism. The next two volumes of *REA*, which are intended to focus on morality in price-setting and on vulnerability, will likely both be published during its 40th anniversary year. Looking beyond, the series will continue seeking new ground for anthropological exploration. As editor, I would like to once again thank all the busy researchers who gave their precious time to serve as anonymous referees, and also those who have contributed articles to the series, for *REA* would not be what it is today without their efforts.

Donald C. Wood
Editor

PART I
PRODUCTION

CULTURAL ECONOMICS AND RAMIFICATIONS OF HOME-BREWING, SELLING AND CONSUMPTION OF ALCOHOL AMONG THE MARAGOLI OF WESTERN KENYA

Edwins Laban Moogi Gwako

ABSTRACT

Purpose – *This longitudinally informed ethnographic work explores the interlocking socioeconomic and cultural roles, changes as well as effects of home-brewed alcoholic beverages in Maragoli society of western Kenya. The informants' emic perspectives enhance existing knowledge and understanding of the commodification of home-brewing of alcohol. The participants' experientially anchored views provide refined insights into how home-brews are influenced by the disintegration of livelihoods and women brewers' need to earn money independently from men's income to meet their financial needs. This work also documents alcohol-related maladaptive aspects including men's misappropriation of funds, malnutrition, domestic violence, sexual promiscuity, rape, prostitution, and disposal of agricultural inputs and produce to obtain money to buy brews.*

Anthropological Considerations of Production, Exchange, Vending and Tourism
Research in Economic Anthropology, Volume 37, 3–32

ISSN: 0190-1281/doi:10.1108/S0190-128120170000037002

Methodology/approach – *This study used a combination of qualitative and quantitative research methods to enhance data quality, validity, reliability, and deep learning of the dynamics and ramifications of home-brewing of alcoholic products.*

Findings – *This study's empirical results show Maragoli brewers' ingenuity in their risk-aversive efforts to: (1) optimize positive benefits and (2) reduce the unintended maladaptive consequences of home-brews.*

Practical implications – *This work demonstrates that brewers are not passive victims of their productive resource constraints. They exercise ingenuity in producing and selling alcoholic beverages to earn a living even though this venture generates unintended harmful outcomes. This calls for interventions by governmental arms, nongovernmental organizations, and community-based support networks to empower brewers and their clientele to venture into alternative enterprises and consumption of less harmful refreshments. Safety-nets should also be in place to minimize vulnerability and social fragmentation attributable to home-brewed alcohol.*

Keywords: Maragoli; ramifications of home-brews; gender roles; women's ingenuity; risk-aversive; Kenya

INTRODUCTION

The brewing of indigenous beer in African societies, fermented mostly from sorghum or millet, was once local but is increasingly big business (Ross, 2013). BBC News (2005) highlights that local brews can provide much-needed money for poor families in Africa. The work of Maoura and Pourquie (2009) documents the nutritional value and impact upon human health. The commodification of home-brews in Africa recirculates wealth from men consumers to women brewers (Colson & Scudder, 1988; Dancause, Akol, & Gray, 2010; Dietler, 2006). Maula (1997) and Dancause et al. (2010, p. 1124) assert that "women adopt beer sales in response both to the appeal of participating in a business venture ('pull' factors) as well as to social or environmental pressures that necessitate earning extra income ('push' factors)."

Heath (1987) argues that "anthropological data, methods, and concepts have contributed significantly over many years to our understanding of the interactions between alcohol and the human animal" (p. 99). The production and use of home-brewed alcoholic beverages have received significant attention from sociocultural anthropologists (Carlson, 1990, 1992; Dancause et al., 2010; Dietler, 2006; Holtzman, 2001; Karp, 1980; Kutalek, 2011; McAllister, 2003; Myhre, 2015; Netting, 1964; Roberts, 2000; Sangree, 1962; Subbo, 2001; Suggs, 1996;

Willis, 2001, 2002, 2010). In many societies in Kenya, "beer was brewed for community celebrations and rituals, and on occasion people got drunk, but not as an end in itself or to forget the pressures of daily life" (Sobania, 2003, p. 8). Alcohol brewing and consumption is measure that has been adopted by individuals in the face of collapsing livelihoods and, especially, women's need to earn money independently from male income (Amuyunzu-Nyamongo & Francis, 2006; Kutalek, 2011; Verma, 2001).

Among the Maragoli, *amatwa* (home-brewed beer also called *amalwa* in the larger Luyia subethnic groups) is one of the diverse income-generating activities in which women engage in order to meet their monetary requirements (Verma, 2001). However, a strong patrilineal structure limits the independence and enterprise of women in this society (Weisner & Abbott, 1977). Evidence suggests a relationship between alcohol and violence, and even documents that alcohol plays a role in causing violent and aggressive responses (Mutongi, 2007, p. 114; Parker & McCaffree, 2013).

The longitudinal ethnographic data collected from the Maragoli is used to examine how brewing, selling, consumption, and availability of beer influence people's daily lives and endeavors. The chapter's emphasis is on the lived and observed experiences of the study participants pertaining to beer activities, behaviors, ramifications, and multilayered strategies that are employed to minimize detrimental effects of beer consumption. In this regard, this study presents a historical and cultural background on the nature of indigenous use of beer as a prelude to gaining a contextualized understanding of multiple dimensions of alcohol brewing among the Maragoli.

BEER BREWING IN THE INDIGENOUS MARAGOLI SOCIETY

Several studies have explored the brewing and use of home-brews in Kenya (Ambler, 1988, 1991; Amuyunzu-Nyamongo & Francis, 2006; Bradley, 1995; Holtzman, 2001; Karp, 1978, 1980; Kilbride & Kilbride, 1990; Levine & Levine, 1977; Levine et al., 1994; Levine, 1982; Orvis, 1997; Osogo, 1966; Roberts, 2000; Sangree, 1962; Sobania, 2003; Subbo, 2001; Wagner, 1949). Ambler (1991) found that "No child was initiated, no marriage was arranged, no planting or harvesting begun, no important case decided without preparation, consumption or offering beer" (p. 166). Home-brewed beer was/is made from maize, millet, or sorghum and virtually any fruit, grain, or vegetable, which will ferment can be transformed into an alcoholic beverage. Tiriki women brewed beer for their menfolk's beer parties, which were an integral part of initiated male sociability, and also of the initiation feasts. The women, however, were never included in the parties (Sangree, 1965).

Beer dominated every social aspect of the indigenous Maragoli way of life. Beer was not simply brewed for commercial purposes. Women brewed maize, millet, and sorghum beer and prepared locally distilled liquor by the natural process of fermentation (Were & Wilson, 1987). Heath (1987) notes that the act of brewing and actual use of local brew symbolized an enormous range of things among the Maragoli. The brewing and drinking of home-made beer had social and ritual relevance which Karp (1980) calls "the role of beer as a mediating symbol" (p. 116). Such a role included various occasions for observing ancestral cults involving supplications and offerings. Occasions for ritual undertakings were very important and all initiated adults were required to participate and to refrain from working in their gardens during the ritual period (Wagner, 1955, pp. 52–53).

Ancestors in Kenyan societies were not worshipped, but they were revered and understood as being able to play an active part in everyday lives of the living (Sobania, 2003). Maragoli people congregated at Mung'oma caves to observe *ovwali* (ritual fire in Maragoli) ceremony twice a year to seek blessings of their ancestors in agricultural activities (Bulimo, 2013). Regular offerings of gifts, libations, and sacrifices were conducted at three levels, namely, family, clan, and locality (society); each homestead had a small hut for these observances. Special ancestral stones were placed inside the hut, and before any beer was drunk in the homestead a little of it was poured on those stones and whenever they made a sacrifice some blood was sprinkled on those stones (Osogo, 1966, p. 143; Sangree, 1962; Sobania, 2003, pp. 34–35). This was important because it was believed that the *ekigingi* (spirits of the family ancestors) needed this food to eat, and would be displeased if not remembered on these special religious occasions. Kilbride and Kilbride (1990) observe that among the Luyia, ancestors, or spirits of the dead people are thought to play a significant role among the living. The *ekigingi* (spirits of the dead) provide warnings, often through dreams, about the proper course of action to avoid difficulty or to endure laborious activities, such as farming (Kilbride & Kilbride, 1990).

In the indigenous Maragoli society, brewing and use of beer was entrenched in religious, social, economic, and political rationalizations. For example, libations and sacrifices affirmed the continuity of the line of descent and ensured the ancestors' support, protection, and spiritual potency, optimized productivity of diverse resources, and fundamentally, the health of the family, and the fertility of the wife or wives (Bulimo, 2013; Carlson, 1990; Were & Wilson, 1987). The Maragoli had a "habit of making sacrifices to ancestors in the event of illness" (Mutongi, 2007, p. 49). Before anyone partook of the first alcohol brewed from the new crop, an alcohol pot of the spirits was placed at the *siro* (king post) of the hut for an overnight stay to receive ancestral blessings (Bulimo, 2013). As Carlson (1990) observes, "... offerings and sacrifices presented to ancestors or gods is a means of recognizing their nearness and expressing the interdependence between two domains that are separated by a maximal status of difference" (p. 307).

Although beer was used to mediate between the spheres of the people's everyday life and the ancestral world, excessive drunkenness, violence, and destructiveness were never tolerated by the Maragoli; in fact, they even condemned such behavior. Moreover, such socially unacceptable behavior annoyed other well-behaved elders, and, in most cases, often resulting in the casting of curses upon ill-behaved persons. Thus, the Maragoli had societal morals and ethics which regulated drinking. The youth were not allowed to drink, as they were expected to herd livestock and continue training as soldiers to protect their society against external aggression (Were & Wilson, 1987, p. 51). Young married men who had no initiated children were only passively allowed to consume beer because drinking was considered the preserve of the elders.

Home-made beer was consumed during negotiations between clans for exchange of bride wealth to formalize marriages with the import of sanctifying the "new bond between families and lineages" (Ambler, 1991, p. 166). In this regard, the consumption of beer "gave symbolic weight to such deliberations" (Ambler, 1991, p. 166), which included, but not limited to, arbitrating, or resolving disputes (peacemaking ceremonies), making decisions pertaining to land, property damage, delinquent bride wealth payments, divorce settlements, assault, warfare, adultery, rape, incest, premarital pregnancy, and lifting curses. Typically, the spilling of a little beer occurred at the beginning of an assembly of elders who convened together to discuss community events and issues. Occasional invitations of Maragoli age-mates for a beer party provided opportunities to consume large quantities of home-brews. These instances reflected the household heads' organizational abilities to access and accumulate enormous amounts of ingredients and mobilize labor required to prepare large volumes of beer. Consumption was very often a male activity that brought together elders and other-initiated men who ate food and imbibed as neighbors from a single beer pot using special *zinjeke* (long straws) made from climber shrubs that grew naturally in the bushes. This display of wealth earned men considerable social respect in society.

Brewing and drinking of beer was used to mobilize work parties to complete specific agricultural or house building tasks, as a refreshment, or as opportunities for village elders to relax, after performing responsibilities bestowed upon them by their society (Levine, 1962; Orvis, 1997; Sangree, 1962; Subbo, 2001). Beer parties marked the completion of the grass thatching of a new house, agricultural task; housewarming parties were held before moving into a new homestead. Such occasions involved the sprinkling of beer across the compound to honor and welcome the presence of the ancestors into the new home while at the same time imploring them to bless the new residence.

Beer consumption was also integral to the welcoming, blessing, and naming of newborn members of society and their initiation into full adult status through circumcision (Osogo, 1966). A child was given an ancestral name during the first ancestral offering (Bulimo, 2013). Olenyo (2011) observes that "Nearly all Lulogooli [Maragoli] personal names have a denotative meaning.

The naming of the children and members of the community is therefore an important occasion, which is often marked by ceremonies in the community" (p. 212). Some names were gradually rejected because their holders had "been associated with societal vices such as: murder, suicide, drunkardness, divorce, alcoholism, robbery and so on" (Olenyo, 2011, p. 216).

Alcohol was also used during burials and other ritualistic ceremonies. Provision of beer to men digging a grave sustained their morale, work ethic, and teamwork (Kilbride & Kilbride, 1990). A significant percentage of mourners also consumed locally brewed beer and, thereafter, danced and threw their shoulders about to allay the grief of the parents and soothe the spirits of the buried member of the society (Osogo, 1966). Sangree (1962) writes that "when a man of property dies, a beer-drinking post-funeral meeting of the lineage and neighborhood was held to honor his memory and settle his estate" (p. 12). Thus, brewing and consumption of beer was a core aspect of the Luyia subethnic groups. The subsequent discussion focuses on the demographic and socioeconomic description of the Maragoli research setting.

STUDY SITE DESCRIPTION, RESEARCH APPROACH, AND METHODS

This chapter draws on a longitudinal ethnographic fieldwork among the Maragoli of western Kenya from July 1995 through December 1996, and July to December 2007. The Maragoli are "horticulturalists who intercrop a variety of grains, trees, roots and vegetables, and who keep some cattle for milk, meat, and bride wealth" (Bradley, 1995, p. 161). High population density and declining land holdings have forced many Maragoli off the land in search of better economic fortunes (Gwako, 2014).

The researcher contacted the administrative officers in the area to obtain basic background information necessary for identifying a research site with representative characteristics of western Kenya, and to enlist their support in compiling a sampling frame of all households in the area. Thereafter, random sampling techniques were used to draw a random sample for detailed investigation of the production, use, and ramifications of home-brews.

Questions pertaining to brewing and drinking of beer were asked to only 53 households with confirmed history of indulgence in production, sell, and/or consumption of home-brewed beer. A total of 23 households, which engaged in brewing beer for commercial purposes, were subjected to in-depth interviews. The research team also conducted focus group discussions with four active women's groups in the area. Thirty-four key informants provided more data on the dynamics of home-brews in their society.

Multiple data collection methods were employed to enhance holistic deep learning and understanding of home-brew dynamics by adding layers of information and using one type of data to validate or refine another (Reinharz, 1992). These methods included participant observation, detached observation, close- and open-ended standard questionnaire interviews, focus group discussions, and key informant interviews. Survey questionnaires were designed, pretested, and revised to improve reliability and validity (King, Keohane, & Verba, 1994; Kirk & Miller, 1986).

Qualitative data were obtained from focus group discussions with members of four active women's groups, in-depth interviews with elderly cultural experts, and participant observations. Focus group discussions were used as a friendly and respectful research method to obtain qualitative data and to engage discussants in debates on sensitive issues, such as rape, domestic violence, and decision-making processes (Morgan & Krueger, 1993). More data were compiled from archival documents, participant and detached observation in dispute resolution meetings, weddings, child naming rituals, circumcision ceremonies, and funeral rites. These culturally contextualized events yielded data and availed numerous opportunities for witnessing the unfolding of multidimensional and interlocking ramifications of home-brews. The results of this study are presented and discussed in the subsequent parts of this chapter.

BREWING AND CONSUMPTION OF BEER IN CONTEMPORARY MARAGOLI SOCIETY

The results of this study confirm widespread brewing and consumption of beer in the study area. As shown in Table 1, there are persisting and emerging new trends in the production and use of beer among the Maragoli. The percentages in Table 1 and in all subsequent tables were calculated from a sample size of 76 women interviewees who provided multiple responses to open-ended questions. The results of this study indicate Maragoli people's continued use of beer to initiate, discuss, and formalize marriage arrangements in their social world. Nearly 97 percent of the study participants reported this persisting use of home-brews as a typical behavior among elderly male members of the society involved in marriage deliberations. They drink beer to cool off after heated bride wealth payment negotiations. Elders involved in such negotiations take intermittent breaks to drink beer to rethink serious issues raised in their deliberations. Data obtained from in-depth interviews affirmed that intermittent breaks in marriage negotiations are used to reevaluate the broad implications of the conclusions of the deliberations on the parents, extended families, and individuals getting married.

Beer plays a significant role in Maragoli funeral rites. It is consumed after an individual is pronounced dead and during the mourning period. This was reported to be the case by about 93 percent of the interviewees who indicated that the elderly men who convened in the homesteads of the deceased

Table 1. Persistence and Change in Brewing and Consumption of Home-Made Beer.

Aspects Reported	Frequency of Mentioning	Percentages
Persistent indigenous dimensions of beer		
Used during marriage arrangements	4	97.3
Used during funerals and burials	71	93.4
Women are main brewers	68	89.5
Used during initiation ceremonies	67	88.1
Used in ancestral worship and sacrifice	64	84.2
Used during peace-making ceremonies	64	84.2
Used for mobilization of work groups	62	81.6
Some elders still organize beer parties	60	78.9
Serves as leisure activity	56	73.7
New dimensions of beer		
Brewing and drinking is highly commodified	75	98.7
More youths drink	73	96.0
Men indulge in commercial brewing	71	93.4
Brewing and drinking of local beer is illegal	69	90.8
Brewing involves adding addiction enhancements	66	86.8
Mobilization of labor requires more than beer brewing	64	84.2
Christians do not allow use of beer in funerals and burials	61	80.2
Some people indulge in drinking as if it is a career	59	77.6
Declining role in marriage arrangements	56	73.7
Declining role in peacemaking ceremonies	30	39.5
Declining role in ancestral worship and sacrifices	25	32.9
Consumption is more frequently associated with violence	24	31.6
More fund-raising and fewer beer parties nowadays	21	27.6

person(s), preferred to drink beer as they made burial arrangements. During the burial ceremony, the grave is dug in the early hours of the morning by men who "take turns digging and while at rest drink beer, which has been provided by the host family" (Kilbride & Kilbride, 1990, p. 101). As Belliard (2011) asserts, beer gives force and strength and is very helpful for working faster.

Nowadays, the burial date is typically announced in advance over the radio and in the daily newspapers. Funerals are usually attended by huge crowds of relatives, colleagues, and friends who make donations of money and foodstuffs for use during the mourning period. The donations are mostly used to buy food, kerosene for lanterns, and to offset hospitalization and funeral expenses.

However, in-depth interviews and participant observations revealed that a significant proportion of the donated cash is spent on purchasing beer for those who hang around to keep the bereaved family company.

The findings indicate that Maragoli women are still the main brewers as per the articulations of nearly 89 percent of the study participants. Beer brewing was mostly the preserve of women in indigenous sociocultural settings (Sangree, 1965). This is no longer the case because men, as reported by about 93 percent of the respondents, have ventured into this activity due to the fast cash generated from it. Most of the female brewers argued that given their low educational levels, they find brewing an excellent strategy for generating income, because it only requires minimal initial capital outlay and yields quick cash returns. Brewing does not require specialized skills, and with the readily available ingredients, as well as a guaranteed ready market, women brewers find it a fast and convenient income-generating activity.

Women brewers have direct access to cash from beer-brewing activities, but their husbands and/or male relatives can demand a share of these earnings (Holmboe-Ottesen & Wandel, 1991). Overall, home-brews allow women to earn money independently from male income, an aspect that has received less significant scholarly attention (Holtzman, 2001). King and Burgess (1993) and Kutalek (2011) document that if women earn money, the nutritious standards of their family members improve because they prioritize food than men do, and are more likely to invest earned cash in their children's education.

Social and cultural practices, such as initiation rites, ancestral veneration, sacrifices, and libations, influence brewing and drinking in Maragoli society as indicated by approximately 88 percent of the study participants. Male circumcision is one of the practices associated with high levels of activity, beer brewing, and consumption. Bulimo (2013) and Wagner (1949) provide a detailed description of this highly regarded occasion that brings Maragoli people together to celebrate the elevation of the male members into higher status. Although a significantly lower amount of beer is consumed nowadays, as compared to the time Wagner conducted his fieldwork, home-brews remain an important aspect of what brings the Maragoli people together to mark this rite of passage. About 84 percent of the study participants also indicated a persisting influence of sociocultural practices in the contemporary use of alcohol in ancestral veneration and sacrifice. This is particularly the case among the conservative elderly members who believe that the ancestors and *wele* (god) will not be at peace with them unless they are offered some beer to drink. These conservatives hold the view that failure to give beer offerings to ancestors and god will unleash their wrath and misfortune on the individuals, their families, clans, or the entire society.

Nearly 84 percent of the study participants reported that brewing and consumption of beer is still used during peacemaking ceremonies organized by the council of village elders to reconcile individuals, families, and clans experiencing conflicts or strained relations. Thereafter, participants drink together from one beer pot using long straws to revitalize and reinforce kinship and group solidarity. Several informants indicated that persons who drink together immediately after being reconciled heal faster from the wounds of their past unpleasant experiences.

The Maragoli still use beer to mobilize work groups as per the testimony of approximately 82 percent of the study participants. This is viewed as a cost-effective way of accomplishing tasks including land preparation, weeding, plucking tea, and building a house. Typically, only very close friends agree to such an arrangement as most people prefer cash payments as observed by about 84 percent of the interviewees. It was noted that mobilization of labor requires more than the brewing of beer "as an incentive for kin to engage in labor parties" (Suggs, 1996, p. 598). On this same subject, Suda (1996) writes that "relatives who may be willing and able to help with household and farm work are increasingly beginning to expect to be paid in cash and rarely in kind" (p. 79).

The interviewed women also indicated that some of the elderly male members of the society continue to organize occasional beer parties which are usually attended by their peers. This was reported by nearly 79 percent of the study participants who noted that it brings elderly age-mates together to socialize and reflect upon the changing dynamics of their society. In fact, some of the elders viewed beer drinking as their main form of leisure activity and a major avenue for establishing and reinforcing trusting friendship transcending other social obligations. It is, therefore, not surprising that nearly 74 percent of the study respondents indicated that the brewing and consumption of beer continues to serve as a leisure activity among the rural elderly residents experiencing fewer recreational options.

Kratz (1994) notes that "any practice that constitutes and carries the force of tradition has considerable scope for individuality and change as well" (p. 291). This is evident in Maragoli where older members clearly recognize changes in the production and use of home-brews. Beer brewing has become a commercialized activity, as illustrated by the responses of close 99 percent of the study participants. Ambler (1991) noted a similar trend among the Kikuyu who increasingly viewed beer "as a commodity" (p. 178). Home brewing of alcohol is a demand-driven activity that produces a commodity which is mostly "marketed as a drink to be drunk for drinking sake" (Suggs, 1996, p. 599). Brewing as an increasing economic activity attracts both men and women's involvement as per the testimony of about 93 percent of the sample.

The increasing commodification of beer-brewing evident in Maragoli society has been noted in other communities in Kenya (Roberts, 2000; Subbo, 2001; Willis, 2002). Because of commodification, alcohol consumption among the Maragoli is no longer the preserve of the elderly. As observed by 96 percent of the respondents, the youth are more frequently involved in drinking due to the commercialization of alcohol. Most of the youth have intermittent access to money earned from engagements in the rapidly spreading cash economy.

Consequently, the indulgence of the Maragoli youth in drinking is a privilege they have earned through the penetration of the cash economy.

As reported by approximately 98 percent of the respondents, the Kenya's laws prohibit the brewing and drinking of beer. However, production, sale, and consumption of beer is widely practiced in both rural and urban areas. This can be attributed to weak legal policing and failure to enforce laws against home-brews by corrupt officers who are either consumers, brewers, or sellers of the same. In most cases, the law enforcement officers accept bribes (in cash and kind) to turn a blind-eye to illegal brewing, selling, and consumption of home-brews.

Brewing increasingly involves the addition of liquid chemicals and other elements extracted from opium and dry battery cells. Approximately, 87 percent of the respondents indicated that the addition of these elements enhances addiction to sustain a steady flow of cash-paying customers. Ethnographic investigation in Maragoli confirmed that addicted individuals indulge in regular and predicable use of alcohol. About 78 percent of the study participants noted that beer drinking itself is tantamount to a career. In some cases, alcoholics end up being nuisances by engaging in violent acts, causing inconveniences to other people as per the observations of nearly 32 percent of the sample. Such behavior is a contributing factor to the prohibition of the consumption of alcoholic beverages during funerals and burials of deceased devoted Christians, as observed by about 80 percent of the subjects. Nearly 74 percent of the study participants also indicated that devoted Christians prefer their children to get married in church weddings because the consumption of alcohol is highly discouraged in such contexts.

Nearly 39 percent of the sample noted that the centrality of beer libations in invoking ancestral moral guardians in peacemaking ceremonies is disintegrating as an increasing number of individuals prefer resolving their problems through the Kenya government's formal judiciary system. Almost 33 percent of the interviewees also reported a decrease in the role of beer in ritual and ancestral recognition. Sangree (1962) notes that "a mystical attitude of almost religious reverence is still widely held by the elders towards locally brewed beer, undoubtedly because of its traditional use in ritual and ceremonial occasions" (p. 16). The Maragoli elders constitute a minority of the population of their contemporary society where a growing number of people pay minimal attention to the power of the ancestral spirits and have essentially lost what Sangree (1962) calls "the traditional feeling of reverence towards beer" (p. 17).

Another new trend is the use of beer to attract and induce people to participate in raising money for students to pursue further studies, either locally or abroad. About 28 percent of the respondents observed that the use of beer in fund-raising events was on the increase in the rural areas. It is clearly evident that the fermenting and use of home-brews has multiple and interlocking consequences in Maragoli society. The subsequent discussions focus on women's perspectives regarding the effects of drinking on the household members.

EFFECTS OF BEER CONSUMPTION ON THE CONSUMERS' HOUSEHOLD MEMBERS

The sampled women expressed diverse views and experiences about the dynamics of alcohol and its effects on consumers in their society (shown in Table 2). These findings are consistent with other studies demonstrating that the production of beer can lead to considerable problems within families and communities (Carlson, 1992; Garine, 2001; Kutalek, 2011; Mutongi, 2007, p. 114; Sobania, 2003, p. 70; Subbo, 2001; Willis, 2010). Some of the study participants had personally experienced the maladaptive aspects of home-brews. A significant number of the participants articulated multidimensional effects of drinking on the nutritional status of the household members. These included an inadequate supply of cooking oil (cited by about 93 percent), inadequate supply of salt (expressed by nearly 92 percent), inadequate supply of sugar (reported by slightly above 89 percent), and inadequate provision of other foodstuffs that are necessary for the sustenance of a balanced nutritional status of household members (voiced by approximately 85 percent). In most cases, failure to provide a nutritionally balanced diet resulted in the malnourishment of some of the household members.

Malnutrition has detrimental effects on the health status of the household members. This is made worse by lack of money to purchase prescribed drugs, as indicated by nearly 83 percent of the interviewees. In most cases, there is no money to pay for the required cost-sharing fee at the health centers before one can be treated, as indicated by about 79 percent of the study participants. Moreover, the male household heads divert significant cash into drinking; thus, leaving the other household members with little or no money for intermittent medical services. This results in the poor health of household members, as reported by approximately 74 percent of the respondents.

Diversion of a significant amount of household resources into beer drinking also affects the general well-being of the household members who end up having inadequate clothing as noted by close to 76 percent, inadequate beddings as reported by about 69 percent, and inadequate furniture for household use as expressed by approximately 54 percent of the study participants. Other affected areas of well-being include inadequate supply of kerosene for lanterns as reported by nearly 43 percent, unhygienic or absence of pit latrines as expressed by about 29 percent, and inadequate provision of shelter for the household members as stated by 21 percent of the sample.

Most study participants associated drinking with denial of their rights in decision making at the household level. It implies that women's "major responsibilities for the household's well-being do not always mean decision-making power within the family" (Karl, 1995, p. 3). This is the case among the Maragoli where slightly above 68 percent of the interviewees said that they were denied rights to decision making regarding use of household labor. About

Table 2. Effects of Beer Consumption on Household Members.

Responses	Frequency of Mentioning	Percentages
Affects nutritional status of members		
Inadequate supply of cooking oil	71	93.4
Inadequate supply of salt	70	92.1
Inadequate supply of sugar	68	89.5
Inadequate supply of other foodstuffs	65	85.5
Affects health status of household members		
Inadequate money for drug purchase	63	82.9
No money for local clinic cost-sharing fee	60	78.9
Poor health status among household members	56	73.7
Affects general well-being of household members		
Inadequate provision of clothing	58	76.3
Inadequate provision of bedding	53	69.7
Inadequate provision of household furniture	41	53.9
Inadequate provision of kerosene for lanterns	33	43.4
Unhygienic or absence of pit latrines	22	28.9
Inadequate provision of shelter	16	21.0
Denial of rights to decision making		
Regarding use of household labor	52	68.4
Regarding use of money	51	67.1
Affects children's schooling		
Failure to pay children's school fees	68	89.5
Failure to purchase required school textbooks	64	84.2
Inadequate provision of school uniforms	62	81.2
Early school drop-rates due to poor parenting	57	75.0
Routine physical and emotional child abuse	37	48.7
Affects spousal relations		
Regular quarrels among spouses	74	97.4
Domestic violence and physical spousal abuse	70	92.1
Sexual harassment and rape	58	76.3
Enhancement of the probability of divorce	46	60.5
Selling of household property		
Radios	33	43.4
Food from granaries	28	38.8
Sometimes even clothes are sold	17	22.4
Irresponsible and sometimes immoral behavior		
Bad role models and mentors to children	43	56.6
Promiscuous and generally loose sexual morals	41	53.9
Transmission of STDs and most likely HIV/AIDS	23	30.3
Incestuous affairs	14	18.4

67 percent of the interviewees also indicated that they were excluded from decision-making processes pertaining to the use of money. This concurs with the observation by Karl (1995) that "in most cases women do not have equal control over the management and allocation of family income" (p. 3). It was clear in the focus group discussions that, while the husbands in Maragoli tend to monopolize decision-making processes, the wives are the major sources of household labor and, indeed, play a significant role in the generation of money. The broad negative implications of this denial of rights to decision making on women's agricultural production are shown in Table 4.

Excessive expenditure of household money on beer consumption affects the children's education and strains spousal relationships in varied ways. For instance, about 89 percent of the subjects indicated that the children's school fees are at times not paid promptly, thus resulting in their expulsion from school. Dibuk (1993) notes that such drinkers "forsake paying children's school fees because their money is spent on beer" (p. 18). Observed disruption of school-based learning is made worse by the parents' inability to purchase the required textbooks because of excessive expenditure on beer as per the expressions of about 84 percent of the sample. Pupils are also expelled from school because they do not have school uniforms (articulated by nearly 81 percent of the study participants), especially in cases involving alcoholic parents, who consistently fail to cater to this requirement. Seventy-five percent of the interviewees reported that some children dropped out of school because of poor parenting, role modeling, mentoring, inspiration, and guidance. It was reported by nearly 49 percent of the sample that drunk parents consistently engaged in physical and emotional abuse of their children.

Alcohol abuse also strained spousal relations. Nearly 97 percent of the respondents disclosed that their families experience regular and predicable quarrels. About 92 percent said that domestic violence and physical spousal abuse are something they frequently encounter in their domestic spheres. Domestic violence is largely a power play with the men exerting their authority and citing culture as a reason permitting them discipline their wives (Amuyunzu-Nyamongo & Francis, 2006).

Among the Maragoli, violence against women which in most cases involves wife-beating and battering is viewed by men as a normal customary practice (Kilbride & Kilbride, 1990). Women in Law and Development in Africa (1990) indicates that "domestic violence and rape are not criminal offences in Africa and the police and courts are unsympathetic towards women" (p. 13). Ambrose (1995) also observes that "on numerous occasions, women are frustrated by police when they make an attempt to exercise their fundamental human rights" (p. 59). The persistence of this practice and its disruptive impact on the smooth running of the family was captured in the most widely read Kenyan English language newspaper (*Daily Nation*, Cutting Edge, March 4, 1997), which posed the following question: "What can you do when a violent drunkard is destroying his family but because he has not actually caused any bodily harm (yet), the police cannot act? His traumatized kids sleep out, scarcely eat, are rarely at school, and his wife has fled in fear. Is there an organization which could advise?" This situation candidly sums up a typical inequality in gender-power relations inherent in the married lives of some couples in patrilineal African societies. Amuyunzu-Nyamongo and Francis (2006) argue that "male power in most Kenyan communities has been steeped in patriarchy that traditionally has been reinforced through rites of passage, bride wealth payments, and patrilocal residence" (p. 221).

Bradley (1997) observes an increase in domestic violence and 60 percent of the women confirming having been beaten by their husbands. Heise (1995) argues that "violence against wives – indeed violence against women in general – is as old as recorded history, and cuts across all nationalities and socioeconomic groups. Every day, thousands of women are raped, assaulted, and sexually harassed" (p. 75). Heise further contends that violence against women is perhaps the most pervasive yet least recognized human rights abuse in the world. Violent acts represent fundamental violations of women's bodily integrity and undermines widely held goals for economic and social development. In most cases, violence against women is grounded on power imbalances between men and women (Heise, 1995, p. 79); it is often about social control and a power bid (Skaine, 1996).

According to Bradley (1995, p. 159), "an atmosphere of scarcity, whether real or perceived, may create tension between men and women who must compete for scarce resources" and sometimes this may culminate in violent behavior. Sexual harassment, which Skaine (1996, p. 11) defines as "unwelcome sexual behavior by one person against another person," was voiced as one of the effects of drinking on household members. In this study, about 76 percent of the interviewees reported sexual harassment and rape by their own husbands which "are not a criminal offence in many parts of Africa" (Women in Law and Development in Africa, 1990, p. 13). This is a clear illustration that women know that rape occurs even within marriage, and it may result in strained spousal relations as well as create a situation conducive to the pursuit of divorce by wives as per the testimony of approximately 60 percent of the sample.

The results of this study concur with the observation by Dibuk (1993) that "women often talk about how their own lives and those of their children are affected by men's drinking because it appropriates household capital" (p. 19). Frequent indulgence in alcohol consumption tempts some individuals to sell various household items raise money to buy beer. This documented by about 43 percent of the study participants who stated that their husbands had sold family radios. Nearly 39 percent of the interviewees reported disposal of household foodstuff from storage granaries and intermittent harvesting and selling of bananas, tomatoes, and onions directly from cultivated plots. Approximately, 22 percent of the subjects talked about extreme cases involving the sale of household members' clothes to obtain cash to buy home-brews.

Wide ranging aspects of irresponsible behavior were reported to be characteristic of alcohol addicts. Such individuals serve as bad role models to their own children, as mentioned by nearly 57 percent of the interviewees. Some of the alcohol addicts engage in promiscuous sexual behaviors, as per the observations of nearly 54 percent of the respondents. Close to 30 percent noted that such loose sexual behaviors facilitate the spread of various sexually transmitted infections and HIV/AIDS. Another 18 percent of the sample stated that some addicts indulged in incestuous affairs. This behavior caused their families social stigma, stress, and embarrassment. We now turn to the effects of brewing, selling, and consumption of beer on the household members of brewers and sellers in the research site.

CONSEQUENCES OF BEER CONSUMPTION ON PRODUCERS' AND SELLERS' HOUSEHOLDS

The brewing, use, and sale of beer have multiple and interlocking consequences on the households. Views pertaining to the influence of beer production and selling on the households involved in this enterprise were compiled, and a summary of the results is shown in Table 3. The findings affirm that the brewing, selling, and drinking of alcohol is a major informal sector activity yielding significant cash income. This is evident from the approximately 97 percent of the women who indicated that households engaged in the enterprise regularly generate money which the beneficiaries used to meet a variety of basic needs. Bradley (1995) observes that "Maragoli women who sell beer are notoriously independent" (p. 163). These women have what Holmboe-Ottesen and Wandel (1991) call "direct access to cash from beer brewing activities" (p. 115). In fact, an informant indicated that sometimes the family members of the brewers and sellers and, especially the husbands drink up the potential profits. If such behavior occurs too often, it leads to domestic violence as per the observations of nearly 95 percent of the study participants. Cases of physical injuries and burns associated with domestic violence, distillation of alcohol, and pouring of hot water to dilute their customers' beer were frequent and noted by nearly 87 percent of the sample.

The testimony of 71 percent of the study subjects revealed that, in some of the alcohol brewing and selling households, husbands may reduce and, in some cases, completely withdraw their financial contributions from household expenses if they think that their wives make sufficient cash from the selling of beer. In such households, where the husband uses the wife's beer-selling cash income as an excuse for withdrawing his share of cash contributions to the family's upkeep, the wife finds herself with familial responsibilities that place excessive demands on her. Nearly 85 percent of the respondents noted that easy availability of alcohol in the brewers' households contributed to alcohol

Table 3. Effects of Beer Brewing and Consumption on the Producer Households.

Responses	Frequency of Mentioning	Percentages
Positive effects		
Source of cash income	74	97.4
Source of cheap domestic labor	65	85.5
Source of cheap agricultural labor	54	71.0
Negative effects		
Encourages spousal domestic violence	72	94.7
Sometimes results in physical injuries	66	86.8
Alcohol addiction	65	85.5
Withdrawal of financial support by husbands	54	71.0
Promiscuous and loose sexual morals	51	67.1
Sexual harassment	49	64.5
Rape and incestuous sexual indulgence	47	61.8
Facilitates spread of STDs and AIDS	44	57.9
Use of child labor in transporting and selling alcohol	44	57.9
Child malnutrition	43	56.6
Physical and emotional child abuse	41	53.9
School dropout	40	52.6
Provides inappropriate environment for child socialization	36	47.4
Children learn to drink alcohol at tender ages	35	46.0
More frequent teenage pregnancies in brewing household	33	43.4
Generally, brewing disrupts smooth running of the family	26	34.2

addiction. This gradually stimulates early drinking habits (cited by 46 percent of the interviewees).

About 47 percent of the sample noted the inappropriateness of the beer-selling environment for children's enculturation. Sobania (2003) notes that "destitute young children in these neighborhoods, who see one or both parents drunk and passed out, can also be found drinking illegal brew in response to the seemingly hopelessness of their conditions" (p. 170). Thus, frequent exposure to the negative impact of drunkenness thwarts the moral development of the affected children. For example, excessively drunk parents intermittently indulge in sexual intercourse in broad delight when their own children are present and even observing the act.

Nearly 53 percent of the respondents observed that beer-selling and -drinking environments induce significant school dropout rates. Other negative effects are child malnutrition as per the observations of close to 57 percent, and child abuse as reported by nearly 54 percent of the sample. One extreme instance of child abuse mentioned by about 58 percent of the sample is the use of children in transporting and even selling alcohol. Children involved in these undertaking gradually drop out of school and learn to drink at very tender ages. The observations of about 34 percent of the sample pointed to the fact that home surroundings that were overwhelmingly characterized by the production and sale of alcohol were disruptive to the smooth running of the family unit.

The beer-selling households have access to cheap domestic labor which is usually volunteered by the drinkers in exchange for beer. About 85.5 percent of the interviewees noted that the cheap domestic labor is utilized in fetching water from the nearby drinking water sources, clearing and maintaining the homestead yard, and splitting firewood. The same brewing and alcohol-selling households usually have access to almost free agricultural labor in return for beer. On this point, 71 percent of the interviewees indicated that a significant number of male drinkers perform various farming tasks in return for beer whenever they are short of cash. The farm tasks performed in exchange for beer generally vary with the agricultural season, but typically include land preparation, planting, weeding, and harvesting.

Other problems associated with drinking, as per the testimonies of nearly 67 percent of the study subjects, included promiscuous and loose sexual morals. The respondents indicated that excessive consumption of alcohol interferes with the drinkers' sense of moral judgment, and lures men and women into indiscriminate sex. Several informants indicated that drunk individuals also tended to be less sensitive in their selection of sexual partners and, especially men were less likely to use condoms for safe sex. This behavior places the affected persons at high risk of being infected with sexually transmitted diseases (STDs) and HIV/AIDS. Moreover, awareness of HIV/AIDS is very high in the study area but the stigma related to this pandemic persists.

About 64.5 percent of the study respondents noted that beer brewers and sellers are also regularly exposed to prostitution in an environment that subjects them to high risks of sexual abuse and disease. In addition, women beer sellers are frequently sexually harassed by their regular male customers; the men sometimes succeed in having sexual affairs with some female sellers, who supplement their beer-selling income by indulging in transactional sex.

It is evident that incidences of rape have increased in an alarming rate (Chazan, Mortimer, Ravenhill, & Rothchild, 1992). The results also indicated that rape and incestuous sexual affairs occurred in the area as per the responses of nearly 62 percent of the sample. Beer-selling households also were reported by about 43 percent of the study participants as experiencing frequent teenage pregnancies. It was observed by nearly 58 percent that sexual indulgence facilitates the spread of STDs and HIV/AIDS. We now turn to the results pertaining to how beer dynamics affect agricultural activities.

IMPACT OF BEER BREWING, SELLING, AND DRINKING ON WOMEN'S AGRICULTURAL PRODUCTION

Women play critical roles in both food and cash-crops production in the developing countries (Bryceson, 1995; Buvinic, Gwin, & Bates, 1996). In Kenya, approximately 80 percent of the women live in the rural areas, where they engage in farming as a major economic activity and contribute over 70 percent of the agricultural labor force (Suda, 1996). Men in Kenya and other parts of Africa "valued their women for their productive labor" (Suggs, 1996, p. 597). Although "the participation of women as the majority group is essential to development in Africa" (Ambrose, 1995, p. 57), the realization of higher agricultural productivity is somehow constrained by the fact that women who provide the bulk of the required farm labor "cannot lend their labor or creative ideas fully when they are burdened with physical and psychological scars of abuse" (Heise, 1995, pp. 75–76). Table 4 shows the negative effects of the scars of abuse associated with the male household heads' alcohol consumption on their wives' agricultural production. Domestic violence is a principal cause of stress in the lives of married women farmers. In most cases, women farmers who suffer physical injuries resulting from domestic violence experience tension

Table 4. Effects of Beer Brewing and Consumption on Women's Agricultural Activities.

Responses	Frequency of Mentioning	Percentages
Productivity reduced by physical injuries	56	73.7
Poor motivation due to frequent tension and stress	53	69.7
Malnutrition results in low energy	52	68.4
Weakened by diseases due to inadequate funds for medication	50	65.8
Beer consumption results in theft of agricultural produce	50	65.8
Diversion of agricultural credit into drinking	48	63.1
Husband resells fertilizer purchased for farm use	47	61.8
Sometimes husband resells household's purchased hybrid seeds	45	59.2
Husband sold some of the hoes, machetes, and spray pumps	42	55.3
High potential agricultural plots either sold or leased out	36	47.4
Absence of husband's labor from farming activities	36	47.4
Husband sells farm produce without consulting wife	34	44.7
Frequent conflicts regarding access to and control of farm income	32	42.1
Women weakened by excessive farm-related workload	29	38.1

and stress, which interfere with their meaningful and productive engagements in farming. Nearly 70 percent of the interviewees indicated that tension and stress usually discourage women's motivation to perform farm work.

Malnutrition affects women farmers' energy levels. As reported by about 68 percent of the sample, households lack nutritiously balanced diets almost on a regular basis because of the diversion of a greater proportion of money into beer drinking. This situation is usually exacerbated by the fact that malnourished individuals tend to be vulnerable to diseases, especially when they have little or no access to medical services due to lack of money. Nearly 66 percent of the sample noted that this trend was undermining women farmers and decreasing their farm productivity. This is notwithstanding the fact that women farmers are generally weakened by the excessive farm-related workload, as expressed by nearly 38 percent of the interviewees. Some of the respondents also indicated that some of the addicted beer drinkers at times end up stealing crops from other people's farms. In most of the instances cited by about 66 percent of the interviewees, maize and bananas were stolen from the women's plots at night and transported to near and distant markets for sale. This habit was reported as having a significant demoralizing effect on the affected women farmers. These results are consistent with the observation that "with consumption comes drunkenness, a decline in labor productivity, and increase in crime and prostitution" (Sobania, 2003, p. 170).

The diversion of agricultural credit into beer drinking affected female farmers' agricultural productivity. It was reported by approximately 63 percent of the study participants that their husbands, who are the holders of land title deeds, receive credit specifically intended for improving agricultural output (Gwako, 2002) but funds are utilized on drinking sprees. This demoralizes wives from investing their full labor in farm level activities. The same holds true for husbands who were reported by nearly 62 percent of the study participants as reselling fertilizer. Close to 59 percent of the sample also said that sometimes alcoholic husbands who need money for beer resell hybrid seeds purchased for planting. Farm implements were also sold to raise money for home-brews as per the testimony of approximately 55 percent of the sample. Such behaviors divert needed inputs for improving agricultural productivity.

The permanent selling and/or temporary leasing out of the households' high potential agricultural land to obtain cash to buy beer also impedes high farm yields. This was articulated by nearly 47 percent of the study participants who also noted that routine indulgence of husbands in beer consumption decreases the time and labor they invest in farming. Other studies have shown that men spend substantial amounts of their time and money drinking, even at the expense of household food security (Amuyunzu-Nyamongo & Francis, 2006; Holmboe-Ottesen & Wandel, 1991). This emerged as problem experienced by some Maragoli households as per the testimony of about 47 percent of the study participants.

In some households, women farmers have minimal incentives to achieve high farm yields because their husbands sell farm produce without consulting them. This habit was cited by nearly 45 percent of the interviewees, out of whom close to 42 percent also indicated that the accompanying scenario becomes even more compounded by conflicts pertaining to access and control of crop income. The paralyzing effects of men's excessive drinking on women's lives and agricultural production are clear and significant. These situations inspired some respondents to explore what Stanley and Wise (1990) call "various avenues to protect themselves and safeguard their interests" (p. 22). The deployment of varied strategic maneuvers by women farmers features prominently in the subsequent discussions.

EFFORTS TO REDUCE THE DETRIMENTAL RAMIFICATIONS OF HOME-MADE BEER CONSUMPTION

Women typically employ a variety of strategies to improve their situation (Clark, 1984). This section examines the ingenuity employed by Maragoli women farmers to avert various detrimental effects of brewing, selling, and consumption of beer on their lives and endeavors. The study participants took actions individually and collectively to deflate the maladaptive aspects of beer from the "standpoint of women's lives" (Scott, 1995, p. 133). Their strategic efforts illuminate the "understanding of women as agents who make choices, have a critical perspective on their own situations, and think and organize collectively against their oppressors" (Mohanty, 1991, p. 21). The results of this study are consistent with the observation that "with the commodification of alcohol, women have frequently benefited from their role as brewers by developing a new source of economic power and independence" (Dietler, 2006, p. 236) resulting from the extra income they earn from male consumers (Colson & Scudder, 1988; Dancause et al., 2010; McCall, 1996).

The innovative interventions articulated by the Maragoli study participants are shown in Table 5. These findings are a clear testimony that women exercise agency "to participate in the events and processes that shape their lives" (United Nations, 1991, p. 6). Suda (1996) points out that "in order to influence further changes in their life situations and also to accelerate the self-empowerment process, increasingly significant numbers of Kenyan women have taken the initiative to mobilize and organize themselves into self-help groups at the grassroots levels" (p. 82). This is one of the most effective strategies women farmers use to reduce the maladaptive aspects related to home-brews in their society. A significant number of the study sample (64.5 percent) observed self-help groups as a crucial and effective strategy for self-empowerment, which boosted the actualization of women's well-being in multiple dimensions.

Table 5. Participants' Solutions to the Effects of Alcohol Use on Women's Lives and Agricultural Activities.

Efforts	Frequency of Mentioning	Percentages
Joined women groups	49	64.5
Participate in formal and informal development committees	43	56.6
Use other people to sell agricultural produce	39	51.3
Safe keeping money with other people	38	50.0
Never disclose to your husband the amount of money you have	36	47.4
Prompt spending/investment of money as soon as one gets it	33	43.4
Christians preach and teach against alcohol consumption	27	35.3
Use songs to condemn spousal abuse and violence against women	23	30.3
Appeal for the enactment of laws that safeguard women's interests	21	27.6
Women's group support for victims of spousal abuse	18	23.7
Use cultural ethos to deal with alcoholic spousal abusers	15	19.7
Use of self-censorship	12	15.8
Encourage use of condoms for safe sex	8	10.5
Divorce	6	07.9

Abwunza (1995) argues that Maragoli women "united to improve women's social, economic and political status, to wage war against illiteracy and ignorance, poor health, poverty and joblessness and to call for government assistance to women's groups for technical, financial and other necessities for progress" (p. 29). Although not all women's groups have registered major successes in accomplishing their original goals, most of them, however, achieved some measure of success. For example, the evidence provided by Abwunza (1995, 1997) clearly shows that the women's group networks in Maragoli have been very instrumental in uplifting their members' well-being and have served as useful avenues for providing much-needed cash in this densely populated area with limited opportunities for paid labor. Abwunza (1995) further reports that as a mechanism for enhancing both social and economic support, women strategically raise "money through singing in choirs or by digging land, selling food and crafts, building schools or churches or cleaning water resource areas" (p. 30). As result of their collective endeavors, Maragoli women have an acknowledged social power to influence various communal aspects of development. As active economic providers for their families and the community, the fruits of their collective efforts are visible in their accumulation of cash, food, blankets, lanterns, utensils, a day's or two days' work for one another, and their ability to borrow, lend, and provide support to each other in times of need, whether occasioned by unexpected guests or by a death (Abwunza, 1995).

Women farmers have been routinely excluded from the distribution of various forms of agricultural benefits, such as extension service and credit that are guaranteed with the land title deeds (Nzomo & Staudt, 1994; Saito & Weidemann, 1991). Women's group movements have been extremely instrumental in facilitating the dissemination of information about family planning, farming techniques, and loans (Gwako, 1997a, 1997b, 1998a, 1998b, 2002). Abwunza (1995) notes that "women gathering in groups share information, for example, details about government directives in old and new laws, or current wages for digging and prices of commodities. Confronting the difficult aspects of subsistence, they discuss agricultural assistance and innovations and mourn the loss of kinship support" (p. 36). This is further testimony that women are very intentional in mobilizing themselves for various purposes, including self-empowerment. Membership in women's groups is highly valued and desired by Maragoli women (Verma, 2001).

The concept of empowerment, as used in this study, refers to "a process of awareness and capacity building leading to greater participation, to greater decision-making power and control, and to transformative action" (Karl, 1995, p. 14). Empowerment and ingenuity were evident in Maragoli society because women were largely involved in self-help groups at both individual and collective levels. These voluntary associations enhance the development of their members' awareness and ability to organize and bring about change and to alleviate the undesirable effects of beer on agricultural production. The concept of self-help groups in this study encompasses "groups that organize individuals to engage in collective action to ameliorate their conditions and, concomitantly, to change the social arena in which they operate" (House-Midamba, 1996, p. 297). These groups are widespread in rural Kenya and have the primary goal of promoting the women's "common social, economic, and political interests by organizing themselves and pooling their resources" (Suda, 1996, p. 82). It is, therefore, apparent that self-help groups in rural Kenya are based on the need of rural women to mobilize effective means for acquiring resources to support their activities.

Women also seek remedial measures through participation. Nearly 57 percent of the sample stated that this entails the involvement and election of women in various development committee meetings and at various levels of the national government's development planning committees. Such a representative usually consults with the women she represents prior to providing input in development planning committee meetings. Women also form and actively participate in informal pressure groups for purposes of articulating their needs to both the government and nongovernmental organizations. These pressure groups include mothers' unions and various professional associations that serve as convenient avenues of vocalizing their views against varied forms of oppression and the offsetting of the negative impact of alcohol consumption on both their lives and agricultural activities.

Women farmers are becoming more careful in concealing their farm produce incomes from their husbands. For example, in situations where husbands gauge their wives' cash incomes through the amount of farm produce sold, their wives use proxies to deliver and sell the products in the local markets. This was cited by close to 51 percent as an effective strategy for avoiding their husbands' demands for cash. Fifty percent of the study participants indicated that they intermittently leave their money with other people to minimize their husbands' chances of getting access to it. About 47 percent of the study subjects refused to disclose to their husbands how much cash they had whenever such information was sought. Slightly above 43 percent of the participants indicated that they sometimes promptly spend the cash they earn to avoid misappropriation by their husbands. There are significant numbers of Christian groups in the area who encourage and actively preach and teach against alcohol consumption to discourage misuse of money. This approach was deemed effective by approximately 35 percent of the participants, who further noted that it involved the joint efforts of church leaders and their followers who frequently conducted Christian outreach missions in the area.

Women are repositories of society's traditional and cultural practices. This is particularly true in Kenya where women are excellent traditional singers and dancers, who are regularly called upon to entertain guests during major functions, such as national holiday celebrations, fund-raising events, and political rallies. Karl (1995) notes that "women play a significant part in the cultural life of their communities as the members of the community who preserve the traditional culture in song, dance, storytelling, art and ritual" (p. 4). Women have, however, become smart enough to use such avenues to articulate unpleasant experiences deriving from practices undermining their well-being. More frequently, as it was pointed out by approximately 30 percent of the study participants, women used such avenues to express their dissatisfaction with their husbands' beer consumption and the undesirable effects associated with the habit. During such occasions, women also sing protest songs directed at discriminative practices of agricultural credit-financing institutions and biased government policies.

Women do not only sing to entertain guests during national holiday celebrations, but they also call for the enactment of laws to safeguard their interests. As mentioned by nearly 28 percent of the sampled participants and frequently highlighted by key informants, the appeal for the enactment of laws protecting women's interests is also pursued by the various professional associations of women, such as bankers and lawyers. These professional associations engage in sensitizing women on their legal rights through seminars, workshops, and printed media on the premise that "if women know the law, they can use it to effect changes in their daily lives by confronting oppressive laws and customs that have resulted in women's subordinate status in society" (Ambrose, 1995, p. 64). About

24 percent of the study participants also indicated that women's self-help groups serve as good support networks for other women who are victims of spousal abuse. Suda (1996) observes that "women also join these groups to provide psychological and physical support to one another, especially during times of crisis" (p. 83).

Married women minimize the maladaptive impact of their husbands' excessive indulgence in alcohol consumption through use of varied cultural ethos as mentioned by nearly 20 percent of the interviewees. Ridicule, generally in the form of jesting and mimicry, is leveled against the individual or clique commonly felt to be indulging in undesirable behavior, and it serves as an important mechanism of social control within the community (Sangree, 1962). Occasionally, women compose and sing protest songs alluding to their spousal abusers and, in extreme cases, they may even refuse to give birth or name their newborn children after abusive alcohol addicts. About 16 percent of the sample mentioned the use of self-censorship as a strategy employed to minimize chances of physical abuse by their spouses. The application of this method usually involves reading the spouse's mood and refraining from behaving in a manner likely to trigger violent behavior. Thus, some Maragoli "women learn to censor their own behavior based on what they think will be acceptable to their husbands or partners" (Heise, 1995, p. 82). The least mentioned and used strategies include requesting the amorous husband to use condoms while indulging in sexual intercourse with the wife (mentioned by only 10.5 percent of the sample) and divorce option which was mentioned by nearly 8 percent of the study participants. However, not a single case of divorce associated with the husband's alcohol addiction was documented in this study. The findings show that Maragoli women use ingenuity to advance their individual and collective well-being.

CONCLUSION

This chapter analyzed the role of beer brewing and drinking in the indigenous Maragoli society and highlighted the changes from brewing and consumption for ritual, ceremonial, and other culturally approved purposes to commercialized ventures. The commodification of beer motivates brewers to add addiction enhancers to attract and sustain a steady flow of paying customers. These ingredients have detrimentally affected the health status of the consumers. The ramifications of brewing, selling, and use of beer are major concerns in Maragoli society.

The findings illustrate Maragoli women's ingenuity in confronting and averting the maladaptive outcomes of excessive alcohol consumption habits. The women's strategic use of multiple mechanisms at different times demonstrates "how Kenyan women have been working for change in their lives" (Suda, 1996, p. 82).

Manifestations of empowerment and agency are, therefore, gradually becoming apparent as women make attempts to resist, "in favor of their own interests, actions of institutions and more powerful individuals who might limit their ability to act" (Bradley, 1995, p. 160). The diverse strategies used by women to foster their individual and collective well-being illustrate that, even though the authority to make decisions officially rests with the men, women may find ways of having their views accepted (Holmboe-Ottesen & Wandel, 1991). Although some women over imbibe, they are more actively involved in efforts to counter excessive consumption of alcohol. The impact of home-brews on Maragoli women cannot be understated. This study has demonstrated these effects in the context of changes within the Maragoli community. Another trend is an increasingly important collective action by Maragoli women and their own empowerment.

The research results also indicate that women have become highly sensitized to their rights as manifested in their strategic assertiveness to overcome the undesirable effects of their husbands' alcohol addiction on both their daily lives and agricultural production. This assertiveness is also linked to women's awareness of their contributions to the economy, which often subjects them to significantly heavy workloads in meeting the needs of their households. Equally significant is the evidence that women find ways and means of ensuring the protection of their group and children's interests. Most of the Kenyan women know that the existence of formal avenues for seeking redress does not necessarily translate into actual protection of their rights, due to lack of good will, as clearly illustrated by cases of the Kenyan police, who often decline to intervene when either violent abuses or disputes are domestic. It is, however, encouraging that Kenyan women are actively working in different ways to overcome persistent barriers anchored in structures of inequality in gender-power relations. The study's cardinal argument, as well as its findings, has challenged the notion that alcohol is only brewed for commercial purposes, and its consumption simply wrought violence, aggression, and other forms of social miseries against women, thus reducing women to helpless, voiceless, and powerless victims.

REFERENCES

Abwunza, J. M. (1995). "Silika—To make our lives shine": Women's groups in Maragoli, Kenya. *Anthropologica, 37*, 27–48.

Abwunza, J. M. (1997). *Women's voices, women's power: Dialogues of resistance in East Africa*. Peterborough: Broadview Press.

Ambler, C. H. (1988). *Kenyan communities in the age of imperialism: The central region in the late nineteenth century*. New Haven, CT: Yale University Press.

Ambler, C. H. (1991). Drunks, brewers, and chiefs: Alcohol regulation in colonial Kenya, 1900–1939. In S. Barrows & R. Room (Eds.), *Drinking: Behavior and belief in modern history* (pp. 165–183). Berkeley, CA: University of California Press.

Ambrose, B. P. (1995). *Democratization and the protection of human rights in Africa: Problems and prospects*. Westport, CT: Praeger.

Amuyunzu-Nyamongo, M., & Francis, P. (2006). Collapsing livelihood and the crisis of masculinity in rural Kenya. In I. Bannon & M. C. Correia (Eds.), *The other half of gender: Men's issues in development* (pp. 219–244). Washington, DC: The World Bank.

BBC News. (2005). Should we drink home brews? Retrieved from http://news.bbc.co.uk/2/hi/africa/4188106.stm

Belliard, F. (2011). Brewing sorghum beer in Burkina Faso: A study in food technology from the perspective of anthropological linguistics. In W. Schiefenhovel & H. Macbeth (Eds.), *Liquid bread: Beer and brewing in cross-cultural perspective* (pp. 171–181). New York, NY: Berghahn Books.

Bradley, C. (1995). Women's empowerment and fertility decline in western Kenya. In S. Greenhalgh (Ed.), *Situating fertility: Anthropological and demographic inquiry* (pp. 157–178). New York, NY: Cambridge University Press.

Bradley, C. (1997). Why fertility is going down in Maragoli. In T. S. Weisner, C. Bradley, & P. L. Kilbride (Eds.), *African families and the crisis of social change* (pp. 227–252). Westport, CT: Bergin & Garvey.

Bryceson, D. F. (1995). *Women wielding the hoe: Lessons from rural Africa for feminist theory and development practice*. Oxford: Berg Publishers.

Bulimo, A. S. (2013). *Luyia of Kenya: A cultural profile*. Bloomington, IN: Trafford Publishing.

Buvinic, M., Gwin, C., & Bates, L. M. (1996). *Investing in women: Progress and prospects for the World Bank*. Baltimore, MD: The John Hopkins University Press.

Carlson, R. G. (1990). Banana beer, reciprocity, and ancestor propitiation among the Haya of Bukoba, Tanzania. *Ethnology*, *29*, 297–311.

Carlson, R. G. (1992). Symbolic mediation and commodification: A critical examination of alcohol use among the Haya of Bukoba, Tanzania. *Medical Anthropology*, *15*, 41–62.

Chazan, N., Mortimer, R., Ravenhill, J., & Rothchild, D. (1992). *Politics and society in contemporary Africa* (2nd ed.). Boulder, CO: Lynne Rienner Publishers.

Clark, M. H. (1984). Women-headed households and poverty: Insights from Kenya. *Signs*, *10*(2), 338–354.

Colson, E., & Scudder, T. (1988). *For prayer and for profit: The ritual, economic, and social importance of beer in Gwembe district, Zambia, 1950-1982*. Stanford, CA: Stanford University Press.

Dancause, K. N., Akol, H. A., & Gray, S. J. (2010). Beer is the cattle of women: Sorghum beer commercialization and dietary intake of agropastoral families in Karamoja, Uganda. *Social Science & Medicine*, *70*, 1123–1130.

Dibuk, S. (1993). European alcohol, history, and the state in Cameroon. *African Studies Review*, *36*, 1–42.

Dietler, M. (2006). Alcohol: Anthropological/archaeological perspectives. *Annual Review of Anthropology*, *35*, 229–249.

Garine, E. (2001). An ethnographic account of the many roles of millet beer in the culture of the Duupa-agriculturalists, (Poli Mountains) Northern Cameroon. In I. De Garine & V. De Garine (Eds.), *Drinking: Anthropological approaches* (pp. 191–204). New York, NY: Berghahn Books.

Gwako, E. L. M. (1997a). Conjugal power in rural Kenya families: Its influence on women's decisions about family size and family planning practices. *Sex Roles: A Journal of Research*, *36*, 127–147.

Gwako, E. L. M. (1997b). Married women's ideal family size preferences and family planning practices: Evidence from rural Kenya. *The Social Science Journal*, *34*, 369–382.

Gwako, E. L. M. (1998a). Polygyny among the Logoli of western Kenya. *Anthropos*, *3*(4/6), 331–348.

Gwako, E. L. M. (1998b). Widow inheritance among the Logoli of western Kenya. *Journal of Anthropological Research*, *54*(2), 173–198.

Gwako, E. L. M. (2002). Property rights and incentives for agricultural growth: Women farmers' crop control and their use of agricultural inputs. In J. Ensminger (Ed.), *Theory in economic anthropology* (pp. 3–25). Walnut Creek, CA: Altamira Press.

Gwako, E. L. M. (2014). Maragoli and Gusii farmers in Kenya: Strong collective action and high prosocial punishment. In J. Ensminger & J. Henrich (Eds.), *Experimenting with social norms: Fairness and punishment in cross-cultural perspective* (pp. 309–336). New York, NY: Russell Sage Foundation.

Heath, D. B. (1987). Anthropology and alcohol: Current issues. *Annual Review of Anthropology, 16*, 99–120.

Heise, L. L. (1995). Overcoming violence: A background paper on violence against women as an obstacle to development. In G. Reardon (Ed.), *Power and process: A report from the women linking for change conference, Thailand, 1994* (pp. 75–95). Oxford: Oxfam Publications.

Holmboe-Ottesen, G., & Wandel, M. (1991). "Wife, today I only had money for pombe," gender and food: Women's bargaining power and agricultural change in a Tanzanian community. In K. A. Stolen & M. Vaa (Eds.), *Gender and change in developing countries* (pp. 93–119). Oslo: Norwegian University Press.

Holtzman, J. (2001). The food of elders, the 'ration' of women: Brewing, gender, and domestic processes among the Samburu of Northern Kenya. *American Anthropologist, 103*(4), 1041–1058.

House-Midamba, B. (1996). Gender, democratization, and associational life in Kenya. *Africa Today, 43*, 289–306.

Karl, M. (1995). *Women and empowerment: Participation and decision making*. London: Zed Books Ltd.

Karp, I. (1978). *Fields of change among the Iteso of Kenya*. London: Routledge & Kegan Paul.

Karp, I. (1980). Beer drinking and social experience in an African society: An essay in formal sociology. In I. Karp & C. S. Bird (Eds.), *Explorations in African systems of thought* (pp. 83–119). Bloomington, IN: Indiana University Press.

Kilbride, P. L., & Kilbride, J. C. (1990). *Changing family life in East Africa: Women and children at risk*. University Park, PA: The Pennsylvania State University Press.

King, F. S., & Burgess, A. (1993). *Nutrition for developing countries*. Oxford: Oxford University Press.

King, G., Keohane, R. O., & Verba, S. (1994). *Designing social inquiry: Scientific inference in qualitative research*. Princeton, NJ: Princeton University Press.

Kirk, J., & Miller, M. L. (1986). *Reliability and validity in qualitative research*. New Park, CA: Sage.

Kratz, C. A. (1994). *Affecting performance: Meaning, movement, and experience in Okiek women's initiation*. Washington, DC: Smithsonian Institution Press.

Kutalek, R. (2011). Ritual use of beer in South-West Tanzania. In W. Schiefenhovel & H. Macbeth (Eds.), *Liquid bread: Beer and brewing in cross-cultural perspective* (pp. 159–169). New York, NY: Berghahn Books.

Levine, R. A. (1962). Wealth and power in Gusiiland. In P. Bohannan & G. Dalton (Eds.), *Markets in Africa* (pp. 520–536). Evanston, IL: Northwestern University Press.

Levine, R. A. (1982). Gusii funerals: Meanings of life and death in an African community. *Ethos, 10*, 26–65.

Levine, R. A., Levine, R. A., Levine, S., Dixon, S., Richman, A., Leiderman, P. H., ... Brazelton, T. B. (1994). *Child care and culture: Lessons from Africa*. Cambridge, NY: Cambridge University Press.

Levine, R. A., & LeVine, B. B. (1977). *Nyansongo: A Gusii community in Kenya*. Huntington, NY: Robert E. Krieger Publishing Company.

Maoura, N., & Pourquie, J. (2009). Sorghum beer: Production, nutritional value and impact upon human health. In V. R. Preedy (Ed.), *Beer in health disease prevention* (pp. 53–60). Burlington, MA: Elsevier Academic Press.

Maula, J. (1997). *Small-scale production of food and traditional alcoholic beverages in Benin and Tanzania: Implications for the promotion of female entrepreneurship*. Helsinki: The Finish Foundation for Alcohol Studies.

McAllister, P. (2003). Culture, practice, and the semantics of Xhosa beer-drinking. *Ethnology, 42*, 187–207.

McCall, M. (1996). Rural brewing, exclusion, and development policy-making. *Gender and Development, 4*, 29–38.

Mohanty, C. T. (1991). Cartographics of struggle: Third world women and the politics of feminism. In C. T. Mohanty, A. Russo, & L. Torres (Eds.), *Third world women and the politics of feminism* (pp. 1–47). Bloomington, IN: University of Indiana Press.

Morgan, D. L., & Krueger, R. A. (1993). When to use focus groups and why. In D. L. Morgan (Ed.), *Successful focus groups: Advancing the state of the art* (pp. 3–19). Newbury, CA: Sage.

Mutongi, K. (2007). *Worries of the heart: Widows, family, and community in Kenya*. Chicago, IL: The University of Chicago Press.

Myhre, C. K. (2015). What the beer shows: Exploring ritual and ontology in Kilimanjaro. *American Ethnologist, 42*, 97–115.

Netting, R. M. (1964). Beer as a locus of value among the west African Kofyar. *American Anthropologist, 66*, 375–384.

Nzomo, M., & Staudt, K. (1994). Man-made political machinery in Kenya: Political space for women? In B. J. Nelson & N. Chowdhury (Eds.), *Women and politics worldwide* (pp. 416–435). New Haven, CT: Yale University Press.

Olenyo, M. M. J. (2011). What is in a name? An analysis of the semantics of Lulogooli personal names. *International Journal of Humanities and Social Science, 1*(20), 211–218.

Orvis, S. (1997). *The agrarian question in Kenya*. Gainesville, FL: University Press of Florida.

Osogo, J. (1966). *A history of the Baluyia*. Nairobi: Oxford University Press.

Parker, R. N., & McCaffree, K. J. (2013). *Alcohol and violence: The nature of the relationship and the promise of prevention*. Lanham, MD: Lexington Books.

Reinharz, S. (1992). *Feminist methods in social research*. New York, NY: Oxford University Press.

Roberts, B. D. (2000). Always cheaply pleasant: Beer as a commodity in a rural Kenya society. In A. Haugerud, M. P. Stone, & P. D. Little (Eds.), *Commodities and globalization: Anthropological perspectives* (pp. 179–196). Lanham, MD: Rowman & Littlefield Publishers.

Ross, O. (2013). Beer you can eat: Africa's homebrew becomes big business. Retrieved from https://www.thestar.com/news/world/2013/10/07/beer_you_can_eat_africas_homebrew_becomes_big_business.html

Saito, K. A., & Weidemann, C. J. (1991). *Agricultural extension for women farmers*. Washington, DC: The World Bank.

Sangree, W. H. (1962). The social functions of beer drinking in Bantu Tiriki. In D. J. Pittman & C. R. Snyder (Eds.), *Society, culture and drinking patterns* (pp. 6–21). New York, NY: Wiley.

Sangree, W. H. (1965). The Bantu Tiriki of western Kenya. In J. L. Gibbs, Jr (Ed.), *Peoples of Africa: Cultures of Africa south of the Sahara* (pp. 43–79). Prospect Heights, IL: Waveland Press.

Scott, C. V. (1995). *Gender and development: Rethinking modernization and dependency theory*. Boulder, CO: Lynne Rienner Publishers.

Skaine, R. (1996). *Power and gender: Issues in sexual dominance and harassment*. Jefferson, NC: McFarland and Company, Inc., Publishers.

Sobania, N. (2003). *Culture and customs of Kenya*. Westport, CT: Greenwood Press.

Stanley, L., & Wise, S. (1990). Method, methodology and epistemology in feminist research process. In L. Stanley (Ed.), *Feminist praxis: Research, theory and epistemology in feminist sociology* (pp. 20–61). New York, NY: Routledge.

Subbo, W. K. (2001). Socioeconomic and cultural implications of alcohol beverages among the Abagusii of western Kenya. In I. De Garine & V. De Garine (Eds.), *Drinking: Anthropological approaches* (pp. 205–211). New York, NY: Berghahn Books.

Suda, C. (1996). The political economy of women's work in Kenya: Chronic constraints and broken barriers. In P. Ghorayshi & C. Belanger (Eds.), *Women, work, and gender relations in developing countries: A global perspective* (pp. 75–90). Westport, CT: Greenwood Press.

Suggs, D. N. (1996). Mosadi Tshwene: The constraints of gender and the consumption of alcohol in Botswana. *American Ethnologist, 23*, 597–610.

United Nations. (1991). *The world's women, 1970–1990: Trends and statistics*. New York, NY: United Nations.

Verma, V. (2001). *Gender, land, and livelihoods in East Africa: Through farmers' eyes*. Ottawa: International Development Research Centre.

Wagner, G. (1949). *The Bantu of north Kavirondo* (Vol. I). London: Oxford University Press.

Wagner, G. (1955). The Abaluyia of Kavirondo. In D. Forde (Ed.), *African worlds: Studies in the cosmological ideas and social values of African peoples* (pp. 27–54). London: Oxford University Press.

Weisner, T., & Abbott, S. (1977). Modernization, urbanization, and stress: A controlled comparison from East Africa. *Journal of Anthropological Studies, 35*(4), 421–451.

Were, G. S., & Wilson, D. A. (1987). *East Africa through a thousand years: A history of the years AD 1000 to the present day*. New York, NY: Africana Publishing Company.

Willis, J. (2001). 'Beer used to belong to older men': Drink and authority among the Nyakyusa of Tanzania. *Africa, 71*, 373–390.

Willis, J. (2002). *Potent brews: A social history of alcohol in East Africa, 1950-1999*. Athens, OH: Ohio University Press.

Willis, J. (2010). Protecting young people: Alcohol, advertising, and youth in Kenya. In A. Burton & H. Charton-Bigot (Eds.), *Generations past: Youth in East African history* (pp. 279–292). Athens, OH: Ohio University Press.

Women in Law and Development in Africa. (1990). *Origins and issues*. Washington, DC: OEF International.

SYNERGISTIC CHANGE AND SMALLHOLDER AGRICULTURE IN PÉREZ ZELEDÓN, COSTA RICA*

Deborah Sick

ABSTRACT

Purpose – *This chapter examines changes in smallholder agriculture in terms of processes of de-agrarianization in a rapidly changing regional economy of Costa Rica long characterized by small-scale commercial coffee farming.*

Methodology – *The study is based on multiple periods (1990–1991, 1993, 2006, 2010–2012) of ethnographic research on household economic strategies among farming families in two districts in the canton of Pérez Zeledón, Costa Rica.*

Findings – *Though occupational multiplicity and non-farm-based livelihoods are on the rise, smallholder agriculture continues to play a substantial role in the livelihood strategies of both young and old and in the regional economy, not* in spite *of these trends, but* because *an expanding business sector and an increase in non-farm employment opportunities are creating a demand for agricultural produce and providing new opportunities for*

*This chapter is a substantially revised, updated, and theoretically re-focused version of an earlier paper which dealt with generational livelihood changes in Pérez Zeledón (Sick, 2014).

Anthropological Considerations of Production, Exchange, Vending and Tourism
Research in Economic Anthropology, Volume 37, 33–59

ISSN: 0190-1281/doi:10.1108/S0190-128120170000037003

smallholders to diversify agricultural production, stabilize their incomes and maintain a significant presence in the regional economy. Specific historic conditions and state policies have been important factors in shaping rural economic change, livelihood strategies and smallholder agriculture in this region.

Research limitations – *Sample sizes are relatively small and some data on children's economic activities were obtained second hand from siblings and/or parents.*

Implications – *This research has implications for policy makers, planners and social activists interested in agrarian change.*

Originality/value – *This research provides an important longitudinal lens on the economic strategies of farming households, processes of de-agrarianization and the persistence of small-scale family farmers in today's world.*

Keywords: Rural development; de-agrarianization; smallholders; agriculture; Costa Rica

INTRODUCTION

The fate of the family farmer has long been the subject of debate among academics, policy makers and social activists. In light of national development policies which promoted the modernization of agriculture and the production of agricultural exports as a means to raise rural incomes and support to industrial growth, family farmers were seen variously as 'subsistence-oriented 'communalists', *unwilling* to embrace capitalism; as helpless victims *overpowered* by the capitalist system; or as backward, inefficient, and 'tradition-bound' producers, *unable* to move successfully into that system' (Sick, 2008a, p. 6). Marxist scholars predicted the demise of the smallholder farmers who would be unable to compete with larger and more powerful producers, while economists and organizations like the World Bank advocated the transition of smallholders into non-agricultural sectors of the economy, so as to leave agricultural land available to be consolidated into larger, more efficient units of production.

While both processes have occurred, smallholders (somewhat surprisingly) persist (Rigg, Salamanca, & Thompson, 2016). Today agriculture continues to provide the foundation for the livelihoods of millions throughout the world. While estimates vary, over 90% of farms worldwide can be classified as family farms[1] (smaller-scale farms that rely predominately on live-in family labour) that produce crops and livestock on roughly 53% of the world's agricultural land (Graueb et al., 2016, pp. 5–6, see also FAO, 2014; World Bank, 2007).

In the new millennium, scholars, practitioners, policy makers and activists have renewed their interest in family farming, not just in terms of their position vis-a vis the modernization of agriculture and transitioning economies, but in recognition that it continues to be the basis of millions of rural livelihoods and the backbone of many regional economies. For many, sustaining smallholder agriculture is 'the best means to promote rural development, sustain rural livelihoods, and ameliorate rural poverty' (Rigg et al. 2016, p. 119). And following the world food crisis of the early 2000s in particular, family farming is increasingly advocated as a significant means of more sustainably contributing to food security. Marking this shift in attitude towards smallholder farming and its potential to alleviate poverty and provide better food security for millions, in 2014 the United Nations launched the International Year of Family Farming (IYFF). Nevertheless, continued rural poverty, high rates of rural out – migration and declines in the relative importance of agricultural production to rural household incomes remind us of the precarious position of family farmers and have raised alarms and their future in today's world.

In this chapter I examine changes in smallholder agriculture in terms of processes of de-agrarianization in Pérez Zeledón, Costa Rica, a canton that since the mid-twentieth century overwhelmingly has been reliant on smallholder coffee production. Drawing on my 1990–1991 ethnographic research with coffee-producing households in two farming districts in the canton, subsequent research on alternative coffee markets in 2006, and a re-study (2010–2012) of a subsample of these same farming households and their now adult children,[2] I analyse the ways in which changing demographic patterns, new socio-cultural trends, diversifying national and regional economies, ever-uncertain international markets and a general shift away from agriculturally based livelihoods are affecting farming households who, for the most part, have been reliant on export agriculture. This longitudinal lens allows for a better understanding of the conditions which have been shaping rural economic change, livelihood strategies and smallholder agricultural production in this region. I argue that while occupational multiplicity and non-farm-based livelihoods (especially among the younger generation) are on the rise in Perez Zeledón, smallholder agriculture continues to play a substantial role in the livelihood strategies of both young and old and in the regional economy, *not in spite of* these trends, but *because* of them.

THE DEMISE OF THE FAMILY FARM? LIVELIHOOD DIVERSIFICATION AND DE-AGRARIANIZATION

Farming is a risky business, especially for smallholders with few resources at their command. Farmers are quick to point out how fickle Mother Nature and markets can be and how risky farming is. The flexibility to channel labour into alternative income-producing activities that is inherent in family farming contributes to the persistence and resiliency of smallholders (see e.g. Netting, 1993). Still, in the last 20 years, a growing body of research has shown that not only have small-scale farming households worldwide increasingly come to rely on diversified income-producing activities, but that many – especially among the younger generation – are leaving agriculture entirely (see e.g. Bah et al. 2003; Barrett, Reardon, & Webb, 2001; Davis et al., 2010; Li, 2009; Ramisch, 2014; Rigg, 2006).

Many scholars argue that increased global competition, weak domestic markets, and shrinking landholdings have made it difficult for small-scale farmers to survive on agricultural production alone. In many parts of the world, lack of land for small-scale farmers to cultivate has been (historically and currently) the result of land grabs by the state, large landowners or agri-businesses (see e.g. Brockett, 1990; McMichael, 2013; North, 1981; Saturnino, Hall, Scoones, White, & Wolford, 2011; Zoomers, 2010). Occupational multiplicity within farming households and trends of 'de-agrarianization' can be read as signs of the vulnerability of smallholders operating within an inherently inequitable global capitalist system in which their relatively weak position vis-à-vis more powerful players whose control resources, commodity networks and policy-making make it difficult for them to survive (see e.g. McMichael, 2006).

Under these conditions, farming families are forced to resort to 'distress diversification', relying on low-paying agricultural wage labour or other non-farm economic activities to re-pay debts or supplement their farming efforts or to leave agriculture altogether as it no longer provides a means to support oneself and one's family. Furthermore, in most of the world' rural regions, non-farm employment that pays a living wage is often difficult to find (see e.g. Li, 2009). Migration to search for wage labour in urban centres or abroad is now common for millions throughout the developing world (see e.g. Cohen, 2004; Gray, 2009; Ramisch, 2014) and is, in many instances, an indicator of the difficulties facing small-scale farmers and their families.

There is indeed a good deal of evidence that smallholder farming households are facing incredible struggles to survive and prosper. Yet, while many scholars see the growing trends of increasing smallholder livelihood diversification and 'de-agrarianization' as harbingers of the demise of family farmers, Rigg, Salamanca, and Parnwell (2012) argue that an increase in occupational multiplicity and a relative decline in returns to agriculture does not necessarily denote a livelihood crisis for rural peoples. A number of studies have indicated that the growing importance of rural non-farm activities in smallholder household economic strategies is not due to economic distress. For many smallholders, occupational multiplicity is a means of improving standards of living. Producing for mere subsistence does not allow rural households to meet their needs in today's world and income diversification provides a way out of mere subsistence level production and what Rigg terms 'old' poverty (2006, p. 194, see also Barrett et al., 2001; Davis et al., 2010). Furthermore, in many regions with growing populations, agricultural land is becoming more scarce and farm sizes are inadequate to support families. In such cases, a rise in rural *non-farm* employment can be a positive means of absorbing excess labour and providing higher wages than agriculture (World Bank, 2007, pp. 202–221).

Research suggests that increasing occupational multiplicity and a shift away from farming in rural Pérez Zeledón is the result of a number of push (necessity-driven) and pull (opportunity-driven) factors (see e.g. Hansson, Ferguson, Olofsson, & Rantamäki-Lahtinen, 2013; Barrett et al., 2001). On the push side these include: diminishing farm size (due to encroachment by large landowners/agri-businesses and/or population growth); increasing production costs; falling crop prices; weak domestic markets and lack of financial and human resources. Pull side factors include: new and/or better-paying employment or business opportunities; attractions and amenities of urban living; better education and improved infrastructure and transportation. Understanding the precariousness of family farmers and the future of small-scale agriculture in light of increasing non-farm related incomes requires an understanding of relative declines in agricultural returns, increases in non-agricultural incomes (e.g. via wage work, petty commodity production and micro-enterprises) and migration as inter-related parts of broad processes of change (Rigg et al., 2012).

Furthermore, we must understand the specific socio-cultural, political, and regional contexts which have shaped smallholder agriculture in particular locales and within which farming families operate. 'Agrarian change is a function of several different drivers that ... structure everyday life and decision-making, ... [including] the nature of the society in question, its population-environment relationship and pressures on resources, and its history of engaging in commodity markets, levels of technology, and other aspects of political and economic history' (Batterbury, 2007, p. 19). National policies towards agricultural production and smallholder producers vary widely as do local and regional infrastructure, environmental conditions and the socio-cultural contexts of production. Smallholder farming families in the Global South vary in the extent to which they have been integrated into market production, ranging from more subsistence-oriented producers who are being increasingly drawn into cash crop production to those smallholder who have long been 'more closely integrated into the global agro-food system' through their participation in agricultural export production (Akram-Lodhi & Kay, 2010, p. 271).

In order to ascertain whether and/or how diversification and de-agrarianization are indeed indicators of the demise of smallholder agriculture requires not just an understanding of these processes from the perspective of household producers and the broader social and historical contexts which have, and are, shaping their decisions, but an understanding of the dialectic processes at work among agricultural and non-agricultural sectors of regional economies (Davis et al., 2010, pp.48–49).

SMALLHOLDER AGRICULTURE IN PÉREZ ZELEDÓN[3]

Historic Context of Coffee Production in Costa Rica

As throughout much of Central America, since the early nineteenth century, coffee has been a key crop and major export earner for Costa Rica. There is no doubt that the production of coffee as a major cash crop has dramatically altered the lives of small farmers in regions that have relied heavily on its production, but its effects on rural people's livelihoods have been varied, shaped by local contexts and historically defined by demographics, social structures, and political cultures (Cardoso, 1977; Paige, 1987; Roseberry, Gudmundson, & Samper, 1995; Williams, 1994). Though Costa Rica was not immune to the social problems and inequities linked to the rapid rise of coffee production, its historical experience with coffee differed significantly from its neighbours. Elsewhere in Latin America thousands of rural families (especially indigenous peoples) were marginalized and disenfranchised as elites used their power to expand existing estates, control processing and export, and enact laws to coerce labour for coffee production.

Several factors affected the ways in which coffee production in Costa Rica impacted smallholder households. First, during the colonial era, Costa Rica was a small, poor, geographically rugged and culturally backward territory and so was largely avoided by most Spanish colonists (Biesanz, Biesanz, & Biesanz, 1982). With very little indigenous labour that could be exploited, all colonists needed to live and work on their farms, rather than administer large estates from urban cities, as was common elsewhere. Thus, when coffee began to flourish in Costa Rica in the mid-1800s, it did so in an environment of *relatively* equitable land distribution and labour scarcity. The newly rising coffee elite found it more profitable to leave most of the land (and risks of production) in the hands of the existing smallholder sector and instead sought to control of the more lucrative aspects of coffee: processing, export and credit (Cazanga, 1987, p. 73, see also Paige, 1987; Samper, 1990; Winson, 1989).

The control of processing, export and credit did afford elites a tremendous amount of power and control over those who produced Costa Rica's coffee, but the Costa Rican state has done much to support smallholders and to use coffee production as a vehicle for national development. For example, in the 1930s coffee producers were able to unite and pressure the state to step in to regulate the maximum per cent of export earnings that processor-exporters could retain as profits and establish minimum prices as processors could pay farmers (Seligson, 1980, p. 36). In the 1950s, when coffee prices were soaring, the state reduced the profit percentage that could be retained by processor-exporters, in essence establishing a 7% ad valorem tax that was then invested in rural infrastructure, education and health care, which benefitted all. Thus, for the most part, state policies in Costa Rica afforded some measure of protection for family-level producers, which allowed a relatively large, rural middle class of smallholders to share in the rewards of coffee production (Sick, 2008a).

Coffee and Smallholders in Pérez Zeledón

The canton of Pérez Zeledón, where I have been conducting research with farming households since the early 1990s, is located 130 km south of the capital of San José. The main route from San José and the densely populated Central Valley is the two lane Pan American highway which runs up and through the Talamanca mountain range and over the rugged Cerro de la Muerte (Hill of Death). Heavy rains and earthquakes frequently leave the road in bad repair and often impassable. In the early 2000s, Costa Rica invested in finishing and improving the Pacific coastal route which has provided an alternative, if somewhat longer route, in and out of the southern region.

In 2011 Pérez Zeledón had an estimated population of just over 140,000 (INEC, 2015) and encompassed both high valley lands surrounding the Río del General (700 m) and the steep volcanic slopes of the Talamancan Mountains, including Mt. Chirripo, Central America's highest peak (3,820 m). With the exception of the main market centre of San Isidro del General (pop. 45, 327), today the canton's 11 districts remain primarily rural farming districts dotted by small hamlets and villages of less than 1,000 inhabitants (Mideplan, 2013).

Coffee, long the mainstay of the regional economy, arrived relatively late in Pérez Zeledón. Rugged terrain and lack of roads discouraged colonization, leaving the canton a sparsely populated frontier region until the mid-twentieth century.[4] By the 1920s, poorer farmers from the over-crowded coffee zones of the *Meseta Central* (the plateau surrounding the capital of San José) had begun making their way to the region to take advantage of available farmland. Though land was suitable for coffee production, with no processing facilities and poor transportation, commercial coffee production was impossible. During this era, farmers produced rice, beans, sugarcane and some coffee for home consumption. Many earned a modest cash income by feeding corn to pigs which they then herded over the mountains to the cities of Cartago and San José to sell or trade for goods unavailable in Pérez Zeledón.

Eager to increase coffee export revenues and anxious to relieve demographic pressures on the crowded Meseta Central, from the 1940s to 1970s, the Costa Rican government encouraged migration to Pérez Zeledón through homesteading opportunities, land redistribution programs and the construction of a coffee-processing factory. Following the completion of the Pan American highway in the late 1940s, thousands of families flooded Pérez Zeledón hoping to engage in coffee production. Coffee prices were good and by the 1980s and early 1990s, the canton was one of the fastest growing coffee-producing regions in Costa Rica. Production was overwhelmingly done by smallholder farming families and processing done locally by one cooperative and several private factories. Export and marketing were heavily regulated by the state. At this time, the state was still heavily vested in coffee exports and most rural households in the canton relied on conventional coffee production[5] as their primary source of income. Prices had been good, and there was little support for other crops or non-conventional coffee production. Thus, by the latter part of the twentieth century, the majority of farming households produced little else other than coffee, not even for their own subsistence needs (Sick, 2008a).

Agricultural commodity markets are known for their volatility. Coffee is a prime example. From 1958 to 1989 producer and consumer nations attempted to temper this volatility through a series of International Coffee Agreements (ICAs) which regulated worldwide production and exports through a quota system. Though prices still fluctuated, for the most part prices remained relatively high.[6] But in 1989, ICO members failed to reach a new agreement. According to Daviron and Ponte (2005), several factors contributed to the breakdown: conflicts among members over free-riders and quotas, an increase in production and sale among non-member countries, a desire among consumer countries to have more access to better quality *arabica* coffee (Brazil dominated production with less-desirable *robusta* varieties), and an end to Cold War tensions and the U.S. fears that weak Latin American economies would spur a rise in communist sympathies (pp. 87–88).[7] With no international regulations on coffee production, producing countries dumped their surpluses on the world market, countries that produced relatively little during the era of ICAs (e.g. Vietnam) dramatically increased production for the world market and prices fell. As a result, throughout the late 1980s and 1990s, Costa Rican coffee-producing households were forced to contend not just with growing populations and pressures on farmland, but with ever-more competitive and volatile global markets and changing consumer preferences. Few alternatives to export-oriented coffee production existed.

At the time of the coffee crisis of the early 1990s the communities of Santa Cruz and Palomas where I was conducting research were each the largest villages within their districts. Both had populations of between 400–500 and smallholder farming – primarily coffee and some sugarcane production (more so in Palomas) – was the principle occupation. Median farm size in each village (typical of the canton as a whole) was just over 2 ha in each. In the early 1990s, households in these two communities, like farming households throughout the country, were struggling to cope with the downturn in the international coffee market. They attempted to do so in a number of ways (see Sick, 1997).

First, many reduced expenditures by decreasing production inputs (commercial fertilizers and pesticides), though the end result was lower yields. At that time organic markets were not well developed. Commercial organic fertilizers were not available and farming households did not produce enough organic waste to convert into fertilizer for commercial coffee production Second, some farmers attempted to diversify agricultural production until coffee prices might recover, but other crops and small-scale livestock production (e.g. garden vegetables, tropical fruits, cattle, pigs) were equally as risky, and processing facilities and access to markets were limited. For example, in the 1980s, agricultural extension agents encouraged farmers to plant an easy-to-grow ornamental cane which is widely used as a houseplant in North America. Several farmers did so, but when the plants were ready for sale, they found the international market saturated, prices were low, and shipping costs so high that there was no commercial value left in the crop. In another case in 1990, one farmer and his son had great plans to bypass the volatility of international markets by producing garden vegetables for sale in the local market town of San Isidro, but they abandoned this plan within a year. Roads were poor and travel time to market long; vegetables were too delicate and spoiled quickly. Finally, a few households attempted to supplement their incomes with 'micro-enterprises' (e.g. selling a few eggs or knitted clothes to neighbours or selling 'weed-eater services' to famers short of labour) (see Sick, 1997). In the early 1990s, this was one of the few ways to supplement farm income as, apart from seasonal coffee harvesting, there were few wage labour opportunities in Pérez Zeledón – either agricultural or non-agricultural.

For the most part, these efforts were insufficient to cope with the severity of the situation. The costs of leaving coffee entirely (a long-term tree crop) were high as coffee represented a considerable investment. Risks of ripping out or selling off that investment for uncertain alternatives were too high and few viable local options for diversifying livelihoods existed. So, during the early 1990s, the majority of households in Palomas and Santa Cruz held on to their coffee, relying on temporary migration and remittances from family members abroad (primarily to the United States) in order to survive (*ibid.*). But the incentive to invest in new trees disappeared almost entirely as few farmers could afford to put more money into a crop that provided little income and as trees aged, yields dropped, and so did coffee incomes.

In typical boom-bust fashion, the market recovered somewhat during the 1990s, but then began to drop again. By 2001 the world price of coffee had dropped to a 100-year-low of US dollar 0.47/lb. For many, this was the straw that broke the camel's back. Unheard of 20 years earlier, farmers throughout Costa Rica were cutting down their coffee in record numbers, removing coffee for other agro-pastoral activities. While this practice was more prevalent in the north-central regions of Costa Rica, in Pérez Zeledón, 29% of the 48 households that I interviewed in Palomas and Santa Cruz in 2010–2012 had cut a portion of their coffee (Sick, 2014).[8] The situation was indeed dire and was one of several inter-related factors contributing to significant regional economic change.

OCCUPATIONAL MULTIPLICITY AND THE EXIT FROM AGRICULTURE

Both Palomas and Sta. Cruz have grown considerably since my initial research in the early 1990s. In 2012, Sta. Cruz's population was nearly double that of 1990 and that of Palomas nearly three times as great. In both, farming remains a key economic activity, though not the primary means of livelihood that it was. Of the 48 households in my 2010–2012 re-study (30 households from the original study plus households of their now adult children) only seven (15%) had left farming altogether to pursue other income-earning ventures. About one-quarter of my sample households were engaged in both farming and wage labour at some point in 2010–2012.

As noted above, attempting to diversify income sources is not a new strategy for farming households in Pérez Zeledón. Data on income sources from households in Santa Cruz, Palomas, and other rural villages in the canton indicate that while some farming households indeed have turned to other sources of income due to severe distress during acute drops in the global coffee market, levels and types of income diversification fluctuate over time and cover a broad spectrum of activities. Discussions with members of farming households in Pérez Zeledón concerning the mix of various wage labour and other types of non-agricultural income-earning activities (e.g. small-business ventures) and farming activities indicate a number of reasons, other than immediate distress, for income diversification today. These include: to improve standards of living, to guard against perceived risks (perhaps in preparation for children leaving farming), and to meet personal preferences, skills and opportunities available to household members. I do not wish to downplay the severity of the impact of the drop in world coffee prices which left many scrambling to find ways to feed their families, but as discussed below, the changing structure of the regional economy of Perez Zeledón is providing opportunities for farming households to diversify in ways that limit their exposure and mediate the impacts of participation in volatile agricultural export markets.

More telling of the transformation of the economy are the generational livelihood data for the 26 extended-family groups that were the focus of the 2010–2012 study.[9] Of the total of 113 adult children (age 16 or older) who were born into households that were engaged in coffee farming in the early 1990s, 24 (21%) rely on agriculture as their primary source of income. Of the remaining 83 economically active adult children who continue to reside in Costa Rica (i.e. not counting the 30 who are full-time students or have migrated abroad permanently) over 70% support themselves through wage labour (primarily non-farm work) and small-business ownership (see Table 1).

As elsewhere, these trends raise concerns about the future of not just farming families, but smallholder agriculture in general, in the canton. Yet, though the data might suggest that family farmers are simply unable to survive and

Table 1. Primary Occupation of Economically Active Adult Children[a] Born into Farming Households in Palomas and Sta. Cruz, Residing in Costa Rica.

Primary Occupation	Farming	Wage Labour			Small Business	Total Non-Farmers
		Ag.	Non-Ag (PT)	Non-Ag (FT)		
Palomas	13	4	4	23	5	36
($n=49$)	(26.5%)	(8.2%)	(8.2%)	(46.9%)	(10.2%)	(73.5%)
Sta. Cruz	11	1	4	17	1	23
($n=34$)	(32.4%)	(2.9%)	(11.8%)	(50.0%)	(2.9%)	(67.6%)
Total	24	5	8	40	6	59
($N=83$)	(28.9%)	(6.0%)	(9.6%)	(48.2%)	(7.2%)	(71.1%)

Source: Author's survey data 2010–2012.
[a]Age 16+.

that small-scale farming is in danger of disappearing, the situation is complex. The data from Pérez Zeledón suggest that these trends are due not just to frustrations with coffee production and the difficulties facing smallholders in general, but to the opportunities provided by the more diversified and dynamic economy of Perez Zeledón in particular and Costa Rica more generally.

The latest coffee crisis has indeed played a big role in livelihood diversification and the move out of agriculture, but two other factors appear to be more directly related to this shift away from farming in general. First, population growth has led to an increase in the number of *minifundia* – landholdings too small to support a family through agriculture alone. The problem of insufficient land or loss of land to more powerful interests is a well-noted phenomenon throughout the developing world and has been responsible for much of the 'distress diversification' and migration noted among scholars and policy makers elsewhere.

While there is no doubt small-scale farmers are at a disadvantage vis-à-vis more powerful actors in Costa Rica, the increase in *minifundia* in Pérez Zeledón is due less to an expansion of large-scale farming and agribusiness than it is to population growth and the division and re-division of landholdings among descendants over several generations. Apart from one large plantation in the southern part of the canton that has existed since the mid-1980s,[10] coffee production and farming in general remains overwhelmingly small-scale and household-based. As noted earlier, the persistence of smallholder agriculture in the region is likely due to early state policies and demographic factors which favoured family farming during the emergence of the coffee economy in the late 19th and early 20th centuries, but a rugged, mountainous environment may also be a factor in the predominance of small-scale farms over large plantations in the region. Whatever the reason, in 2006, 66% of the 3,991 farms in the canton had 1–10 ha of land; average farm size in the canton is 3.4 ha (INEC, 2007).

Combined with a prolonged and devastating downturn in coffee prices and increasing production costs by the early 2000s, many had opted to get out of farming altogether. While I have heard of some farmers elsewhere in the canton who sold their lands due to economic distress, this was the case for only one of my sample households, a man in his mid-40s who became too ill to work his farm and had no savings from his meagre coffee earnings. In need of cash, in the early 2000s he sold his 1.4 ha of coffee to his brother. With no land and only a grade six education, since his recovery this man has been working as a day-labourer for others in the village. His wife works part-time cleaning a church and one daughter as a babysitter for their other married daughter (in a different household) who works full-time in a hair salon in San Isidro.

Such cases do highlight the precariousness of family farming and show how some must leave farming due to severe economic distress. And indeed for many family farmers throughout the world this has been the case. But as noted above, economic distress is not always the driving factor in diversification or an exit from agriculture. In Pérez Zeledón, a major factor *pulling* people away from farming (especially the younger generation) has been an increase in entrepreneurial and non-farm employment opportunities within the canton. Twenty years ago, few steady employment opportunities existed (either within or outside of agriculture) and the growth potential of small businesses was limited by a relatively small population with little disposable income. Migration, either national, or more commonly to the United States, was really the only option for staying afloat when coffee prices dropped (Sick, 1997, 2008a).

In the last decade, the structure of the economy has changed dramatically. Of particular note, rates of migration have dropped significantly. While more than 50% of sample households in the early 1990s had at least one family member working abroad, today only 13% of sample households fit this profile, and more than half of these permanently reside abroad and do not regularly send remittances home. Starting in the early 2000s, increased vigilance against illegal immigrants in the United States (the prime destination for Costa Rican migrants) and that country's recession made working there difficult and dangerous, and large numbers of migrants returned home to Pérez Zeledón. With them they have brought new skills, tastes, and aspirations. Many also brought savings for home improvements, the purchase of a vehicle, or investment in local businesses.[11]

Today, state investment in infrastructure has meant paved roads throughout the canton, decreasing travel times significantly between rural district centres and San Isidro. Public bus service is good, and many individuals now own cars, all of which make it possible for rural residents to commute to work in San Isidro on a daily basis. This new mobility means that many residents of Palomas and Santa Cruz are able to work in the town of San Isidro, which has grown and diversified considerably since the early 1990s. In addition to government offices, the regional hospital, and health care providers, the town and its immediate peri-urban area boasts dozens of small- and medium-scale businesses, hotels, several medium-size food processing and distribution centres, and secondary and post-secondary schools. While many jobs are in the lower-paying service sector, demand for professionals, white collar workers, and skilled labour, such as teachers, nurses, welders and construction workers, has also been steadily increasing throughout the canton. These jobs provide good wages. In fact, five of my sample households had sold all of their coffee lands because they had other stable incomes and said that they did not have time or inclination to farm. In these cases, the sale of agricultural land cannot be read as a sign of distress, but rather as a measured economic strategy to pursue full-time what they believed to be more desirable and sustainable economic opportunities.

Demand for new goods and services, coupled with new transportation and communication technologies, have facilitated the creation and expansion of small businesses, particularly in the market centre of San Isidro, but also within more rural areas such as Palomas and Sta. Cruz. One in particular, a bamboo furniture shop begun by one family on the outskirts of Santa Cruz in the late 1980s is an example of a successful local business providing employment in the countryside. It now sells its furniture nationally and even exports bamboo to the United States and Nicaragua. This expansion has required more labour and in 2010 the business employed 20 people. Following on the success of this business, four other family owned and operated furniture workshops which have opened in hamlets near Santa Cruz. Though neither Santa Cruz nor Palomas attract many tourists, there is a small family-run hotel and karaoke bar just outside of Santa Cruz that was built by a returned migrant. In recent years, a few foreign tourists have begun staying there, but as yet there is no noticeable tourism presence in either Palomas or Santa Cruz. The number of small, family-owned businesses that have appeared in Palomas in the last decade is even greater. There, the main road is now dotted with home-front clothing stores, *pulperias* (local convenience stores), mechanic shops and garages, a bicycle repair shop, hair salon, small butcher shops and a bakery/pizzeria.

These businesses have been financed in a number of ways.[12] Though a few have used personal savings or pension incomes to begin their business ventures, among my sample households most of these businesses were initially capitalized with money made working abroad or by relatives with well-paying full-time jobs. For example, one farmer's son (who works as a teacher in a nearby village) financed the construction of a small gym in Palomas which his younger brother manages. He also financed his father's bicycle repair shop. Two of my sample households financed their businesses by selling their coffee lands. One woman explained that coffee was just too expensive to grow, required too much dirty and difficult work, and in the end did not pay well. So, she sold the land she had inherited from her father and started a small clothing/household goods store in a spare room of her house. For her, selling her land was not a forced action due to severe distress, but rather a choice to establish a means of supporting herself that she found more suitable and desirable.

Finally, as is common in many parts of the rural Global South, those who can are investing in their children's education, hoping that they will be able to secure stable, well-paying jobs that will contribute to the household and provide a more stable livelihood for their children and grandchildren (see e.g. Li, 2009). A growing number of young adults are continuing their education beyond primary and even secondary school. According to one report, 46.2% of the population of Pérez Zeledón have at least a secondary education (Mideplan, 2013). In the districts of Palomas and Sta. Cruz, rates of secondary education are somewhat lower (31.5% and 30.5%, respectively (*ibid.*)). Among my 2010–2012 sample, 6% of adult children aged 16 or older in Palomas and 22% in Sta. Cruz were full-time students. Nevertheless, many parents in these rural villages are encouraging their children to continue with their education and some independent adults are returning to school on their own initiative. Secondary school degrees (uncommon in the previous generation) have allowed many to find employment in shops, services industries, businesses, banks and schools in the canton (Sick, 2014, p. 45).

Finally, following the trend seen throughout much of the world, many children are showing no interest in farming. Two older farmers explained that they had sold all their coffee lands because they wanted to retire and none of their children were interested in farming. Younger, middle-aged parents in one household were facing a similar future. None of their children have shown an interest in taking over their 6 ha farm, so they are doing what they can to send their children to local universities to study, but wondering what will become to the farm as they get older.

THE END OF SMALLHOLDER AGRICULTURE PÉREZ ZELEDÓN?

This increase in non-agricultural wage labour and small businesses is significant, but small-scale agricultural production continues as the main livelihood strategy for a significant number of rural households and a pillar of the regional economy. Of the 48 farming households re-interviewed in 2010–2012, 39 households (81%) continue to rely on farming as their main livelihood activity. Of their economically active adult children who now have their own households, nearly 30% listed farming as their main economic activity (26.5% in Palomas and 32.4% in Sta. Cruz). This is certainly a substantial decrease from 20 years ago, but does it represent the beginning of the end for smallholder agriculture in the region? Perhaps, but a number of new avenues of production for smallholders have opened up which have the potential of re-invigorating the agricultural sector and provide new opportunities for small-scale family farmers in the region.

Diversified Coffee Markets

Since the collapse of the ICA, the international coffee market has become more competitive and volatile. Though coffee production in Costa Rica has declined significantly in the last two decades and many have given it up entirely, the Costa Rican state has invested in efforts to rejuvenate coffee farms by assisting with the replacement of aging coffee trees with younger stock (SEPSA, 2016, p. 7) and in Pérez Zeledón it remains the dominant crop for farmers in the region. Prices have continued to rise. In 2011 the composite price of non-Colombian milds (the coffee produced in Costa Rica) reached $2.71 lb, though had dropped again, to $1.60/lb in 2015 (ICO, n.d.).

Today's international coffee market is also considerably more diversified, with consumers demanding that the market differentiate among various qualities, including taste and the environmental and social impacts of production. Though these markets remain relatively small, they are growing rapidly and provide new niches particularly for small-scale producers. In addition, in the 1990s, Costa Rica relaxed many of its export regulations, providing opportunities for individual producers and coffee cooperatives to sell directly to specialty coffee buyers without having to go through state-level exporting organizations.

The gourmet market is the fastest growing and most lucrative of these specialty markets. In today's global economy, discriminating buyers will pay top prices for high-quality coffee, especially for quality *arabicas* produced in the higher elevations of Pérez Zeledón. Prices vary, but range from $0.20 more per pound to hundreds of dollars per pound more than conventional coffee. While some coffee producers in Pérez Zeledón are beginning to benefit from sales to the gourmet market, according to Smith (2009) in general Costa Rica has been slow to transform its processing system to accommodate demands of the gourmet system. Still, during my research visits in 2010–2012, Coopeagri, the region's largest cooperative, was focusing more on single-farm certified coffee to meet the demands of the gourmet market and a number *micro beneficios* (processing plants) had been established in the region by smaller groups of farmers funded by a variety of governmental and non-governmental organizations.

Another potentially lucrative alternative to conventional coffee production is organic coffee. Demand for organic coffee has been steadily growing worldwide and prices are substantially higher than that of conventional coffee. Nevertheless, while I did encounter a handful of farmers who were experimenting with organic and agro-ecological coffee production, few in Pérez Zeledón have yet to venture into non-conventional coffee production in a significant way. Few farms in this region produce enough organic waste to provide sufficient fertilizer for their coffee and while farmers today do have more access to commercially produced organic fertilizers, credit for organic fertilizers is not as readily available and farmers continue to note the lower yields and higher labour costs of organic production.

Since the mid-twentieth century, various alternative trade movements, of which FairTrade is perhaps the most well-known, have been working to temper the inequities and uncertainties facing small-scale farmers who produce for global markets. For many farming families, alternative trade networks, such as FairTrade, are providing new markets specifically aimed at improving profitability of coffee production for smallholders, and many are benefitting (see e.g. Jaffee, Kloppenburg, & Monroy, 2004; Lyon, 2007; Murray, Raynolds, & Taylor, 2003). FairTrade and other alternative niche markets have provided coffee-producing households with other options and thus have provided some measure of income security for family farmers. Nevertheless, as I have noted elsewhere (Sick, 2008a, 2008b), FairTrade and alternative coffee markets *alone* have not been able to significantly been able to improve incomes of coffee-producing households in Pérez Zeledón (see also Smith, 2007 for the southern region of Costa Rica). In my frequent trips through Costa Rica over the course of the last decade, I've noted an ever-changing number of specialty logos on coffee being sold in the country, including FairTrade, Rainforest Alliance, Bird Friendly, and Carbon Neutral. There are multiple reasons farmers are wary of, and frequently change, certification for alternative markets. 'Ethical' markets remain relatively small, consumer 'values' are fickle, and not all pay a guaranteed minimum price to producers. FairTrade does, but consumer demand for FairTrade coffee is still relatively low. Producers must pay the costs of certification, yet typically cannot sell all of their crop to FairTrade at guaranteed prices (Sick, 2008b).

Furthermore, and perhaps more importantly, while gourmet, FairTrade, and other alternative niche markets for the region's coffee do provide better alternatives for smallholders than conventional coffee production they nevertheless remain tied to global markets and the whims of distant consumers. Coffee-producing households remain tied to the booms (which can be very good) and busts of a volatile international agricultural commodity.

Lastly, it is worth noting that within Costa Rica, coffee consumption is on the rise, spurred in large part by its booming tourism industry. North American and European tourists are by and large heavy coffee drinkers and the tourist fascination with coffee as part of Costa Rica's cultural heritage is sparking interest in farm tours which help to provide additional income to cash-strapped smallholders (see e.g. Howitt, 2014). But domestic coffee consumption is also increasing among Costa Rica's growing and more prosperous middle and upper classes. Previously reserved exclusively for the export market, today a huge variety of high-quality Costa Rican coffees are for sale in stores, restaurants, and a growing number of coffee shops throughout the country. Though Café Britt, a large private coffee producer dominates sales at Costa Rica's Juan Santamaria International Airport, many coffee farmers' cooperatives such as Coopeagri in Pérez Zeledón are tapping into the growing tourist and domestic consumer markets either with direct sales of roasted coffee in stores or through more 'value-added' sales of brewed coffee in their own modern, Wi-Fi equipped coffee shops. While these sales are miniscule compared to export sales, they do provide more value-added income to the crop and an alternative to volatile export markets.

Diversifying Farming

Farmers have long recognized that producing a diversity of crops helps protect against the vagaries of markets and Mother Nature and provide a measure of income stability. Those Pérez Zeledón are no exceptions, yet, as noted above, until relatively recently, there were few viable options for doing so. Today, sugarcane – for refined granulated sugar or *dulce* (crude brown sugar milled in domestic *trapiches*) – remains a significant secondary crop for many farmers, but other avenues of production are opening up which take advantage of increased demand for agricultural produce from national, regional, and village consumers.

Following trends elsewhere in the country, several farmers in Pérez Zeledón began in varying degrees to raise beef and dairy livestock (and to a lesser extent pigs). Keeping a single household dairy cow, or the few head of beef cattle pastured in the highlands and sold to cover costs of 'special' occasions or emergencies was not uncommon in the past (Sick, 2008a), but growing domestic demand for dairy, beef, and pork, coupled with better roads and transportation, new regional processing facilities, and new storage technologies have made meat and dairy production more attractive. Today farmers are raising livestock not just to meet subsistence needs, but for village, regional, and national markets.

Ten households in my 2010–2012 re-study (21%) removed their coffee specifically in order to diversify their agro-pastoral activities in some way. In one case, the male-head of household and three of his siblings cut their combined 10 ha of coffee and bought 20 head of beef cattle, which were cared for by this man. They told me they have no desire to return to coffee production. But raising livestock carries its own risks. For example, at the height of the coffee crisis of the early 2000s, one young family cut 2 ha of coffee to raise dairy cows. They began with one cow to provide milk for the household and for sale to neighbours to help them put food on the table during these stressful economic times. The venture went well and they then expanded to three cows and within three years had expanded to 10. They took out a loan to purchase a refrigerated storage tank and began selling milk to a local milk producers' association as well as homemade cheese to neighbours. But after two years, they found that tending dairy cows required larger labour inputs (milking and providing fodder for a larger herd, transporting milk to the processing factory) and entailed more risk than they had expected. When several of their cows suddenly and unexplainably died within the span of just a few weeks, the family decided to abandon commercial dairy production, selling off the remaining cows to re-pay their loans (keeping just one cow to provide milk for the household), and invested in re-juvenating their aging coffee fields.

Most farmers in the region have attempted to wean themselves away from coffee and diversify through the production of other crops. Two farmers (one in Palomas and one in Santa Cruz) removed some of their coffee trees in order to plant *mamon chino* (rambutan, a popular type of tropical fruit) trees in anticipation of growth for both export and domestic markets. A new fruit-producers association has been formed in the canton and is working on developing networks for the sale of fresh, as well as processed (jams and juices), 'exotic' fruits such as the *mamon*.

Not all diversification has come at the expense of coffee. The biggest avenue for diversification for smallholders in the region is the growing demand for agricultural produce *within* the canton and to some extent, within rural villages. This includes the sale of what I term 'wild domesticates' – the many fruits and tubers that have long grown among coffee trees and around homes and do not require additional land, labour or other inputs – and the more lucrative *hortalizas* (garden vegetables and herbs) which require specialized growing conditions and care. While some farming households have pulled out coffee to grow the potentially more lucrative *hortalizas* (this is particularly so in the higher elevation village of San Gerardo de Rivas), *hortaliza* production carries its own risks, and for the most part, farmers in Palomas and Sta. Cruz are experimenting with *hortalizas* on a relatively small-scale basis on unused lands around their homes.

Thus far, farmers' attempts to tap into the emerging regional market for *hortalizas* have been varied. Most are working on a trial-and-error basis. Poor soils, brutal summer sun, and harsh winter rains make production of garden vegetables tricky (and risky). One relatively new method has been the construction of low-tech greenhouses (*invernaderos*): simple wooden frames with open sides and a roof of heavy clear plastic. These vary in size from a few square metres to hundreds of square metres. Greenhouses are found extensively in the higher elevations around Mt. Chirripo where tomato production is big, but are increasingly being used by farmers elsewhere in the canton who are experimenting with the production of lettuce, cilantro, parsley and various other leafy vegetables for sale in San Isidro. This technology has facilitated the viable commercial production of garden vegetables in the region, but while relatively inexpensive, even low-tech greenhouses require some level of capital investment.

A few farmers have taken advantage of niches that, for the moment, have made market garden production profitable and sustainable. One notable example is a family in Palomas that cut about 0.25 ha of coffee to build a roadside greenhouse in which they grow lettuce, cilantro, and other leafy vegetables for sale to the residents of Palomas and villages beyond who pass by on their daily commute to/from their jobs in San Isidro. The family has a ready market at hand and does not have to worry about transport costs. As the owner explained, 'people want healthier food. It is cheaper to grow it here and people don't have to go all the way to San Isidro to buy it'.

In another case, a family living on the mountain slopes several kilometres from Santa Cruz has specialized in the production of cilantro for sale to restaurants and supermarkets in San Isidro. While this operation is slightly larger than most (about 0.5 ha) it is still a rather low-cost investment. The family uses organic fertilizer that it produces itself from organic material and cow manure. The crop is planted so as to provide a continuous yield and produce is taken by motorcycle every day to sell in San Isidro.

Two factors seem to be driving this demand for agricultural produce within the canton. First, the increase in wage labour-based livelihoods means a larger number of non-food producing households, many who now have more disposable income, thus increasing demand for local foodstuffs. Second, dietary habits are changing in Pérez Zeledón. While these changes include a shift towards more nutritionally questionable processed foods, at the same time, more families now regularly include a number of garden vegetables in their diets than they did 20 years ago. Rice and black beans remain the foundation of any meal and are typically accompanied by one of many varieties of local tubers (e.g. yucca). But a growing diversity of foods has entered people's diets including a wider variety of garden vegetables, such as lettuce, tomatoes, chilies and cabbage. Several factors may have contributed to dietary changes: higher disposable incomes among wage-labourers, public efforts to improve diets, migrants returning from the United States with new taste preferences, and/or the presence of foreign tourists and ex-pats in the canton. Whatever the reason, it is clear that consumption of high-value garden vegetables is on the rise, providing a new local market for farmers. As noted earlier, one of the biggest problems facing smallholder producers attempting to grow market vegetables has been poor transportation and crop spoilage. Better road conditions and more affordable vehicles, due to lowering of import duties, mean that farmers are now able to get their crops to markets before they spoil, thus allowing many to take advantage of increasing domestic demand in ways they previously could not.

National markets are also providing an avenue for diversification. A burgeoning urban population in and around the capital of San Jose in the Central Valley has increased demand for agricultural produce there. State investments in better roads and transportation now allow farmers in rural districts of Pérez Zeledón to get produce to this more lucrative market in San Jose and the Central Valley before they spoil. While garden vegetables are produced in abundance within the Central Valley, there is a demand for tropical fruits (e.g. bananas, citrus, mamon, papaya) which grow more readily in the southern climes such as Peréz Zeledón.

A family-operated fruit transport business in Santa Cruz is of particular interest as it demonstrates the potential synergy between entrepreneurial enterprise and new avenues for smallholder production. Starting with one old car in the mid-1990s, this family now owns two large half-ton trucks. They buy tropical fruit from farmers throughout the southern *brunca* region of Costa Rica and sell it to retailers in San Jose. Not only has this become a thriving business for this family, but farmers in Santa Cruz and surrounding districts now have a commercial outlet for tropical fruits which have long grown in and around their coffee fields and homes. Previously there was no way to deal with surplus. Most was given away and much just rotted. Though most farmers said that they usually just sold a few bunches of bananas or boxes of oranges at a time, two households were actually planting some of their unused land in orange trees in order to supply this market.

These new avenues for farming families to diversify and expand their operations offer opportunities that did not exist 30 years ago, but some caution is in order. As with the many alternatives with which farmers previous have experimented (Sick, 1997), new avenues also come with risks as we saw above in the example of the young family who cut some of their coffee to raise dairy cows. New crops and agro-pastoral products require new skills, knowledge, and networks to develop, and over-saturation can occur in domestic markets as well as international ones. This happened in 2009–2010 when dozens of families began to produce lettuce to sell to markets and restaurants in San Isidro. Hopeful farmers quickly learned that local markets are also volatile. Over-production in the region led to a drop in prices, and because lettuce is time-sensitive, many people found their lettuce bolting to seed before they could sell.

CONCLUSIONS: TRANSFORMATIVE SYNERGIES AND FAMILY FARMING

Since the twentieth century, coffee production and exports have been the basis of the regional economy of Pérez Zeledón; consequently the livelihoods of farming households have long been tied to a volatile international export market. Though coffee remains the dominant crop for most farmers of the region and a cultural symbol of Costa Rican identity, the economy of Pérez Zeledón is undergoing dramatic transformations. Most farming households today rely on various mixtures of agricultural and non-agricultural incomes, and many young adults from farming households are leaving – or hoping to leave – farming altogether. While these trends might be taken as indicators of the demise of smallholder agriculture in Pérez Zeledón, family farming in the canton remains strong. Regional and household data from over 20 years suggest that smallholder agriculture continues to play a substantial role in the livelihood strategies of both young and old in the regional economy, not *in spite* of these trends, but *because* of them. An expanding business sector and an increase in non-farm employment opportunities are creating a demand for agricultural produce and providing new opportunities for smallholders to diversify agricultural production.

Viewed from a micro socio-economic perspective, occupational diversification can be understood as a means for members within farming households to guard against risk and ensure some measure of material well-being. This logic extends to ties among closely related households as well. Familial and personal ties of reciprocity mean that members of farming households can provide close relatives and friends in households who have abandoned farming altogether in favour on non-farm work with agricultural products; in return, those with secure jobs might provide cash and/or social connections to members of farming households as needed. While such intra- and inter-household mutual support and obligations certainly are important functions of occupational multiplicity, of equal importance is the inter-sectoral synergy that is occurring at the regional level.

Yes, decreasing farm size, increasing costs of production, volatile markets and falling commodity prices have certainly played a role in the decline in agriculture, but the 'pull' factors – the emergence of attractive and accessible employment opportunities *in the region* – have been the force behind the changes we are seeing. As Rigg et al. (2016) note about similar transformations in Asia, 20 years ago rural dwellers in Pérez Zeledón 'had few *easily available* alternatives to family farm-based work' (p. 124, emphasis added). Driven in large part by population growth (rather than the expansion of large-scale farming and agri-businesses) and facilitated by state investments in infrastructure and education, over the course of the last two decades the growth in *locally accessible* non-farm economic activities has created a sector of consumers who are driving demand for fresh foodstuffs. This increased demand for agricultural products and goods and services of all kinds do not stem from a 'dispossessed peasantry', but from a growing new rural middle class with more disposable income than the previous generation had. Rather than struggling to survive on *minifundia*, this cohort of wage-earners is able to support local farmers' efforts to provide food.

Thus, the livelihoods of those engaged in various forms of agricultural and non-agricultural activities are intricately inter-related, not just at the household level in which diversification is part of household economic strategies, but – and perhaps more importantly – at the regional level, where occupational diversification has created complementary sectors within the broader regional economy. The growth of the non-farm sector does not necessarily come at the expense of smallholder agriculture, but rather may have come to its rescue as the food needs of a growing sector of the population now removed from food production are providing new opportunities for smallholders who have long been struggling with the volatilities of a distant and volatile international commodity market. Thus, many small-scale farming households today are surviving and in large part even prospering, not in spite of the flight from agriculture into wage labour employment, but because of it.

Socio-economic change does not happen in a vacuum. The flourishing of accessible non-farm employment opportunities in Pérez Zeledón as well as the ability of local smallholders to step in to meet growing local demand for foodstuffs is the result of several factors. As noted earlier, the Costa Rican state historically helped to foster the survival of small-scale family farmers. More recently, investments in paved roads, public transportation and the infrastructure for new information and communication technologies throughout the canton allow not only rural residents to easily commute to jobs in the main market town of San Isidro, but also farmers to safely deliver fragile, yet high-value crops to urban consumers within the canton and elsewhere in the country. Though most farming households in Pérez Zeledón have chosen not to get out of coffee production entirely (as it can be a very lucratic crop and one they know well), perhaps one of the greatest benefits of these new avenues of production is that farmers now have opportunities to become a bit less reliant on distant and volatile global commodity markets.

Costa Rica has long been noted for its universal public education system and educational opportunities in Pérez Zeledón have continued to improve. San Isidro now has branch campuses of three universities and several technical schools of various types. The data from Pérez Zeledón show that parents are increasingly investing in education for their children – and even themselves – in order to take advantage of the growing job opportunities outside of agriculture. But educational opportunities are benefitting farming households in other ways as well. As one farmer explained to me, he has hopes that his son will study agricultural economics and management at university so that he would be better equipped to manage their farm when he came of age.

Finally, at the regional level, farming families in Pérez Zeledón have a strong and politically active presence. Coopeagri, the region's largest and most influential agricultural cooperative, has been instrumental in guarding the interests of smallholders in the face of more powerful private coffee-processing and exporting companies. By working to directly establish coffee contracts with few intermediaries, providing affordable credit and inputs, investigating and supporting sustainable alternatives to coffee production, and by negotiating with the state to provide landless labourers with access to land with long-term leases, this innovative farmers' cooperative (unlike many) has been instrumental in preserving the smallholder presence in the canton (Sick, 2008a).

Rural livelihoods in Pérez Zeledón are undergoing enormous change, change linked to a number of international, national and regional factors, mostly beyond the control of smallholder farmers and their families. Yet, despite uncertainties, transformations in the regional economy of Pérez Zeledón, the national Costa Rican economy, and international markets do hold some hope for smallholders to more actively shape their own futures. As Netting (1993) noted, flexibility is the hallmark of smallholder households. In Perez Zeledón, most farming households are combining new opportunities within and outside of agriculture, with the variously profitable, yet known, practice of coffee production. The transformations taking place within the regional economy may serve not only to preserve and strengthen the agricultural base of the region, but together with a growing non-farm sector, may provide the basis for further rural economic growth, diversification, and food security for a growing population.

This story does not end here. In Peréz Zeledón, as elsewhere in the developing world, we are witnessing the transformation of an agrarian economy. While data from over 20 years of research with farming households in Pérez Zeledón does provide needed insight into longer term processes of rural economic change, these data, too, only tell a (somewhat larger) piece of an on-going story. There are no guarantees that this synergy will persist. Conventional economic models predict that non-farm wage work will absorb excess labour. While this currently seems to be the case, there are already indications of an over-supply of skilled labour in the canton. As noted above, most young people today have at least a secondary degree and an increasing number are going on to university and technical schools. As education levels in the canton rise, competition for better jobs is becoming fierce and young people and their parents are beginning to worry that even those with more education will not be able to find jobs in the canton. Conventional economic models also predict (and advocate) that as non-farm wage work absorbs excess labour, smallholdings will eventually be subsumed into larger, more efficient farms. While this doesn't seem to be the trend at the moment, there is no guarantee that this will not happen. For example, the canton's only large agri-business, the Dole pineapple plantation in the southern part of the canton, could decide to expand and entice nearby smallholders to sell their farms. Likewise, as is already happening to some extent around Chirripo National Park, farmers might be enticed by the promises of tourism to convert their farms to recreation or conservation areas, though tourists also drive demand for fresh produce. How this will all play out in the long run remains to be seen.

Nevertheless, there is reason to be cautiously optimistic about the ability of smallholders to not only survive, but to prosper in Pérez Zeledón. The possibility of growth in non-farm wage work in conjunction with a strong and dynamic smallholder sector, rather than accompanied by the demise of the smallholder and the rise of large plantation style operations, is not out of the question. While we cannot assume that smallholder agriculture is necessarily a better option than large-scale agriculture in providing for food security in a region, a large and vibrant sector of smallholders *can* provide the basis of a dynamic society (Goldschmidt, 1978; Rosset, 2000; Van der Ploeg, 2014). In Pérez Zeledón, a region historically dominated by family farming rather than large scale agri-businesses, smallholders are poised not only to take advantage of opportunities provided by new niches in international and domestic coffee markets, but they are at the ready to step in and gear production to take advantage of synergistic opportunities that have arisen in a regional economy where non-farm employment is rapidly increasing and diversifies the scope of their agricultural activities. Through the ability to more widely diversify their avenues of agricultural production, smallholders in Pérez Zeledón seem well positioned to maintain a significant presence in the region for many years to come.

NOTES

1. Definitions of what constitutes 'family farms' vary. While the small size of landholdings is often acknowledged as a key characteristics, relevance of size of landholdings varies according to the nature of the resources and type of farming. The reliance on predominantly family labour is generally recognized as the more salient feature of family farming.

2. In 1990–1991 I conducted a series of formal and informal interviews with 36 farming households in Palomas and 40 farming households in Santa Cruz (both are pseudonyms). From 2010 to 12, I conducted a re-study with a sub-sample of 30 of these original farming families (15 in each village) and their now adult children, as well as a select sample of households not related to households in the original study. These included three households in Palomas (two of which were primarily business owners), two in Santa Cruz (farming households), and five in the village of San Gerardo at the base of Mt. Chirripo. Both qualitative and quantitative data were collected in each study in order to gauge trends as well as people's perceptions and motivations for the decisions they were making. While there are limitations in terms of sample size and missing data for some family members, formal interviews, informal conversations and observations over 22 years provide a fairly comprehensive account of household economic strategies and livelihood changes in these two communities.

3. Much of the following section is a summary of material drawn from Sick (1997) and Sick (2008a).

4. Costa Rica does not have the large indigenous populations found elsewhere in Central America.

5. Conventional coffee production entails the use of hybrid coffee varieties coupled with the use of chemical fertilizers, pesticides and herbicides.

6. Prices reached an all-time high of US$3.40 in 1977 (Trading Economics, n.d.)

7. I suspect that non-renewal of the agreement was also linked to growing neo-liberal trends and general de-regulation of markets worldwide.

8. Two households cut old, poorly producing or diseased trees but had decided not to re-plant as coffee prices were too low, but said that they would re-plant if prices recover; two others cut their coffee because they were now small-business owners with neither time nor inclination to care for coffee.

9. Some of these adult children households were purposefully included in the 2010–2012 sample; data on other related child and sibling households not in the 2010–2012 sample were provided by family members interviewed.

10. This plantation originally produced coffee, but converted to pineapple in the early 2000s.

11. I am told that the growing illegal drug trade is also pumping cash into the economy, but I have had no way of exploring to what extent this may be so.

12. While I was able to obtain some information on financing of business from interviews, the data are spotty. Most of what I have come to understand about how new and expanding businesses have been financed comes from anecdotal evidence and hearsay. Sources of finance include: migrant remittances and savings; credit from coffee-processing companies (supposedly for investment in coffee, but sometimes used for investment in other enterprises); profits from existing enterprises; savings from salaried employment; sale of farmland and profits from illegal drug trade that is growing in the region.

ACKNOWLEDGEMENTS

This research was funded by a grant from the Canadian Social Science and Humanities Research Council. Additional funds were provided by the University of Ottawa. The author would like to thank the many farming families who have given generously of their time and knowledge. She would also like to thank anonymous reviewers of this manuscript for their insightful comments and suggestions for revisions.

REFERENCES

Akram-Lodhi, A. H., & Kay, C. (2010). Surveying the agrarian question (part 2): Current debates and beyond. *Journal of Peasant Studies*, *37*(2), 255–284.

Bah, M., Cissé, S., Diyamett, B., Diallo, G., Lerise, F., Okali, D., ... Tacoli, C. (2003). Changing rural–urban linkages in Mali, Nigeria and Tanzania. *Environment and Urbanization*, *15*(1), 13–23.

Barrett, C. B., Reardon, T., & Webb, P. (2001). Nonfarm income diversification and household livelihood strategies in rural Africa: Concepts, dynamics, and policy implications. *Food Policy*, *26*, 315–333.

Batterbury, S. (2007). *Rural populations and agrarian transformations in the global south*. CICRED Policy Paper No. 5. Paris: Committee for International Cooperation in National Research in Demography.

Biesanz, R., Biesanz, K., & Biesanz, M. (1982). *The Costa Ricans*. Prospect Heights, IL: Waveland Press.

Brockett, C. (1990). *Land, power, and poverty: agrarian transformation and political conflict in Central America*. Boston, MA: Unwin Hyman.

Cardoso, C. (1977). The formation of the coffee estate in nineteenth-century Costa Rica. In M. Deas, C. Smith, & J. Street (Eds.), *Land and labour in Latin America* (pp. 165–202). Cambridge: Cambridge University Press.

Cazanga, J. (1987). *Las cooperativas de caficultores en Costa Rica*. San José: Universidad de Costa Rica.

Cohen, J. (2004). *The culture of migration in Southern Mexico*. Austin, TX: University of Texas Press.

Daviron, B., & Stefano, P. (2005). *The coffee paradox: Global markets, commodity trade, and the elusive promise of development*. London: Zed Books.

Davis, B., Winters, P., Carletto, G., Covarrubias, K., Quiñones, E., Zezza, A., ... & Digiuseppe, S. (2010). A cross-country comparison of rural income generating activities. *World Development*, *38*(1), 48–63.

FAO (2014). *FAO The state of food and agriculture 2014: Innovation in family farming*. Rome.

Goldschmidt, W. (1978). *As you sow: Three studies in the social consequences of agribusiness*. Montclair, NJ: Allanheld, Osumn (Reprinted on 1947).

Graueb, B., Jahi Chappell, M., Wittman, H., Ledermann, S., Bezner Kerr, R., & Gemmill-Herren, B. (2016). The state of family farms in the world. *World Development*, *87*, 1–15.

Gray, C. (2009). Rural out-migration and smallholder agriculture in the southern Ecuadorian Andes. *Population and Environment*, *30*(4–5), 193–217.

Hansson, H., Ferguson, R., Olofsson, C., & Rantamäki-Lahtinen, L. (2013). Farmers' motives for diversifying their farm business: The influence of family. *Journal of Rural Studies*, *32*, 240–250.

Howitt, J. (2014). Livelihood strategies, ecotourism, and changing environmental values in a Costa Rican village. In D. Sick (Ed.), *Rural livelihoods, regional economies, and processes of change* (pp. 125–144). Routledge ISS Studies in Rural Livelihoods. London: Routledge.

ICO (International Coffee Organization) (n.d.). *Prices paid to growers in exporting countries*. Retrieved from http://www.ico.org/historical/1990%20onwards/PDF/3a-prices-growers.pdf. Accessed on December 26, 2016.

INEC (Instituto Nacional de Estadísticas y Censos de Costa Rica). (2007). *Censo Cafetalero Turrialba y Coto Brus 2003*, Valle Central y Valle Central Occidental 2004, y Pérez Zeledón, Tarrazú y Zona Norte 2006. San Jose, Costa Rica. Retrieved from http://www.inec.go.cr/sites/default/files/documentos/agropecuario/publicaciones/reagropeccensocaf2003-2006-01.pdf

INEC (Instituto Nacional de Estadisticas y Censos de Costa Rica). (2015). *Indicadores Demográficos Cantonales. 2013*. San Jose, Costa Rica, June 2015.

Jaffee, D., Kloppenburg, J., & Monroy, M. (2004). Bringing the "moral charge" home: Fair trade within the North and within the South. *Rural Sociology*, *69*(2), 169–196.

Li, T. (2009). Exit from agriculture: A step forward or backward for the rural poor. *Journal of Peasant Studies*, *35*(3), 629–636.

Lyon, S. (2007). Maya coffee farmers and fair trade: Assessing the benefits and limitations of alternative markets. *Culture & Agriculture*, *29*(2), 100–112.

McMichael, P. (2006). Peasant prospects in the neoliberal age. *New Political Economy*, *11*(3), 407–418.

McMichael, P. (2013). Land grabbing as security mercantilism in international relations. *Globalizations*, *10*(1), 47–64.

MIDEPLAN. (2013). *Datos socioeconónmicos del cantón Pérez Zeledón*. Slideshare. Dirección Región Brunca. Retrieved from https://www.slideshare.net/carszgull/datos-generales-del-cantn-de-prez-zeledn. Accessed on March 1, 2017.

Murray, D., Raynolds, L., & Taylor, P. (2003). *One cup at a time: Poverty alleviation and fair trade coffee in Latin America*. New York, NY: The Ford Foundation.

Mwandha, J., Nicholls, J., & Sargent, M. (1985). *Coffee: The international commodity agreements*. Brookfield, VT: Gower.

Netting, R. (1993). *Smallholders, householders: Farm families and the ecology of intensive, sustainable agriculture*. Stanford, CA: Stanford University Press.

North, L. (1981). *Bitter grounds: Roots of revolt in El Salvador*. Toronto: Between the Lines.

Paige, J. (1987). Coffee and politics in Central America. In R. Tardanico (Ed.), *Crises in the Caribbean Basin* (pp. 141–189). Beverly Hills, CA: Sage.

Ramisch, J. (2014). 'We will not farm like our fathers did': multilocational livelihoods, cellphones, and the continuing challenge of rural development in western Kenya. In D. Sick (Ed.), *Rural livelihoods, regional economies, and processes of change* (pp. 10–35). Routledge ISS Studies in Rural Livelihoods. London: Routledge.

Rigg, J. (2006). Land, farming, livelihoods, and poverty: Rethinking the links in the rural south. *World Development*, *34*(1), 180–202.

Rigg, J., Salamanca, A., & Parnwell, M. (2012). Joining the dots of agrarian change in Asia: A 25 year view from Thailand. *World Development*, *40*(7), 1469–1481.

Rigg, J., Salamanca, A., & Thompson, E. (2016). The puzzle of East and Southeast Asia's persistent smallholder. *Journal of Rural Studies*, *43*, 118–133.

Roseberry, W., Gudmundson, L., & Samper, M. (1995). *Coffee, society, and power in Latin America*. Baltimore, MD: Johns Hopkins University Press.

Rosset, P. (2000). The multiple functions and benefits of small farm agriculture in the context of global trade negotiations. *Development*, *43*(2), 77–82.

Samper, M. (1990). *Generations of settlers: Rural households and markets on the Costa Rican frontier, 1850-1935*. Boulder, CO: Westview Press.

Saturnino, B., Hall, R., Scoones, I., White, B., &. Wolford, W. (2011). Towards a better understanding of global land grabbing: An editorial introduction. *Journal of Peasant Studies*, *38*(2), 209–216.

Seligson, M. (1980). *Peasant of Costa Rica and the development of agrarian capitalism*. Madison, WI: University of Wisconsin Press.

SEPSA (Secretaría Ejecutiva de Planificación Sectorial Agropecuaria) (2016). *Informe de gestión del sector agropecuario y el desarrollo de los territorios rurales*, Mayo 2015–Abril 2016. San Jose, Costa Rica.

Sick, D. (1997). Coping with crisis: Costa Rican households and the international coffee market. *Ethnology*, *36*(3), 255–275.

Sick, D. (2008a). *Farmers of the golden bean: Costa Rican households, global coffee, and fair trade*. DeKalb, IL: Northern Illinois University Press.

Sick, D. (2008b). Coffee, farming families, and fair trade in Costa Rica: New markets, same old problems? *Latin American Research Review*, *43*(3), 193–208.

Sick, D. (2014). The new face of the countryside: Agriculture and generational livelihood strategies in rural Costa Rica. In D. Sick (Ed.), *Rural Livelihoods, regional economies, and processes of change* (pp. 36–57). Routledge ISSS Studies in Rural Livelihoods. London: Routledge Press.

Smith, J. (2007). The search for sustainable markets: The promise and failures of Fair Trade. *Culture & Agriculture*, *29*(2), 89–99.

Smith, J. (2009). Shifting coffee markets and producer responses in Costa Rica and Panama. *Research in Economic Anthropology*, *29*, 101–124.

Trading Economics. (n.d.). *Coffee*. Retrieved from http://www.tradingeconomics.com/commodity/coffee. Accessed on May 15, 2013.

Van der Ploeg, J. (2014). Peasant-driven agricultural growth and food sovereignty. *The Journal of Peasant Studies*, *41*(6), 999–1030.

Williams, R. (1994). *States and social evolution: Coffee and the rise of national governments in Central America*. Chapel Hill, NC: University of North Carolina Press.

Winson, A. (1989). *Coffee and democracy in modern Costa Rica*. Toronto: Between the Lines.

World Bank. (2007). *World development report: agriculture for development 2008*, Washington, DC: World Bank.

Zoomers, A. (2010). Globalization and foreignization of space: seven processes driving the current global land grab. *Journal of Peasant Studies*, *37*(2), 429–447.

TRANSITION TO FARMING MORE LIKELY IN A LAND OF PLENTY

Serge Svizzero

ABSTRACT

Purpose – *This chapter is about the theories explaining the transition from foraging to farming. It aims to establish which links exist between the traditional theories – based on push/pull models – and the micro-founded approaches developed since the 1980s. More precisely, it asks how the latter may contribute, as the former did, to defining a macro-narrative of the transition to farming.*

Methodology/approach – *While they were providing a global narrative of the Neolithic revolution, the push and pull models have been progressively dismissed. Recent research is diverse, but it is all based upon human behaviour or micro-founded. We critically examine three of these approaches which focus either on foraging behaviour, or on the initial domestication of plants and animals, or on the evolution of social institutions related to ownership.*

Findings – *We demonstrate that these recent micro-founded approaches only provide a partial vision of the transition to farming. Despite this limit, they conciliate push and pull explanations in a single framework. Moreover, they confirm a conclusion held by tenants of pull models: the transition to farming is more likely to have occurred in a resource-rich environment such as the one associated with complex hunter-gatherers. Some archaeological evidence from the Levant is provided to support our claim.*

Anthropological Considerations of Production, Exchange, Vending and Tourism
Research in Economic Anthropology, Volume 37, 61–84

ISSN: 0190-1281/doi:10.1108/S0190-128120170000037004

Value – *This research chapter provides a useful overview of the differing approaches to the behavioural, environmental and economic factors that led to the shift to farming from foraging. Its value lies in the way it presents and evaluates differing positions derived from differing scales of analysis and types of evidence.*

Keywords: Human foraging behaviour; initial domestication; property rights; Neolithic revolution; sharing; niche construction

INTRODUCTION

The transition from foraging to farming, or the origin of agriculture, is one of the most debated topics in the academic literature (Bellwood, 2005). Until the 1980s there was an early or traditional vision of this transition. For various reasons the academic research of these three last decades has contributed to the emergence of a recent or new vision of this transition (Price & Bar-Yosef, 2011; Svizzero & Tisdell, 2014).

The differences between the two visions are quite numerous. Until the 1980s all the traditional theories could be classified into two opposite groups usually called 'push' and 'pull' models. For each theory of these two groups, the origins of agriculture were explained by mono-causal factors such as resource depletion, population pressure, changes in social organization, and cognitive changes (Bender, 1978; Binford, 1968; Childe, 1936; Cohen, 1977). In contrast, recent approaches tend to favour explanations based on multi-causal factors (Bowles & Choi, 2013; Price & Bar-Yosef, 2011; Smith, 2015; Zeder, 2009). More precisely, it has become clear that the whole transition was not, as it was previously thought, a long and progressive or gradual process. Although it is still considered to have been very long, the process is now seen more as a case of punctuated equilibrium. Moreover, recent approaches point out that local histories heavily influence outcomes occurring in any given locale, such as the transition to farming. This new vision has had two consequences. On the one hand, foraging and farming are now considered only as polar cases of a long-term process. Thus, the focus has shifted from these polar cases to the vast middle ground in which foraging and farming were coexisting either side by side or even together. The former situation has led to studies related to contact and exchange between HG (Hunter-Gatherers) and farmers, or the so-called 'neolithization process'. The latter situation, also called 'mixed economies' (Smith, 2001), has led to a shift of the main point of interest. Most research which were before about the origins of agriculture now focus on initial domestication of plants and animals (Smith, 2015; Zeder, 2015), one of the main features of agrarian societies. It is thus useful to refer, according to Price and Bar-Yosef (2011, p. s165), to the definitional distinctions between foraging (gathering wild resources), cultivation (planting morphologically wild plants), farming (planting genetically domesticated plants), and agriculture (where farming is the majority of the diet).

These changes from the traditional to the new vision are themselves the result of methodological changes. Although the literature is still dominated by archaeologists and anthropologists, a growing part of it is now taken by contributions from other disciplines (geneticist, economist, etc.). This change has contributed to the evolution of the various approaches about the origin of agriculture.[1] In addition, new techniques, such as genetic analysis based on DNA, have provided new data, even on already existing archaeological records. New methods, and hence new data have contributed to the emergence of new ideas and new results. The discovery of new archaeological sites has also contributed to this shift.

In this context, the main difference between the traditional and the new vision is about the scale level of each approach. The traditional vision was based on a global or macro approach. Its aim was to provide a 'macro-narrative' able to provide a convincing and – as much as possible – universal explanation of the origins of agriculture. While human behaviour – related to either foraging or farming – was present, it was implicit in most cases. The focus was more on macro-causes – such as climate change or population pressure – and on macro consequence, namely the introduction of farming. Thus, the main point of debate was to know whether such introduction was intentional or constrained, i.e. due to forced adaptation. The contributions of the new vision have emphasized on human behaviour, i.e. on a micro approach rather than on a macro approach. These contributions have been especially concerned with three main topics. The first is about human foraging behaviour, the second about human/environment interaction, and the third about social institutions in prehistoric societies. These micro-founded contributions have provided a more detailed and accurate understanding of the past. However, and this is the natural shortcoming of micro-founded approaches, each contribution only provides a partial explanation of the transition from foraging to farming. It is thus the aim of this chapter to provide a link between the traditional and the new vision of the origins of agriculture. Indeed, push and pull models have been supplanted by the new contributions. However, push or pull explanations are still relevant per se, especially if they are supported by the micro-founded contributions of the new vision. In other words, do the micro-founded contributions of the new vision may be used to provide a macro-narrative of the transition and in particular, when compared to the traditional vision, do they strengthen the conclusions of push or pull explanations?

TRADITIONAL THEORIES OF THE TRANSITION TO FARMING AND THEIR LIMITS

Until the 1980s or so, most of the various theories about the origins of agriculture and dealing with ancient HG could be classified into two groups.

For the first group of theories, the shift to agriculture was the result of forced human adaptation. In other words, 'push models' or scenarios were directly influenced by the Darwinian or neo-Darwinian approach. In such context, the causal factor could be of various origin. However, since it had to introduce a constraint on HG's lifeway, it could be presented as an imbalance between edible food resources provided by the nature and the HG's diet need for their subsistence. Such imbalance could be the result of two independent (but possibly contemporaneous) reasons: resource depression and population pressure. Resource depression was, and still is, very popular among scholars (Bar-Yosef, 2011; Childe, 1936; Dow, Reed, & Olewiler, 2009; Richerson, Boyd, & Bettinger, 2001) probably because it may primarily result from a true external force, namely climate change (Roberts, 2004). Population pressure is a good but now less popular candidate (Binford, 1968; Cohen, 1977, 2009; Keeley, 1988). Indeed, according to a Malthusian perspective, the population grows faster than food resources and, therefore, the imbalance previously highlighted inevitably occurs after a while. However, such conclusion can be challenged or at least weakened. Indeed, and according to Boserup (1965), population pressure in agrarian societies – without leading to starvation – stimulates technological innovation and thus food resources are, on average, available in sufficient quantities to sustain population growth. By extending such conclusion to foraging societies, the Malthusian conclusion can also be challenged. Another shortcoming of the population pressure explanation is that archaeological records tend to confirm that agriculture was very difficult in its early Age (Berbesque, Marlowe, Shaw, & Thompson, 2014; Bowles, 2011; Harlan, 1992), or in other words that HG were on average far from starvation, even though they did experience starvation periodically. Finally, while climate change is nowadays quite easy to measure (through various new techniques), the population level of prehistoric HG is much more difficult to assess, especially because most HG had a nomadic way of life.

For the second group of theories, the transition to agriculture was unconstrained, i.e. was the result of HG's deliberate choice. Contrary to 'push models', these 'pull models' emphasized on internal factors or endogenous process within HG societies (Bender, 1978; Hayden, 1990). Social competition, through the mean of social feasting, was one of the main explanations. The feasting model posits that intensive agriculture was the necessary result of ostentatious displays of power. To regularly throw feasts as a means of exerting dominance, large quantities of food had to be assembled. Thus, foragers found advantages in farming because it provided a larger and more regular food surplus than foraging and thus was more useful to sustain feasting and therefore to socially promote the organizers of such events. Unfortunately, such explanation faces a chronological problem: although it may explain why HG prefer farming, when the latter already exists, it does not really give the reason of how and why farming may emerge in an HG society.

From the previous statement, it appears that mono-causal factor theories – either push or pull models – have been progressively dismissed. In fact, none of these theories can be fully rejected but none of these can be considered as a universal explanation of the origin of agriculture. Regional studies of the numerous (at least 10) independent centres where agriculture has been invented have demonstrated that some factors were more relevant than others at some period of time, and conversely. Such studies have also shown that the transition was not progressive and gradual, as it was previously thought. Indeed, while it is certain that the transition from foraging to farming was very long – as confirmed by time required for the domestication process (Larson et al., 2014; Zeder, 2015) – it is well described by a punctuated equilibrium, i.e. a process in which periods of rapid change are followed by long periods of stasis, and even sometimes by period of reversion to foraging (Bellwood & Oxenham, 2008; Smith, 1993). In other words, between the two extreme – foraging and farming – there is a vast and diverse middle ground. The latter can be described either as the persistence of HG economies (Svizzero & Tisdell, 2015) or as the existence of mixed economies, i.e. of economies including farming but in which subsistence is mainly (at least 50%) based on foraging. Smith (2001) has labelled such situation as 'low-level food production'. While for push–pull models the central question was 'why agriculture has emerged', the central question for mixed economies is now 'why they have persisted'. Once again, such mixed economies can be viewed according to two opposite ways, either as the result of HG's necessary adaptation or as HG's deliberate choice. If it is considered as the result of HG's adaptation, then mixed economies are an unstable situation, i.e. a simple stage in the evolution process from foraging to farming and their study is therefore of less importance (Bellwood & Oxenham, 2008; Bowles & Choi, 2016).

THE MULTIPLE AND EVOLVING GOALS OF HUMAN FORAGING BEHAVIOUR

Foraging behaviour is universal among living species. For non-human, as well as for human, foraging is crucial because it directly influences their fitness, and therefore the ability to survive and to reproduce. While such biological goal is unique for animals, it is not for human. Indeed, human foraging behaviour is also motivated by two other fundamental goals (Svizzero, 2016a).

First, there exists an economical goal. According to this goal, natural resources, either edible or not, are foraged in order to be exchanged for other resources (goods, services or cash). In other words, foraging provides income through trade or exchange and this income is afterward used by its owner to satisfy various needs which are not necessarily related to subsistence, i.e. that can be independent of the biological goal. One should note that archaeological records of trade or exchange, even on long distance, are numerous from the pre-Neolithic period (e.g. ornaments or tools made from precious stones, shells, etc.) (Tykot, 2004). According to the typology introduced by Polanyi (1944), i.e. whatever the form – reciprocity, distribution or market exchange – underlying such exchange, the biological goal of foraging is not necessarily dominant or even present.

Second, there exists a socio-cultural goal. Indeed, foraging activities can be part of a ritual or a religious practice. In other words, the main goal is neither biological nor economical, but it is related to either culture and heritage or social prestige. Once again, rituals and religious beliefs have been developed in the pre-Neolithic period as testified for instance by cave paintings, carvings of non-utilitarian objects (e.g. Venus) or even by the building of some monuments (e.g. Göbekli Tepe). Moreover, in all foraging societies (and even beyond) hunting has always been associated with social competition and prestige. This was especially true for pre-Neolithic foragers since hunting was the only mean to get animal food. We recall that even though foraging societies are considered as egalitarian, there was some degree of labour division and specialization based on gender. While the men were hunters, the role of female labour in foraging economies tends to gravitate almost exclusively to the role of plant-product provisioning, the manufacturing of perishable technological items from plant products, or the processing of animals killed by men.[2] Hunting was therefore a male activity and even in an egalitarian society a good hunter had special advantages such as more mating. Most hunter-gatherers prefer to hunt for big game, even though big game is treated as common property of the band regardless of who kills it. Social approval, prestige, and competition for wives seem to be adequate incentives to get males to hunt for the whole band (Hawkes, 2001). For instance, Hawkes (1991) uses the Ache people of Paraguay as evidence for the 'Show-off hypothesis', i.e. the concept that more successful men have better mate options.

For all foragers, including pre-Neolithic HG, these three goals – biological, economical, socio-cultural – were present but at various degrees. Foraging must therefore not be viewed as the consequence of only one or two of these three goals. Indeed, if foraging is only motivated by the biological goal, then HG are assumed to behave as animals, i.e. they modify their diet in response to variation in their natural environment (Weisdorf, 2005; Winterhalder & Kennett, 2006). Such Darwinian vision is at the centre of the push models described previously. Conversely, if the biological goal is neglected, i.e. if foraging is mainly explained by the economical and/or the socio-cultural goal, then any change in the diet (and subsequently the introduction of farming) results of HG's choice, either in order to increase the income provided by trade or to satisfy socio-cultural values. In other words, push and pull explanations do not have different origin, they are linked, i.e. they are both the possible outcome of human foraging behaviour. In fact, when one goal is dominant, one group of theories is more relevant, while it is the other group when the considered goal is dominated but still present.

The same conclusion holds about mixed economies. As stated previously, these economies mix foraging and farming. It is thus possible that people farm for their subsistence and trade what they forage, as it seems to be the case in many traditional societies living in the Southeast Asian region (Morrison, 2005; Svizzero, 2016b). Conversely, they may consume what they forage and trade what they farm, for instance the Mikea of Madagascar trade the maize they grow (Kelly, Rabedimy, & Poyer, 2004).

HUMAN/ENVIRONMENT INTERACTION AND NICHE CONSTRUCTION THEORY

One of the recent developments associated with foraging behaviour defined at the individual level is the interaction of human and the environment. At the core of this approach is the debate about initial domestication, i.e. how and why it has happened (Smith, 2015; Zeder, 2015). However, domestication defined as the 'morphological or genetic changes in plant and animal species' (Price & Bar-Yosef, 2011, p. s165) can be viewed as the ultimate outcome of an interaction process between human and his environment. From a theoretical point of view, such process – the central feature of the Anthropocene – is clearly described by niche construction theory (NCT) (Smith & Zeder, 2013).

Niche Construction Theory

NCT is a new conceptual approach (Odling-Smee, Laland, & Feldman, 2003). Its aim is the study of human/environment interaction and it is derived from the developments of Behavioural Ecology. NCT was developed directly out of macroevolutionary theory in the mid-1980s. Contrary to the Darwinian and neo-Darwinian approaches, NCT centres on the issues of directionality and intent in evolution. In other words, adaptation is considered as being symmetrical, i.e. human adapt to environmental changes (as in the Darwinian approach) but human also adapt the environment according to their needs. Thereby Odling-Smee et al. (2003) argue that niche construction is universal and should be regarded, alongside natural selection, as a second major participant in evolution. During the last decades NCT has been extensively used by scholars – especially those focusing on the prehistoric period – in order to describe human behaviour such as foraging or farming (Rowley-Conwy & Layton, 2011), its impact on the environment and biodiversity (Boivin et al., 2016; Smith & Zeder, 2013) and several episodes of human evolution such as the Neolithic revolution (Smith, 2007, 2011, 2012, 2015; Zeder, 2009, 2011, 2015) and its spread (McClure, 2015).

From Free Environment to Initial Domestication

Since domestication is the ultimate stage of an evolutionary sequence in which human masters the nature, the first stage is when the nature evolves freely, i.e. without human intervention. Then, human's predation – as done by HG – is introduced and of course it has an impact on the nature. For pre-modern humans – those that were living before the mastery of fire, about 400.000 BP – it seems reasonable to assume that foraging had an impact on the environment but that such impact was involuntary. With the passage of time, from the lower Palaeolithic to the Mesolithic, HG have however introduced the management of the wild resources they foraged. Such management is defined as the 'manipulation and some degree of control of wild species (plants or animals) without cultivation or morphological changes' (Price & Bar-Yosef, 2011, p. s165). Various techniques (watering fields, tending tubers, fire-stick agriculture, incomplete harvest of seeds, etc.) can be considered as the management of wild resources and thus also as forms of proto-agriculture (Pryor, 2004). Among the latter techniques, the use of fire by HG – either in order to eliminate some plants and to facilitate the growing of others; or to attract game in freshly created meadows – has probably had the larger anthropogenic impact during the prehistoric period. According to such perspective, hunting and forest fragmentation are correlated as open-space promote sustained hunting. Indeed, most large game (deer, elk, etc.) have an important part of their diet which consists of the twigs, shoots, and leaves of low growing shrubs and bushes. Therefore, their population densities are low in climax forest situations where a closed canopy has been established, and are high in early successional situations that have small areas of varying types, producing maximum edge areas between habitat zones. As a result, human clearance of vegetation would actually have improved their habitat and increased carrying capacity levels. We have various evidence that the niche construction efforts of small-scale human societies may modify vegetation communities in ways that result in the capture of a larger percentage of an ecosystem's total biotic energy. For instance, Smith (2009) provides explanation on how the white-tailed deer (*Odocoileus virginianus*) was managed by hunters in the Mississippi River Valley corridor.

The next stage in this evolutionary process motivated by niche construction is cultivation. It is defined as the intentional preparation of the soil for planting wild plants. The equivalent situation for animal is taming, a human–animal interaction such that reared animals may return to the wild easily and even they may interbreed with those still living in the wild (some animals, e.g. reindeers, have been tamed but never domesticated until nowadays). It should be noted that, in addition to wild plants, cultivation may also concern domesticated plants. In such case, the ultimate stage of the process – namely domestication, as previously defined – is reached.

Domestication and Cultivation: Related but Not Dependent

The evolutionary sequence previously described, from free environment to domestication, provides two important advantages. First, the evolution from any stage to the subsequent is clearly described by NCT. In other words, Human Behavioural Ecology (HBE) has during the last two decades led to the emergence of two competing approaches. Optimal foraging theory, and its application to foragers, namely the Diet Breath Model (DBM) (Winterhalder & Kennett, 2006) is well suited to explain – according to forager's behaviour based on energy optimization – the optimal choice between foraging and farming but once the latter already exists. However, and compared to NCT, the DBM is unable to explain the how and the why of agriculture, i.e. the occurrence of initial domestication (Smith, 2015; Zeder, 2009, 2015). Second, initial domestication is easier to identify – through the studies of plant and animal remains – rather than to date the origins of agriculture. Indeed, agriculture is when farming and/or herding predominate the activities of a particular community and determine the main diet. So, the boundary line between farming and agriculture is always blurred because both situations are defined at a macro level.

The evolutionary sequence towards initial domestication do not imply such drawback mainly because it is defined at a micro level. While the various studies and research about initial domestication improve our understanding of the past, they do not provide an accurate picture of the transition from foraging to farming. This major shortcoming comes from the fact that there are two processes but defined at different scales. Therefore, there is no clear one-to-one correspondence between both processes. Two cases illustrate this correspondence problem. On the one hand, it is likely that some plants or animals are domesticated but do not lead necessary to farming or herding. In other words, and as illustrated by the dog domestication (*Canis familiaris*), domesticates may exist in a foraging society (Schmölcke, 2013). On the other hand, cultivation – as previously defined – may occur without the use of domesticated plants while it is clearly a form of food production. In other words, food production without domesticates is possible. Both cases show that the two processes – initial domestication through NCT, and the transition from foraging to farming – are intertwined but are not dependent. Thereby domestication is neither a sufficient nor a necessary condition for cultivation to occur.

SOCIAL ORGANIZATION AND INSTITUTIONS RELATED TO OWNERSHIP

In the academic literature about the sources of economic development in modern as well as in societies of the far past, there are two schools of thought related to the classical opposition between nature and culture. Even though such distinction is quite artificial and finds few support among modern anthropologists, it is nevertheless useful in order to introduce our purpose in this section. For the former school, what is determinant for the economic development to occur is the presence of natural resources (mainly plants and animals suitable for domestication) and therefore of the associated bio-geographic conditions (Olsson & Hibbs, 2004). For the latter, what is crucial is the role of institutions (government, market, property rights, etc.) (Acemoglu & Robinson, 2012; North, 1990). Of course, both – nature and culture – have a huge influence on economic development. For societies of the far past, such as prehistoric societies, the influence of natural resources is obvious. However, the role of institutions should not be neglected or even minimized. Of course in such societies the number of institutions is quite reduced compared to what existed, for instance, in the complex societies emerging from the Early Bronze Age. However, there is a social institution which was present even in pre-Neolithic societies, namely the rules related to ownership (Earle, 2000). Ownership refer to the regime of property rights.[3] However the latter is changing with the passage of time. More precisely, new property rights develop in a society when the benefits of having them exceed the costs of getting them (Demsetz, 1967; North, 1990). While Demsetz (1967) argued that costs and benefits affect the development of property rights, he believed that community preferences also had a bearing, especially as to the 'form' of the rights. An additional query, about 'how' property rights are introduced in a given society, is considered in the section 'Recent Theories and Levantine Archaeological Evidence Support "Pull Explanations"'. Before we turn to the evolution of property rights during the prehistoric period, one should note that such social shifts are particularly difficult to demonstrate archaeologically (see e.g. Shennan, 2011). Earle (200, pp. 49–53) has identified four largely independent sources of archaeological evidence in order to study property, namely the improvement and movements of cultural objects, the patterning of warfare, the patterned distribution of people and objects and marking of both land and objects.

From Open-Access Resources to Exclusive Property Rights

Ownership is related to resources defined in a broad sense. In the 'first stage' of modern human evolution, we may assume that ownership had no real meaning, i.e. resources were under open-access. Such Eden situation is however quite utopian. Indeed, in the subsequent stage of evolution, the one associated with simple HG societies, ownership already existed. Although private property already existed among HG – through deference to possession – and concerned personal items such as clothes, weapons, tools and settlements, land and its standing resources stocks were considered by HG as commons even after the Neolithic revolution (Krier, 2009; Lee & Daly, 2004). Thus, in simple foragers societies ownership mainly took the form of what can be indifferently[4] called sharing, primitive communism or common property regime. According to Benz (2010, p. 7), sharing can be defined *as the act of dividing up resources and goods, or participating in services, communal events, and experiences* and it exists in different forms of reciprocity. Sharing is not a given biological fact, but a culturally established norm. It is a feature of any group of mobile HG. Indeed, it is commonly agreed that sharing was a central feature of pre-Neolithic societies in which HG were simple foragers. Moreover, sharing is remained the central feature of 'modern HG' societies, even though foraging is not for them the only method they use to get food resources (Lee, 2004; Lee & Daly, 2004). In fact, generalized reciprocity is a fundamental characteristic of small-scale human societies of immediate-return foraging systems[5] rather than an adaptation developed because of displacement or isolation. Two main reasons explain the existence of sharing – as a social rule – among HG.

The first reason is related to risk reduction. For HG, foraging is social and, in addition, it also includes a unique element (compared to what non-human foraging animals do), the creation of resource pooling systems (Delton & Robertson, 2012) also called 'sharing' or 'common sharing'. In this type of social foraging, people contribute when they have excess resources and receive some provisions when in need. The latter may occur either because foraging is very risky – by nature it provides returns featured by high variance – or because injury and illness can prevent a person of foraging for extended periods. At least six different theories have been proposed to explain the existence and patterning of intra-group food sharing (Gurven & Jaeggi, 2015; Kaplan & Gurven, 2005); however, the outcome of risk reduction is consistent with all six. In other words, some foragers adopt risky strategies because they know that if their hunt fails, they will nevertheless have food provided by the members of their band and through the sharing system.

The second reason is linked to HG's mobility. Indeed, in the traditional view about pre-Neolithic foragers (Kelly, 1995), it is often assumed that HG had a nomadic way of life. Such situation is a consequence of the low productivity of the technology they used – namely foraging – in order to get their subsistence.

When HG are nomads, the constraints associated with transportation imply that ownership is restricted to the minimum they may carry with them, i.e. to personal belongings (clothes, tools, weapons). In other words, for everything – except personal belongings – HG were living in an economy where natural resources were in open-access. Because HG were living in bands, it is more likely that the access to these resources, especially food resources (the animals to be hunted or vegetation to be gathered), was not open to all but was restricted by sharing or communal rules.

When both reasons previously described – risk reduction and nomadism – are still present but less important, the social institution related to ownership is changing. Indeed, there is a gradual shift from sharing or common property rights towards exclusive property rights. Indeed, when they adopt a sedentary lifeway, the HG modify their foraging strategy and focus on intensification. Thus, the benefits of sharing as a means of risk reduction are decreasing. As a social institution sharing is therefore less defending against those attempting to assert new property rights such as private ownership. The only requirement for the latter to exist is about the characteristics of the resources themselves. The more they are divisible and excludable, the more likely is the existence of private property rights. The ultimate stage of the evolutionary sequence is therefore featured by the generalization of property rights. In other words, at this stage property rights are related to all material resources (food and non-food resources), knowledge as well as land.

The Coevolution of Foraging and Sharing

The reduction in risk related to starvation as well as the adoption of a sedentary way of life are two main features of agrarian societies. In other words, it seems there exists a close connection between the introduction of exclusive property rights and the advent of agriculture. Such conclusion has already been claimed several decades ago (North & Thomas, 1977; Smith, 1993). More recently, it has also been claimed in a model developed by Bowles and Choi (2013, 2016), and recent numerical simulations of such model (Gallagher, Shennan, & Thomas, 2015) have confirmed the necessary coevolution of property rights and farming. The reasons explaining the latter can be indirectly deduced from the reasons explaining the coevolution of sharing and foraging. In fact, when a Western conception of self and selfishness is assumed – such as the one underlying the *homo oeconomicus* – we may consider two reasons for explaining such coevolution.

First, the sharing rules can be interpreted as an implicit tax on the food resources harvested by HG (Chakraborty, 2007). Such tax lowers the marginal return to resource harvesting, which reduces effort and increases the stock of wild resources. In other words, foraging does not necessarily lead to overexploitation of wild resources: sharing avoids waste of food and favours resource conservation because it reduces foragers' incentives to extract wild resources.

Second, a fundamental input in the foraging process is Traditional Ecological Knowledge (TEK) and its transmission among foragers is closely associated with the norm of sharing. Because foraging is risky, any HG has a strong incentive to share his TEK with the members of his band. Indeed, if in some circumstances his hunt fails, he may nevertheless get some food – through the sharing system – provided by another HG with whom he has previously shared his TEK. Thereby TEK is clearly a public good; its production and transmission across foragers and generations of foragers are socially beneficial. However, and as any public good, any HG has no incentive to innovate, i.e. to produce 'new TEK' because the rewards of such innovation have to be immediately shared with all the others HG. We may thus conclude by claiming that TEK is likely under-produced in HG societies. In other words, and as clearly stated by North and Thomas (1977. p. 241), *When common property rights over resources exist, there is little incentive for the acquisition of superior technology and learning.*

Property Rights and Farming: Linked but Not Dependent

Both reasons previously stated show that the sharing system, which is ubiquitous in mobile HG societies, reduces the incentive to do additional work as well as the incentive to innovate through, for instance, the invention of new TEK. One should however note that the transition to agriculture requires the opposite, i.e. additional effort as well as innovation. Indeed, the development of agriculture requires substantial effort, especially in its early Ages, for forest clearance, irrigation system, tillage, etc. Likewise, the transition to agro-pastoralism requires innovation in order to ensure the taming and the domestication of wild animals (e.g. wild goat, sheep, etc.) as well as the cultivation of wild plants (e.g. wild cereals, pulses, etc.) and their subsequent domestication. In other words, the transition to agriculture seems to necessitate the gradual disappearance of sharing and the introduction of exclusive property rights. However, the previous conclusion presents some shortcomings, as illustrated by the following two cases.

First, property rights were present in some foraging societies labelled as complex HG (Finlayson, 2009; Price & Brown, 1985; Sassaman, 2004; Svizzero, 2014). In these societies, private property rights existed about some locally concentrated valuable resources (e.g. an orchard, a well, a quarry of precious stone, a marine coastal site with abundant shellfish, etc.). Indeed, specific locations within the resource-catchment area that offer high resource abundance and predictability were likely to be the subject of clear and strongly enforced control of access (Smith, 2012). Private property rights may also concern people themselves since slavery existed in some complex HG societies of the American Northwest coast. In fact, and according to the terminology introduced by Woodburn (1982), in any foraging economy with delayed return, HG have first to incur some investment (e.g. to build a fish weir) before being able to get food procurement. Therefore, and by assuming that they behave as defined by the *homo oeconomicus* premise, HG have incentive to build such infrastructure only if they may later own the product obtained from it. More generally, these societies of complex HG were hierarchical and featured by socio-economic inequalities. Thus, adult hunters, ritual leaders and corporate groups were probably the main violators of the principle of sharing in their desire to accumulate commodities and power. This is why HG have introduced property rights in their society. In other words, the process of commodification – the establishment of productive milieus and value systems – is often considered as the main characterization of the neolithization since it is implied by productive activities associated with agro-pastoralism (Gebel, 2010). However, the commodification of territory, water, and nature itself already occurred during the pre-Neolithic period in complex HG societies, i.e. in societies in which there was no food production. As stated by Shennan (2011, p. 920) about the existence of ownable resources, what matters are resource permanence and the potential of ownership in terms of divisibility and excludability, i.e. conditions that can be fulfilled in foraging as well as in farming economies, even though the latter provides the most obvious basis for such purpose.

Second, in its early Age agriculture was a production process using mainly labour, in addition to land of course. Therefore, most farming activities – such as forest clearance, tillage, harvesting, building an irrigation system, etc. – had to be done collectively. Intensive herding, especially of large animals, and farming require cooperation and reciprocity on a level above the nuclear family. In other words, in early Age agrarian societies the property regime was more likely close to common property than to exclusive property rights.

With exclusive property rights in some foraging societies, and common property rights still present among early farmers, the two previous cases demonstrate that there is not a one-to-one correspondence between the adoption of property rights and the advent of agriculture. In other words, the introduction of exclusive property rights is neither a sufficient nor a necessary condition for agriculture to emerge.

RECENT THEORIES AND LEVANTINE ARCHAEOLOGICAL EVIDENCE SUPPORT 'PULL EXPLANATIONS'

In the preceding sections, we have identified three different evolutionary sequences. These sequences could be labelled as developmental rather than evolutionary since there is no necessary imperative that one step be required before another can be taken.

The human manipulation of the environment – also called niche construction – has led to the following sequence (Fig. 1).

The interaction between humans leads to the adoption of social institutions. In the prehistoric period, the rules pertaining to ownership were present for sure and likely one of the main social institutions. We have then identified the evolutionary sequence in Fig. 2.

Both previous sequences help us to improve our understanding of the far past. However, they are diachronic and in addition none of them have a one-to-one correspondence with the following macro sequence featuring the Neolithic revolution (Fig. 3).

Despite this conclusion, the two evolutionary sequences related, respectively, to human/environment interaction and to social institution shed new light on the transition from foraging to farming. Indeed, we have demonstrated that the various macro theories (the push/pull models) about this transition could be

Free Environment / Predation with involuntary impact / Management of Wild Resources /
Cultivation without domesticated plants (or herding of tamed animals) /
Cultivation with domesticates, or Farming -Rearing of domesticated animals /
Agriculture

Fig. 1. The Evolutionary Sequence Provided by Niche Construction.

Open-access Resources /
Sharing or Common property rights /
Exclusive or Private property rights

Fig. 2. The Evolutionary Sequence Associated with the Rules Related to Ownership.

Foraging or Hunter-Gatherer societies (food procurement only through predation) /
Mixed economies (or low-level food production) /
Farming societies or agro-pastoralism (food production dominates human diet)

Fig. 3. The Evolutionary Sequence from Foraging to Farming.

explained within a unique methodological framework (see the section 'The Multiple and Evolving Goals of Human Foraging Behaviour'). This is because human foraging behaviour is motivated by multiple goals and that according to the relative weight of each of these goals, a theory is more relevant than the other. However the previous conclusion leaves us with a central query: which goal – underlying human foraging behaviour – is more likely associated with the transition from foraging to farming? In other words, is it push or pull explanations which are the best tailored to explain the origin of agriculture?

The latter question may also be formulated as follows: is the transition to agriculture more likely to occur either in an environment with few edible natural resources or in a resource-rich environment (a land of plenty)? For push explanations, it is the former situation which is relevant. Indeed, since the transition to farming results from human adaptation to an external constraint, food shortages – being due to resource depression and/or to population pressure – are more likely to occur in a resource-poor environment. Although this conclusion seems to be obvious, it can be challenged according to the recent developments of the academic literature we have previously presented. In addition to the latter, we also provide some archaeological evidence from the Levant which also support our claim.

Indeed, in the Near East – more precisely the Levant – as well as in the Yangtze River Valley corridor in China, Sub-Saharan Africa, eastern North America, and Mexico, very early evidence domestication of a range of different species comes from settlements situated in very rich-resource zones associated with river valleys, lake margins, and springs (Smith, 2007). The Levant is one of those unique places where the transition from HG to farmers occurred locally, so it is possible to observe the whole sequence of these processes within the region as a whole. For these reasons the neolithization of the Levant has been studied for several decades and has given rise to various interpretations and theories. It is now widely agreed that our current vision of the neolithization in the Levant has deeply changed since the last two decades (Kuijt & Goring-Morris, 2002; Zeder, 2009, 2011). Some of these changes tend to confirm the theory we have presented in the previous sections. Before turning to evidence related to domestication and to ownership, we may first highlight the fact that the Levant was a land of plenty. Indeed, it appears that the places where settlement took place in southwestern Asia (e.g. Abu Hureyra, Mureybet, Eynan, Göbekli Tepe) were at the time exceptionally rich in plant and animals resources that could be foraged without mobility.

The Evolution of Human Manipulation of the Environment

According to the evolutionary sequence associated with human/environment interaction, it is niche construction which has led to the transition between the different stages and, ultimately, to the initial domestication of plants and animals. Such construction is based on experimentation and trial-and-error process. As clearly stated by Price and Gebauer (1995, chapter 1), populations in a high-risk environment will seldom try new subsistence strategies that bear even greater risk of failure. New strategies are initiated in situations where risk is affordable. In other words, human/environment interaction leads to the view that agriculture was adopted in areas of relatively abundant resources.

For the Levant, it is commonly agreed that members of Late Natufian and PPNA communities were intentionally manipulating, managing, and cultivating plant resources in a previously unprecedented manner in the Near East and elsewhere. However, debate continues on the issue of the existence and role of domesticated versus cultivated plant resources within PPNA communities.

For the Natufian, their subsistence modes were based primarily on the intensification of hunting and gathering and associated processing techniques. While it clearly appears that the Natufian does exhibit intensification of plant collection, there is no evidence for intentional plant cultivation. Concerning animals, the domestication of the dog is attested during the Natufian and even before. Indeed, grey wolves, the source species, are asserted to have first evolved into dogs in East Asia ca 15,000 BP, during the latter stages of the most recent Ice Age (Savolainen et al., 2002). However, there is no other example of animal domestication during that period. Some degree of management of wild boar is claimed during the late Natufian period and the subsequent PPNA period (Vigne, Carrére, Briois, & Guilaine, 2011). In fact, signs of initial management of morphologically wild future plant and animal domesticates appeared even before 11,500 BP. In other words, a long period of increasingly intensive human management preceded the manifestation of morphological change in managed crops and livestock (Zeder, 2011). This is because the morphological change may have occurred quite late in the domestication process and can therefore no longer be considered as a leading-edge indicator of domestication. Therefore, it is a context of human niche construction which gave rise to co-evolutionary relationships between humans and certain species that eventually resulted in the domestication of the latter.

During the PPNA period small-scale cultivation started in alluvial plains but the plant remains recovered were not always of species that were soon to be domesticated locally. During the PPNB, communities subsisted primarily on domesticated plants and animals. Besides farming and herding, hunting and fishing were still present as well as some mobile foraging groups. Cereals and lentils were the main domesticated plants. By the late PPNB, about 75% of animals were domesticated goats and sheep. It now seems that plant and animal domestication occurred at roughly the same time. Despite the previous statement, it is only towards the end of the Late Neolithic that subsistence throughout the region became based mostly on domesticated plants and animals.

The Evolution of the Forms of Ownership

According to the evolutionary sequence of interactions between humans, changes in social institution – namely the rules of ownership – have led to the final stage, i.e. to the introduction of exclusive property rights related to material resources, information and land. Some authors (Bowles & Choi, 2013) have claimed that such evolution necessitated a coevolution of property rights and farming. However, and even though they could have coevolved, one still have to explain how and why property rights have emerged. In fact, we have recall that some HG societies were featured by the abundance of natural resources. In most cases these abundant natural resources were the main contributor to human diet (e.g. wild cereals, shellfish, sea mammals, land snails, anadromous fish, etc.). Thus, in these complex HG societies the sharing rules have progressively vanished even before the introduction of food production. Once again it is in a rich-resource environment that property rights have first appeared (see also Svizzero, 2016c).

In light of recent archaeological research, it seems likely that institutional and cultural changes associated with sedentism preceded and facilitated the emergence of farming in southwest Asia, and more precisely in the Levant. For some authors (e.g. Bender, 1978), these changes – sedentism and later the introduction of farming – were imposed to commoners by an extractive political elite. Archaeological as well as ethnographic HG evidence confirm the existence in pre-Neolithic communities of structures – or political institutions – that allowed collective decision making and enforcement of norms. However, there is little evidence that such communities (of either foragers or farmers) were at the hands of extractive elite, i.e. no evidence that sedentism, property rights or farming were imposed by an elite. In fact, it now seems that settlement and the associated transition to institutions that favoured farming may have been facilitated by collective action of a relatively non-hierarchical sort of the type commonly observed in HG groups (Bowles, 2015). These social innovations probably included an enhanced domain of private property rights to several domains (Earle, 2000; Goring-Morris & Belfer-Cohen, 2011; Kuijt & Goring-Morris, 2002; Shennan, 2011; section 4) even though making inferences about prehistoric property rights is problematical.

First, we may infer the existence in the Levant of property rights in raw materials sources (e.g. precious stones, bitumen, salt, etc.).

Second, it may concern dwellings. The early Natufian settlements were large well-built structures that were surely occupied by units larger than nuclear families. Subsequently a shift from common to private property occurred. For instance, the evidence of burials under the floors of dwellings (in Abu Hureyra, 9,400–7,000 BP) is interpreted as the existence of family rights to private property (Bowles, 2015). The scale of individually spaced oval semi-subterranean residential units is also indicative of nuclear family residences and reflected by the presence of grinding and pounding installations within each domestic unit.

Third, the storage of cereals (gathered, then cultivated and thereafter domesticated) also gives us insights about the transition from common to private property. Although storage was probably also in baskets suspended from beams, well-constructed external silos are found in several Levantine sites. For instance, during the PPNA (11,500–11,000 BP) early granaries (e.g. at Dhra') were between houses, i.e. in extramural locations (Kuijt & Finlayson, 2009). A thousand years later they had shifted inside houses as dedicated storage rooms.

Fourth, reared animals, especially cattle (*Bos taurus*) (because they can be used for various purposes,[6] i.e. for their meat and hide, traction, and the dairy products), are an important form of property. The presence of numerous cattle bones remains on the site of the earliest farming societies provides evidence of private property in cattle even though herd of cattle can be managed communally.

Fifth, land is of course another important form of property. The intensive use by farmers of small areas of land also points to the existence of private property rights.

CONCLUSION

The transition from foraging to farming is mainly explained by theories which, in their traditional (or mono-causal factor) or more recent presentation, are dichotomized between push and pull models. First, we have demonstrated that such dichotomy was dubious: i.e., that it was the result of the macro approach of the Neolithic revolution adopted by most scholars until the early 1980s. With a micro approach, based on the multiple goals of human foraging behaviour, both groups of theories are consistent. Second, and although they are consistent, this does not mean that they both are relevant. While push models have emphasized the emergence of farming in marginal environments, recent research – on niche construction leading to initial domestication, and on social institutions[7] as explaining the adoption of property rights – reaches a conclusion similar to pull models, but for a different (and more relevant) reason. Indeed, the transition to farming was more likely to occur in complex HG societies, i.e. for HG living in a land of plenty. Of course, such conclusion does not minimize the importance of other important factors in the transition from foraging to farming such as the availability of proto-domesticates or the existence of harvesting and processing technologies. It is however important since, as claimed by push models – which are more numerous than pull models – agriculture is often viewed as an evolutionist answer (in the Darwinian sense), i.e. as a forced human adaptation to environmental changes.

NOTES

1. See for instance the special issue 'The origins of agriculture: New data, new ideas' published in *Current Anthropology*, 52, Suppl. 4, October 2011.

2. Such gender-specific strategies are however based on stereotypes (Waguespack, 2005).

3. A question pertaining to property rights is how they are acquired. In the legal and philosophic literature on this topic, there are two views – through first possession and through labour. Though this problem is also important we do not consider it in the sequel of this chapter.

4. Demsetz (1967) pictured three "idealized forms of ownership" – communal, private and state. The first he took to be ownership by all members of a community, and the last to mean ownership by a governing authority (such as the state and a village). As to 'private ownership', usually he took it to mean ownership by a single individual. In the present chapter however we do not distinguish between communal and state ownership.

5. This assertion only concerns ancient HG and does not include other small-scale societies such as complex HG or horticultural societies.

6. As stated by the so-called 'Secondary Products Revolution'.

7. It should be noted that for some authors (e.g. Shennan, 2011), social institutions can also be viewed as the result of human niche construction.

ACKNOWLEDGEMENT

The author wishes to thank three anonymous reviewers for their comments and suggestions on an earlier version of this chapter. The usual *caveat* applies.

REFERENCES

Acemoglu, D., & Robinson, J. (2012). *Why nations fail: The origins of power, prosperity, and poverty*. New York, NY: Crown Publishers.

Bar-Yosef, O. (2011). Climatic fluctuations and early farming in West and East Asia. *Current Anthropology*, *52*(S4), S175–S193.

Bellwood, P. (2005). *First farmers: The origins of agricultural societies*. Oxford: Blackwell.

Bellwood, P., & Oxenham, M. (2008). The expansions of farming societies and the role of the neolithic demographic transition. In J.-P. Bocquet-Appel & O. Bar-Yosef (Eds.), *The neolithic demographictransition and its consequences* (pp. 13–34). Dordrecht: Springer.

Bender, B. (1978). Gatherer hunter to farmer: A social perspective. *World Archaeology*, *10*, 204–222.

Benz, M. (2010). The principle of sharing: An introduction. In M. Benz (Ed.), *The principle of sharing. segregation and construction of social identities at the transition from foraging to farming* (Vol. 14, pp. 1–18). Studies in Early Near Eastern Production, Subsistence, and Environment. Berlin: Ex oriente.

Berbesque, J. C., Marlowe, F. W., Shaw, P., & Thompson, P. (2014). Hunter-Gatherers have less famine than agriculturalists. *BiologyLetters*, *10*, 20130853. doi:10.1098/rsbl.2013.0853

Boivin, N. L., Zeder, M. A., Fuller, D. Q., Crowther, A., Larson, G., Erlandson, J. M., Denham, T., & Petraglia, M. D. (2016). Ecological consequences of human niche construction: Examining long-term anthropogenic shaping of global species distributions. *PNAS*, *113*(23), 6388–6396.

Binford, L. R. (1968). Post-Pleistocene adaptations. In L. R. Binford & S. R. Binford (Eds.), *New perspectives in archaeology* (pp. 313–341). Chicago, IL: Aldine.

Boserup, E. (1965). *The conditions for agricultural growth: The economics of agrarian change under population pressure*. Chicago, IL: Aldine.

Bowles, S. (2011). Cultivation of cereals by the first farmers was not more productive than foraging. *Proceedings of the National Academy of Sciences*, *108*(12), 4760–4765.

Bowles, S. (2015). *Political hierarchy, economic inequality & the first southwest Asian farmers*. SFI Working Paper No. 2015-06-015.

Bowles, S., & Choi, K. (2013). The holocene revolution: The co-evolution of private property and farming. *Proceedings of the National Academy of Sciences*, *110*(22), 8830–8835.

Bowles, S., & Choi, K. (2016). *The neolithic agricultural revolution*. Santa Fe Institute Working Paper 2016-09-016.

Chakraborty, R. N. (2007). Sharing culture and resource conservation in hunter-gatherer societies. *Oxford Economic Papers*, *59*(1), 63–88. doi:10.1093/oep/gpl025

Childe, V. G. (1936). *Man makes himself*. London: Watts.

Cohen, M. N. (1977). *The food crisis in prehistory: Overpopulation and the origins of agriculture*. New Haven, CT: Yale University Press.

Cohen, M. N. (2009). Rethinking the origins of agriculture. *Current Anthropology*, *50*(5), 591–595.

Delton, A. W., & Robertson, T. E. (2012). The social cognition of social foraging: Partner selection by underlying valuation. *Evolution and Human Behavior*, *33*, 715–725.

Demsetz, H. (1967). Toward a theory of property rights. *American Economic Review*, *57*, Paper & Proceeding, 347.

Dow, G. K., Reed, C. G., & Olewiler, N. (2009). Climate reversals and the transition to agriculture. *Journal of Economic Growth*, *14*, 27–53. doi:10.1007/s10887-009-9038-x

Earle, T. (2000). Archaeology, property, and prehistory. *Annual Review of Anthropology*, *29*, 39–60.

Finlayson, B. (2009). The 'complex hunter-gatherer' and the transition to farming. In N. Finlay, S. McCartan, N. Milner, & C. Wickham-Jones (Eds.), *From bran flakes to bushmills: Papers in honour of Professor Peter Woodman* (Vol. 1, pp. 175–188). Prehistoric Society Research Papers. Oxford: Oxbow Books.

Gallagher, E. M., Shennan, S. J., & Thomas, M. G. (2015). Transition to farming more likely for small, conservative groups with property rights, but increased productivity is not essential. *Proceedings of the National Academy of Sciences*, *112*(46), 14218–14223.

Gebel, H. G. K. (2010). Commodification and the formation of Early Neolithic social identity. The issues as seen from the southern Jordanian Highlands. In M. Benz (Ed.), *The principle of sharing. Segregation and construction of social identities at the transition from foraging to farming*. (Vol. 14, pp. 35–80). Berlin: Ex oriente.

Goring-Morris, N., & Belfer-Cohen, A. (2011). Neolithization processes in the Levant. The outer envelope. *Current Anthropology*, *52*(S4), s195–s208.

Gurven, M., & Jaeggi, A. V. (2015). Food sharing. In R. Scott & S. Kosslyn (Eds.), In *Emerging trends in the social and behavioral sciences* (pp. 1–12). New York, NY: Wiley.

Harlan, J. R. (1992). *Crops and man*. Madison, WI: American Society of Agronomy.

Hawkes, K. (1991). Showing off tests of an hypothesis about men's foraging goals. *Ethology and Sociobiology*, *12*(1), 29–54.

Hawkes, K. (2001). Is meat the hunter's property? Big game, ownership, and explanations of hunting and sharing. In C. B. Stanford & H. T. Bunn (Eds.), *Meat-eating and human evolution* (pp. 219–236). Oxford: Oxford University Press.

Hayden, B. (1990). Nimrods, piscators, pluckers, and planters: The emergence of food production. *Journal of Anthropological Archaeology*, *9*, 31–69.

Kaplan, H., & Gurven, M. (2005). The natural history of human food sharing and cooperation: A review and a new multi-individual approach to the negotiation of norms. In H. Gintis, S. Bowles, R. Boyd, & E. Fehr (Eds.), *Moral sentiments and material interests: The foundations of cooperation in economic life*. Cambridge, MA: MIT Press.

Keeley, L. H. (1988). Hunter-Gatherer economic complexity and "Population Pressure": A cross-cultural analysis. *Journal of Anthropological Archaeology*, *7*, 373–411.

Kelly, R. L. (1995). *The foraging spectrum: Diversity in hunter-gatherer lifeways*. Washington, DC: Smithsonian Institution Press.

Kelly, R. L., Rabedimy, J. F., & Poyer, L. (2004). The Mikea of Madagascar. In R. B. Lee & R. H. Daly (Eds.), *The Cambridge encyclopaedia of hunters and gatherers* (pp. 215–219). New Delhi: Cambridge University Press.

Krier, J. E. (2009). Evolutionary theory and the origin of property rights. *Cornell Law Review*, *95*, 139–160.

Kuijt, I., & Finlayson, B. (2009). Evidence for food storage and predomestication granaries 11,000 years ago in the Jordan Valley. *Proceedings of the National Academy of Sciences*, *106*, 10966–10970.

Kuijt, I., & Goring-Morris, N. (2002). Foraging, farming, and social complexity in the pre-pottery neolithic of the southern Levant: A review and synthesis. *Journal of World Prehistory*, *16*(4), 361–440.

Larson, G., Piperno, D. R., Allaby, R. G., Purugganan, M. D., Andersson, L., Arroyo-Kalin, M., ... Fuller, D. Q. (2014). Current perspectives and the future of domestication studies. *Proceedings of the National Academy of Sciences*, *111*(17), 6139–6146.

Lee, R. B. (2004). Power and property in twenty-first century foragers: A critical examination. In T. Widlok & T. Wolde (Eds.), *Power and equality: Encapsulation, commercialization, discrimination* (pp. 16–31). Oxford: Berg Publishing.

Lee, R. B., & Daly, R. H. (2004). Introduction: Foragers and others. In R. B. Lee & R. H. Daly (Eds.), *The Cambridge encyclopaedia of hunters and gatherers* (pp. 1–19). New Delhi: Cambridge University Press.

McClure, S. (2015). The pastoral effect. *Current Anthropology*, *56*(6), 901–910.

Morrison, K. D. (2005). Historicizing foraging in Asia: Power, history, and ecology of Holocene hunting and gathering. In M. Stark (Ed.), *An archaeology of Asia* (pp. 279–302). New York, NY: Basil Blackwell.

North, D. C. (1990). *Institutions, institutional change and economic performance*. Cambridge: Cambridge University Press.

North, D. C., & Thomas, R. P. (1977). The first economic revolution. *The Economic History Review*, Second Series, *30*, 229–241.

Odling-Smee, F. J., Laland, K. N., & Feldman, W. (2003). *Niche construction* (Vol. 37). Monographs in Population Biology. Princeton, NJ: Princeton University Press.

Olsson, O., & Hibbs, D. (2004). Geography, biogeography, and why some countries are rich and others are poor. *Proceedings of the National Academy of Sciences*, *101*(10), 3715–3720.

Polanyi, K. (1944). *The great transformation: The political and economic origins of our time*. New York, NY: Farrar & Rinehart.

Price, T. D., & Bar-Yosef, O. (2011). The origins of agriculture: New data, new ideas. An introduction to supplement 4. *Current Anthropology*, *52*(S4), The Origins of Agriculture: New Data, New Ideas, S163–S174.

Price, T. D., & Brown, J. (1985). *Prehistoric hunter-gatherers: The emergence of cultural complexity*. San Diego, CA: Academic Press.

Price, T. D., & Gebauer, A. B. (1995). New perspectives on the transition to agriculture. In T. D. Price & A. B. Gebauer (Eds.), *Last hunters - First farmers. New perspectives on the prehistoric transition to agriculture*. Santa Fé, NM: School for American Research.

Pryor, F. (2004). From foraging to farming: The So-Called "Neolithic Revolution". In A. J. Field (Ed.), *Research in economic history* (Vol. 22, pp. 1–41). Greenwich, CT: JAI Press.

Richerson, P. J., Boyd, R., & Bettinger, R. L. (2001). Was agriculture impossible during the Pleistocene but mandatory during the Holocene? A climate change hypothesis. *American Antiquity*, *66*(3), 387–411.

Roberts, N. (2004). Postglacial environmental transformation. In P. Bogucki & P. J. Crabtree (Eds.), *Ancient Europe; 8000 BC-1000 AD Encyclopaedia of the Barbarian World* (Vol. I, pp. 126–131). New York, NY: Charles Scribners & Sons.

Rowley-Conwy, P., & Layton, R. (2011). Foraging and farming as niche construction: Stable and unstable adaptations. *Philosophical Transactions of the Royal Society B, 365*, 849–862.

Sassaman, K. E. (2004). Complex hunter-gatherers in evolution and history: A North American perspective. *Journal of Archaeological Research, 12*(3), 227–280.

Savolainen, P. et al. (2002). Genetic evidence for an East Asian origin of domestic dogs. *Science, 298*(5598), 1610–1613.

Schmölcke, U. (2013). The evidence for hunting dogs from Mesolithic times up to the Viking Age from a zoological point of view – A survey. In O. Grimm & U. Schmölcke (Eds.), *Hunting in northern Europe until 1500 AD. Old traditions and regional developments, continental sources and continental influences* (pp. 175–183). Neumünster: WachholtzVerlag.

Shennan, S. (2011). Property and wealth inequality as cultural niche construction. *Philosophical Transactions of the Royal Society B, 366*, 918–926.

Smith, B. (2001). Low-Level food production. *Journal of Archaeological Research, 9*, 1–43.

Smith, B. D. (2007). Niche construction and the behavioral context of plant and animal domestication. *Evolutionary Anthropology, 16*, 188–199.

Smith, B. D. (2009). Resource resilience, human niche construction, and the long-term sustainability of pre-columbian subsistence economies in the Mississippi river valley corridor. *Journal of Ethnobiology, 29*(2), 167–183.

Smith, B. D. (2011). General patterns of niche construction and the management of "wild" plant and animal resources by small-scale pre-industrial societies. *Philosophical Transactions of the Royal Society B, 366*, 836–848.

Smith, B. D. (2012). A cultural Niche construction theory of initial domestication. *Theoretical Biology, 6*, 260–271.

Smith, B. D. (2015). A comparison of niche construction theory and diet breadth models as explanatory frameworks for the initial domestication of plants and animals. *Journal of Archaeological Research, 23*, 215–262.

Smith, B. D., & Zeder, M. A. (2013). The onset of the Anthropocene. *Anthropocene, 4*, 8–13.

Smith, V. L. (1993). Humankind in prehistory: Economy, ecology and institutions. In T. L. Anderson & R. T. Simmons (Eds.), *The political economy of customs and culture* (pp. 157–184). Lanham, MD: Rowman & Littlefield Publishers Inc.

Svizzero, S. (2014). Pre-Neolithic economy. *History of Economic Ideas, XXII*(2), 25–40.

Svizzero, S. (2016a). Foraging wild resources: Evolving goals of an ubiquitous human behavior. *Anthropology, 4*(161). doi:10.4172/2332-0915.1000161

Svizzero, S. (2016b). Foraging wild resources and sustainable economic development. *Journal of Economics and Public Finance, 2*(1), 132–153.

Svizzero, S. (2016c). Population pressure and the transition to agriculture. *Global Journal of Human-Social Science, 16*(2), 7–12.

Svizzero, S., & Tisdell, C. (2014). Theories about the commencement of agriculture in prehistoric societies: A critical evaluation. *Rivista di Storia Economica, 3*, 255–280. doi:10.1410/78237

Svizzero, S., & Tisdell, C. (2015). The persistence of hunting and gathering economies. *Social Evolution and History, 14*(2), 3–25.

Tykot, R. H. (2004). Trade and exchange. In P. Bogucki & P. J. Crabtree (Eds.), *Ancient Europe; 8000 BC-1000 AD Encyclopaedia of the Barbarian World* (Vol. I, pp. 65–71). New York, NY: Charles Scribners & Sons.

Vigne, J.-D., Carrére, I., Briois, F., & Guilaine, J. (2011). The early process of mammal domestication in the Near East: New evidence from the Pre-Neolithic and Pre-Pottery Neolithic in Cyprus. *Current Anthropology, 52*(S4), S255–S271.

Waguespack, N. M. (2005). What do women do in large-game hunting societies? The organization of male and female labor in foraging societies: Implications for early paleoindian archaeology. *American Anthropologist, 107*(4), 666–676.

Weisdorf, J. L. (2005). From foraging to farming: Explaining the Neolithic revolution. *Journal of Economic Surveys*, *19*, 561–586.

Winterhalder, B., & Kennett, D. J. (2006). Behavioral ecology and the transition from hunting and gathering to agriculture. In D. J. Kennett & B. Winterhalder (Eds.), *Behavioral ecology and the transition to agriculture* (pp. 1–21). Berkeley, CA: University of California Press.

Woodburn, J. (1982). Egalitarian societies. *Review of Man*, *17*(3), 431–451.

Zeder, M. A. (2009). The Neolithic Macro-(R)evolution: Macroevolutionary theory and the study of culture change. *Journal of Archaeological Research*, *17*, 1–63.

Zeder, M. A. (2011). The origins of agriculture in the near East. *Current Anthropology*, *52*(S4), The Origins of Agriculture: New Data, New Ideas, S221–S235.

Zeder, M. A. (2015). Core questions in domestication research. *Proceedings of the National Academy of Sciences*, *112*(11), 3191–3198.

PART II
EXCHANGE

LONG-DISTANCE EXCHANGE AND CENTRALIZED POLITICAL POWER IN PRECOLUMBIAN AMERICA

Kathryn M. Hudson and John S. Henderson

ABSTRACT

Purpose – *Relationships between long-distance exchange, especially of luxury goods, and the centralization of political power represent a fundamental dimension of political and economic organization. Precolumbian American societies, outside familiar European contexts that have shaped analytical perspectives, provide a broadened comparative field with the potential for more nuanced analysis.*

Methodology/approach – *Analysis focuses on four cases that vary in political centralization, institutional complexity, and geographic scale: Ulúa societies without political centralization; small Maya states; Aztec; and Inka empires. Emphasis on relationships between principals and agents highlights the potential of social practices to perform the functions often associated with state institutions*

Findings – *In the Ulúa region, commerce flourished in the absence of states and their concomitants. The very wealth of Ulúa societies and the unusually broad dispersion of prosperity across social segments impeded the development of states by limiting the ability of local lords to intensify their status and convert it to political power. Intensity of market activity and long-distance exchange does not correlate well with the florescence of states. Less*

Anthropological Considerations of Production, Exchange, Vending and Tourism
Research in Economic Anthropology, Volume 37, 87–114

ISSN: 0190-1281/doi:10.1108/S0190-128120170000037005

centralized and non-centralized political systems may in fact facilitate mercantile activity (or impede it less) in comparison with states.

Originality/value – *These cases frame a useful perspective on the organizational configuration of long-distance trade. Informal social mechanisms and practices can be an alternative to state institutions in structuring complex economic relations. The implications for understanding trajectories of societal change are clear: the development of states and centralized political organization is not a prerequisite for robust long-distance commerce.*

Keywords: Andes; long-distance trade; Mesoamerica; political centralization; principal–agent problem

Analyses of the structures of exchange networks involving pre-industrial societies with state-level political systems typically focus on the roles of state institutions and on how groups near the core of centralized political power shape economic interaction. A proper analysis of how exchange relates to political systems requires attending to contexts in which state institutions may not have the expected economic functions. It also demands consideration of systems in which complex and far-flung economic systems operated beyond the compass of state institutions or in their absence altogether.

In the mid-20th century, Polanyi and his colleagues (Polanyi, Arensberg, & Pearson, 1957) called attention to the need for better frameworks for analyzing the broad range of economic organizations, institutions, and processes encountered by economic historians. Though anthropologists mostly adopted the substantivist perspective (Dalton, 1969, 1975), Rotstein (1970, p. 117) could still observe in 1970 that

> to focus attention on different kinds of economic institutions and on ways of distinguishing among them ... requires, in the first instance, a broader frame of reference for the study of the human economy than the one we possess. Our present conceptual tools, originating as they do from the study of modern market economies, carry their own special advantages in illuminating these economies; but they carry equally their own inherent bias and limitations in the selection and interpretation of economic phenomena from other cultures ... Such limitations are characteristic of all conceptual systems; we can only attempt to become conscious of them and then to proceed beyond existing limits.

His comments are still salient in relation to archeology: broader comparative perspectives offer substantial potential for more nuanced analysis (see Oka & Kusimba, 2008 for a review of archeological approaches to trade and Feinman & Garraty, 2010 for a broader consideration of economic frameworks in archeological thought, mainly in relation to markets).

Ancient America offers a rich field for the comparative enterprise that is required for this kind of analysis, since precolumbian states and their economic systems and institutions were structured by principles and values quite different from their European and west Asian counterparts. Ethnohistorians quickly seized on key elements of Polanyi's arguments. Murra (1956) characterized the economic organization of the Inka state in terms of reciprocity and redistribution and Chapman (1957) identified Mesoamerican trade centers as ports of trade. Brown (1977a, 1977b), adopting a more strictly archeological approach, identified the Valley of Guatemala as a potential port of trade controlled jointly by the rulers of Kaminaljuyu and San Antonio Frutal and frequented by merchants from Central Mexico as well as the Maya highlands.

An initial enthusiasm for classifying institutions and even whole economies in Polanyi's terms faded quickly as Americanists moved beyond simple notions of causal relations between long-distance trade and the state (Garraty, 2010; Webb, 1975, pp. 26–27), but the legacy of Polanyi's ideas has continued to condition economic perspectives on ancient American societies in other ways. Though they have been slow to undertake serious exploration of Polanyi's observation (1963, p. 31) that real economies are likely to involve complex and varied blends of reciprocity, redistribution, markets, and administered exchange (Berdan, 1978, 1986, 1988; Gasco & Berdan, 2003; Salomon, 1987 are notable early exceptions), Americanists have been very much inclined to conceptualize long-distance exchange and markets in relation to one another and to situate them in the context of states and their institutions (Fargher, Heredia Espinoza, & Blanton, 2011, pp. 321–322; Feinman & Garraty, 2010, p. 169; Kowalewski, 2012, p. 215). The degree to which states managed markets and sponsored trade has been an enduring concern. The focus on linkages among political systems and economic institutions has sometimes obscured the importance of delineating the distinctive features of particular economies.

Interest in world systems theory (Wallerstein, 1974, 1980) as a framework for understanding inter-regional interaction brought with it a renewed interest in long-distance exchange as an explanatory factor in economic history. A central feature of world systems perspectives is that asymmetrical exchange networks constitute a key mechanism by which cores dominate peripheries. Vigorous critiques (Hall, Kardulias, & Chase-Dunn, 2011; Harding, 2013; Kardulias & Hall, 2008; McGuire, 1996; Stein, 1999, 2002) have tempered the initial popularity of world systems theory. Key tenets of this perspective – that exploitive exchange restructures the political economies of peripheries, that peripheries are simpler than cores in every way, and that peripheries are entirely dependent on cores for inspiration and innovation – can rarely be demonstrated in the archeological record. Strong versions of world systems theory are of dubious relevance in pre-capitalist contexts, and even weak versions are often generalized to articulate with other kinds of paradigms (see Hudson & Henderson, 2014).

A sharp resurgence of interest in markets among archeologists during the second decade of the 21st century has brought renewed attention to the relationships between markets and long-distance exchange and to the ways in which they articulate with state political organization. Methodological concerns, particularly the problem of identifying marketplaces and market exchange archeologically (Dahlin, Jensen, Terry, Wright, & Beach, 2007; Hirth, 2010; King, 2015a; Stark & Garraty, 2010; Stark & Ossa, 2010) are a major theme, but current archeological thinking about markets involves a thorough reexamination of theoretical approaches to markets in ancient economies (Blanton, 2013; Blanton & Fargher, 2010; Feinman & Garraty, 2010; Garraty, 2010; Hirth & Pillsbury, 2013). Concomitant attention to systematics, including definitions of institutions and processes, has made it easier to address relationships among markets, long-distance exchange, and state institutions.

Reactions to Polanyi still loom large in the recent re-thinking of archeological approaches to economies. Embeddedness – the degree to which economic institutions must be understood in the context of social institutions and practices – is a recurrent theme (Blanton, 2013; Blanton & Fargher, 2010; Feinman & Garraty, 2010, pp. 172–174; Feinman & Nicholas, 2010; Garraty, 2010, p. 89). The notion that markets and other economic institutions are socially embedded is widely accepted as an abstract theoretical proposition; exploration of that embeddedness has much to contribute to the understanding of the workings of particular economies.

Below, we examine long-distance exchange in four precolumbian American societies, with particular attention to the ways in which it was structured by social institutions and social practices. The focus is on long-distance trade – commercial transactions, as distinct from other kinds of exchange – especially in terms of the roles of specialized long-distance merchants. Long-distance merchants often acquired goods in distant markets and sometimes operated in local markets, but for the most part market exchanges involved other merchants. The articulation of long-distance trade with institutions of centralized political authority is emphasized in the context of relationships among social actors, not in connection with sponsorship of trade or the issue of management of the economy.

Three cases focus on long-distance trade in the context of states with varying degrees of centralization of power and territorial scales. Long-distance trade was not a major feature of the Inka imperial economy, though exchange systems that had developed in conquered societies were allowed to continue to function when they could be turned to state advantage. In contrast, markets and exchange were highly developed in the Aztec empire. Long-distance trade was almost entirely in the hands of a socially distinctive class of specialized merchants, the *pochteca*, whose economic activities reflect the complex interrelations of markets, long-distance trade, formalized state-level exchange, and other forms of political action. Maya long-distance trade was also in the hands of specialized merchants, often from royal families. The lower Ulúa valley in northwestern Honduras was deeply involved in long-distance trade, but in sharp contrast to the other cases political power there was not centralized. In all four cases, long-distance trade was very much focused on costly exotic materials and manufactures.

Concepts and issues familiar from European contexts – principals, agents, differential information, risk, incentive, contracts, money – take on very different forms in the context of these precolumbian economies, none of which was highly monetized. Other salient parameters must be recognized. One of the most interesting dimensions of exchange involves the issue of how those involved in exchange relations deal with the risk that their agents may cheat or renege on commitments. This "principal–agent problem," a preoccupation of much analysis of exchange in other contexts, has attracted almost no attention from Americanists, perhaps in part because so much of the economic literature focuses on quantifying the optimal degree of risk-sharing between principals and agents or on implications for organization theory and political science (Eisenhardt, 1989; Grossman & Hart, 1983; Miller, 2005; Myerson, 1982).

Consideration of the relationships between principals and agents is useful in highlighting important dimensions of long-distance trade that are sometimes overlooked, in particular the potential of social practices to perform functions often assumed, at least implicitly, to be associated with formal state institutions. In most precolumbian states, societal scale was relatively small, and even in large imperial formations, effective societal scale in the context of exchange systems was not great. We suggest that the degree to which exchange was structured by principles usually thought to be overshadowed by formal political and economic institutions in state societies – notably kinship relations and notions of proper social behavior – has been underappreciated.

The history of long-distance exchange in the lower Ulúa valley provides a particularly interesting perspective on these linkages. At the time of the Spanish invasion in the 16th century, archeological and historical data show that valley communities were key nodes in far-flung exchange networks but that state political organization and social stratification were absent. Archeological evidence documents strong continuities in these respects: political systems never involved the centralization of power and the region had been involved more or less continuously in long-distance exchange for some three millennia. Informal social mechanisms and practices are perfectly adequate to structure complex economic relations. The poor correlation between intensity of commercial activity and the florescence of states elsewhere in Mesoamerica (Blanton, Kowalewski, Feinman, & Finsten, 1993; Stark & Ossa, 2010) suggests the possibility that some facet of the non-centralized political formations in the lower Ulúa valley may have facilitated mercantile activity (or at least inhibited it to a lesser degree). Contemplating the inverse – that the organization of long-distance trade in the lower Ulúa valley might have inhibited the development of states – is particularly intriguing. It might offer a way of accounting, in part, for the otherwise surprising absence of centralized political power and social stratification in a resource-rich region that maintained close relationships with neighboring Maya states during the Classic period (ca 300–850 CE).

LONG-DISTANCE EXCHANGE IN LATE PREHISPANIC STATES

Tawantinsuyu: The Inka Empire

Tawantinsuyu, by far the largest political formation of precolumbian America, grew from a small regional polity in the Cuzco basin of southern highland Peru at the beginning of the 15th century to an empire embracing a territory that stretched from southern Colombia to Central Chile 100 years later (D'Altroy, 2015b; Morris & von Hagen, 2011; Shimada, 2015). Administrative control within this vast domain was astonishingly tight, given the absence of writing, thanks to an army of bureaucrats and their effective use of *khipu* (*quipu*) knotted cord records.

Murra's (1956) analysis of economic organization in the Inka world emphasized redistributive aspects of the state economy to the virtual exclusion of other mechanisms. At regional and local levels, Murra (1968, 1971) saw reciprocity and a pattern of vertical complementarity – involving the maintenance of enclaves in areas with resource potentials different from those of the home community or region – as the factors structuring production and exchange. Murra's views were so influential during the second half of the 20th century that there seemed little room in the Inka world – perhaps not in the pre-Inka Andes – for any kind of market activity or for long-distance exchange carried on by merchants (as opposed to casual exchange in contexts such as religious pilgrimages). Recent scholarship has substantially moderated Murra's extreme position regarding markets and merchants in Tawantinsuyu, acknowledging that both were implicated in pre-Inka Andean economies and that neither was fully suppressed by the Inka (Burger, 2013; D'Altroy, 2015a; D'Altroy & Earle, 1985; Mayer, 2013; Rostworowski, 1999; Stanish & Coben, 2013). Merchants and markets were present in the Andes and both were implicated in the economy of Tawantinsusyu, though they were largely suppressed in favor of redistributive institutions.

Imperial uniformity seems to have been the ideal, but the Inka sometimes found it expedient to tolerate departures from economic norms and institutions of the Cuzco core (Rostworowski, 1970, p. 160; Salomon, 1987, p. 63). Just as local lords were often left in place – circumscribed by Inka garrisons, administrators, and transplanted groups loyal to Cuzco – so too useful non-Inka economic institutions sometimes continued to function, subject to imperial manipulation. The best-documented examples involve long-distance exchange systems at the margins of the empire that could supply critical goods that were beyond the reach of imperial conquest and tribute. Some sumptuary goods flowed through the tribute system and others were produced in Cuzco by transplanted craftsmen, but these mechanisms did not supply all of the exotic luxury items deemed essential by the state. *Spondylus* shell, a prime material for elite jewelry and essential for offerings to a host of state deities, provides the clearest example. The southernmost source of *Spondylus* was located in coastal Ecuador, far beyond the limits of early Tawantinsuyu, and the empire was never successful in controlling the coast of northern Ecuador where the best beds were located (Fig. 1).

The south coast kingdom of Chincha, whose lords were famous for their wealth, especially precious metals, was an early focus of Tawantinsuyu expansion (Murra, 1987; Rostworowski, 1970; Sandweiss, 1989). Specialized Chincha merchants sailed north at least as far as Ecuador, where they traded for *Spondylus*, gold, and emeralds; they organized llama caravans into the southern highlands, where they acquired copper and probably silver and coca leaves. Many of their transactions involved money in the form of pieces of copper used for payments and as a standard of values; gold and silver also had a fixed value relation (Rostworowski, 1970, p. 171; Sandweiss, 1989, p. 30). Chincha merchants were likely the providers of *Spondylus* for the Inka in pre-imperial times.

Following the incorporation of Chincha into Tawantinsuyu – apparently without direct military conquest (Rostworowski, 1970, pp. 142–143; Sandweiss, 1989, pp. 17–18) – its lords and merchants maintained a considerable degree of privilege and autonomy. Part of the reason may have been religious authority and prestige stemming from Chincha's special connection to the powerful pilgrimage center at Pachacamac (Rostworowski, 1970, p. 142; Sandweiss, 1989,

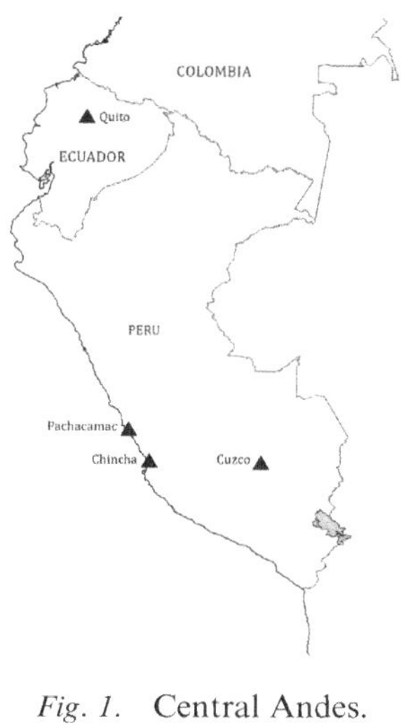

Fig. 1. Central Andes.

pp. 16–17), but economic considerations were critical. The Spaniards who met and imprisoned Atawallpa in Cajamarca at the beginning of the European invasion, learned that the ruler of Chincha was the only lord in Tawantinsuyu, apart from the Inka himself, who was permitted to be carried in a litter because, as Atawallpa also told them, he had "100,000 [innumerable] rafts on the sea" (Rostworowski, 1999, p. 209). The merchants who sailed them continued their activities under Tawantinsuyu rule. Not only did they have special tribute status, but they also continued to trade in sumptuary goods outside the state economy, acquiring gold and emeralds for the lords of Ica (Rostworowski, 1970, pp. 144–160). *Spondylus* shells were primarily destined for Cuzco; they are rare in Chincha archeologically (Sandweiss, 1989, p. 32). The value of reliable access to *Spondylus*, along with other northern goods that no doubt flowed to Tawantinsuyu along with them, evidently outweighed the fact that long-distance trade was not a feature of the economic organization the Inka sought to establish.

Beyond their occupational specialization, merchants formed a highly distinctive social group in Chincha (Rostworowski, 1970). Their relationship to the Chincha lord as agents, which remained in place under Inka rule, was direct and highly personalized. Though Colonial period documents speak of 6,000 merchants in Chincha, the majority of these were porters, crewmen, and other support staff. Everywhere in the Andes clothing, headgear, jewelry, and body modification – including cranial modification and tattooing – were distinctive indicators of regional, community, and social identity. Merchants would have stood out clearly from fishermen and farmers, the other major occupational groups in Chincha, and their activities would have been correspondingly easy for principals to monitor. They would have also been easily identifiable and trackable outside the valley (Rostworowski, 1970, pp. 149–150).

Under the Inka, monitoring would have been even easier, both for the Chincha lord and for the new Cuzco principals. Tawantinsuyu's intensification of patterns of distinctive dress and bodily ornamentation is most famously reflect in the *orejones* ("big ears"), who wore large earspools to mark their identity as high-ranking Cuzco nobles. On one occasion, the Inka is said to have dressed *orejones* (who staffed his elite military guard) as merchants in order to facilitate their intelligence-gathering (Rostworowski, 1970, p. 149). In addition, movement was restricted and monitored: only those authorized by the state could travel and the suspension bridges that made efficient travel in the highlands possible were strictly controlled. Merchants, probably a significant proportion of travelers, were a particular focus of monitoring (Murra, 1956, pp. 246–248; Rostworowski, 1970, pp. 147–148); a Spanish invader investigating the road system reported that

> those who come and go pay tolls in the very things that they carry; and no one can take a load out of town if he did not bring one in. ... No traveler can enter or leave with a load by any other road that the one where the guard is, under penalty of death. (Francisco de Xerez, cited in Murra, 1956, p. 247)

As suppliers of key state goods, Chincha merchants would have dealt directly with high-ranking officials in Cuzco, many of whom were close kin of the Inka. Though outside the normal system of tribute obligation, their activities would not have escaped the attention of the bureaucratic corps and their *khipu* records (Rostworowski, 1999, p. 154). Since the Chincha lords were required to spend several months a year in Cuzco (Sandweiss, 1989, p. 19), they were in effect hostage guarantors of their merchant agents. Administrative institutions and less formal political and social mechanisms were in place to minimize risk for Inka principals. Because *Spondylus*, the critical item provided by Chincha merchants, was consumed mainly in state ritual, demand for it was substantially less outside Cuzco and provincial state installations. The potential for merchant misfeasance was thereby limited, so that risk for the Inka principal was partly self-limiting. A further consideration with respect to risk is that Chincha merchants, in addition to their long-distance trading, may have served state political ends; their counterparts along the northern fringe of Tawantinsuyu certainly did (see below). To the degree that these functions were important to the Inka, risk attached to merchants' exchange activities was of reduced concern.

In northern Ecuador and southern Colombia, long-distance exchange focused on *Spondylus*, gold, and coca leaves was in the hands of another specialized merchant group, the *mindalá* (Salomon, 1987; Topic, 2013). Some of the sumptuary goods they acquired were for sponsoring lords, but they also traded them in local markets. Their transactions employed two forms of money: gold buttons (*chagual*) and beads of *Spondylus* or bone (*chaquira*) (Salomon, 1987, p. 70).

Tawantinsuyu expanded into this region late and administrative control was always less firm than in regions to the south, but Inka rule had a far greater impact on the *mindalá* than on their Chincha counterparts. An additional half century of expansion and experience incorporating different organizational systems into the empire may have made the Inka more inclined to modify or eliminate pre-existing institutions and processes that departed from Cuzco norms. Nonetheless, the Inka tolerated continuing *mindalá* merchant activity, in part because the goods they channeled to the state were of value; they had access to the best *Spondylus* beds along the north coast of Ecuador beyond imperial control. It is also clear that the Inka found it useful to make the *mindalá* agents of statecraft (Salomon, 1987, pp. 70–73).

The *mindalá* constituted a distinct social group before and after the Inka conquest, living in separate neighborhoods under the authority of their own leaders and almost certainly marked by distinctive dress. One *mindalá* barrio in Quito still had 26 households and a clear corporate identity 50 years after the Spanish invasion (Salomon, 1987, pp. 64–69). The *mindalá* stood outside both local and Inka systems of administration and tribute, acting as agents for local lords and for Inka overlords. Bureaucratic institutions and social mechanisms were available to allow both kinds of principals to monitor and control the long-distance exchange *mindalá* undertook on their behalf. In addition, Tawantinsuyu supervision of marketplace exchange provided surveillance of their extra-state trading as well (Salomon, 1987, p. 70).

It is also very clear that Inka intervention in *mindalá* affairs served political ends. Carefully inhibiting some *mindalá* activities and facilitating others fostered the gradual emergence of influential regional lords who could function as agents of indirect rule (Salomon, 1987, pp. 72–73). This political advantage may have rivaled the provision of luxury goods to the state as a motive for tolerating the nonconforming institutions of long-distance exchange. To the degree that this was so, the importance of any residual risk in principal–agent relations would have been diminished.

Triple Alliance: The Aztec empire

The roots of the Aztec empire lay in an alliance formed about 1425 by Tenochtitlan, Texcoco, and Tlacopan to end the political dominance of the Tepanecs of Azcapotzalco in the Basin of Mexico (Fig. 2). By the time of the Spanish invasion, slightly less than a century later, the Triple Alliance controlled most of western Mesoamerica and was dominated by Tenochtitlan. The Triple Alliance intervened minimally in the administration of its provinces so

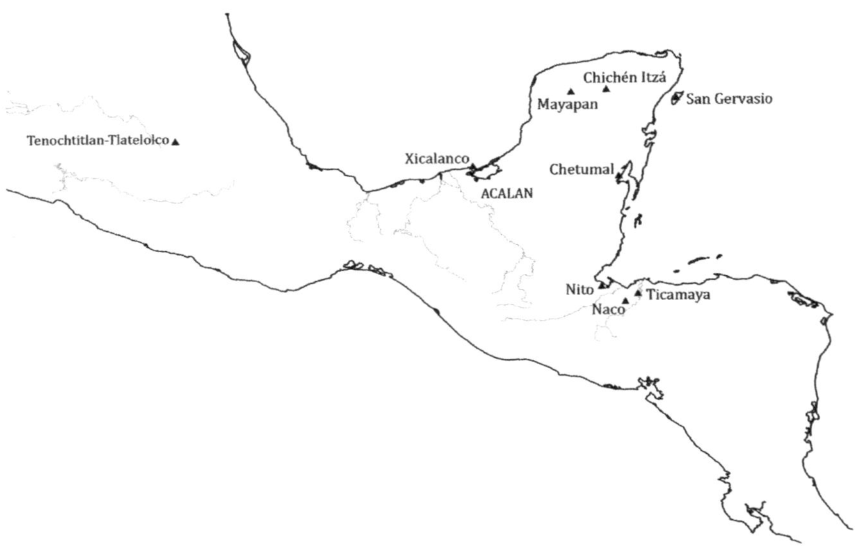

Fig. 2. Mesoamerica.

long as tribute and other goods flowed as expected (Berdan, 2014; Smith, 2003).

Relationships among tribute, redistribution, long-distance trade, marketplace exchange, and reciprocal exchange at the level of local political and social entities were complex and varied (Berdan, 2014; Nichols, 2013). Most provinces owed regular tribute payments – consisting largely of sumptuary goods, but including food, textiles, and construction materials as well in the case of provinces near the core – to one or more of the ruling cities. Other provinces provided sumptuary goods to the Triple Alliance on a non-tributary basis. These unscheduled deliveries of unspecified goods had something of the character of gift exchange, though an element of coercion was certainly involved (Berdan, 1994, p. 307). Markets were well developed throughout the Aztec world (Berdan, 2014, pp. 114–128). Spanish invaders, who observed the market in Tlatelolco – located on the same island as Tenochtitlan – while it was still functioning in indigenous mode were astonished by the variety and quality of goods for sale as well as by the maintenance of order (Díaz, 1963, pp. 232–233; Sahagún, 1950–1971, Bk8, 10). Local agricultural produce, wild plant and animal foods, raw materials, regional craft products, and an array of exotic materials and manufactured goods all flowed through this and smaller markets in every Basin of Mexico city. Prices were not fixed across the board but the state did exercise regulatory control in some contexts. Long-distance trade was almost entirely in the hands of specialized merchants, the *pochteca*, who channeled goods into the state redistribution system and into markets as well (Sahagún, 1950–1971, Bk9).

Pochteca were socially distinct from other groups in Central Mexico. They were organized in guild-like groups, which occupied specific neighborhoods (*calpolli*) in 12 of the chief cities of the Basin of Mexico (Berdan, 1986, 1988; Nichols, 2013; van Zantwijk, 1985, pp. 132–143). *Calpolli* were municipal administrative units as well as residential districts and most were characterized by strong kinship relations among residents. The path to a merchant occupation began with birth into a *pochteca* family in a *pochteca calpolli*. Administrative functions within the *calpolli* were exercised by *pochteca* officials; in Tenochtitlan and Tlatelolco, principal *pochteca* were formally recognized by the lord, known as the *tlatoani* ("speaker").

Pochteca are best known for their specialization in and control of long-distance trade in costly luxury goods, but they engaged in an array of other economic activities (Berdan, 1986, 1988; Isaac, 1986). Only 5 of the 12 *pochteca* guilds undertook expeditions to commercial centers beyond the frontiers of the empire and they were also active in distant markets within the empire, where members of the other guilds traded. *Pochteca* routinely operated in the imperial core as well, supplying craftsmen with raw materials, supplying regional markets with exotic goods required for tribute, converting goods to merchandise suitable for distant trade (Berdan, 1986, 1988; Isaac, 1986; Nichols, 2013). While *pochteca* specialized in high-value luxury goods, they sometimes dealt in bulk goods, which were mainly handled by regional merchants who occasionally dealt in wealth items. *Pochteca* policed themselves, with high-ranking guild members presiding over inquiries into merchant wrong-doing and they also served as market officials, at least in Tlatelolco, punishing irregularities and perhaps ensuring adherence to fixed prices (Sahagún, 1950–1971, Bk8, p. 67).

It can be difficult to separate them analytically from regional merchants, but all *pochteca* focused on the acquisition of exotic costly goods from distant regions. Some *pochteca* engaged regularly in and dominated trade in sumptuary items beyond the imperial frontiers, and their activities included "gift"-like exchange, formalized state-level exchange, and other forms of political action as well. Sometimes *pochteca* operated as agents of the state; they undertook exchange as agents for the *tlatoani*, for other *pochteca*, or for the *calpolli*, and they traded on their own behalf on a large scale. The cost of the feasts hosted by senior *pochteca* is a clear indication that they accumulated considerable wealth beyond the commissions paid by the *tlatoani* (Sahagún, 1950–1971, Bks4, p. 60;5, p. 154;9, pp. 7–8, 45–61).

The *pochteca* of Tenochtitlan and Tlatelolco were famous for their dealings in commercial centers along the fringes of Triple Alliance territory, especially in Xicalanco on the Laguna de Términos at the edge of the Maya world. Xicalanco was certainly a commercial hub, but it was not quite the classic port of trade that Chapman (1957) imagined. Merchants came from distant regions to trade for luxury goods at Xicalanco, but the local population was deeply involved as well and exchange of local quotidian items was active. The lords of Xicalanco provided a secure environment in which merchants could conduct their business; they even provided an escort for Aztec *pochteca* to conduct them safely from the edge of Triple Alliance territory to Xicalanco itself. But at other times, Aztec troops were garrisoned there, and the center cannot be said to have been self-consciously maintained as neutral territory by interested states (Sahagún, 1950–1971, Bk9).

Pochteca expeditions to Xicalanco sometimes involved exchange undertaken as agents for the *tlatoani* as well as trading on their own behalf. Procedures surrounding the departure and return of caravans were elaborate. They involved a careful specification of the goods consigned by the *tlatoani* and the trade items that were the merchants' own. In some cases, *pochteca* would take the *tlatoani*'s goods to the market in Tlatelolco and convert them to merchandise more suitable for exchange at the destination. *Pochteca* of Tenochtitlan and Tlatelolco traveled together in large groups under the authority of a senior merchant and sometimes with a military escort. Departures were formally announced in public.

Not all of the exchanges effected by *pochteca* can be classed as trade. Some of the exchanges with the lord of Xicalanco on behalf of the *tlatoani* seem more like formalized political-diplomatic exchanges (Sahagún, 1950–1971, Bk9, pp. 18–19). *Pochteca* also performed a variety of political functions for the state, often providing military intelligence and occasionally acting as *agents provocateurs*, inviting an attack which could become the prelude to imperial military action (Berdan, 1978, p. 186; Sahagún, 1950–1971, Bk9).

Pochteca returning to Tenochtitlan from a merchant venture sometimes brought the goods they had acquired directly to the *tlatoani*'s palace. On other occasions, they deposited their merchandise at the residence of a well-respected neutral *pochteca* who had no interest in that particular caravan. In either case, a ritualized display of goods in the context of a feast, often accompanied by a formal acknowledgment of the merchant's fiduciary roles, had the character of a public accounting (Sahagún, 1950–1971, 9:5–6, 27–32).

Prescribed behaviors surrounding merchant ventures facilitated monitoring of *pochteca* activities, particularly by principals within the merchant community. Indeed, *pochteca* were said never to have gone anywhere alone (Sahagún, 1950–1971, 9:24). In the case of individual or corporate *pochteca* principals, the agency of long-distance merchants was subject to the norms of kinship and of the "guild." Principal–agent relationships between *pochteca* and the state were mediated by the chief merchants designated by the *tlatoani*, and were highly personalized. Political roles of the *pochteca* were of considerable value to the state and the salience of risk associated with their agency in long-distance exchange was correspondingly reduced.

Maya Kingdoms of Northern Yucatan

In sharp contrast to Central Mexico and the Andes, there were no large territorial states in eastern Mesoamerica (Henderson, 1997; Sharer & Traxler, 2005). Political geography in the Maya world revolved around small territorial polities. Following the disintegration of the sphere dominated by Mayapan in the 15th century, small independent city-states dotted the northern Yucatan peninsula. Most of them were intensively involved in long-distance exchange, and active maritime networks ringed the peninsula, extending along the base of the Gulf of Mexico in the west and to the Bay of Honduras in the east (Andrews, 1990; Roys, 1957, 1972; Sabloff & Rathje, 1975). Preparation for a trading venture at Chetumal on the east coast in 1532 suggests that large merchant canoe fleets plied coastal trade routes (Chamberlain, 1948, p. 117). The largest and most prosperous towns were located on the coast or maintained port outposts there. Several can be considered major commercial centers, though none fits Chapman's (1957) port of trade template.

Long-distance exchange systems focused on costly exotic materials and manufactures, but utilitarian goods such as obsidian were important as well. This trade was controlled by specialized merchants distinct from other commercial specialists (King, 2015b; Tokovinine & Beliaev, 2013, p. 170). Long-distance traders were often (perhaps always) members of royal families and in at least some cases, rulers were characterized as great merchants. Cortés reported that, in Acalán in southwestern Yucatan, "there is no other chieftain in the land except the most prosperous of the merchants, and the one who does most trading by sea" (Pagden, 1971, pp. 367–368). Less than a century earlier, the son of the lord of Mayapan was said to have survived the takeover of the city because he was in Honduras on a trade venture (Tozzer, 1941, p. 39). Most of the items handled by specialized long-distance traders were sumptuary goods essential for royal legitimation.

Maya merchants were active in Xicalanco in the west. Acalán, just inland, was an independent commercial center, but its access to the sea would have passed through or very near Xicalanco, so its merchant lord likely had an enclave there. He certainly maintained a quarter at Nito, a commercial center far to the south on the Gulf of Honduras under the supervision of his brother (Pagden, 1971, p. 368; Scholes & Roys, 1968). The lord of Chetumal, had factors and perhaps warehouses in the lower Ulúa valley (Roys, 1957, p. 162; 1972, pp. 116–117; Sheptak, 2013, p. 64). There is little doubt that other Yucatecan lords adopted the same strategy, maintaining enclaves in distant commercial centers where critical goods could be obtained. Permanent installations in distant ports ensured that the royal principal could maintain very effective surveillance of trading activity. Yucatecan royal courts were small and long-distance exchange was in the hands of rulers themselves and nobles who were close kinsmen, so that principal–agent relationships were intensely personal and embedded in the context of kinship relations.

These cases encompass tremendous differences in geographic scale, institutional complexity, and degree of political centralization. In orthodox perspectives, they represent the full range of variability in political systems involving significant mercantile activity. The Ulúa region broadens the comparative perspective even further to include a context without state institutions.

LONG-DISTANCE EXCHANGE WITHOUT CENTRALIZED POLITICAL POWER AND SOCIAL STRATIFICATION: THE LAND OF ULÚA

In the Ulúa sphere, along the southeastern fringe of Mesoamerica (Henderson & Hudson, 2012, 2015), invasion-period societies were not politically centralized, but they were nonetheless deeply involved in long-distance trade. The political reach of Ulúa chiefs was localized, but flourishing agricultural and craft production and valuable regional resources made their towns thoroughly prosperous. They were active participants in exchange networks linking them with their Maya neighbors to the north and west and with lower Central America to the east and south.

Long-term archeological investigations in the lower Ulúa valley and adjacent regions document a comparable political and economic landscape during earlier

Fig. 3. Lower Ulúa Valley and Adjacent Region.

periods as well (Fig. 3). During the late Classic period, in the second half of the first millennium CE, it is quite clear that state political formations were absent, but that long-distance exchange was very active. Material reflections of invasion-period Ulúa political and economic systems can be enriched with delineations of institutions and social actors drawn from Colonial period documentary sources. The resulting reconstruction of long-distance exchange and its political and economic context can be used, with appropriate caution, to flesh out the hazier view of Classic period organization that is based solely on the patterning of material remains.

Largely because of the absence of states and the material manifestations of their institutions of royal legitimation and power maintenance – grand palaces, temples dedicated to royal ancestors and patron deities, monumental royal portraits, and hieroglyphic texts that aggrandized royal persons – Mayanists have constructed the Ulúa region as a non-Maya periphery of the Maya world. This image of Ulúa societies, often phrased in the language of world systems theory, is not congruent with the archeological record in the lower Ulúa region (Henderson & Hudson, 2015, pp. 15–16). Societies in the region were not subordinate to a Maya core as a function of asymmetrical exchange networks. Political economies were not re-structured by interaction with the hypothetical core and there is no evidence that innovation sprang from an external font. The effect of the orthodox peripheral perspective is to eliminate Ulúa societies from the comparative framework and to envision an economic and political landscape far simpler than it actually was.

The Ulúa region provides a particularly interesting perspective on long-distance trade in the absence of centralized political organization. The different forms assumed by problems of risk management and principal–agent relationships in this context signal interesting structural differences between state and non-state economic contexts. Political control of trade and markets is obviously not an issue. Social relations rather than state institutions constrained the actions of principals and agents. Ulúa economies thus offer a fertile field in which to explore relationships between the form and intensity of long-distance trade on the one hand and state institutions and other concomitants of the centralization of political power on the other hand.

The town of Naco in the Ulúa region – famous as the land of gold, quetzal feathers, and cacao – was a major destination for Yucatecan traders (Henderson, 1977; Sheptak, 2013; Wonderley, 1981). Overland and maritime networks linked the region with Maya towns as far west as the Gulf of Mexico. Copper was available in the Chamelecón valley near Naco, and gold deposits occur approximately 50 kilometers upstream. Quetzal birds inhabit the cloud forests west of the lower Ulúa valley. The quality of the cacao produced on extensive Ulúa plantations was famous throughout Mesoamerica (Bergmann, 1969). Merchants from northern and eastern Yucatan maintained agents and installations in the valley to secure access to Ulúa cacao (Roys, 1957, p. 162; 1972, pp. 116–117; Sheptak, 2013, p. 64; Tozzer, 1941). So important was the Ulúa cacao trade to Nachan Can, the lord of Chetumal, that he sent a fleet of 50 war canoes to help valley lords repel Spanish invaders (Chamberlain, 1953, pp. 53–57; Tozzer, 1941, p. 8). Shortly after colonial control was established, lords of Yucatecan towns arrived in Naco to ask the Spanish governor to safeguard their long-standing and lucrative Ulúa trade (Chamberlain, 1953, p. 78). Lower Ulúa valley towns were still paying tribute to the Spanish colonial administration in cacao late in the 16th century (Sheptak, Joyce, & Blaisdell-Sloan, 2010, p. 157).

Goods surely moved in the context of political and social relations as well. On his fourth voyage, Columbus encountered a large canoe off the north coast of Honduras, carrying more than two dozen people and an array of valuable goods: cacao, decorated cotton garments, swords edged with obsidian, stone axes, copper bells, axes, and knives, and crucibles for melting copper (Las Casas, 1875, pp. 109–110; MacNutt, 1912, p. 317). The orthodox interpretation, that it was a merchant vessel, may well be correct; the cargo is consistent with a commercial venture, and the substantial number of women and children among the passengers might have been a merchant's family. The apparent inability of anyone aboard to speak any of the languages that functioned as commercial *linguae francae* along the coast of Honduras and Yucatan, however, does make the merchant vessel interpretation less likely (Sheptak, 2013, p. 74). The canoe could just as well have been ferrying an elite family with gifts to a visit with relatives in a distant town or carrying the emissaries of a lord with goods for a diplomatic exchange. The uncertainty provides a useful reminder that it can be very difficult to distinguish trade from other forms of long-distance exchange.

Naco, the largest town in the region, was located well inland along the Río Chamelecón some 15 kilometers southwest of the point where the river enters the lower Ulúa valley proper. Clusters of public structures, elaborate residences, and smaller domestic buildings stretch for several kilometers along the left bank of the Chamelecón (Schortman & Urban, 2011; Wonderley, 1981). Naco's architectural core – a compact zone of public structures, including a ball court, surrounded by residences of varying size and degrees of elaboration – lay along both banks of the Río Naco, a small tributary of the Chamelecón. This part of the community alone extended over more than 150 hectares between 1250 and 1525 CE. At the time of the Spanish invasion, the town probably had a population approaching 10,000 (Henderson, 1977; Schortman & Urban, 2011; Wonderley, 1981, p. 5). Of the towns in the Ulúa region, Naco was certainly the best known in distant regions. It was the most prominent commercial center, but there are no grounds for identifying it as politically dominant on a regional scale, suggestions to the contrary in a few Colonial period documents notwithstanding (Henderson, 1977, p. 371).

Other towns in the region, particularly some of those in the lower Ulúa valley proper, were also active participants in networks of long-distance trade. Ticamaya (also called Quitola and Quitamay in early Colonial period documents; and corresponding to an archeological site sometimes called Rancho Irés) was the most prominent (Blaisdell-Sloan, 2006; Sheptak, 2013; Wonderley, 1984a). The archeological remains at Ticamaya are buried by alluvial deposits so its architecture cannot be directly compared with Naco. Auger and shovel tests and geophysical prospection indicate a substantial community, but distinctly smaller in area than Naco; documents suggest a much smaller population (Blaisdell-Sloan, 2006; Sheptak, 2013). At the time of the Spanish invasion there were at least a dozen other substantial towns in the lower Ulúa valley proper and many more in adjacent regions (Sheptak, 2013, fig. 2).

In general, archeological data confirm the accounts of long-distance trade in documentary sources. Archeologists have documented a few pieces of copper at Naco (Schortman & Urban, 2011, p. 232) and a copper fishhook at Ticamaya, along with a piece of sheet copper that may be from the Colonial period (Blaisdell-Sloan, 2006, p. 172). Reports of copper and tumbaga (a gold-copper alloy) artifacts looted from Naco and lower Ulúa valley sites suggest that metal was not rare in invasion-period communities. A cache of several hundred copper bells, many with distinctive zoomorphic and anthropomorphic forms, and several small copper sheets were discovered in a cave in the Naco region early in the 20th century (Blackiston, 1910). Copper deposits in the local area and extensive evidence of copper smelting at nearby El Coyote indicate that copper artifacts were produced locally (Urban, 2016; Urban, Shugar, Richardson, & Schortman, 2013). Copper bells similar to those in the cave cache found at San Gervasio on the island of Cozumel off the northeast coast of Yucatan (Paris, 2008, p. 62) identify one of the ports through which Ulúa goods passed on their way to towns in the interior of Yucatan. Very similar anthropomorphic and zoomorphic bells from the main cenote at Chichén Itzá (Paris, 2008, p. 47) were imported from the Ulúa region. Many copper bells found at Mayapan have proportions of trace elements matching those from the cave cache (Root, 1962, p. 398). Sheet copper, tumbaga, and gold likely came to Mayapan from the Ulúa region as well (Paris, 2008).

Obsidian, the exchange item best reflected in archeological record, can serve as a rough proxy for the intensity of long-distance trade in the Ulúa region. A spike in obsidian frequencies at Naco coincides closely with the town's emergence as a prominent commercial center in the Late Postclassic period, increasing 25-fold at 1250–1300 CE and doubling again a century later (Wonderley, 1981, pp. 250, 308). Some obsidian from El Venado and a few other sources in the lower Ulúa region was used locally, but obsidian was imported in large quantities from southeastern Guatemala and probably passed on to Yucatecan merchants. Much of Naco's obsidian, including the great majority of the material found in the town's core (Schortman & Urban, 2011; Wonderley, 1981), came from Ixtepeque source in the highlands of Guatemala. Obsidian used at Ticamaya came overwhelmingly from Ixtepeque as well (Blaisdell-Sloan, 2006, pp. 240–241, 344–348).

As might be expected, obsidian was heavily used at the major centers in the region. Obsidian represents between 83% and 93% of lithics used in different parts of Naco (Schortman & Urban, 2011; Wonderley, 1981). At Ticamaya, it was the only material used for chipped stone tools (Blaisdell-Sloan, 2006; Sheptak et al., 2010, p. 152). Residents of much smaller Ulúa communities had access to obsidian as well; obsidian amounted to 67% of lithic material at El Remolino (Wonderley, 1984b).

Other imports are difficult to identify in the archeological record in large part because they consisted of highly perishable materials. Colonial period documents identify cotton textiles, honey, salt, and slaves as the major imports from Yucatan (Roys, 1972). Exports correspond well to historical accounts. The cargo of the canoe encountered by Columbus included cacao, obsidian tools, copper bells and cutting tools, and metallurgical crucibles, all likely Ulúa exports, along with decorated cotton garments, a known import from Yucatan.

Invading Spaniards identified Çoçumba as the most prominent lord in the lower Ulúa region. He certainly controlled Ticamaya and other mid-valley towns, but there is no evidence that he dominated the lords of towns elsewhere in the valley (Sheptak, 2013, pp. 82–83). García de Celis (cited in Sheptak, 2013, p. 64) called him "el gran mercader del cacao," indicating that, like his counterparts in Yucatan, he was personally engaged in long-distance trade.

Concerns about risk were quite different for Çoçumba and other Ulúa principals than they were for their Yucatecan counterparts. Ulúa towns were relatively small. Çoçumba's agents, who may have been very few, were close kin, likely members of his own household. Relationships with them were close, personal, and governed by kinship norms. Moreover, it is not clear that Çoçumba and other valley merchant lords often (or ever) sent agents on long-distance trading ventures; there were substantial foreign commercial establishments in the lower Ulúa valley. Attracting merchants from elsewhere, minimizing the need to dispatch agents far from home, is a very effective way to manage risk associated with agents. Monitoring agents' trading activities becomes a very simple matter.

The archeological record indicates some fluctuation in the intensity and patterning of exchange, but lower Ulúa valley communities were linked with distant communities for most of the three millennia preceding the emergence of Naco and Ticamaya as commercial centers (Beaudry-Corbett et al., 1993; Henderson & Hudson, 2012, 2015). The profound cultural changes that transformed political and economic organization in the southern Maya lowlands in the Terminal Classic period (between about 850 and 1000 CE) affected the Ulúa region in much the same way, making it difficult to track continuities, but Classic period communities seem to have participated in long-distance exchange networks in much the same way as their Postclassic period descendants. Obsidian import followed similar patterns, though there were shifts in the intensity with which particular sources were exploited. Elsewhere in the Maya world, changes in obsidian trade were more radical (Golitko, Meierhoff, Feinman, & Williams, 2012) and have sometimes been identified as a major causal factor in the transformation process.

Classic period political organization did not involve the centralization of political power. Travesía in the lower Ulúa valley, Los Naranjos on the north shore of Lake Yojoa, and La Sierra in the Naco valley were large and prosperous centers, but there is no basis for interpreting any of them as the capital of a state. Smaller towns of varying sizes and many villages and hamlets suggest that the lower Ulúa valley population was substantially larger in the Classic period than it was at the time of the Spanish invasion. At the end of the Late Classic period, as processes of transformation took hold in the valley, settlement systems were radically simplified and Cerro Palenque emerged as a major population center.

As in the Postclassic period, obsidian was a major import and was extensively used in sites of all sizes. La Unión, within the Ulúa region, was the major source, followed by Ixtepeque and El Chayal in the highlands of Guatemala, and La Esperanza in southern Honduras (Joyce, Shackley, McCandless, & Sheptak, 2004). A very few pieces of green obsidian came ultimately from the Pachuca source in Central Mexico. Jade, from the middle Motagua valley to the northwest, and *Strombus* and *Spondylus* shells, from both the Caribbean and Pacific coasts, were used for beads and other items of adornment. A few jade plaques carved in styles typical of the Maya lowlands and northwestern Costa Rica and a gold or tumbaga figure of the kind manufactured in lower Central America have been found cached with Ulúa marble vessels (Luke, 2010, pp. 43–44).

Imagery and chemical analysis indicates that cacao was cultivated during the Classic period and it was very likely an important export item. Elaborately painted polychrome pottery was exported from various parts of the Ulúa region to Maya communities to the north and west. Ulúa polychromes were very costly in terms of the labor and expertise required to fashion and paint them. Like obsidian, they were in wide domestic use – even in small houses with no indications of expensive construction features. Prosperity was evidently very general in the lower Ulúa valley. Carved marble vessels, manufactured in the lower Ulúa valley in the vicinity of Travesía, were sent to Ambergris Caye, Altun Ha, and San José in Belize and to Uaxactún in the Petén lowlands in Guatemala. Ulúa marbles were also exported to the south and east, to northern Nicaragua, and to the Guanacaste region of northwestern Costa Rica (Luke, 2002).

Many of these patterns were already in place a millennium earlier (Henderson & Joyce, 2006; Henderson, Joyce, Hall, Hurst, & McGovern, 2007; Joyce & Henderson, 2001, 2007, 2010a, 2010b; Joyce et al., 2004). The valley's engagement in the Olmec world in the centuries from about 1100 to 600 BCE involved trade as well as social exchange. The great bulk of obsidian came from La Unión and other regional sources; Ixtepeque and El Chayal provided smaller quantities. Jade was already acquired from the middle Motagua valley. Chemical evidence indicates that cacao was already used to mark special occasions, and it may have become an important export by this time.

The earliest known valley residents were importing obsidian during the early second millennium BCE, mainly from La Unión and other nearby sources, with much smaller quantities from La Esperanza (Joyce et al., 2004). Technological and stylistic features of the first documented pottery reflect intense interaction with distant communities beginning before 1500 BCE. Cacao was in use and almost certainly under cultivation by about 1300 BCE.

DISCUSSION AND CONCLUDING REMARKS

These cases are useful in framing a comparative perspective on the organizational configuration of trade in luxury goods and its implications for understanding trajectories of societal change. That long-distance exchange in towns like those of the lower Ulúa valley and in the small Maya regional states of late precolumbian Yucatan was embedded in the context of personal and kinship relations and constrained by social norms is not a surprise. It is, though, easy to lose track of the fact that the effective social scale of exchange activity can be quite small even in very extensive territorial states.

Precolumbian states met the organizational challenges that accompanied centralized political power, territorial growth, and geographically expanded long-distance trade in varied ways. Maya states in Yucatan dealt with the risk associated with principal–agent relations largely by keeping them in the family. Long-distance exchange was in the hands of rulers themselves and their close relatives, so that social norms and sanctions and the prescriptions associated with kinship relations performed functions elsewhere assigned to formal state institutions.

The extent to which principles usually thought to characterize small-scale social organization are important at much larger scales, even at an imperial scale, is underappreciated. The Triple Alliance and Tawantinsuyu – the two largest political formations in precolumbian America – approached long-distance exchange and its attendant risk through varied blends of social and political, informal and institutionalized, principles and constraints. Long-distance exchange was controlled by well-defined groups set apart by separate residence and by distinctive elements of dress and bodily ornament. Institutional mechanisms – bureaucracies and their *khipu* records, restrictions on travel in Tawantinsuyu; constraints on *pochteca* movement and prescribed formal behaviors that amounted to public accounting in the Triple Alliance – facilitated monitoring and control of the actions of agents in long-distance exchange.

Chincha merchants and *mindalá* operated largely outside Tawantinsuyu imperial administrative organization, because they were foreign and operated according to cultural principles that did not fit easily into the uniform organizational system the Inka sought to impose. Incorporating groups with different established systems into imperial administration was a serious and growing problem for the Inka, but nonconforming merchants were tolerated mainly because of economic and political value. *Pochteca*, culturally Aztec, nonetheless lived in their own *calpolli*, were subject to their own administrative systems, and mostly acted outside Triple Alliance administrative frameworks. They provided important political as well as economic benefits to the *tlatoani* and the state. In both cases, much of the surveillance and control of long-distance trading activity was performed by social groups outside state administrative institutions: by local lords in Chincha and Ecuador, by the *pochteca* guilds in the Basin of Mexico. The nexus between these extra-imperial systems and the state was highly personalized in the relationship between the Chincha lord and the Inka and between the principal *pochteca* and the *tlatoani*. Moreover, long-distance merchants were coopted by Triple Alliance rulers and the Inka and made instruments of statecraft. To a very great degree, their political usefulness outweighed whatever residual risk remained in principal–agent relationships.

The lower Ulúa valley provides an example of long-distance exchange flourishing on a very extensive scale in the absence of formalized political and economic institutions. Contemplating such issues as risk and its management in relation to the identities of principals and agents and the forms of interrelationships among them is particularly interesting in this context. It throws the potential of social and kinship institutions to facilitate long-distance trade into sharp relief. That is, it is a reminder that embeddedness in social relations can be an alternative to state economic institutions.

Ulúa lords, like all those who seek positions of elevated rank, required exotic raw materials and manufactures for redistribution to favored and loyal groups and especially for display as costume elements and other personal accouterments that lent them an air of distinction and so helped to maintain and build influence. Unusually favorable environmental circumstance – suitability for cacao production for export and local availability of valuable resources, especially quetzal feathers, jade, copper, and gold – made the lower Ulúa valley a magnet for long-distance merchants and allowed Ulúa lords to satisfy these needs without expanding the scope of their own agents' operations. Social and kinship mechanisms and doxa can carry much of the burden often borne by formalized institutions, effectively monitoring agent behavior and ensuring faithfulness to fiduciary responsibilities.

The lower Ulúa valley data certainly make it obvious that centralized political organization is not a prerequisite for large-scale long-distance trade. Elsewhere in Mesoamerica – notably Oaxaca (Blanton, Kowalewski, Feinman, & Finsten, 1993) and the Gulf coast (Stark & Ossa, 2010) – intensity of market activity and long-distance exchange does not correlate well with the florescence of states. Less centralized and non-centralized political systems may in fact facilitate mercantile activity (or impede it less) in comparison with states. It might even be argued that the importance of long-distance exchange in the lower Ulúa valley actually inhibited the centralization of political power there. Mechanisms for the provision of the most basic exotic raw material, obsidian, to lower Ulúa valley households had already been in place for at least half a millennium by the time communities in the region had any experience of centralized political power when they began to interact with distant communities in the Olmec world at about 1100 BCE. Cacao was cultivated in the lower Ulúa valley before that time, probably centuries before, and presumably was an important focus of the exchange that soon brought jade to at least some households. Quetzal feathers, available in nearby zones of cloud forest, were also likely exports.

Though it is uneven, the archeological record suggests overwhelming continuity through the period following the dissolution of the Olmec world (ca 500 BCE). In the Classic period (after about 300 CE), these mechanisms and networks intensified and expanded and there is every indication of a considerable prosperity, very generally distributed among residents of the valley. Every household consumed obsidian from distant sources in substantial quantities, along with costly Ulúa polychrome pottery. Jade and other imported materials used to make jewelry and ornaments were also quite broadly available. By about 800 CE, on the threshold of the Terminal Classic transformation, exchange of a few items – imported carved jade plaques and tumbaga ornaments, exported carved marble vessels – appears to have been in the hands of high-status individuals and probably most often took the form of gift exchange among families vying for distinction in their home communities. There is no evidence for a clearly defined elite segment of lower Ulúa society, and there is certainly no case to be made that such a group controlled long-distance trade, which had flourished for many centuries in the absence of such developments. At first glance, the failure of state political organization to develop in the lower Ulúa valley, whose communities maintained intense interaction with regional states in the Maya world to the west and north, seems anomalous. It is possible that the very wealth of the region, the flourishing of the long-distance trade it supported on the foundation of social institutions, and the unusually broad dispersion of prosperity across social segments so limited the ability of local lords to intensify their status and convert it to political power as to impede the development of states.

Whether this is so or not, it is useful to maintain a sufficiently broad perspective – on long-distance exchange and its various forms, on principal–agent relations and the salience of associated risk, and on mechanisms of surveillance and control – to embrace these examples. They provide a healthy reminder that the functions of familiar European institutions and structures can be accomplished by quite different institutional arrangements and social mechanisms.

REFERENCES

Andrews, A. P. (1990). The role of trading ports in Maya civilization. In F. S. Clancy & P. D. Harrison (Eds.), *Vision and revision in Maya Studies* (pp. 159–167). Albuquerque: University of New Mexico Press.

Beaudry-Corbett, M. P., Caputi, P., Henderson, J. S., Joyce, R. A., Robinson, E. J., & Wonderley, A. W. (1993). Lower Ulúa region. In J. S. Henderson & M. P. Beaudry-Corbett (Eds.), *Pottery of prehistoric Honduras: Regional classification and analysis* (pp. 64–135). Los Angeles, CA: UCLA.

Berdan, F. F. (1978). Ports of trade in Mesoamerica: A reappraisal. In D. L. Browman (Ed.), *Cultural continuity in Mesoamerica* (pp. 179–198). The Hague: Mouton.

Berdan, F. F. (1986). Enterprise and empire in Aztec and early Colonial Mexico. In B. L. Isaac (Ed.), *Economic Aspects of Prehispanic Highland Mexico* (pp. 281–302). Greenwich: JAI Press.

Berdan, F. F. (1988). Principles of regional and long-distance trade in the Aztec empire. In J. K. Josserand & K. Dakin (Eds.), *Smoke and Mist: Mesoamerican Studies in Memory of Thelma D. Sullivan* (pp. 639–656). Oxford: British Archaeological Reports.

Berdan, F. F. (1994). Economic alternatives under imperial rule. In M. G. Hodge & M. E. Smith (Eds.), *Economies and Polities in the Aztec Realm* (pp. 291–312). Albany: State University of New York, Institute for Mesoamerican Studies.

Berdan, F. F. (2014). *Aztec Archaeology and Ethnohistory*. New York, NY: Cambridge University Press.

Bergmann, J. (1969). The distribution of cacao cultivation in pre-Columbian America. *Annals of the Association of American Geographers*, *59*(1), 85–96.

Blackiston, A. H. (1910). Recent discoveries in Honduras. *American Anthropologist*, *12*(4), 536–541.

Blaisdell-Sloan, K. (2006). *An archaeology of place and self: The Pueblo de Indios of Ticamaya, Honduras (1300-1800 AD)*. PhD dissertation. University of California, Berkeley.

Blanton, R. E. (2013). Cooperation and the moral economy of the marketplace. In K. G. Hirth & J. Pillsbury (Eds.), *Merchants, markets, and exchange in the pre-Columbian world* (pp. 23–48). Washington, DC: Dumbarton Oaks.

Blanton, R. E., & Fargher, L. F. (2010). Evaluating causal factors in market development in premodern states: A comparative study, with critical comments on the history of ideas about markets. In C. P. Garraty & B. L. Stark (Eds.), *Archaeological approaches to market exchange in ancient societies* (pp. 207–226). Boulder, CO: University Press of Colorado.

Blanton, R. E., Kowalewski, S. A., Feinman, G. M., & Finsten, L. M. (1993). Ancient *Mesoamerica: A* Comparison of Change in Three Regions (2nd ed.). Cambridge: Cambridge University Press.

Brown, K. L. (1977a). The Valley of Guatemala: A highland port of trade. In W. T. Sanders & J. W. Michels (Eds.), *Teotihuacan and Kaminaljuyu: A study in prehistoric culture contact* (pp. 205–395). College Park, PA: Pennsylvania State University Press.

Brown, K. L. (1977b). Toward a systematic explanation of culture change within the Middle Classic Period of the Valley of Guatemala. In W. T. Sanders & J. W. Michels (Eds.), *Teotihuacan and Kaminaljuyu: A study in prehistoric culture contact* (pp. 411–440). College Park, PA: Pennsylvania State University Press.

Burger, R. L. (2013). In the realm of the Incas: An archaeological reconsideration of household exchange, long-distance trade, and marketplaces in the pre-Hispanic Central Andes. In K. G. Hirth & J. Pillsbury (Eds.), *Merchants, markets, and exchange in the pre-Columbian world* (pp. 319–334). Washington, DC: Dumbarton Oaks.

Chamberlain, R. S. (1948). *The Conquest and Colonization of Yucatan: 1517-1550*. Carnegie Institution of Washington, Pub. 582. Washington.

Chamberlain, R. S. (1953). *The Conquest and Colonization of Honduras: 1502-1550*. Carnegie Institution of Washington, Pub. 598. Washington.

Chapman, A. M. (1957). Port of trade enclaves in Aztec and Maya civilizations. In K. Polanyi, C. M. Arensberg, & H. W. Pearson (Eds.), *Trade and market in the early empires* (pp. 114–153). Glencoe: Free Press.

D'Altroy, T. N. (2015a). Funding the Inka empire. In I. Shimada (Ed.), *The Inka Empire: A multidisciplinary approach* (pp. 97–118). Austin, TX: University of Texas Press.

D'Altroy, T. N. (2015b). *The Incas* (2nd ed.). Malden, MA: Wiley Blackwell.

D'Altroy, T. N., & Earle, T. K. (1985). Staple finance, wealth finance, and storage in the Inka political economy. *Current Anthropology*, *26*(2), 187–206.

Dahlin, B. H., Jensen, C. T., Terry, R. E., Wright, D. R., & Beach, T. (2007). In search of an ancient Maya market. *Latin American Antiquity*, *18*(4), 363–384.

Dalton, G. (1969). Theoretical issues in economic anthropology. *Current Anthropology*, *10*(1), 63–102.

Dalton, G. (1975). Karl Polanyi's analysis of long-distance trade and his wider paradigm. In J. A. Sabloff & C. C. Lamberg-Karlovsky (Eds.), *Ancient civilization and trade* (pp. 63–132). Albuquerque: University of New Mexico Press.

Díaz del Castillo, B. (1963). *The conquest of New Spain*. London: Penguin Books.

Eisenhardt, K. M. (1989). Agency theory: An assessment and review. *The Academy of Management Review*, *14*(1), 57–74.

Fargher, L. F., Heredia Espinoza, V. Y., & Blanton, R. E. (2011). Alternative pathways to power in late Postclassic highland Mesoamerica. *Journal of Anthropological Archaeology*, *30*, 306–326.

Feinman, G. M., & Garraty, C. P. (2010). Preindustrial markets and marketing: Archaeological perspectives. *Annual Review of Anthropology*, *39*, 167–191.

Feinman, G. M., & Nicholas, L. M. (2010). A multiscalar perspective on market exchange in the Classic period Valley of Oaxaca. In C. P. Garraty & B. L. Stark (Eds.), *Archaeological approaches to market exchange in ancient societies* (pp. 85–98). Boulder, CO: University Press of Colorado.

Garraty, C. P. (2010). Investigating market exchange in ancient societies: A theoretical review. In C. P. Garraty & B. L. Stark (Eds.), *Archaeological approaches to market exchange in ancient societies* (pp. 3–32). Boulder, CO: University Press of Colorado.

Gasco, J., & Berdan, F. F. (2003). International trade centers. In M. E. Smith & F. F. Berdan (Eds.), *The postclassic Mesoamerican world* (pp. 109–116). Salt Lake City, UT: University of Utah Press.

Golitko, M., Meierhoff, J., Feinman, G. M., & Williams, P. R. (2012). Complexities of collapse: The evidence of Maya obsidian as revealed by social network graphical analysis. *Antiquity*, *86*(332), 507–523.

Grossman, S. J., & Hart, O. D. (1983). An analysis of the principal-agent problem. *Econometrica*, *51*(1), 7–46.

Hall, T. P., Nick Kardulias, P., & Chase-Dunn, C. (2011). World-systems analysis and archaeology: Continuing the dialogue. *Journal of Archaeological Research*, *19*, 233–279.

Harding, A. (2013). World systems, cores, and peripheries in prehistoric Europe. *European Journal of Archaeology*, *16*(3), 378–400.

Henderson, J. S. (1977). The Valle de Naco: Ethnohistory and archaeology in northwestern Honduras. *Ethnohistory*, *24*, 363–377.

Henderson, J. S. (1997). *The world of the ancient Maya* (2nd ed.). Ithaca, NY: Cornell University Press.

Henderson, J. S., & Hudson, K. M. (2012). The southeastern fringe of Mesoamerica. In D. L. Nichols & C. A. Pool (Eds.), *The Oxford handbook of Mesoamerican archaeology* (pp. 482–494). New York, NY: Oxford University Press.

Henderson, J. S., & Hudson, K. M. (2015). The myth of Maya. In H. Kettunen & C. Helmke (Eds.), *On methods: How we know what we think we know about the Maya* (pp. 7–24). Markt Schwaben: Verlag Anton Saurwein.

Henderson, J. S., & Joyce, R. A. (2006). Brewing distinction: The development of cacao beverages in Formative Mesoamerica. In C. L. McNeil (Ed.), *Chocolate in Mesoamerica: A cultural history of Cacao* (pp. 140–153). Gainesville, FL: University Press of Florida.

Henderson, J. S., Joyce, R. A., Hall, G. R., Hurst, W. J., & McGovern, P. E. (2007). Chemical and archaeological evidence for the earliest cacao beverages. *Proceedings of the National Academy of Sciences*, *104*(48), 18937–18940.

Hirth, K. G. (2010). Finding the mark in the marketplace: The organization, development, and archaeological identification of market systems. In C. P. Garraty & B. L. Stark (Eds.), *Archaeological approaches to market exchange in ancient societies* (pp. 227–247). Boulder, CO: University Press of Colorado.

Hirth, K. G., & Pillsbury, J. (2013). Merchants, markets, and exchange in the pre-Columbian world. In K. G. Hirth & J. Pillsbury (Eds.), *Merchants, markets, and exchange in the pre-columbian world* (pp. 1–22). Washington, DC: Dumbarton Oaks.

Hudson, K. M., & Henderson, J. S. (2014). Life on the edge – Identity and interaction in the Land of Ulúa and the Maya World. In J. Ikäheimo, A.-K. Salmi, & T. Äikäs (Eds.), *Sounds like theory* (Vol. 2, pp. 157–171). Monographs of the Archaeological Society of Finland. Helsinki: Archaeological Society of Finland.

Isaac, B. L. (1986). Notes on obsidian, the pochteca, and the position of Tlatelolco in the Aztec empire. In B. L. Isaac (Ed.), *Economic aspects of prehispanic highland Mexico* (pp. 319–343). Greenwich: JAI Press.

Joyce, R. A., & Henderson, J. S. (2001). Beginnings of village life in eastern Mesoamerica. *Latin American Antiquity*, *12*(1), 5–23.

Joyce, R. A., & Henderson, J. S. (2007). From feasting to cuisine: Implications of archaeological research in an early Honduran village. American Anthropologist, *109*(4), 642–653.

Joyce, R. A., & Henderson, J. S. (2010a). Being "olmec" in Early Formative period Honduras. *Ancient Mesoamerica*, *21*(1), 187–200.

Joyce, R. A., & Henderson, J. S. (2010b). Forming Mesoamerican taste: Cacao consumption in Formative period contexts. In J. E. Staller & M. D. Carrasco (Eds.), *Pre-Columbian foodways: Interdisciplinary approaches to food, culture, and markets in ancient Mesoamerica* (pp. 157–173). New York, NY: Springer.

Joyce, R. A., Shackley, M. S., McCandless, K., & Sheptak, R. N. (2004). Resultados preliminares de una investigación con EDXRF de obsidiana de Puerto Escondido. In *VII Seminario de Antropología de Honduras "Dr. George Hasemann"* (pp. 115–129). Tegucigalpa: Instituto Hondureño de Antropología e Historia.

Kardulias, P. N., & Hall, T. (2008). Archaeology and world-systems analysis. *World Archaeology, 40*, 572–583.

King, E. M. (Ed.). (2015a). *The ancient Maya marketplace: The archaeology of transient space*. Tucson, AZ: University of Arizona Press.

King, E. M. (2015b). The ethnohistoric evidence for Maya markets and its archaeological implications. In E. M. King (Ed.). *The ancient Maya marketplace: The archaeology of transient space* (pp. 33–66). Tucson, AZ: University of Arizona Press.

Kowalewski, S. A. (2012). A theory of the ancient Mesoamerican economy. *Research in Economic Anthropology, 32*, 187–224.

Las Casas, B. d. (1875). *Historia de Indias* (Vol. 3). Madrid.

Luke, C. M. (2002). Ulua *style marble vases*. PhD dissertation. Cornell University, Ithaca.

Luke, C. M. (2010). Ulua marble vases abroad: contextualizing social networks between the Maya world and lower Central America. In C. D. Dillian & C. L. White (Eds.), *Trade and exchange: Archaeological studies from history and prehistory* (pp. 37–57). New York, NY: Springer.

MacNutt, F. A. (1912). *De Orbe Novo: The eight decades of peter Martyr d'Anghiera*. New York, NY: G. P. Putman's Sons.

Mayer, E. (2013). In the realm of the Incas. In K. G. Hirth & J. Pillsbury (Ed.), *Merchants, markets, and exchange in the pre-columbian world* (pp. 309–317). Washington, DC: Dumbarton Oaks.

McGuire, R. H. (1996). The limits of world-systems theory for the study of prehistory. In P. N. Peregrine & G. M. Feinman (Eds.), *Pre-Columbian world systems* (pp. 51–64). Madison: Prehistory Press.

Miller, G. J. (2005). The political evolution of principal-agent models. *Annual Review of Political Science, 8*, 203–225.

Morris, C., & von Hagen, A. (2011). *The Incas: Lords of the four quarters*. New York, NY: Thames and Hudson.

Murra, J. V. (1956). The economic organization of the Inca State. PhD dissertation. University of Chicago, Chicago.

Murra, J. V. (1968). An Aymara Kingdom in 1567. *Ethnohistory, 15*, 115–151.

Murra, J. V. (1971). El "control vertical" de un máximo de pisos ecológicos en la economía de las sociedades andinas. In J. V. Murra (Ed.), *Visita de la Provincia de León de Huanuco (1562)* (pp. 429–476). Huanuco: Universidad Nacional Hermilio Valdizán.

Murra, J. V. (1987). Existieron el tributo y los mercados antes de la invasión europea. In O. Harris et al. (Eds.), *La participación indígena en los mercados surandinos*. La Paz: Centro de Estudios de la Realidad Económica y Social.

Myerson, R. B. (1982). Optimal coordination mechanisms in generalized principal-agent problems. *Journal of Mathematical Economics, 10*, 67–81.

Nichols, D. L. (2013). Merchants and merchandise: The archaeology of Aztec commerce at Otumba, Mexico. In K. G. Hirth & J. Pillsbury (Eds.), *Merchants, markets, and exchange in the pre-Columbian world* (pp. 49–83). Washington, DC: Dumbarton Oaks.

Oka, R., & Kusimba, C. M. (2008). The archaeology of trading systems, Part 1: Towards a new trade synthesis. *Journal of Archaeological Research, 16*, 339–395.

Pagden, A. R. (trans. and ed.). (1971). *Hernán Cortés: Letters from Mexico*. New York, NY: Grossman.

Paris, E. H. (2008). Metallurgy, Mayapan, and the Postclassic Mesoamerican world system. *Ancient Mesoamerica, 19*(1), 43–66.

Polanyi, K. (1963). Ports of trade in early societies. *Journal of Economic History, 23*(1), 30–45.

Polanyi, K., Arensberg, C. M., & Pearson, H. W. (Eds.). (1957). *Trade and market in the early empires*. Glencoe: Free Press.

Root, W. C. (1962). Report on the metal objects from Mayapan. In H. E. D. Pollock, R. L. Roys, T. Proskouriakoff, & A. L. Smith (Eds.), *Mayapan, Yucatan, Mexico* (pp. 391–399). Washington, DC: Carnegie Institution of Washington. Publication 619.

Rostworowski de Diez Canseco, M. (1970). Mercaderes del Valle de Chincha en la época prehispánica: un documento y unos comentarios. *Revista Española de Antropología Americana, 5*, 135–178.

Rostworowski de Diez Canseco, M. (1999). *History of the Inca Realm*. New York, NY: Cambridge University Press.

Rotstein, A. (1970). Karl Polanyi's concept of non-market trade. *Journal of Economic History, 30*(1), 117–126.

Roys, R. L. (1957). *The Political Geography of the Yucatan Maya*. Carnegie Institution of Washington, Pub. 613. Washington.

Roys, R. L. (1972). *The Indian background of Colonial Yucatan*. (New ed.). Norman: University of Oklahoma Press.

Sabloff, J. A., & Rathje, W. L. (Eds.) (1975). A study of changing pre-Columbian commercial systems: The 1972-1973 seasons at Cozumel, Mexico. Peabody Museum, Harvard University.

de Sahagún, B. (1950–1971). *Florentine Codex: General History of the Things of New Spain* (12 Vols.) (C. E. Dibble & A. J. O. Anderson, Trans.). Lake City, UT: School of American Research and University of Utah Press.

Salomon, F. (1987). A north Andean status trader complex under Inka rule. *Ethnohistory, 34*(1), 63–77.

Sandweiss, D. H. (1989). The fishermen of Chincha, Peru: An archaeological investigation of late Prehispanic Coastal specialization. PhD dissertation. Cornell University, Ithaca.

Scholes, F. V., & R. L. Roys (1968). *The Maya Chontal Indians of Acalán-Tixchel: A contribution to the history and ethnography of the Yucatan Peninsula*. (New ed.). Norman: University of Oklahoma Press.

Schortman, E. M., & Urban, P. A. (2011). *Networks of power: Political relations in the late postclassic Naco Valley, Honduras*. Boulder, CO: University Press of Colorado.

Sharer, R. J., & Traxler, L. P. (2005). *The ancient Maya* (6th ed.). Stanford, CA: Stanford University Press.

Sheptak, R. N. (2013). Colonial Masca in motion: Tactics of persistence of a *Honduran* indigenous community. PhD dissertation. Universiteit Leiden, Leiden.

Sheptak, R. N., Joyce, R. A., & Blaisdell-Sloan, K. (2010). Pragmatic choices, Colonial lives: Resistance, ambivalence, and appropriation in northern Honduras. In M. Liebmann & M. S. Murphy (Eds.), *Enduring conquests: Rethinking the archaeology of resistance to Spanish Colonialism in the Americas* (pp. 149–172). Santa Fe: SAR Press.

Shimada, I. (Ed.) (2015). *The Inka Empire: A multidisciplinary approach* (pp. 97–118). Austin, TX: University of Texas Press.

Smith, M. E. (2003). *The Aztecs* (2nd ed.), Oxford: Blackwell Publishers.

Stanish, C., & Coben, L. S. (2013). Barter markets in the pre-hispanic Andes. In K. G. Hirth & J. Pillsbury (Eds.), *Merchants, markets, and exchange in the pre-Columbian world* (pp. 419–434). Washington, DC: Dumbarton Oaks.

Stark, B. L., & Garraty, C. P. (2010). Detecting marketplace exchange in archaeology: A methodological review. In C. P. Garraty & B. L. Stark (Eds.), *Archaeological approaches to market exchange in ancient societies* (pp. 33–58). Boulder, CO: University Press of Colorado.

Stark, B. L., & Ossa, A. (2010). Origins and development of Mesoamerican marketplaces: evidence from south-central Veracruz, Mexico. In C. P. Garraty & B. L. Stark (Eds.), *Archaeological approaches to market exchange in ancient societies* (pp. 99–126). Boulder, CO: University Press of Colorado.

Stein, G. J. (1999). *Rethinking world-systems: Diasporas, colonies, and interaction in Uruk Mesopotamia*. Tucson, AZ: University of Arizona Press.

Stein, G. J. (2002). From passive periphery to active agents: emerging perspectives in the archaeology of interregional interaction. *American Anthropologist*, *104*(3), 903–916.

Tokovinine, A., & Beliaev, D. (2013). People of the road: Traders and travelers in ancient Maya words and images. In K. G. Hirth & J. Pillsbury (Eds.), *Merchants, markets, and exchange in the pre-Columbian world* (pp. 169–200). Washington, DC: Dumbarton Oaks.

Topic, J. R. (2013). Exchange on the equatorial frontier: A comparison of Ecuador and northern Peru. In K. G. Hirth & J. Pillsbury (Eds.), *Merchants, markets, and exchange in the pre-Columbian world* (pp. 335–360). Washington, DC: Dumbarton Oaks.

Tozzer, A. M. (Ed.) (1941). Landa's Relacion de las Cosas de Yucatan. Peabody Museum Papers No. 18. Harvard University, Cambridge.

Urban, P. A. (2016). Political economy in late and terminal classic southeastern Mesoamerica: Putting the El Coyote copper smelting workshop in its regional context. *Economic Anthropology*, *3*, 240–253.

Urban, P. A., Shugar, A. N., Richardson, L., & Schortman, E. M. (2013). The production of copper at El Coyote, Honduras: Processing, dating, and political economy. In A. Shugar & S. Simmons (Eds.), *Archaeometallurgy in Mesoamerica: Current approaches and new perspectives* (pp. 77–112). Boulder, CO: University of Colorado Press.

van Zantwijk, R. (1985). *The Aztec arrangement: The social history of Pre-Spanish Mexico*. Norman: University of Oklahoma Press.

Wallerstein, I. (1974). The modern world system *I.*. New York, NY: Academic Press.

Wallerstein, I. (1980). The modern world system *II*. New York, NY: Academic Press.

Webb, M. C. (1975). The flag follows trade: An essay on the necessary interaction of military and commercial factors in state formation. In J. A. Sabloff & C. C. Lamberg-Karlovsky (Eds.), *Ancient civilization and trade* (pp. 155–209). Albuquerque: University of New Mexico Press.

Wonderley, A. W. (1981). Late postclassic excavations at Naco, Honduras. PhD dissertation. Cornell University, Ithaca.

Wonderley, A. W. (1984a). Rancho Irés phase (Colonial) test excavations. In J. S. Henderson (Ed.), *Archaeology in Northwestern Honduras: Interim Reports of the Proyecto Arqueologico Sula* (Vol. I, pp. 67–79): Latin American Studies and Archaeology Programs, Cornell University.

Wonderley, A. W. (1984b). Naco phase (Late Postclassic) test excavations. In J. S. Henderson (Ed.), *Archaeology in Northwestern Honduras: Interim Reports of the Proyecto Arqueologico Sula* (Vol. I, pp. 26–66): Latin American Studies and Archaeology Programs, Cornell University.

MARKETS OF THE HEART: WEIGHING ECONOMIC AND ETHICAL VALUES AT TEN THOUSAND VILLAGES

Laurel Zwissler

ABSTRACT

Purpose – *This project explores tensions at the heart of the fair-trade organization Ten Thousand Villages. I investigate the ways in which this organization attempts to balance concerns of North American staff and volunteers, to care for artisans abroad, and to incorporate expansion plans in the face of challenges raised by the recession.*

Methodology/approach – *This chapter draws on fieldwork with stores in Toronto (2011–2012) and ongoing fieldwork (summer 2014 and 2015) with the flagship store in Ephrata, Pennsylvania.*

Findings – *Members express continuing tension between the organization's founding Mennonite values and the more recent orientation chosen by leadership, to compete successfully in "regular" retail space against non-fair-trade brands. Store staff and volunteers perceive Villages' buying practices, meant to provide "fairness" to producers in the developing world, as somewhat inconsistent with the treatment of North American store employees. Corporate leadership is mainly focused on ameliorating poverty abroad, rather than framing the organization's work in a broader social justice context, which store staff and volunteers expect.*

Anthropological Considerations of Production, Exchange, Vending and Tourism
Research in Economic Anthropology, Volume 37, 115–135

ISSN: 0190-1281/doi:10.1108/S0190-128120170000037006

Originality/value – *At a time of increasing dialogue about alternative value systems that expand notions of economic worth, the fair-trade movement offers a useful model for one attempt to work within the market system to ameliorate its damages. Understanding how one organization negotiates its own competing value systems can provide useful perspective on other revaluation projects.*

Keywords: Fair trade; artisan; Ten Thousand Villages; social justice; Mennonite; ethnography

INTRODUCTION

This project seeks to explore tensions at the heart of the fair-trade organization Ten Thousand Villages. Advocates of fair trade emphasize the movement's potential to ameliorate the risks of global capitalism for small-scale producers (Besky, 2014; Jaffee, 2007; Littrell & Dickson, 2010; Lyon & Moberg, 2010). Villages' fair-trade model promotes an alternative value system that includes the well-being of producers in calculating what products are worth monetarily (Brown, 2013; Lyon, 2006; McMurtry, 2009). Yet, the organization operates as a business within the global economy and is subject to the rules of the often-risky market.

Over the past few decades, experimentation seeking viable alternatives to exclusively profit-driven corporate value systems has increased. In addition to fair trade, various other formulations expand notions of economic worth beyond the profit motive of free-trade capitalism. "Triple bottom line" models factor the well-being of workers and the environment, along with profit, into equations of success (Elkington, 1997). B Corporations disrupt a common binary and seek profit as well as social responsibility (B Lab, 2016). All three models work within existing economic and political structures with an aim to disrupting the exploitation of workers and the environment that has historically resulted from mainstream economic practices. In this context, the fair-trade movement offers a useful model for one such attempt to work within the market system and adapt to its ethical risks (De Neve, Luetchford, & Pratt, 2008).

While some recent and important work has focused on the practical effects of fair-trade projects for producer communities (Besky, 2014; Jaffee, 2007; Lyon, 2011) and on consumer attitudes and practices (Brown, 2013; Doane, 2010), this project focuses on the interface between corporate strategies to promote fair-trade consumption and the sometimes-competing moral visions of those staff and volunteers, also themselves consumers, who have to carry out those strategies. Looking at Ten Thousand Villages from the perspectives of staff and volunteers on the sales floor, those who mediate between corporate planners and actual customers, provides a glimpse of the places where contrasting values collide most directly. Understanding how one organization mediates its own competing value systems can provide useful perspective on other revaluation projects. What kinds of value conflicts arise when global markets are used to undo the harm caused by them? In this chapter, I explore three registers of negotiation in relation to the fair-trade mission of Ten Thousand Villages: economic, self-identity, and ethical.

TEN THOUSAND VILLAGES VALUES

Past its 70th year, Ten Thousand Villages was founded when American Mennonite, Edna Ruth Byler, visited a women's sewing collective in Puerto Rico in 1946. Struck by the poverty she witnessed there, she brought embroidery back to Pennsylvania and sold it to friends and fellow church members to try to get the Puerto Rican women a better price for their work. Her informal networks burgeoned into an international NGO, growing from a non-profit, wholly owned by the Anabaptist relief organization, the Mennonite Central Committee, into an independent partner organization. The stores sell crafts, food, and decorative items that are part of projects through which producers in the developing world are compensated with a living wage, a process explicitly envisioned as promoting international development (Myers, 2013).

This chapter draws on fieldwork with stores in Toronto, Canada (2011–2012), and ongoing fieldwork with the flagship store in Ephrata, Pennsylvania (summer 2014 and 2015). All participants have been assigned pseudonyms. These two fieldwork sites contrast with each other not only in nationality, but in their representation of urban and rural communities, their distance from or closeness to the centers of corporate decision-making, and their constituency of relatively new, religiously diverse staff, volunteers, and customers, or long-term Mennonite-oriented community participants. This contrast helps convey a sense of the competing interests the institution is trying to balance, but also highlights core priorities that transcend these differences. Ten Thousand Villages Canada and Ten Thousand Villages USA are somewhat independent, but decisions in the USA corporate headquarters often influence the direction both take in terms of marketing, relationships with supply groups, and branding. A major way this leadership is conveyed is through the participation of both American and Canadian staff at the annual Manager Meetings, always held in Ephrata, at which strategic plans for the year are unveiled, communicated, and practiced.[1]

Villages as an organization understands its main role as reducing financial risks for producers in the developing world and it communicates that role to employees, volunteers, and consumers in North America. However, within the broader context of the economic recession (Surowiecki, 2014), corporate leadership must deal with the uncertainty of its own existence within an unpredictable retail market; they must balance their commitment to care for others abroad with expectations to care for their domestic staff living under a bad economy at home (Jefferson, 2015). The recession has thrown into question some of the tacit assumptions within the Villages worldview: that life in North America is always more fortunate than life in the developing world; that living-wage work is available to North Americans; that the inevitable excesses of the economy here can be redirected to ameliorate poverty abroad.

ECONOMIC AGENCY IN THE FACE OF "CAPITALISM"

Feminist geographers Gibson-Graham caution that, in collapsing many different economic practices into the category of capitalism, both theorists and practitioners feed a hegemonic narrative that there is a single, inescapable global economic system and it is "capitalist." Such a totalizing narrative parades as empirically descriptive, but is, in reality, prescriptive, foreclosing performances of anti-capitalist and non-capitalist economic actions. Even in defining alternative economic actions against the monolith of "capitalism," critics feed its power to make alternatives invisible or subsume them within its broader category (Gibson-Graham, 1996). A major goal of their work is to find diverse ways out of this dominant discourse.

Their critique raises important questions about how my participants understand themselves as economic agents (Gibson-Graham, Cameron, & Healy, 2013). These questions involves participants' perceptions of the larger economic systems, which they consider mainstream or at least dominant and against which they are trying to provide alternatives, and understandings of the actions of the Ten Thousand Villages organization. It also includes reflections on their own roles as individual economic agents: as consumers, certainly, but also as paid and unpaid laborers, salespeople, cashiers, marketers, and public relations promoters.

Tensions within the broader fair-trade movement are also evident within Villages, especially in the different orientations of corporate staff and long-term store staff and volunteers. Corporate staff, many of whom have been brought into the organization more recently from business schools and non-fair-trade companies, generally share the perspective that capitalism is a tool. As Lyon writes, "Recent years have witnessed a move toward market-friendly approaches to international development, such as fair trade, as poverty is increasingly viewed as the simple result of a lack of effective integration into the market economy" (Lyon, 2011, p. 15). In the perspective of corporate leaders, this tool has historically been inadvertently deployed in ways that harm the most marginalized, but it can also be consciously deployed in ways that help vulnerable people.

The fair-trade model of the organization mobilizes market transactions to channel money toward those who would normally have trouble accessing it, due to lack of availability of materials, time, and buyers. The ultimate goal, from corporate perspective, of a relationship with an artisan group, is to work with members to develop marketing and production strategies that enable them to compete independently in the global market. In other words, while this strategy only works on the scale of long-term relationships, the ultimate goal of those long-term relationships is for the artisan group to out-grow them. I am reminded of this goal whenever I come across items, from producer groups that I am familiar with from the Villages stores, in other, non-fair-trade retailers. Building diverse, external client lists is explicitly part of the Villages corporate model for developing artisan groups.

However, in the views of many long-term staff and volunteers, capitalism is an overwhelming global system of unequal exchange and is, therefore, inherently exploitative. As Lyon articulates this critique, "By facilitating the incorporation of 'marginal' populations into market economies, the shifting development focus, of which fair trade is a key component, may indirectly serve neoliberal state goals" (Lyon, 2011, p. 15). These stakeholders understand Villages' role as mitigating the structural violence brought on by unequal exchange, but are leery of equating market participation with empowerment.

There is a bit of productive miscommunication between store participants and Villages' institutional authority. Volunteers often do not explicitly dwell on the connection between the fair-trade relationships fostered by Villages and the end goal of artisan groups graduating as self-sufficient agents in global markets. It is not that volunteers begrudge the artisans' independence. In fact, when I ask about the value of Villages' mission, volunteers routinely cite autonomy, dignity, and self-determination for artisans as crucial factors. However, they also understand traditional market forces as causing the lack of these options in the first place. If, from the perspective of volunteers, the global market system itself is inherently exploitative, it is difficult to cheer the incorporation of more people into it, even if their participation now comes on their own terms. Given these different understandings of the moral weight of market capitalism, it is not surprising that different actors within the organization emphasize different aspects of the project.

WHAT VULNERABILITIES ARE VISIBLE?

In addition to underlying conflicts about the purpose of their shared commitment to fair-trade, there are also tensions within the organization about responsibility to members in North America, as compared to artisans abroad. During my fieldwork, a frequent topic of discussion among store staff was which stores had recently closed and which were in danger of closing. At the 2015 manager meetings, the "State of the Village" presentation by the CEO included the news that several American stores had closed over the past year, but that a few new ones had opened. The report also included the news that sales had been flat for the past four years, which was disappointing but comparatively good news in contrast to the hit they took with the recession (Ten Thousand Villages, 2015).

The new challenges that the recession raises for the organization emphasize continuing tension between its founding Mennonite Christian values and the more recent orientation promoted by leadership: the goal to compete successfully in "regular" retail space against non-fair-trade brands such as Pottery Barn, Pier 1, and Crate and Barrel. Attempts to expand market share are driven by desire to help as many artisans as possible. However, there is also concern on the part of corporate that the only way to survive as a company is to attract new customer demographics, especially those with more money to spend and younger people, who can replenish a loyal, but aging customer base. Like the leaders of many companies, Villages' leaders have their eyes on millennial consumers.

Members of Ten Thousand Villages have varying levels of comfort around participation in market capitalism, even in their highly modified form. This discomfort derives both from traditional Mennonite teachings, which caution against being too involved in worldly affairs as distractions from religious truths, and from the same liberal values that undergird fair-trade projects more generally. Of course, attitudes toward religion and economics blend in myriad ways. Even within Christianity, approaches range from Prosperity Gospel brands that emphasize enthusiastic spending on faith that God will return the investment (Coleman, 2011; Luca, 2011), through Catholic alternatives to capitalism focused on collectivism (Nanini, 2011), and explicit critique of neo-liberal globalization, borne from Liberation theology, among progressive congregations (Zwissler, 2018). Like the foundations of Ten Thousand Villages, religious networks continue to provide connections between artisans and consumers around the world (Cochrane, 2015; Zwissler, 2018).

In my fieldwork, I found that many long-term volunteers and some staff greet evidence that Villages is successfully competing at "regular" retail with ambivalence and, therefore, they are often slow to embrace top-down plans to emulate other companies' marketing and merchandising practices, for fear of losing what they see as Villages' unique identity. That identity is grounded in Villages' practices, understood as providing "fairness" to producers, such as commitment to repeat orders, providing half-payment in advance, providing full payment in advance in cases of emergency, such as the flooding in Pakistan in 2010 and the earthquake in Nepal in 2015. However, these same practices, which are so important to the identity of the company for those who have contributed for a long time, are at times perceived as inconsistent with the organization's treatment of North American store employees. Most are part-time and paid less than they perceive peers in more traditional retail settings as receiving. Implicit messages, also common to other non-profit environments (Benz, 2005), are that Villages cannot afford to pay more and that employees receive extra benefit beyond remuneration by being able to do fulfilling work. This element of volunteerism is further promoted by the presence in store environments of actual volunteers, who perform nearly all the same tasks as paid employees.

Concern about fair treatment of North American employees was expressed in various ways during my fieldwork. For example, while we were discussing a conflict that had broken out among volunteers, Sandra, the manager at the Toronto store, became exasperated at, what she saw as unfair expectations for her assistant manager to have resolved it. Sandra said, "She's nineteen years old and paid $20,000 a year!" Sandra's frustration, at least in part, was the disconnect between what volunteers expected of her inexperienced, part-time employee and what Sandra felt she could be fairly expected to do, based on her age and financial compensation. The intense emotional care-taking volunteers expected struck Sandra as unfair given Carrie's job description and salary.

Margot, a long-term but part-time employee at the Ephrata store, said of her situation: "You know, it's a real choice to decide to be poor and it's not easy. It has not been easy for me. At all. Because I love to travel. I don't need a fancy car, to live in a fancy house, but I want to travel and I want to buy books and, you know, the stuff that matters to me." Yet she does choose to stay because, as she said, "You wouldn't even have to call it religious to say that it needs to be work that matters to me, some kind of transformative work, and you can come at that from lots of different angles, but for me it is [religious]." She continues to work at Villages, despite not making the kind of money she would like to, because it offers an opportunity to engage in work that is meaningful to her. However, she does see it, if not as a sacrifice, then at least as a conscious choice to, as she put it "be poor."

Likewise, as corporate administrators strategize more high-end items designed to attract a hipper and more affluent clientele, long-term contributors sometimes feel alienated and priced-out. From their perspective they find themselves, not selling the cute arts-and-crafts decorations they have been used to, but suddenly expected to sell upscale home decor items that they could not afford to buy themselves. As Margot related:

> I was looking at the new items for August on-line and I thought "What?!" I would say at least half of the new products coming in are things that I would never be able to buy, unless I wanted to make a really big investment. I would really like to have one of those [recycled] sari [bed] covers, but whoah! That's too much! And [a volunteer] who is here doing the sale, her viewpoint too was, "I'd love to buy a tablecloth here or something, but I can't afford it!" And so I think, when I was looking at it yesterday I thought, "What are they thinking?"

As corporate management seeks to draw new people into the stores, those that have been there feel neglected and uncertain. Especially in the face of perceived low wages from the company, staff like Margot worry that their contributions go unseen by corporate decision-makers, who are excited by new promotional plans that reflect higher-end lifestyles. Yet, it is also revealing that staff like Margot and volunteers do expect to be able to afford the products they sell, in contrast to many producers and salespeople across industries, both in developing and developed countries. In the end, members worry that there is a disconnect between new plans for marketing expansion and the traditional values of the organization, which have up until now made them feel more central.

REFRAMING VALUE: REDUCING ARTISAN RISK THROUGH RELATIONSHIPS

Practitioners of fair trade articulate it as an alternative to free-market capitalism, which they understand to be exploitative. In this perspective, when the market it presented as a space where ethics are inapplicable, economic transactions become, inevitably, unethical (Goodchild, 2002). Free-market exchanges favor those with the most money and power and with the least threat to their survival. As a result, free trade drives down prices to the lowest with which producers can be forced to agree, "market price" or "what the market will bear" (Fridell, 2007; Jaffee, 2007).

In contrast, fair-trade models aim to level disparities in exchanges between producers, distributors, and consumers, operating to ensure equality between actors in the production/consumption chain. This contrasts, in the perception of fair-trade advocates, with charity, which they see as crucial in short-term situations of crisis or disaster, but as a problem when implemented long-term. Ongoing charity with no plans to change donor/recipient relationships is seen as a stop-gap measure within a broken system, as self-aggrandizing to providers, and as demoralizing for recipients. Nonetheless, it is important to note that the fair-trade vision of ethical transactions between equals in an international community is often also subverted by similar political power imbalances between the developed and developing world (Dolan, 2008). Furthermore, fair traders still operate within a global economic system built on capitalist mechanisms that default to free-trade models.

Fair-trade worldviews posit transcendence of traditional political boundaries and require a shift in thinking about an individual's place in the market economy. Sandra, the manager at the Toronto store, calls this shift, "reframing," asking people to change their understanding of economic consumption from thinking about how much they can get for the least amount of money to thinking about how much went into a product and what that time and labor should be worth, how the producer should be compensated (Gibson-Graham et al., 2013). This personalizes purchases: a consumer is no longer buying items from a faceless corporation or an abstract marketplace, but directly from real people to whom she or he has ethical obligations created by the purchase (Berlan, 2008).

Traditional Villages' values focus on connections between consumers and producers. Materials available for purchase within the stores are presented to staff, store volunteers, and customers with accompanying narratives about their countries of origin and the localized development projects with which they are connected. Producer narratives transform items into symbols of the human beings who created them and to whom, the stories strongly imply, their potential purchasers are already in relationship.

Artisan stories are shared through marketing material, volunteer training, on-line listings, in-store special events that feature producers or Villages' staff, as well as through sales interactions. These details are supplemented by photographs of artisans, sometimes working on their products, sometimes just smiling at the viewer. In perusing a physical store or in visiting the website, customers can learn about the artisan collectives that make the products they are browsing, see pictures of laborers, and read personal stories from people who belong to the artisan groups. Examples of items sold in Ten Thousand Villages stores include oriental rugs purchased through the Bunyaad project that supply the name and village of each weaver, the Level Ground coffee packages that feature pictures on the front of the bags, with stories about the producers on the back, and photographs of artisans that are displayed throughout stores next to items they worked on. Behind each object is a person in the developing world to whom consumers in the West have pre-existing ethical obligations.

This process of representing the producer responsible for the creation of a commodity can be read as a kind of "defetishization," reconnecting consumer goods to their origins in human labor (Lyon, 2006), sometimes the labor of specific human beings with names and life histories (Luetchford, 2008).[2] Personal connections posited by fair-trade worldview are promoted in several ways by the Villages organization. Products are not simply products, dropped fully formed onto shelves, but are *produced*, created by real people who do work, have families to support, and have dreams for the future. To emphasize the skill and labor that goes into creating their handicrafts, Ten Thousand Villages deliberately uses the language of "artisans" to describe their suppliers, vocabulary I echo here. As Antrosio and Colloredo-Mansfield (2014, p. 125) articulate, this implies not just workers, but skilled specialists who "bring something extra" to their creations. In bringing producers into the picture, fair-trade organizations encourage consumers to consider themselves in relationship to people they might otherwise consider strangers, or not think about at all (De Neve et al., 2008).

For example, in his blog at the Villages website, the director of the Bunyaad rug project, with whom I worked at the Ephrata store, writes, "On behalf of our artisans throughout Pakistan, I thank you for caring about people around the world that many of you have never met but whose artistry and creativity grace many of your homes. People that share the same goals in life that most of you have – for peace, for security and for the joys of family" (Bunyaad, 2010).

Through its emphasis on the skill of producers and item quality, as well as rhetorics of shared human experience, such as the desire to be able to support one's family, the organization deliberately replaces models of aid-as-charity, and instead promotes alternative discourses of independence, equality, and authentic value. In doing so, the organization frames consumer capitalism not as separate from, but inextricably part of, an ethical economy in which all actors, regardless of their level of awareness, are already active participants. Whether they are conscious of it or not, economic consumers are engaged in social exchanges that carry moral weight through their effects on the well-being of other people and the environment.

CHALLENGING "NORMAL" TRADE

In encouraging consumers to think about producers and factor their well-being into the worth of a product, to include the cost of supporting human rights into what is considered a reasonable price, fair-trade organizations offer an implicit, and occasionally explicit, criticism of free-market systems.[3] This is an area in which customers can sometimes offer resistance. For example, as I helped Carrie, the assistant manager in the Toronto store, display rugs for a potential buyer, she was giving a standard spiel, which includes the information that they are produced with all-adult labor.

While many customers find this an important selling point, the man to whom we were showing the rugs stopped her. "Wait, why is it bad to let kids work? Isn't it better for the family to get more money?" Carrie responded that working prevents children from going to school and getting the education they need to break the cycle of poverty. She further explained that the rug-group, Bunyaad, invests in communities, building schools and educating the children of the adult workers they employ, giving them a way out of the forced choice of either having enough money to feed their families or being able to send their children to school. She closed by saying that, if you give parents a choice of having their kids work or go to school, overwhelmingly they choose to educate their children. The customer disengaged from the conversation, looked at a few more rugs and left without purchasing. As non-confrontational as Carrie had been, the conversation nonetheless seemed to rub him the wrong way.

Carrie talks about the difficulty of successfully reframing the conversation of value. "For people who have always had money, it's hard to get them to think about who makes their stuff." Referring to a frequent customer who buys big-ticket items, but is always fishing for price reductions, Carrie said, "She just doesn't get it. That's money out of people's hands. It's not cool to constantly ask for discounts."

CAN A SUBSUMING SYSTEM BE SUBVERTED?

Drawing on Saba Mahmood's use of Foucault's "subjectivation," in which, "… the very processes and conditions that secure a subject's subordination are also the means through which she becomes a self-conscious entity and agent" (2005, p. 17), I want to turn to ways in which fair-trade advocates' resistance is shaped by the very forces they seek to counter. Fair-trade consumers practice both boycott and inducement, redirecting their spending from companies that do not practice fair trade to those that do. This politically motivated economic practice nonetheless takes place within a larger system that is designed around free-trade assumptions. Fair-trade artisans, distributors, and customers work together to mitigate the negative effects of the system from within, leaving the larger structures intact (Fridell, 2007). Therefore, fair trade serves as an idiosyncratic alternative deployment of, rather than a total challenge to, global capitalism.

The tension is not lost on my participants and plays out most explicitly as the company has been shifting closer to a more mainstream corporate model in its retail promotion, while still maintaining its reliance on volunteers. For example, just before Canadian Thanksgiving (in October), I was speaking with Sandra about the approaching Christmas season. She said, "It's earlier and earlier each year and that can cause problems for some people." I asked if she meant asking artisans to make Christmas items earlier in the year, but she said that it was actually a problem for staff and volunteers, who resisted the newly imposed corporate model of retail seasons, especially pushing Christmas buying.

She said that a lot of managers and volunteers had left over the past five years as the company restructured and changed its focus to be more in-line with a traditional sales model. To illustrate, she related that she had been on a video conference with managers from across Canada when they were discussing how to encourage people to purchase add-on items, a familiar practice in retail. One of the participants, "a *manager* of one of the stores!" said that she didn't like that idea, "'I don't want to encourage consumption.' But we're working for the artisans. That's how we help them. We get people to buy their products. So there's a lot of ambivalence right now."[4]

The ambivalence also comes out in other ways. Carrie, the assistant manager, has mentioned several times that she is uncomfortable selling to particular middle-aged, white women whom she believes are compulsively shopping in the manic phase of manic-depression. She says "I want to tell them, 'This isn't good for you. Having this won't make you feel better,'" but she has not gone so far as to actually say such things. I have noticed, however, that she often encourages such women to put items on hold, rather than purchase them immediately, and then calls them a week later to ask if they still want them. Frequently they do not and the items go back on the sales floor.

Additionally, I watched Deborah, who also runs a church program for street-involved people, talk a newly sober woman in rough clothes out of buying expensive gifts for a reunion with her sister, to whom she had not spoken in years. As they talked, Deborah asked if she had been to one of the drop-in dinners her church provided down the street. "Yes. Oh, you're the pastor's wife!" Deborah encouraged her to go to the church that night, mention her name as the person who had sent her over, and ask them for a winter coat, a blanket, a day planner, and a notebook to journal in. Instead of the large purchases for which the customer had initially come, when she left, Deborah had placed a single decorative pillow, the least expensive in the store, on hold for her to pick up on Monday before she left for the bus station.

As Sandra articulated above, fair-trade organizations do need people to spend money in order to provide support to their producers. Marta is the former manager at another Toronto Ten Thousand Villages location and now works in the Canadian head office in New Hamburg, Ontario. She shared that it is sometimes a challenge to get store volunteers on board with this idea. She said, "It's good to talk to customers about the issues, but you need to make the sale."

Feminist ethnographers, such as Marla Frederick (2003), R. Marie Griffith (1997) and Saba Mahmood (2005), urge scholars to disrupt the tempting dichotomy of complicity versus rebellion in their analysis of relationships between subjects and the dominant systems with which they interact.[5] Trying to define specific choices as either pure resistance or accommodation flattens out complex social and personal negotiations for the sake of maintaining artificially separate analytical categories. So it is with my participants and their fair-trade practices. In advocating a moral imaginary in which consumers in the West are already in relationship with and have pre-existing ethical obligations toward producers in the developing world, they challenge the atomization of neo-liberal economic models. And, like other fair-trade activists, my participants are not able to fully shed a capitalist framework; their resistance must work within the systems of power that also contribute to the problems they are trying to solve (Goodchild, 2009).

THE ETHICAL DANGERS OF "FAIRWASHING"

One of the places the systems of capitalist consumption may push back against the fair-trade ideal is by co-opting its marketability and lowering standards for what can be included in the category. My participants are concerned that in educating the public to consider fair-trade issues, customer interest may be hijacked by those who do not necessarily support global justice values, a process called "fairwashing" (Brown, 2013). As consumers increasingly prioritize issues of economic justice, it is easy for individual merchants or large corporations to claim that they are engaging in ethical trade without really doing anything differently. This is exemplified by the concerns about the Fair Trade USA's, formerly TransFair USA, decision to certify plantation-grown products and break from Fair Trade International (FLO) (Besky, 2014, pp. 26–27; Brown, 2013, pp. 11–16), but is also reflected in less publicized and smaller-scale practices.

For example, as we were decorating the Toronto store's Christmas trees on Halloween, to get ready for November, a young couple came in and perused some of the ornaments. They started talking with Carrie about what fair trade means. The woman related, "I was in another store and he said that his products were fair-trade, but he was selling these knitted toys, a mama monkey and a baby monkey, for $10. Now I knit, and I know how much work went into those. It would take me a long time to make something like that and he was selling them for $10! How can that be fair trade?"

Sandra, the manager, joined the conversation, "Well, unfortunately I can't speak for other vendors, but we are part of third-party certification programs that guarantee that we are meeting minimum standards." Carrie showed the customers a package of coffee with the "Fair Trade" logo, given by the World Fair Trade Organization (World Fair Trade Organization, 2014). "Our coffee producers are currently paid 26% above the fair trade minimum."[6]

"So they get minimum wage?" the young man asked.

Carrie responded, "It's difficult to talk in terms of Western minimum wage. If we paid producers in Western terms, they would be millionaires within their communities and that would be a problem there." He seemed perplexed, but they did leave with some purchases and the promotional pamphlet Sandra offered them.

Even when distributors mean well, they are not always well educated about best practices. Marta, the former manager from another location who now works at corporate in Canada, is originally from another country and, since working for Ten Thousand Villages, she has made several trips back to visit artisans there. She says that one of the most important things that Villages does is guarantee future orders, rather than just taking what producers have on hand. The security of recurring orders allows producers to invest in their homes and make plans for the future. Even an organization that wants to help and engages in ethical negotiation with producers can still unintentionally perpetuate a feast-and-famine cycle, in which producers never know where their next order will come from.

However, there are also over-arching critiques of the efficacy of fair-trade projects, even those that meet international certification standards, which themselves can perpetuate neo-liberal power imbalances (Dolan, 2008). Besky's poignant deconstruction of how fair-trade practices have actually undermined the welfare of workers on Darjeeling tea plantations is one example (2014). Despite the historical emphasis within the fair-trade movement on cooperative communities of small farmers, Darjeeling plantations were certified as exceptions in the

1990s. Required price premiums for community development, when translated into an indentured plantation system, go toward worker support that was formerly legally required of the owners by the government. That financial obligation is now funded by the community premiums, while worker wages remain unchanged. Rather than being subject to democratic community deliberation, the fair-trade premiums in this case provide subsidy to plantation owners, who in turn use the projects they underwrite to argue for rolling back legal obligations to their workers (Besky, 2014, p. 134).

Lyon's study of women's disenfranchisement within a Guatemalan coffee cooperative is another example (2011). Lyon discovered that, despite certification requirements to increase and value women's participation, women were not included in decision-making and their concerns were not taken seriously by the broader, male-dominated collective. Certification compliance spot-checks were conducted in parachute fashion, so there was no way for inspectors to develop a clear understanding of gender dynamics within the group. Despite this, the coffee that the cooperative produced was marketed under promises of improving women's lives. Lyon cautions that the marginalization of women in this particular fair-trade project should not be taken as representative of all contexts; she cites several projects in other places that have found ways to promote women's participation and leadership. However, the example starkly demonstrates the need for different certification compliance mechanisms (Lyon, 2011, p. 110).

It can also be easy in a Western context for fair-trade vendors to support fair trade as an abstract concept, but remain disengaged from social justice issues at home. Talking in the break room, seasoned Toronto volunteer Deborah related to me that the previous week her husband, Bob, a pastor, had been working on his sermon in a local cafe that serves fair-trade coffee. In her story, a homeless man whom Bob knows was trying to get his attention through the window, but he was absorbed in his papers. The man started to open the door to speak to him when the manager ran to the entrance and started yelling, "You can't come in here! I told you not to come in here!" Bob packed up his Bible and papers and got up to leave. He turned to the manager and said, "If you're going to do fair-trade, you can't treat people like dirt. That was my friend." The guy just looked at him; he didn't know what to say. Summing up her point, Deborah said, "Fair trade means you have to treat *everyone* fairly. This here [sitting in the back], this is easy. Out there, it's hard," she gestured toward the sales floor and the street beyond the store windows.

Deborah is concerned that fair trade is becoming just another consumer trend, one that requires very little of people ethically. For her, fair trade loses its moral edge if it is not connected to a larger social justice worldview, in which multiple forms of social inequality can be made visible and rectified. This concern is somewhat supported by Brown's research on fair-trade consumers in Philadelphia, PA (2013). While some were passionate, well-informed, and deeply committed to only purchasing fair-trade items, others mixed their fair-trade purchases with discounted deals from places like Target, a practice which Brown finds hypocritical. At least in my work, this practice seems fairly widespread. When my partner and I began my fieldwork stint volunteering in Ephrata, people were anxious that we would be bored in such a small town and made various suggestions about sightseeing and activities. Several Villages staff made a point of telling us about the nearby destination outlet mall. I admit to being taken aback, in such a pointed fair-trade space, that people were encouraging us to shop for non-fair-trade deals.

I suggest, however, that rather than declaring mixed purchasing immoral, it is more useful to explore what forces contribute to it. The relatively high cost of fair-trade goods coupled with comparatively low income of store staff and many volunteers may be part of the answer. Nonetheless, Brown argues that in his research, even customers with a household income of $200,000 felt that they did not have enough money, at least not enough to spare on a fully fair-trade lifestyle, even though they expressed interest in the well-being of the producers of their purchases.

In pinpointing access to global markets as the key to economic success for artisans in the developing world, the discourse of Villages' corporate leaders block the stories of those who already have access. The case of part-time staff in the retail stores, such as Margot, above, is one example. Besky argues that, despite good intentions, the fair-trade movement perpetuates a "Third World agrarian imaginary," which objectifies geographically distant and ethnically different others, imagining that it is contact with modernity, in the form of colonialism and industrialization, that has made their lives difficult. The solution is to help them return to a prior state of harmony with nature and their ancestral practices (Besky, 2014, pp. 29–31). This fantasy is easier to project onto people far away, whose lives can be dissolved into the romantic soft-focus of "cultural difference," than with those who are close to home, in one's community and able to speak directly for themselves. For North American store staff and volunteers, who see customers and coworkers struggling to make ends meet or are doing so themselves, narratives that economic development will solve global poverty contradict their personal experiences.

Herein lies an important blind-spot within the corporate narrative, one which draws on neo-liberal mission of market expansion (Fridell, 2007; Lyon, 2011). Discursively, poverty is only visible far away, in the developing world. From the perspective of many store staff and volunteers, such as Deborah, if the overall project of the organization is social justice, which they believe it to be, then poverty among immediate community members should be able to be seen, discussed, and remedied.

Nonetheless, no one, corporate leader, store staff, or volunteers, would argue that not being able to purchase a desirable item or take a vacation is *the same as* not being able to eat or to educate one's children. However, these issues of scale get lost in a discourse that posits protected access to global markets (Fridell, 2007), in the form of fair trade, as the main answer to global poverty.

Put bluntly, which I must stress it never is, if poverty exists within the developed world, the very system into which fair-trade projects are working to incorporate artisans, how can the same system eliminate poverty in the developing world for the long-term? Also, if in the corporate frame real "poverty" is eliminated by development, then what is it that North American members are seeing in the faces of homeless people or food-insecure children in their communities?

RELATIONS OTHER THAN RESCUE?

A further area of tension arises around the very nature of fair-trade's marketability. Villages promotes its narratives of producer/consumer interconnectedness in a social context with a long history of colonialist discourses (Zwissler, 2012) and therefore runs risks of being subsumed by or even perpetuating them. While artisan-group liaisons and Villages' corporate leadership strive to emphasize the relationship between volunteers, customers, and producers as reciprocal,[7] there are competing tendencies that promote counter-narratives of western rescue and third-world helplessness. These are fed not only by historical stereotypes, but also by the marketing campaigns of other non-profit groups, campaigns which draw on images of crying, fly-plagued children or starving mothers. For example, consider the historical campaigns for Christian Children's Fund (now Childfund and advertising differently) and World Vision, which continues to use images of dirt and tears, interspersed with more upbeat images (World Vision, 2015), or even the marketing of some fair-trade organizations (Berlan, 2008). Villages deliberately works against these kinds of portrayals: their pictures feature healthy, smiling adults, often actively engaged in artistic labor; they are literally "productive."

There is only so much Villages can control what consumers, volunteers, and even staff, take away from the company's consumer education projects. For all the effort that goes into presenting artisans with dignity, sometimes this is overwhelmed by prior expectations. As one illustrative example, from among the over sixty artisan groups that the company works with in 38 countries, there is one that explicitly works with survivors of the sex trade in Bangladesh and includes related information in narratives about its products, mainly soap and repurposed sari items. In a presentation to a gathering of retired women visiting the rug room in Ephrata, a newly hired assistant manager, Ashton, a refugee from previous job at a Calvin Klein store in the nearby outlet mall, showed several different products and told some artisan stories to accompany them. Among the products was a purse from this artisan group.

Ashton had mentioned to me beforehand that he was nervous about the presentation; the volunteer coordinator, who normally would give the talk, was out that day and he and the other newer hires were uncertain how it was supposed to go. This nervousness came out in his responses to questions the women asked about different products and their origins. When he wasn't certain about details, he would go back to talking about the mission of Villages more generally and got himself into a cycle where almost every product, including the rugs, connected back to saving women from prostitution, "It's important so they won't, you know, have to sell their bodies," he said. This was very different from the usual marketing and educational materials, to the point where, after the presentation was over, I turned to a rug-room staffer, Emma, and asked what she thought about Ashton's talk.

Andy, a son of the founder of the Pakistani rug artisan group and someone who grew up around the Lahore rug warehouse, joined us to process the experience. "I was going to say, I don't know who he's talking about, but the women who make these rugs would be very offended by that. They would not like the idea that if they didn't do this, they would be prostitutes!" Emma speculated that Ashton was drawn to the anti-sex-slave rhetoric because it is current in popular culture and because it resonates with others' expectations. She pointed out that it *did* seem to work on his audience; the women snapped to attention when he mentioned it, seemed especially interested in the original purse he had showed them, and nodded their heads when he would come back to the topic. Nonetheless, Emma decided she would go talk to Ashton about over-generalizing the issue in future presentations.

I share this story because it highlights the challenge of trying to persuade people emotionally with ethical rhetoric – you as a consumer owe something to the people who make your goods – without resorting to manipulations that reinforce colonialist discourses (Berlan, 2008; Besky, 2014; Dolan, 2008). It also draws attention to competing approaches, not only between Villages' and other organizations' appeal models, but also within Villages itself. While the message from the top of the organizational hierarchy focuses on artisan empowerment and ownership of local development programs, this message is filtered through many lenses: artisan groups, North American store and warehouse volunteers, store staff, corporate headquarters staff, and customers. Each of these groups, and the communities and individuals within them, interpret marketing materials and narratives in their own ways, some of which are progressive, some of which are condescending, and some of which are a mixture of both.

This demonstrates that, at the same time that the marketing of fair-trade products draws on models of defetishization, there are also ways that "fair trade" itself becomes a commodity (McMurtry, 2009, p. 33). In emphasizing not the inherent qualities of a product, but instead the process through which it was produced, distributed, and made available to the consumer, fair trade discourses can "refetishize" products, providing new forms of mystification (Doane, 2010, p. 230). As part of this dynamic, the producers themselves may become objectified, assumptions about who they are and what they have experienced in their lives become part of the desirability of a particular product. As Sarah Lyon writes, "Fair trade consumers are called to ethical action through demonstrations of cultural difference, not sameness" (2006, p. 458).

One of the many challenges for Villages is trying to balance these interpretations in a way that is best for the artisans and the organization; how do you educate people about the developing world without alienating them to the point where they will not buy artisan products anymore (Brown, 2013, pp. 131–136)? If saving women from sex-work is what gets consumers motivated to buy, which ultimately serves the interests of the very people they are objectifying, how do you opt out of this construction? If harm-reduction is a selling feature, there is potential to fetishize *certain kinds* of harms over others. In the case above, the danger of prostitution seemed more salient for Ashton and his audience than the dangers of hunger or a lack of education.

CONCLUSION

Villages' mission is to help producers develop the resilience necessary to weather the uncertainties inherent in a globalizing economy. At the same time, awareness of its own precarity in the marketplace has resulted in increased investment by corporate leaders, both financial and psychological, in looking more like a traditional retail business. Through newsletters and updated trainings, corporate decision-makers explain to staff and volunteers their position that this is the best way to engage new customers, whose money can be directed to artisans in support of Villages' mission, and to ensure the organization's long-term viability.

Using the market to mitigate the impacts of economic globalization also opens up the organization to being influenced in turn, which many long-time members fear will be for the worse. For example, despite a narrative that Villages stores should support each other and work together, not compete like other retail chains, a number of stores across North America were closed over the past few years in a turn of corporate downsizing. This includes the Toronto store location where I conducted fieldwork. Last time I had coffee with the former manager, she told me she has become a real estate agent and is actually much happier with the work.

The possibility of counter-influence creates concern on the part of long-term stakeholders, staff and volunteers, that the company may be changing too much to continue to reflect their values. They make their own decisions about what is ethically acceptable within the larger organizational structure. They must consider whether to go along with a new retail model that encourages conspicuous consumption that they see as contradicting the values that built the organization in the first place. They must choose whether to challenge colonial discourses that position Western consumers as rescuing third-world producers, at the risk of losing sales that would benefit those very people. They must measure the value of sticking with an organization in the midst of transition, at the risk of being undervalued, as Margot often feels, or even being let go, as Sandra and her store members were. Yet, while I encountered anxiety in my conversations with participants, they also expressed hope that the organization can reintegrate its market goals and service values in such a way that navigating economic uncertainties need not perpetuate ethical conflicts.

The tensions between corporate plans and community members' reactions highlight a problem shared across businesses trying to insert social and environmental responsibility into economic practice, that is, the problem of commodifying ethical values. Those relationships Villages constructs, artisan smiles, educated children, become commodities with specific dollar values, determined, essentially, by how much more consumers are willing to pay above market price for items also available in non-fair-trade retailers. The questions with which Ten Thousand Villages, as an organization, is struggling revolve around whether that kind of economic commodification is ever acceptable and under what circumstances. Is complicity in consumption and various forms of fetishization the ethical price Villages' North American community members must pay for facilitating artisan admittance to the benefits of the global economy? Is it ever morally acceptable to just whole-heartedly play retail to win?

NOTES

1. I attended the 2015 meetings.
2. For accounts of disconnection between the acquisition of artisan photographs and the marketing claims to which they are attached, see Dolan (2008, p. 281) and Besky (2014, p. 126).
3. For criticism of the efficacy of this model, see Graeber (2001).
4. Personal conversation. October 1, 2011. Emphasis hers.
5. Considering agency from beyond the binary of accommodating or resisting structures of power is central in their work, but see especially Frederick (2003, pp. 5–6, 212–220), Griffith (1997, pp. 199–213), and Mahmood (2005, pp. 5–32).
6. See also Ten Thousand Villages, Canada (2011).
7. On the limits of such reciprocity, see Doane (2010).

REFERENCES

Antrosio, J., & Colloredo-Mansfield, R. (2014). Risk-seeking peasants, excessive artisans: Speculation in the Northern Andes. *Economic Anthropology*, *1*(1), 124–138. doi:10.1002/sea2.12008

B Lab. (2016). Welcome. *B Corporation*. Retrieved from https://www.bcorporation.net/

Benz, M. (2005). Not for the Profit, but for the Satisfaction? Evidence on Worker Well-Being in Non-Profit Firms. *Kyklos*, *29*(17), 155–177. doi:10.1111/j.0023-5962.2005.00283.x

Berlan, A. (2008). Making or marketing a difference? An anthropological examination of the marketing of fair trade cocoa from Ghana. In G. De Neve, P. Luetchford, J. Pratt, & D. C. Wood (Eds.), *Hidden hands in the market: Ethnographies of fair trade, ethical consumption, and corporate social responsibility* (Vol. 28, pp. 171–194). Research in Economic

Anthropology. Bingley: Emerald Group Publishing Limited. doi:10.1016/S0190-1281(08)28008-X

Besky, S. (2014). *The Darjeeling distinction: Labor and justice on fair-trade tea plantations in India*. Berkeley, CA: University of California.

Brown, K. R. (2013). *Buying into Fair Trade: Culture, morality, and consumption*. New York, NY: NYU Press.

Bunyaad. (2010). *Dear Fair Trade friends. Ten thousand villages: Pakistan flood*. Retrieved from http://rugs.tenthousandvillages.com/

Cochrane, L. (2015). Addressing global economic inequalities in local ways in Senegal's artisanal workshops. *Economic Anthropology*, *2*(2), 250–263. doi:10.1002/sea2.12029

Coleman, S. (2011). Prosperity unbound? Debating the "Sacrificial Economy". In L. Obadia & D. C. Wood (Eds.), *The Economics of religion: Anthropological approaches* (Vol. 31, pp. 23–45). Research in Economic Anthropology. Bingley: Emerald Group Publishing Limited. doi:10.1108/S010-1281(2011)0000031005

De Neve, G., Luetchford, P., & Pratt, J. (2008). Introduction: Revealing the hidden hands of global market exchange. In G. De Neve, P. Luetchford, J. Pratt, & D. C. Wood (Eds.), *Hidden hands in the market: Ethnographies of Fair Trade, ethical consumption, and corporate social responsibility* (Vol. 28, pp. 1–30). Research in Economic Anthropology. Bingley: Emerald Group Publishing Limited. doi:10.1016/S0190-1281(08)28001-7

Doane, M. (2010). Relationship coffees: Structure and agency in the fair trade system. In S. Lyon & M. Moberg (Eds.), *Fair trade and social justice: Global ethnographies* (pp. 229–257). New York, NY: NYU Press.

Dolan, C. S. (2008). Arbitrating risk through moral values: the case of Kenyan fairtrade. In G. De Neve, P. Luetchford, J. Pratt, & D. C. Wood (Eds.), *Hidden hands in the market: Ethnographies of fair trade, ethical consumption, and corporate social responsibility* (Vol. 28, pp. 271–296). Research in Economic Anthropology. Bingley: Emerald Group Publishing Limited. doi:10.1016/S0190-1281(08)28012-1

Elkington, J. (1997). *Cannibals with Forks: The triple bottom line in the 21st century*. Oxford: Capstone.

Frederick, M. F. (2003). *Between Sundays: Black women and everyday struggles of faith*. Berkeley, CA: University of California Press.

Fridell, G. (2007). *Fair trade coffee: The prospects and pitfalls of market-driven social justice*. Toronto: University of Toronto Press.

Gibson-Graham, J. K. (1996). *The end of capitalism (as we knew it): A feminist critique of political economy*. Oxford: Blackwell.

Gibson-Graham, J. K., Cameron, J., & Healy, S. (2013). *Take back the economy: An ethical guide for transforming our communities*. Minneapolis, MN: University of Minnesota Press.

Goodchild, P. (2002). *Capitalism and religion: The price of piety*. London: Routledge.

Goodchild, P. (2009). *The theology of money*. Durham, NC: Duke University Press.

Graeber, D. (2001). *Toward and anthropology of values; the false coin of our dreams*. New York, NY: Palgrave.

Griffith, R. M. (1997). *God's daughters: Evangelical women and the power of submission*. Berkeley, CA: University of California Press.

Jaffee, D. (2007). *Brewing justice: Fair trade coffee, sustainability, and survival*. Berkeley, CA: University of California Press.

Jefferson, A. (2015). "Not what it used to be": Schemas of class and contradiction in the Great Recession. *Economic Anthropology*, *2*(2), 310–325. doi:10.1002/sea2.12033

Littrell, M. A., & Dickson, M. A. (2010). *Artisans and fair trade: Crafting development*. West Hartford, CT: Kumarian Press.

Luca, N. (2011). Multi-level marketing: At the crossroads of economy and religion. In L. Obadia & D. C. Wood (Eds.), *The economics of religion: Anthropological approaches* (Vol. 31, pp. 217–239). Research in Economic Anthropology. Bingley: Emerald Group Publishing Limited. doi:10.1108/S010-1281(2011)0000031012

Luetchford, P. (2008). The hands that pick fair trade coffee: Beyond the charms of the family farm. In G. De Neve, P. Luetchford, J. Pratt, & D. C. Wood (Eds.), *Hidden hands in the market: Ethnographies of fair trade, ethical consumption, and corporate social responsibility* (Vol. 28, pp. 143–169). Research in Economic Anthropology. Bingley: Emerald Group Publishing Limited. doi:10.1016/S0190-1281(08)28007-8

Lyon, S. (2006). Evaluating fair trade consumption: Politics, defetishization and producer participation. *International Journal of Consumer Studies, 30*(5), 452–464. doi:10.1111/j.1470-6431.2006.00530.x

Lyon, S. (2011). *Coffee and community: Maya farmers and fair-trade markets*. Boulder, CO: University of Colorado.

Lyon, S., & Moberg, M. (2010). What's fair? The paradox of seeking justice through markets. In S. Lyon & M. Moberg (Eds.), *Fair Trade and Social Justice: Global Ethnographies* (pp. 1–23). New York, NY: NYU Press.

Mahmood, S. (2005). *Politics of piety: The Islamic revival and the feminist subject*. Princeton, NJ: Princeton University Press.

McMurtry, J. J. (2009). Ethical value-added: Fair trade and the case of cafe femenino. *Journal of Business Ethics, 86*, 27–49. doi:10.1007/s10551-008-9760-x

Myers, P. (2013). Does fair trade promote international development?. *Journal of Markets and Morality, 16*(1), 251–257.

Nanini, R. (2011). A catholic alternative to globalization? The Compagnia Delle Opere. In L. Obadia & D. C. Wood (Eds.), *The economics of religion: Anthropological approaches*. (Vol. 31, pp. 47–76). Research in Economic Anthropology. Bingley: Emerald Group Publishing Limited. doi:10.1108/S010-1281(2011)0000031006

Surowiecki, J. (2014). System failure: Institutions, incentives, and collective folly. *Economic Anthropology, 1*(1), 17–29. doi:10.1002/sea2.12001

Ten Thousand Villages. (2015). *Annual report: April 1, 2014–March 31, 2015*. Retrieved from http://www.tenthousandvillages.com/media/wysiwyg/downloads/Annual_Report_2014-15.pdf

Ten Thousand Villages, Canada. (2011). Direct trade in a free trade world. *The Villager: Ten Thousand Villages Newsletter*. February/March 1. Retrieved from http://resources.tenthousandvillages.ca/cdn/pdfs/TTVStore2103CrowchildNewsletter2011febmar.pdf

World Fair Trade Organization. (2014). Our product label. *WFTO*. Retrieved from http://wfto.com/standard-and-guarantee-system/our-product-label

World Vision. (2015). *Syrian children and the refugee crisis*. Retrieved from https://www.worldvision.org/news-stories-videos/faqs-war-syria-children-and-refugee-crisis

Zwissler, L. (2012). Feminism and religion in North America: Intersections between western activism, theology and theory. *Religion Compass, 6*(7), 354–368. doi:10.1111/j.1749-8171.2012.00363.x

Zwissler, L. (2018). *Religious, feminist, activist: Cosmologies of interconnection*. Lincoln, NE: University of Nebraska Press.

PROVISIONING, SHOPPING AND PRODUCTIVE LEISURE AT NORTH MARKET, COLUMBUS, OHIO

Lisa Marie Beiswenger and Jeffrey H. Cohen

ABSTRACT

Purpose – *The purpose of this chapter is to show the multi-faceted nature of shopping behavior at North Market and to develop the concept of productive leisure as a way of examining and reframing Daniel Miller's* Theory of Shopping.

Methodology/approach – *This chapter utilizes Daniel Miller's* Theory of Shopping *as a starting point to understand the dimensions of shopping at North Market. It draws upon survey data collected by North Market, as well as participant observations and informal interviews conducted by the authors.*

Findings – *Much of the shopping at the market goes beyond simple provisioning, thrift, and treats, and instead fits into a hybrid category we call "productive leisure." Productive leisure occurs when individuals complete productive tasks during their leisure time. It maximizes thrift-time by completing productive tasks during leisure and in response to or in connection with finding a reward (treat). In the case of shoppers at North Market, many customers are using their leisure time to provision.*

Originality/value – *This chapter presents a new way of thinking about shopping at public markets and could potentially serve to help public markets*

Anthropological Considerations of Production, Exchange, Vending and Tourism
Research in Economic Anthropology, Volume 37, 137–154

ISSN: 0190-1281/doi:10.1108/S0190-128120170000037007

redefine their role in local food systems and in the greater community. More broadly, this chapter provides a unique insight into how and why people use public markets.

Keywords: Shopping; markets; provisioning; leisure; thrift; Ohio

INTRODUCTION

Lisa Beiswenger recently visited North Market on a beautiful February day. She arrived about 10 minutes before opening, and there were already a dozen people waiting for the doors to open. As she waited, she reflected on her first visit. That late-summer day, over 6 years earlier, was equally sunny, albeit considerably warmer. On that day, there was a farmers' market, and she had to wend her way through the throngs of people, young and old, to get into the market. The market was buzzing as patrons struck up conversations with strangers, greeted old friends, and celebrated the bounteous offerings. The morning in February was more subdued, but the guests were no less happy to be at the market. Just as a child reached toward the door to test whether it would open, an employee appeared, unlocked it, and the waiting guests excitedly entered. After the market had been open for an hour, Beiswenger walked to a restaurant on the second floor. While waiting for her food, she watched a family of five – a mother, father, two teenagers, and a young child – gather around a table. The patriarch was showing the family his purchases as they ate. He talked about the meals he would make for the week, and Beiswenger was struck by how enthusiastic he was.

North Market is located between Downtown and the Short North neighborhood in Columbus, Ohio. Housed in a renovated farm machinery warehouse, the market is home to 34 vendors, including butchers, bakers, a green grocer, snack shops, a fish monger, a cheese shop, and a plethora of prepared foods. The first iteration of North Market opened in 1876, a few blocks from its current location, and served as a place for local producers and buyers to conduct business.

The ethos of the market today emphasizes locality, sustainability, and boasts a million visitors a year (North Market – About Us, 2012). In the description of the market, they explain:

> More than 30 merchants vend a wide variety of fresh, local, authentic food. Offerings include organic produce, grass-fed beef, pork, lamb and goat, pastured poultry, sustainably raised seafood, locally roasted coffee, baked goods, cheeses, flowers and other artisan food items. The Market also provides an international selection of freshly prepared foods, authentic ethnic specialties, distinctive gifts and personable service from its merchant owner operators. (North Market, 2017)

MILLER'S THEORY OF SHOPPING

To understand shopping at North Market, our analysis models and tests Miller's theory of shopping. First, we explore the meaning of provisioning at North Market. Second, we examine how thrift becomes a concept among shoppers in general and at North Market in particular. Third, we analyze the role shopping for treats plays, and finally, we explore how provisioning, thrift, and treat are interrelated with ideas of entertainment and free-time to create framework for "productive leisure."

Daniel Miller defines three dimensions of shopping in his book *A Theory of Shopping* (1998): the treat, provisioning, and thrift. Provisioning encompasses the bulk of shopping. It includes the purchasing of clothes, personal care items, and general grocery items. Provisioning takes care of a shopper's immediate needs and is typically "highly routinized" and consists of regular trips to a local supermarket (Miller, 1998, p. 44). Miller's second category of shopping, thrift, takes into account the strategies that a shopper uses to save money and time as they provision.

Many people balance concerns that include time, taste, value, and source as they make decisions over their purchases. Thrift is not always about price, but is manifest in different ways individuals shop. Thrift encompasses short- and long-term strategies that are divided between a focus on immediate needs and the future.

Personal provisioning covers the necessities of modern existence, and thrift balances a shopper's time and energies; the treat is more complicated. Miller defines "the treat" as "any special purchase made with respect to a particular individual or group, often including the shopper" (1998, p. 5). A treat can be immediate, small, and simple like a bar of chocolate purchased to reward a well-behaved child. A treat can also be complicated and expensive and built around a trip to the department store where the shopper can purchase with "no reason behind it other than the desire to possess" (Miller, 1997, p. 45), a vacation or a weekend excursion. Ultimately, treats are a small portion of the actual shopping experience and are best understood as a personal indulgence which "help to define the rest of shopping as based around sacrifice and need" (Miller, 1997, p. 45).

While Miller's theory (1998) illuminates most shopping, there are choices that govern shopping habits and do not fall neatly into his triad. North Market represents a locus where people can provision, practice thrift, and find a treat; it is also a vibrant venue for entertainment and a prime location for what we call "productive leisure." Productive leisure occurs when individuals complete productive tasks during their leisure time. Productive leisure is a hybrid category of shopping that exists between the treat and thrift. It maximizes thrift, including the time spent shopping, by completing productive tasks during leisure activities and in response to or in connection with finding a reward (treat). In the case of shoppers at North Market, many customers use their leisure time to provision.

Many customers who come to North Market for special events, including the Food and Ohio Wine Event, find themselves in the midst of a farmer's market and will often make the most of their visit by provisioning.

Productive leisure parallels the hybrid shopping described by Bardhi and Arnould (2005). They argue that shopping at thrift stores and flea markets carries qualities of provisioning, thrifting, and hedonism. They find that thrifting takes an economic experience and transforms it into a hedonistic expression of self as it fulfills a consumer's fantasies for fulfillment (Bardhi & Arnould, 2005). We argue that like Bardhi and Arnould's hybrid shopping, productive leisure combines provisioning and thrift as consumers plan for their futures.

North Market is a public space well suited for the study of provisioning, thrift, the treat, and productive leisure. Its vendors fall into six categories: desserts/snacks, groceries, cookware/gifts, toiletries/cleaning, prepared foods, and beverages. The market contains vendors who specialize in goods that must be prepared before they can be consumed. The Greener Grocer, The Fish Guys, Curds & Whey, and North Market Poultry & Game all sell foods to take home and prepare. For consumers who want to purchase toiletries while shopping for their bread and chicken, there is Better Earth, a vendor specializing in vitamins, incense, souvenirs, and a limited selection of earth-friendly cleaning supplies. North Market has just about everything for consumers. At the same time, the presence of vendors who trade in snacks and desserts, such as Jeni's Splendid Ice Cream and Pam's Popcorn, define North Market as a destination for those shoppers.

The prepared foods vendors add another dimension to the shopping experience at North Market. These merchants sell meals to be eaten on the premises or carried-out. They reside in the area between provisioning and the treat. Prepared foods are provisional and replace the food and efforts consumers would make if they had to shop and cook. Prepared foods are treats as well, saving consumers time and effort and creating an opportunity to experience foods that are different and a break from the norm (Au & Law, 2002; Chang & Hsieh, 2006).

MEET NORTH MARKET

A public market is a "group of locally owned, primarily owner operated, private retail businesses leasing space in a shared facility with an emphasis on fresh foods and community services" which is open throughout the year (Brown, 2001, p. 660). The social dynamics of public markets have changed significantly since public markets appeared in the United States. Early public markets served to differentiate and emphasize class divisions: upper class families and individuals held priority at the start of the day with access to fresh, high-quality goods, middle-class shoppers arrived later, while the lower classes visited to shop for what was left at the end of the day.

Today's markets, by contrast, are cosmopolitan with a diversity of customers (Anderson, 2004). Vendor dynamics have also changed. In the earlier days of public markets, most vendors were producers, selling goods they had a hand in producing. Most modern public market vendors, by contrast, resell goods they do not make and which may not have been locally produced (Brown, 2001, p. 660).

North Market includes a collection of vendors selling meats, seafood, poultry, produce, pastries, prepared foods, and bread. When a visitor enters North Market, its charm is evident. First, the conglomeration of culinary smells hits: the sour tang of lemon from the Greek food vendor, the fragrant spices from the Indian food stall, and aromatic star anise from the pho shop. The more subtle sweet bitterness of chocolate truffles hits next, followed by the yeasty smell of baking bread. The vendors are arranged around the perimeter of the market, with a two-sided row of vendors in the center. A bright red staircase at the northwest side of the building leads up to the second floor and tables for diners. From the balcony, the visitor can watch the market below. The organization of the market invites the visitor to partake in the wares and absorb the spectacle which can be simultaneously overwhelming, comforting, and entertaining. The vendors are friendly and courteous, always willing to offer suggestions, and the foods they offer are delicious and diverse. A visitor sees in the market a glimmer of a time when shoppers relied on it for a majority of their food. It is imagined nostalgia recalling events from a bygone era that they never experienced firsthand (Jinhua & Chen, 1997). The sights, smells, tastes, and sounds of the market, in Theodore Bestor's words "endow [the market] with a sense of place, a social identity, a structural order, and a historical memory, as well as an economic purpose" (2004, p. 38).

At the time of our study, North Market contained 34 permanent vendors inside the warehouse with additional vendors filling outdoor pavilions during "Farmers' Market Saturdays" throughout the summer (North Market – Meet the Market, 2009). We divided the permanent vendors into six categories with some overlap:

Desserts/Snacks: Jeni's Splendid Ice Cream, Mozart's North Market Bakery, Pam's Market Popcorn, Pure Imagination Chocolatier, Taste of Belgium, and The Candy Shack

Prepared Foods: Barry's New York Deli, Best of the Wurst, El Paraiso, Experessly Market Bakery & Bistro, Firdous Express, Flavors of India, Heil's Family Deli, Holy Smoke BBQ, Lac Viet Market, Nida's Sushi at North Market, Pastaria, and Sarefino's Pizzeria and Deli.

Grocery/Cook at Home: Bluescreek Farm Meats, CaJohn's Flavor & Fire, Curds & Whey, The Greener Grocer, North Market Poultry & Game, Omega Artisan Baking, Pastaria Seconda, and The Fish Guys.

Cookware/Kitchen Supplies/Gifts: Better Earth's Beyond Beads, Market Blooms, The Source by Wasserstrom, and North Market Cookware.

Household Cleaning/Toiletries/Herbal Supplements: Better Earth

Beverages: A Touch of the Earth, Bubbles: The Tea and Juice Company, and Grapes of Mirth

DATA

In 2009, North Market conducted a survey of customers for strategic long-range planning. The online survey allowed any North Market customer with Internet access to complete the questionnaire. Respondents were entered into a draw for a North Market gift card. Over 1,200 surveys were completed by customers. During the summer of 2011, Lisa Beiswenger met with David Wible, the Executive Director of North Market, to discuss a possible research project examining how customers use the market. After he heard our proposal, Mr. Wible offered us access to the data from the 2009 survey. While the goals of the survey and the direction of our research did not mesh perfectly, there was sufficient overlap to provide a firm footing for exploration.

We also conducted participant observations at the market and informal interviews with customers over the course of 3 months in late 2011 and early 2012. Twelve informal interviews with customers were conducted, typically while they were eating, waiting in line, or walking through the market. Participant observations were conducted from the floor level of the market, the second floor balcony, and outside the market by Lisa Beiswenger and Krystle Klein, our research assistant.

Data – Customers and Spending at North Market

According to the survey, the typical North Market customer is a young, professional woman who spends between $10.99 and 24.99 at the market. She usually visits the market on Saturdays – the most common day for a customer to visit – and identifies herself as a shopper/diner who may also attend select special events. Like most of the visitors to the market (84%), she lives in Columbus metro area and visits the market at least once every other month, but probably more often.[1] While a handful (8%) of customers estimated their 2009 income as less than $25,000 a year, 39% of customers report earning between $50,000 and $100,000 a year, and another 22% reported earning more than $100,000 (Fig. 1). Just under half (47%) of all respondents report spending between $10 and 25 per visit at North Market (Fig. 2), and spending tends to parallel a household's income.

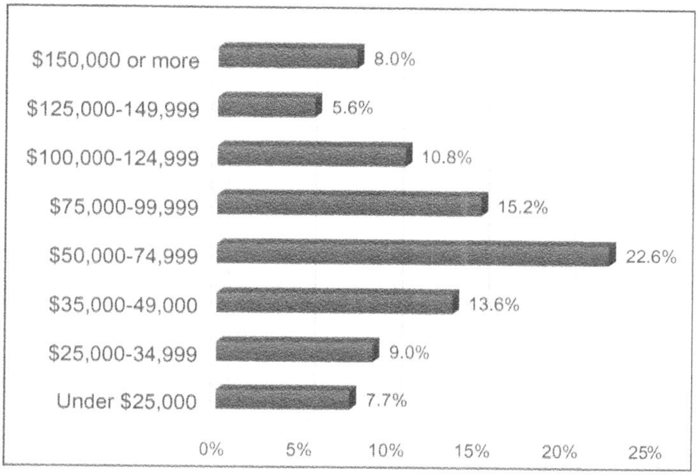

Fig. 1. Estimated Household Income for 2009.

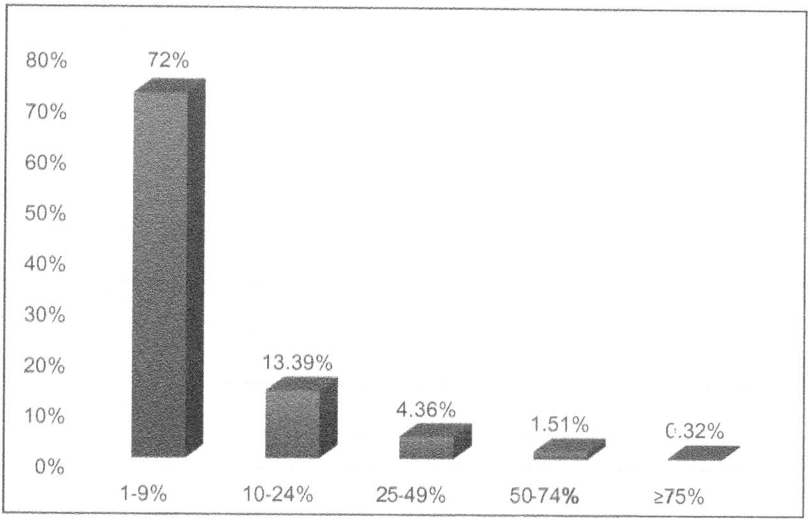

Fig. 2. Respondents' Answers to the Question, "What Percent of Your Household Shopping Is Done at North Market?".

The survey asked the respondents to categorize their behavior at the market and indicate whether they were "shopping," "dining," or attending "special events" to discover how customers categorized their trips to North Market. A majority (76%) of respondents indicated that they were diners and purchased prepared foods to eat at the market. Visitors to the market for shopping included 67% of respondents, while 48% visited to attend "Special Events." North Market hosts a number of special events throughout the year, and these visitors attended at least one event in the year before they completed the survey. Many visitors noted they participated in more than one activity at the market, about one-quarter (24%) combined shopping and dining, and about one-third (32%) shopped, dined, and attended special events (Figs. 3 and 4).

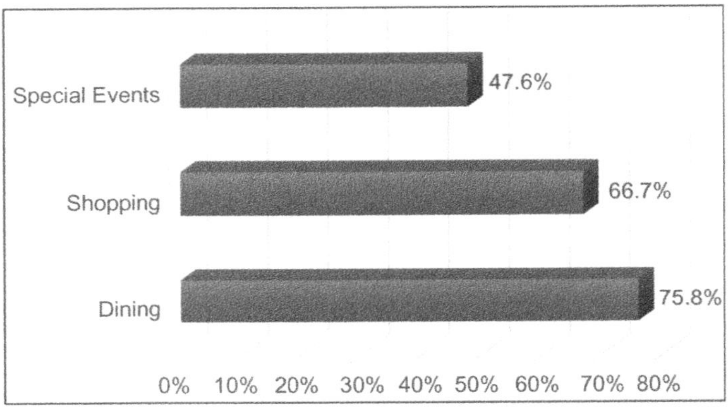

Fig. 3. Customers Were Asked If They Considered Themselves Shopping Customers, Dining Customers, and/or Special Events Customers.

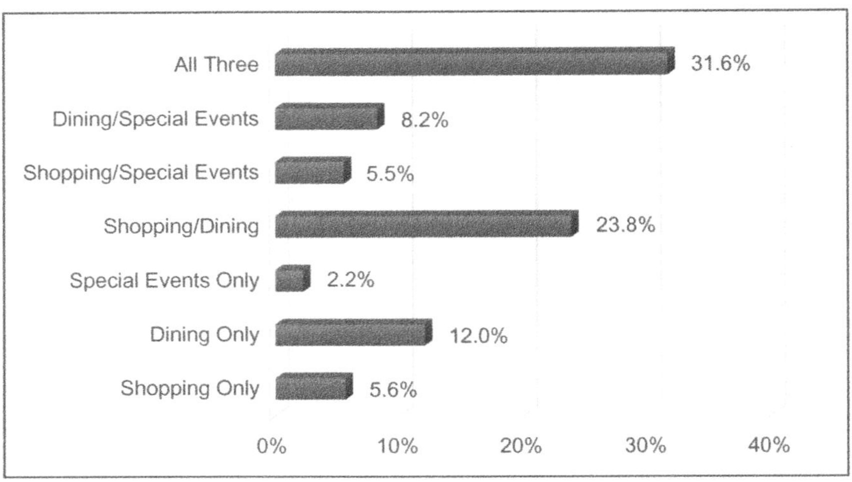

Fig. 4. Customers Were Asked If They Considered Themselves Shopping Customers, Dining Customers, and/or Special Events Customers. This Figure Separates Their Answers into Seven Discrete Categories.

Table 1. The Name of Each Vendor, Accompanied by the Percent of Respondents Who Indicated that Vendor as One of the Five They Visited Most Frequently (Fig. 5 Is a Graphic Representation of This Data).

Jeni's Splendid Ice Cream	47.50%	Bubbles	10.50%
The Greener Grocer	21.60%	Best of the Wurst	7.40%
Flavors of India	20.50%	Pam's Popcorn	7.40%
Omega Artisan Baking	17.40%	CaJohn's	6.30%
The Fish Guys	17.40%	A Touch of Earth	5.70%
Firdous Express	17.10%	Heil's Family Deli	5.50%
Pastaria	16.90%	Taste of Belgium	5.30%
Lac Viet Market	16.60%	Holy Smoke BBQ	4.80%
Sarefino's Pizzaria	15.80%	Pastaria Seconda	4.30%
Curds &Whey	15.40%	Pure Imagination Chocolatier	4.30%
Bluescreek Farm Meats	15.30%	North Market Cookware	3.50%
North Market Poultry & Game	15.00%	Expressly Market Bakery	3.20%
Mozart's North Market Bakery	13.50%	El Paraiso	2.90%
Grapes of Mirth	12.80%	The Candy Shack	2.80%
Market Blooms	12.40%	The Source by Wasserstrom	2.70%
Barry's New York Deli	12.30%	Better Earth	2.10%
Nida's Sushi	11.90%	Better Earth's Beyond Beads	0.80%

Nearly half (48%) of those surveyed responded that they visit Jeni's Splendid Ice Cream when asked to name the five North Market vendors they visited most frequently. The next most frequently visited shop was The Greener Grocer (22%), followed by Flavors of India (21% and see Table 1). Over twice the number of respondents indicate visiting Jeni's Splendid Ice Cream than the next most popular vendor, The Greener Grocer; however, when divided categorically according to types of goods sold – desserts/snacks, prepared foods, grocery/cook at home, etc. – a majority of respondents indicate that they purchased prepared foods while at North Market. The next most common category was grocery followed by desserts/snacks (Fig. 5, Table 1), indicating that guests engage in productive leisure while at the market.

ANALYSIS

People shop for a variety of reasons. Personal motives for shopping include the fulfillment of socially expected roles (being a good spouse/parent and satisfying the needs of the family), diversion or entertainment, to alleviate boredom or loneliness, or for physical activity (Bardhi & Arnould, 2005; Chang & Hsieh, 2006;

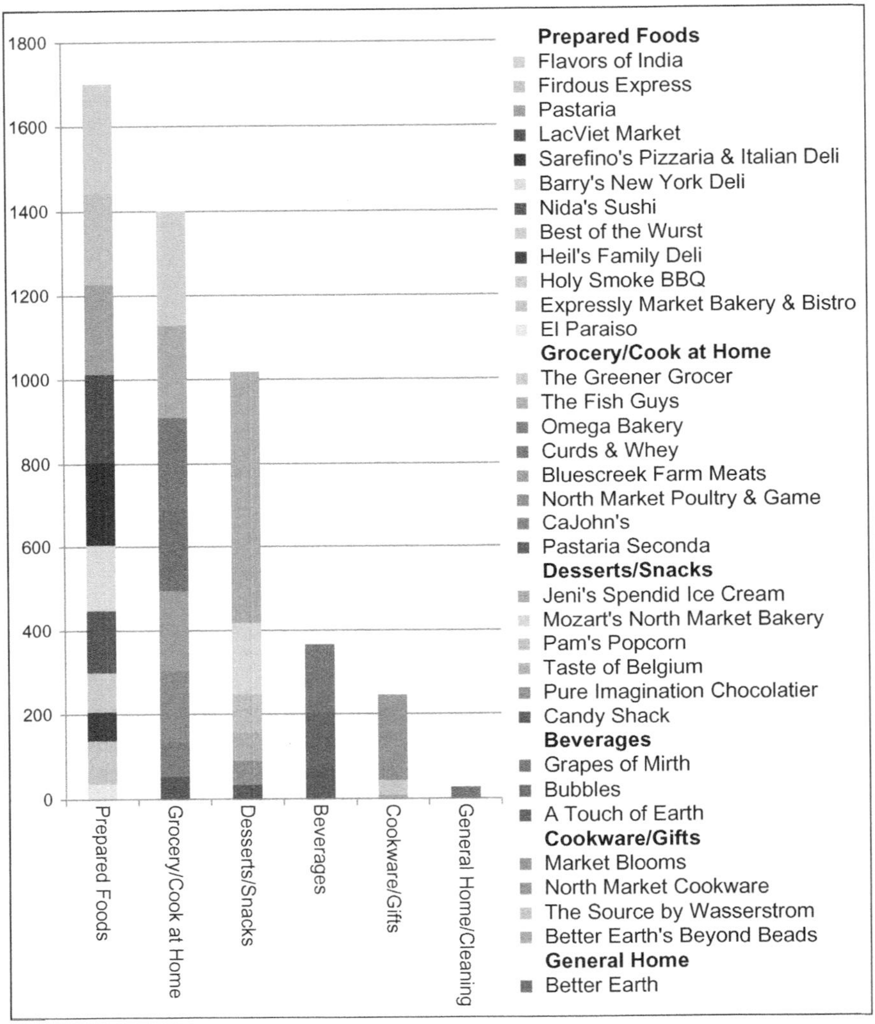

Fig. 5. Respondents' Responses to Being Asked Which Five Merchants They Visit Most Frequently, Organized by the Types of Goods Each Vendor Primarily Sells. Each Vendor Is Represented by a Different Color and Organized into the Categories of Goods Sold. Percentages for This Figure Can be Seen in Table 1.

Miller, 1997; Woodruffe-Burton, 2002). There are also social motives for shopping: shopping can provide an opportunity to socialize with friends and strangers. Browsing through the aisles a shopper can be drawn to the attraction of a good bargain (Bardhi & Arnould, 2005; Woodruffe-Burton, 2002).

Using Miller's (1998) framework as a foundation, we can follow how shopping in the North market and productive leisure capture the structure, meaning, and interrelation of provisioning, the treat, and thrift. Miller notes, a person may buy a treat because it is a bargain or they may go to the high-end store for provisional shopping as a treat because these types of purchases are something extraordinary or something beyond mere provisioning (Miller, 1998). Building on his ideas, we argue that shopping often becomes a leisure activity and serves as a foundation for other activities including exercise, bargain hunting, and socializing with friends (Bäckström, 2011; Bardhi & Arnould, 2005; Jansen-Verbeke, 1987). The point of shopping, particularly as a leisure activity, is to have an enjoyable time that moves the shopper away from the pressures of daily life.

Shopping ranks among the major categories of tourists' expenditure (Jansen-Verbeke, 1998; Littrell, Paige, & Song, 2004), and over 33% of money spent by tourists is dedicated to food (Williams, Williams, & Omar, 2014, p. 4). While vacationing, food is a necessity – tourists must eat – and it is more, becoming a leisure activity and setting for treats, the practice of thrift and adventure. Gastro-tourism is a relatively new concept meant to capture the growing importance of food tourism and is "defined as the intentional pursuit of appealing, authentic, memorable, culinary experiences of all kinds, while traveling internationally, regionally or even locally" (Williams et al., 2014, p. 4).

Gastro-tourists seek more than fuel for the body: they seek unique food experiences. The search for food as both sustenance and an adventurous treat is an exceptional illustration of productive leisure, and gastro-tourism is evident among visitors to North Market. A visitor from Mt. Washington, Kentucky said, "I mainly come to eat and to look around ... love the atmosphere". Another from Charlotte, North Carolina mentioned that she makes a point of stopping at the market when visiting her brother in Columbus, exclaiming "What can I say? It's a highlight of my visits to Columbus!" Gastro-tourists do not have to come to the North Market from out of town or far; for those who live nearby, it can serve as a destination spot. When asked how he would improve the market, 39-year-old customer from a Columbus suburb explained, "Highlight the merchants and collective spirit that make the North Market special and unique and worth the drive down from the suburbs. I love the North Market and it is a great cultural asset to Columbus. However, it is a bit of a pain to drive down from Worthington."

Provisioning

Provisioning encompasses the bulk of a shopper's experiences (Miller, 1998). Generally, it includes the purchase of personal care items, household items, groceries, and clothes. Provisional shopping takes care of immediate needs, and, it consists of regular trips to a local supermarket to purchase food and household items for fairly immediate consumption throughout the week (Miller, 1998, p. 44).

Many customers indicate that they would like to provision more at North Market, feel as if the market is either too expensive or does not fulfill all of their needs, necessitating trips to additional grocery stores. Holly, a regular customer who lives in the nearby Weiland Park neighborhood explains, "If I could do all of my shopping at the North Market I would. I only go to the grocery store anymore to buy things like toilet paper and light bulbs. Being able to get items like this at the North Market would be fantastic because it's a much nicer experience." Bob also wishes the market was more of a "one-stop shop." He would "love nothing more than to shop the market and not have to go to Kroger and Giant Eagle."

Thrift

Thrift encompasses all of the strategies that a shopper uses to save money and time while shopping, but is North Market a place where people go to practice cost-conscious shopping? Of the 33% of survey respondents that indicated that they do not consider themselves shopping customers, only 4% indicated that cost was the major deterrent; however, the story is more complex.

To discover whether cost is a factor at North Market, we compared prices between the goods at North Market and other local food stores (Table 2). First, we identified stores that compete with North Market for customers. We selected eight local stores where a customer might do provisional shopping: Giant Eagle (Neil Avenue), Kroger (High Street), Wal-Mart (Main Street), Target (Olentangy River Boulevard), Trader Joe's (Easton, OH), Whole Foods (Upper Arlington, OH), Fresh Market (Henderson Road), and Hill's Market (online). We also chose one convenience store, Turkey Hill, where shoppers might stop for emergency provisional items on their way home or if they realize they need something quickly. These grocery stores fell into two categories: "conventional grocery stores" (Wal-Mart, Giant Eagle stores, Target, Kroger, and Turkey Hill) and "elite/specialty markets" (Hill's Market, Fresh Market, Whole Foods, and Trader Joe's).

At each store, we recorded the price of 13 items: Granny Smith apples, bananas, oranges, cucumbers, carrots, chicken, ground beef, milk, peanut butter, eggs, dish washing detergent, laundry detergent, and toilet paper. These items were selected because they are all available at North Market, and they represent a diverse array of items including produce, shelf stable items, and household items.

Table 2. Comparison of Prices in All Three Categories to Conventional Grocery Stores and Elite/Specialty Grocery Stores.

	Produce Total	Protein/Dairy Total	Household Total	Total
Turkey Hill (Broad St., Columbus)	$7.11	–	$7.13	–
Wal-Mart (Main St., Columbus)	$5.35	$11.09	$4.12	$20.56
Kroger (High St., Columbus)	$5.81	$13.20	$5.50	$24.51
Giant Eagle (Neil Ave, Columbus)	$7.59	$13.09	$5.26	$25.94
Target (Olentangy River Blvd., Columbus)	$6.37	$12.39	$9.52	$28.26
Trader Joes (Easton, OH)	$8.01	$13.65	$11.97	$33.63
Whole Foods (Upper Arlington, OH)	$9.07	$17.05	$10.77	$36.89
Hill's Market (Online)	$8.67	$18.15	$13.27	$40.09
North Market (Spruce St., Columbus)	$9.79	$22.16	$14.97	$46.92
Fresh Market (Henderson Rd., Columbus)	$10.16	$17.25	$24.97	$52.38

There is a limit to what the market offers; for example, flour, name brand cereals, canned goods, and even some types of produce that are common at conventional grocery stores are absent from the market. In order to avoid seasonal changes, we visited the stores in a relatively short time span – between January 11, 2012 and January 27, 2012. To mimic shopping on a budget, and in order to be as consistent as possible, we noted the cheapest option at each location regardless of package size or product quality.

Ultimately, we found that the prices at North Market were considerably higher than those at conventional grocery stores. The total cost of our goods at North Market was over twice that of the least expensive location (Wal-Mart). The price of our shopping excursion at North Market totaled $47.92, while the same items were only $20.56 at Wal-Mart. The price difference was apparent in all items, but it was most apparent in the cost of general household items. At North Market, our general household items were triple the cost at Wal-Mart. The differences are due to many things including the variety of products available at Wal-Mart, its size, commanding position in negotiations and presences around the country to name just a few (and see McMillan, 2012).

While the prices at Wal-Mart were lower than those at North Market for most grocery items, North Market prices were much closer to those found in elite grocery stores, specialty stores, and among stores that practiced an ethos of sustainability and a celebration of locally sourced items. Fresh Market was the only store that was routinely more expensive than North Market. The total cost of the items on our shopping list was $46.92 at North Market. At Fresh Market, the same items cost just over $52, a 9% increase in the price.

Not surprisingly, cost was the third most common complaint in the survey and our interviews. Customers felt that the products were good, but that they were too expensive, and several respondents recommended starting a loyalty program to support and reward frequent visitors. In short, North Market is generally a more expensive option. Nevertheless, thrift is about more than money and often reflects planning and a series of decisions concerning issues that range from the moral to health and well-being. When a customer is at North Market for a special event or lunch, they are also often practicing thrift as they purchase raw foods or grocery items for consumption later. In other words, North Market provides an opportunity to multitask and many customers multitask while they visit. As seen in Figs. 3 and 4, 60% of survey respondents indicated that they are shopping/dining visitors, shopping/special events visitors, or shopping/dining/special events visitors (24%, 6%, and 31%, respectively).

At lunchtime on weekdays, the majority of visitors to the market are people who work nearby. These visitors are joined by an occasional group of college students, tourists, or adults with children in tow. Although the primary purpose for visiting the market for these patrons was lunch, many of the diners also made purchases as they provisioned for future meals. During one observation, an office worker instructed her compatriots to return to work without her as she turned to visit a vendor to pick up a few items. She proceeded to stop at the bread, wine, and poultry vendors.

Individuals multitasked during and around our interviews as well. One customer, a college student who identifies as primarily a diner, explained that she likes to buy prepared food from Taste of Belgium and Flavors of India but will often buy from the farmers' market as well. Another customer explained that he likes to purchase special items from The Fish Guys and Omega Artisan Baking, but mostly visit North Market to attend special events or for prepared foods he can eat as meals.

Some customers suggest that the market might stock more daily goods and become a one-stop site for shopping. Hugh, a 33-year-old survey respondent, pointedly stated, "Make it possible that this could be the only stop on a grocery trip. I'm tired of running around town to hit each place that has what I need (poultry here, bread there, produce yet somewhere else...)." Steve, a 29-year-old who identifies as a dining/shopping/special events customer, explained,

"My wife and I often go to the market on Sundays to buy food for a Sunday night meal with friends. We go and wander and just plan the meal as we walk, more often than not we end up having to make a second stop." These customers want to conserve their time and complete all of their shopping in one trip, preferably at North Market, but with the current composition of vendors, this is impossible.

The Treat

While there is overlap between treats and provisioning, generally a treat is something special that can take many forms. A treat may be a chocolate bar that is a reward for completing a task or a stop at a specialty shop for something unique. Time for leisure, and space for a break from the everyday, can also become a treat. Leisure is time free from the obligations of labor (De Grazia, 1964). It is, in its own way, an indulgence or a reward for completing the obligations which are necessary for survival.

The key to a treat is whether the activities that surround it are a necessity or a choice. When shopping is a necessity, it is likely to be viewed as work; it is the work that accompanies provisioning. However, when a shopper has the freedom to browse and wander they exercise free expression (Campbell, 1998; Jansen-Verbeke, 1987). The freedom that comes with leisure and the opportunity to walk around the market is a draw for many visitors and perhaps expressed most clearly by visitors who attend a special event at North Market. The annual Food and Ohio Wine event is one example. Visitors have the opportunity to taste some wine and browse the vendors' stands with little pressure and no obligation to make a purchase.

In 2011, the first day of the event coincided with *Farmers' Market Saturday*, and many visitors wandered between the event and the farmers' stands. The opportunity to absorb the surroundings and freely move about the market is a treat for visitors who have completed their formal, working weeks. For some people, being surrounded by like-minded individuals who are enjoying an excursion may also be a treat. These like-minded individuals might be friends or strangers, but all are united in their enjoyment of the market.

Eating out or purchasing prepared foods for consumption at home or at work can also be another form or kind of treat. Miller argues that dining out is "understood as a treat in the sense of a personal indulgence for the shopper" (Miller, 1998, p. 43). "Eating out" does not have to be a formal or structured occasion. It can be as simple as stopping at a particular store for a cup of coffee or having a meal at a food court attached to a shopping establishment. Similarly, eating out may be a treat because it represents a departure from the labor of cooking a meal for oneself or for one's family (Barbas, 2002). Indeed, role of eating out as a treat was clear in some of our interviews. Peter, who identified as a dining/shopping customer, explained that he brings his family to the market to treat themselves. He went on to explain, "We love it, and when we take the kids it feels like we are on a vacation and like to spend the day there."

Productive Leisure

Although North Market is a place where many customers spend their leisure time, it is not exclusively used for that purpose. More than 60% of the visitors to North Market indicate that they combine their reasons to visit as they shop, dine, and attend special events. At North Market, customers who pick up a few items for future consumption while attending events or dining are practicing thrift, by using their leisure time not only to relax but also to provision, meet with friends and family, and connect with community.

In the evenings, productive leisure is more nuanced because customers often stop at multiple locations as they travel through the market. We visited the market in the evening to observe shoppers and vendors interact. We noticed that a family of four arrived at the market together, divided to get their meals from different vendors, and reassembled in the balcony dining area where they ate together. After dinner, the family divided again to purchase desserts – two decided to buy Jeni's Splendid Ice Cream and two decided to indulge in Belgian waffles at A Taste of Belgium. Before leaving, the parents purchased some produce and meats. This relaxing dinner removed the burden of cooking and gave the family an opportunity to dine together as a unit. The parents also took the opportunity to provision for future food preparation at home.

Kim told a similar story. She comes to the market every Saturday for breakfast and to visit with friends and has done this for years. While at the market, she shops at Bluescreek Farm Meats. She told us that she would like to shop more at The Greener Grocer, but finds it too expensive. Nevertheless, her weekly excursion gives her an opportunity to dine with friends, enjoy a break in her normal schedule and buy the foods necessary for the coming week.

CONCLUSION

This study advances Miller's theory of shopping by demonstrating the hybrid nature of the market as a locus for both leisure and productive shopping where consumers satisfy their needs and sometimes fantastic wants. On one hand, there are vendors who trade in snacks and desserts; while on the other hand, the market also contains vendors who specialize in goods which must be prepared before they are consumed. The prepared food vendor has a role in serving customers who wish to provision and those who wish to treat themselves to something special. Ultimately, the majority of guests at North Market engage in multiple activities while at the market. They are not exclusively attending events or dining, they are engaging in "productive leisure." These customers are using their leisure time not only to relax but also to procure produce, meats, grocery items, and household goods.

In order to understand the role of the market in the wider community, it is important to understand how the role of the market has shifted. The public market, initially born out of necessity, still has a role in American society; however, in the case of North Market, that role has evolved from one primarily centered around provisioning to one centered on leisure. Thus, this study has broader implications. (1) It can assist public markets across the United States clarify their role in the local community and assist in the development of strategic plans for future development. (2) It can help markets, governments, and tourism authorities when planning promotional activities, and (3) it can help to bolster local food systems by providing insight for cross-promotional activities and events.

NOTE

1. The survey noted that 62% of respondents visited the market at least once every other month, and 22% visited 20 or more times per year.

ACKNOWLEDGMENTS

We are grateful for support from The Ohio State University Food Innovation Center, North Market and both its current and former directors: Mr. Rick Harrison Wolfe and Mr. David Wible, North Market Executive Director, the anthropology department at Ohio State University, Drs. Douglas Crews, Dorothy Noyes, and Anna Willow; and Krystle Klein who served as our research assistant during fieldwork for this project.

REFERENCES

Anderson, E. (2004). The cosmopolitan canopy. *Annals of the American Academy of Political and Social Sciences*, *595*, 14–31.

Au, N., & Law, R. (2002). Categorical classification of tourism dining. *Annals of Tourism Research*, *29*(3), 819–833.

Bäckström, K. (2011). Shopping as Leisure: An exploration of manifoldness and dynamics in consumers shopping experiences. *Journal of Retailing and Consumer Services*, *18*(3), 200–209.

Barbas, S. (2002). Just like home: "Home Cooking" and the domestication of the American restaurant. *Gastronomica*, *2*(4), 43–52.

Bardhi, F., & Arnould, E. J. (2005). Thrift shopping: Combining utilitarian thrift and hedonic treat benefits. *Journal of Consumer Behavior*, *4*(4), 223–233.

Bestor, T. C. (2004). *Tsukiji: The fish market at the center of the world.* Berkeley, CA: University of California Press.

Brown, A. (2001). Counting farmers markets. *Geographical Review*, *91*(4), 665–674.

Campbell, C. (1998). Consumption and the rhetorics of need and want. *Journal of Design History*, *11*(3), 235–246.

Chang, J., & Hsieh, A. T. (2006). Leisure motives of eating out in night markets. *Journal of Business Research*, *59*, 1276–1278.

De Grazia, S. (1964). *Of time, work and leisure*. Garden City, NY: Anchor Books.

Jansen-Verbeke, M. (1987). Women, shopping and leisure. *Leisure Studies*, *6*(1), 71–86.

Jansen-Verbeke, M. (1998). The synergism between shopping and tourism. In W. F. Theobal (Ed.), *Global tourism: The next decade* (2nd ed., pp. 428–446). Oxford: Butterworth-Heinemann.

Jinhua, D., & Chen, J. T. H. (1997). Imagined nostalgia. *Boundary 2*, *24*(3), 143–161.

Littrell, M. A., Paige, R. C., & Song, K. (2004). Senior travelers: Tourism activities and shopping behaviors. *Journal of Vacation Marketing*, *10*(4), 348–362.

McMillan, T. (2012). *The American way of eating: Undercover at Walmart, Applebee's, farm fields, and the dinner table*. New York, NY: Scribner.

Miller, D. (1997). Consumption and its consequences. In H. McKay (Ed.), *Consumption and everyday life* (pp. 13–64). London: Sage.

Miller, D. (1998). *A theory of shopping*. Ithaca, NY: Cornell University Press.

North Market – About Us. (2012). North Market. Online. Retrieved from http://www.northmarket.com/about-us. Accessed on 28 January 2012.

North Market – Meet the Market. (2009). North Market. Online. Retrieved from. http://web.archive.org/web/20090417234907/http://www.northmarket.com/meet-the-market. Accessed on 28 January 2012.

North Market. (2017). *North Market*. Retrieved from http://www.northmarket.com/. Accessed on 12 February 2017.

Williams, H. A., Williams, R. L. Jr., & Omar, M. (2014). Gastro-tourism as destination branding in emerging markets. *International Journal of Leisure and Tourism Marketing*, *4*(1), 1–18.

Woodruffe-Burton, H. et al. (2002). Towards a theory of shopping: A holistic framework. *Journal of Consumer Behavior*, *1*(3), 256–266.

RELATIVE CUSTOMERS: DEMAND-SHARING, KINSHIP AND SELLING IN SOLOMON ISLANDS

Rodolfo Maggio

ABSTRACT

Purpose – *This chapter contributes to drawing Melanesian ethnography out of the exoticizing interest for gift exchange and demand-sharing. Furthermore, it provides an analytical perspective from which it is possible to conceptualize the manipulation of gift and commodity logics as mutually compatible frameworks. Rather than seeing them as contradictory, this perspective enables the theorization of shared calculative agencies that are becoming increasingly common in contemporary Melanesia.*

Methodology/approach – *The chapter draws on 13 months of ethnographic fieldwork in Gilbert Camp, a peri-urban settlement on the outskirts of Honiara, Solomon Islands with a focus on the domestic moral economy of its inhabitants.*

Findings – *The people of Gilbert Camp are confronting a difficult economic and moral dilemma. On the one hand, they are at constant risk of financial failure because of their general conditions of scarcity. On the other, they face the prospect of disrupting some of their much-valued social relationships because such scarcity prevents them from fulfilling their cultural obligations. In order to avoid both risks, they make use of their financial competence and cultural creativity to set up strategies that save them money and preserve these relationships. Situated at the interface between kinship and market*

Anthropological Considerations of Production, Exchange, Vending and Tourism
Research in Economic Anthropology, Volume 37, 155–175

ISSN: 0190-1281/doi:10.1108/S0190-128120170000037008

values, these strategies contribute to achieving the kind of 'good' life that they see as the correct balance between financial prosperity and morality.

Originality/value – *Current negotiations over the meaning of buying, selling and taking are changing the values of contemporary sociality in Honiara, Port Vila, and other Melanesian cities. Tradestores simultaneously supply households with food and money, create a sense of sharing, and limit the demand-sharing and the taking of* wantoks. *Hence they create the conditions for the resolution of tensions over the incompatibility of values of kinship and market that confront the inhabitants of Melanesian cities. Household tradestores thus constitute a major site of these negotiations, and they provide a unique vantage point from which to look at the moral and economic processes that are leading to the future identity of urban Melanesia.*

Keywords: Demand-sharing; kinship; market; scarcity; Solomon Islands; urban Melanesia

INTRODUCTION

The people of Gilbert Camp (see Fig. 1), a settlement on the outskirts of Honiara, the capital city of Solomon Islands, habitually declare: 'Honiara is hard' (*Honiara hemi had*). What they mean by that is not simply that it is hard to get by. More generally, they mean it is hard to live a 'good' life as they try to solve complex problems such as the incompatibility between the values of the city and those of their island of origin.

Most of the residents of Gilbert Camp (85%) originate from Malaita. They began migrating to Honiara towards the end of the Second World War

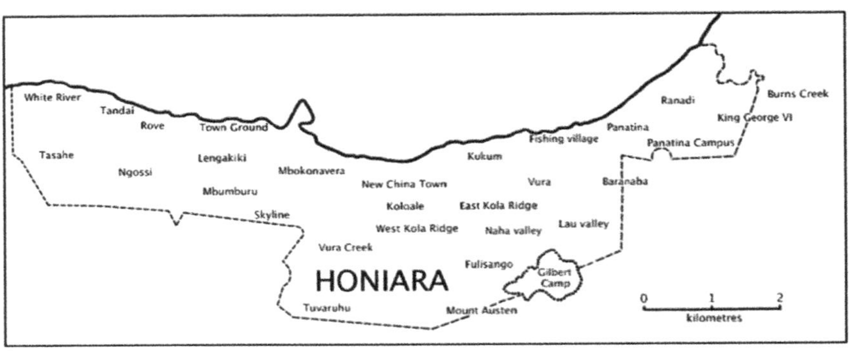

Fig. 1. Gilbert Camp and the Honiara Town Boundary.

(Moore, 2004). Malaita is still 'home' (*hom*) for them, but at the same time they are trying to transform Gilbert Camp into a place where they can live well. That requires a skilful manipulation of economic and moral values. In the peri-urban context these settlers are confronted with the need to make ends meet while simultaneously uphold the principles that they consider fundamental to their Malaitan culture. Their challenge, thus, is to solve this incompatibility in order to live a 'good' life.

Living a 'good' life (*gud laef*) implies many daily struggles for the inhabitants of Gilbert Camp. They must ensure subsistence for their immediate families but in a way that allows for the maintenance of harmonious social relations between kin, neighbours, friends and members of the various religious communities, including Roman Catholic Church, Seventh-Day Adventists, United Church, Jehovah's Witnesses and five different Pentecostal churches; they struggle to voice their concerns over the security of their settlement because government officials and 'landowners' perpetuate a legacy of confusion about the issue of landownership and residency rights in Honiara (Maggio, 2016b; cf. Allen, 2012; Foukona, 2015); they need to find ways to regulate life in the settlement in terms of both state and customary law, for there is no state-based systems of resolution of customary disputes when these arise among members of the community (Maggio, forthcoming); even their religious affiliation can be a source of tension with members of other denominations, although they also make use of Christianity to cope with tensions resulting from clashes of values such as autonomy and relatedness (Maggio, 2016a).

Prima facie a statement such as 'Honiara is hard' might suggest that living on the outskirts of the capital city corresponds to a continuous struggle to live according to the values of unity, cooperation, sense of belonging and quality of life that Malaitans associate with *hom* (cf. Blunt & Dowling, 2006; Chapman, 1978; Rapport & Dawson, 1998; Strathern, 1985). Table 1 lists some of the statements in which Gilbert Camp residents express such belonging as opposed to Honiara.

However, taking these statements at face value would not account for why more and more migrants keep coming (see Fig. 2), settling down, investing resources in long-term life projects, and adapting their lifestyles to the urban context (cf. Calestani, 2012).

In order to lead what they consider a 'good' life, the residents of Gilbert Camp attempt to take control of and modify the notion of 'good' according to the new priorities of their urban condition. That requires a daily effort to negotiate tensions between seemingly incompatible values, such as the economic value of the marginal profit and the moral value of sharing. That indicates the extent to which they *want* to live in Honiara, and especially how they want to live. What is 'hard' about Honiara, in other words, is not life itself, but the efforts that settlers make to realize the 'good' life. That is an indispensable part of their existence, though one yet to be achieved.

Table 1. Indigenous Statements about *hom* and Honiara.

hom	Honiara
'We don't use money'	'You need money for everything'
'We know everybody'	'A lot of "different" people'
'It's the place we belong to'	'It's the place where we work'
'The food is good'	'The food is bad'
'We own the land'	'We do not own the land'
'Everybody is the same'	'There are a lot of mixed colours'
'If I take your food, we share'	'If I take your food, I steal'
'We live following our culture'	'We follow the way of white man'
'We know our culture'	'We forget our culture'
'We speak Kwara'ae'	'We mix Pidgin and Kwara'ae'
'It is the land of our ancestors'	'It is not the land of our ancestors'
'Young people respect the elders'	'There is no respect for the elders'
'We have our chiefs'	'We don't know our chiefs'
'We are a community'	'We are related, but not really'
'We eat *kumara*'	'We eat *kassava*'
'One village, one church'	'Many different religions'
'People do not make noise'	'People make a lot of noise'

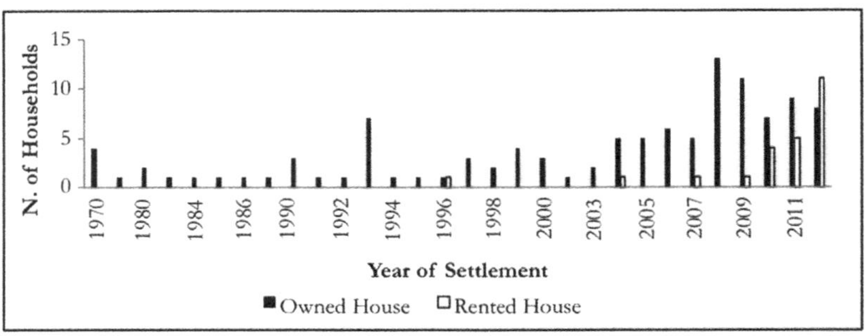

Fig. 2. Number of Households Settled between 1970s and 2012.

Focussing on the Kwara'ae people, the largest ethno-linguistic group of Gilbert Camp (see Table 2), I investigated these efforts in a set of social situations, namely the negotiations over the allocation of resources, the multiplicity of land claims, the compensation meetings organized to solve community disputes, and the relations between Christianity, gender roles and the domestic moral economy of the Gilbert Camp household (Peterson & Taylor, 2003). I argue that there is no contradiction between contemptuous statements about Honiara and the decision to reside in town as long as one looks

Table 2. District of Origin of Migrant Households to Gilbert Camp.

District	1970–1990	1990–2003	2003–2012	Total	%
Kwara'ae	12	21	45	78	57
Baegu		1	7	8	5
Lau		1	7	8	5
'Are'are			4	5	4
Sa'a		1	4	5	4
Western		1	4	5	4
Fataleka		1	3	4	3
To'abaita		1	3	4	3
Kwaio			3	3	2
Langalanga			3	3	2
Makira			3	3	2
Baelelea			2	2	2
Guadalcanal			2	2	2
Isabel			2	2	2
Choiseul			1	1	1
Central		1	1	1	1
PNG		1		1	1
Total	12	29	94	135	100
%	8	22	70	100	

at both as illustrations of the intense commitment of Gilbert Camp residents to live according to values that emerge in a process of constant and arduous negotiations.

The tensions resulting from the incompatible values of monetary accumulation and social relatedness are the focus of this chapter. One of the ways in which the people of Gilbert Camp seek to resolve such incompatibility is a saving strategy (cf. Annis, 2010, pp. 75–106; Mariz, 1994; 81–162; Sjørup, 2002, p. 25) deployed as domestic commercialization of food stocks. Such a strategy shows how market logics can be manipulated in the domestic context without necessarily resulting in the erosion of social relationships that many scholars have warranted following the argument originally advanced by Aristotle (Bohannan, 1959). Another way consists of the creation of fictive kinship relationships on the basis of credit ratings with respect to unrelated tradestore customers. Shop owners regard the reiterated capacity to pay a debt contract by buying on credit as increasing the relational proximity between debtor and creditor, thereby turning a series of supposedly impersonal interactions into relations with kinship-like qualities. What the two strategies suggest is that, in conditions of scarcity, the impersonal and arithmetical character of monetary transactions introduces a quantifiable and regimented formulation of individual responsibility and, at the same time, a form of shared agency (Bratman, 2013).

Such an interpretive direction could easily be read as a contribution to the classical argument against *homo economicus* (Malinowski, 2002, 1922; Polanyi, 1957; Sahlins, 1972, 1985, 1992). But it is not meant to de-emphasize the presence of marginal utility in the rationale behind the above-mentioned strategies. Calculation and monetary accumulation can, I argue, be explained as emerging from a shared agency rather than an instrumental objectification of human relationships. The exchange of commodities can be regarded as fundamentally distinguished from the exchange of gifts, but only as long as the inner motives of the exchange partners are assumed to be limited to the exchange regime itself (Gregory, 1982). Assuming, to the contrary, that the motives of the exchange partners can be multiple, diverse, and of equivalent analytical relevance, it is possible to argue that the exchanges of commodities analysed in this chapter constitute instances of engagement with the values of an 'arrival city and pacific hybrid living space' (Moore, 2015), whereby people in conditions of scarcity equate their objects while at the same time concretizing the values of their relationships

The aim of this chapter thus is to provide a representation of a localized system of economic and moral dynamism characterized by the interaction of capitalist and non-capitalist values interlocking in accordance to recent developments in the history, geography and demography of urban Solomon Islands. Recently, this kind of moral and economic dynamism has been observed in other parts of Melanesia, as illustrated in the work of anthropologists Chris Gregory (1982), Karen Sykes (2008), Keir Martin (2013), and others (McCormack & Barclay, 2013; Weinberger & Wallendorf, 2012). That has engendered a progressive shift from the 'centrality of gift exchange' in Melanesia (Carrier, 1992). Although a pre-existing interest for tradestores and other kinds of businesses (*bisnis*) was already evident (Connell, 1978; Curry, 1999; Grossman, 1986) most recently a new and growing body of ethnographic reports about demand-sharing (Peterson, 1993, p. 861), with particular reference to household stores and corner shops has been emerging (Eby & Thomas, 2016; Saxe & Esmonde, 2004; Sharp, 2016). For example, Knut Rio, in a forthcoming collection focused on urban Melanesia and edited by Christine Jourdan and Lamont Lindstrom, analyses household stores in Port Vila (Vanuatu) and argues that they constitute a form of resistance against the impersonal relations that foreign forms of commodity exchange engender. At the same time, they attempt to control and/or fence off aggressive forms of demand-sharing by the part of *wantoks* (Nanau, 2011).

Looking at the household store as a site of negotiation of both qualities of relationships and quantities of goods, a useful contribution can be advanced to the anthropological theory of value (Graeber, 2001) and the 'good life' (Fisher, 2014; Matthews & Izquierdo, 2008). Calculation in market-influenced contexts is a fundamental human activity devoted to the control of uncertainty and risk.

Interpreting it as a site of negotiation where shared agencies let market values penetrate and adapt to their contexts does not necessarily mean resuscitating the economic man. The Gilbert Camp residents who exchange commodities have no way to ensure that their strategies will result in monetary growth. The quality of the relationship in which they enter in the context of the exchange is precarious; only time will tell them if they are relative or customers to each other. But the calculative character of their shared agency takes into consideration both profit and the value of the relationship. That's because, as it will become clear, the interpenetration of kinship logics and accumulation strategies results from sharing the risk of monetary failure. Profit from these particular transactions is a possibility, but one which depends heavily on the quality of the relationships, and vice versa.

THE ECONOMY OF GILBERT CAMP – A QUICK OVERVIEW

Gilbert Camp residents are migrants or children of migrants. They normally do not own the land upon which they reside, nor have any right to use it. It follows that the first characteristic that should be taken into account is that, in most cases, lack of land property results in a recurrent drain of money. When settlers refuse to pay the landowner, their Temporary Occupation License, or a Fixed Term License, they might save some money, but live in a continual lack of security.

Secondly, the cost of food is rather high.[1] As an article published on the national newspaper Solomon Star headed 'Cost of living in Honiara [is] unbearable' (Kauhue, 2011). Accordingly, there is a general disproportion between the amount of money and the number of mouths to feed in the average Gilbert Camp household. The average income that the members of one typical household manage to generate is 1,225 Solomon Islands Dollars (SBD) fortnight (about £108). Considering that three adults and four children live in an ordinary household, it follows that each person has slightly more than one pound a day to survive.

Thirdly, school fees, transports and consumables are very expensive too. This third aspect is not just a local, isolated occurrence. Rather, it is a national problem. Despite all the natural resources with which the Solomon Islands are endowed, the economy has not grown during the last decade. The population, in contrast, has grown with the second fastest growth rate in the Pacific (2.7% in 2008,[2] 2.59% in 2011[3]). The country suffered a severe economic regression around 2000; and the so-called 'Ethnic Tensions'[4] and the subsequent civil unrest contributed to worsening the general economic situation. Between 1998 and 2002, the gross domestic product decreased by about 24%. Thus, the population kept growing in a context of economic and political decline that resulted in raising commodity prices and the withdrawal of public services. Because of a general lack of investments and an increasing number of people placing further demand on already stretched services, Solomon Islanders live in a condition of worse general well-being compared to their Pacific neighbours.[5]

In Gilbert Camp, residents who can rely on a paid job in town and a piece of land to cultivate are relatively well off. In contrast, those who only have their job or their garden are ultimately dependent on the market for their subsistence. It is not surprising, therefore, that their entire lives pivot around the difficult task of generating an income, nor that this relatively small amount of money is entirely spent to get by.

In order to cope with the high costs of food, about 80% of the Gilbert Camp settlers cultivate a horticultural garden. Those who own the house where they live tend to cultivate more often (84%) than those who rent accommodation (63%). That seems to suggest that in order to cultivate, residents prefer or need to be living in relatively stable conditions. Also, renters need to work to pay their rent, and might just not have enough time to cultivate. In both cases, vegetable production is not only used for home consumption, but also for sale. Those cultivators who turn into market sellers usually avoid intermediaries in order to secure higher returns (cf. Genova, Kriesemer, Neave, Jaw-Fen, & Weinberger, 2010; Kastom Gaden Association, 2005). However, since most settlers do cultivate a garden, the demand for horticultural products is limited. As a consequence, income-generating activities of other sorts are very common in Gilbert Camp, ranging from selling cakes to printing labels on t-shirts.

The most hardworking among the residents manage to make a relatively considerable amount of money by simultaneously cultivating, working in town, and running a few income-generating activities. Clement, for example, works in the early morning as a pastor for one of the local churches, as a clerk in the afternoon, and in the evening he takes care of his poultry, piggery, and a small store he built in front of his house. All this, in addition to his garden. Tom, to take another example, regularly receives commissions from schools and churches to print labels on T-shirts. There are several printing services in town, but Tom's prices are extremely competitive: he does not pay taxes, nor does he pay collaborators. He does not spend much on materials either, as most of his tools are homemade. The final product might not be perfect, but it will do. Tom is also a teacher at the Naha Elementary School. He always gets the commission for the annual football tournament of the school, when more than 150 T-shirts are needed. When he is not busy with his work and T-shirt prints, he takes care of a store that he built in front of his house, just like Clement.

The store, or *maket haus*, is probably the most common income-generating activity in Gilbert Camp. It consists of four walls of usually unpainted timber, roofed with corrugated iron, and a few shelves displaying products ranging from toilet paper to sugar to notepads and even USB memory sticks. Most affluent storekeepers install cold storage facilities, sometimes to refrigerate minced meat, but most often to make 'ice lollies' with water and cordial.

Mobile phone top up is also a very common service offered by these stores, at the price of 1 or 2 SBD.

From the point of view of the settlers, the *maket haus* is the easiest way to make a profit with relatively little labour. So easy, that stores have been mushrooming all over the place during the last decade. Along the 700 metres of a segment that runs on the main road between the top of the hill where Gilbert Camp begins and the old rain tree where it ends (see Fig. 3), I counted 25 *maket haus*. That means an average of one shop every 28 metres. The reason is clear. Money is a constant subject of discussion and silent preoccupation among migrants in Honiara. In Gilbert Camp, on several occasions, I observed a Kwara'ae man studying what his neighbour was doing in order to make some extra-cash. In this respect, a man who worked in a *maket haus* once told me, *mifala olsem copycat*, literally 'we are all copycats'.

That does not mean that everybody will succeed. Clement, for example, after a few years following his daily schedule, is now pretty well off compared to his fellow settlers. When he came to live in Honiara, he wanted to make money like everybody else. Unlike many less skilful businessmen, he quickly learnt to coordinate multiple activities. That is also thanks to his wife Betty, who takes care of the *maket haus* while he is away.

Clearly household subsistence is not based solely on production. Cooperation is fundamental because it is through the coordination of multiple activities that households become self-reliant. However, a fundamental contradiction lies between the production of food and money and the maintenance of 'good' social relations. Gilbert Camp residents state rather unanimously that each household

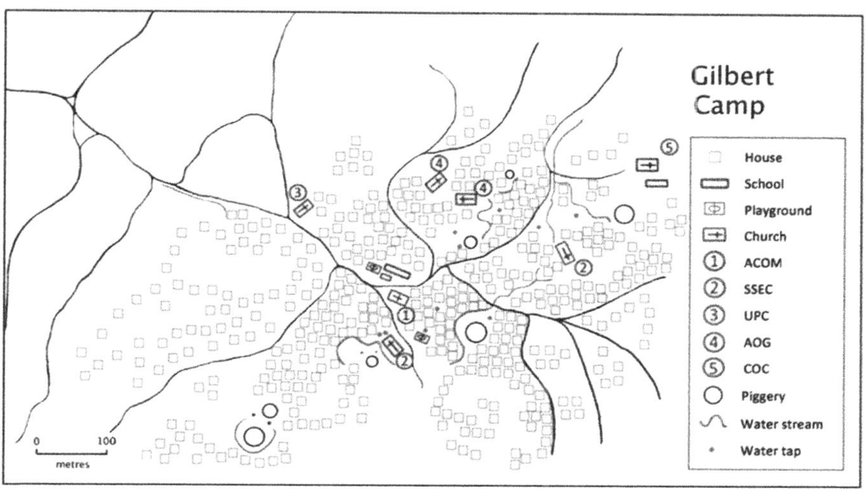

Fig. 3. Topography of Gilbert Camp.

should be economically autonomous: householders must produce their own food and money and shall not rely on resources produced by members of other households. However, to live a life they call 'good' they must also create and maintain 'good' social relationships with the members of their community, which depends largely upon the circulation of resources such as food and money. Hence, a 'good' life requires a certain degree of mutual dependence between autonomous households.

It follows that the picture of a set of interconnected households begins to appear. On the basis of the principle of household self-reliance, householders help each other with their different skills. The mutual dependence between these individuals, however, connects the household with other households, because of the interaction of each individual with other householders that are outside of the supposedly autonomous household, and on whom they depend to a certain extent. And yet people would never say that their household is not autonomous. It appears that, rather than a series of either autonomous or related households, each household is negotiating a tension between the value of autonomy and the value of relatedness.[6]

Gilbert Camp residents create and maintain such relatedness largely as a result of transactions of food and money that are accomplished through sharing, selling on credit and sending gifts to people living in their district of origin. However, sometimes it is hard to perform these transactions because of lack of resources. Finding a balance between economic necessity and the values of relatedness as conceptualized in *kastom* (cf. Browne & Milgram, 2008; Foster, 2005; 210) constitutes a great challenge for them. In order to make their economic necessities compatible with their moral values, they use their productive energy, their knowledge of *kastom*, and their creativity to harmonize these values with economic necessity. That illustrates their commitment to transform Gilbert Camp into a place where they can live a 'good' life, whereby 'good' social relationships are necessary for them as much as food and money are necessary for household subsistence and self-reliance. People obviously need food and money to survive. But, to paraphrase a Biblical proverb in Melanesian fashion, people do not live by cassava alone.

The two strategies described in the following sections exemplify these daily efforts to live a 'good' life by working hard and maintaining 'good' relationships notwithstanding the basilar incompatibility between the limited availability of resources in autonomous households and the need to concretize the value of relatedness with transactions of food and money. The ways in which these transactions are constructed suggest that there is a connection between Gilbert Camp as a historically and geographically specific socio-economic context and the creative response its people elaborate in order to cope with conflicting priorities that emerge from that particular context. Sitting on the town boundary that separates the city from the rest of Guadalcanal, the geographical location of Gilbert Camp is indeed an effective metaphor of different coexisting moralscapes (Peterson, 2001).

DOMESTIC TRADESTORES: TURNING RELATIVES INTO CUSTOMERS

In Gilbert Camp, it has become rather common to see residents buying retailed products from stores that are physically part of their own households. Even though it is a co-resident relative who has originally bought the stock of wholesale products and who re-sells them at a dearer price per unit, this is not necessarily considered as inappropriate. This form of domestic commercialization of food stocks is understood as a strategy that prevents the appropriation of the marginal profit by someone located beyond the limits of the household. It is therefore understood as a practice intended to reinforce the household itself.

That is suggested by three features. Firstly, the person who has originally bought the products at the wholesale distributor has to pay for any product that he or she wishes to consume from the domestic stock, just like anybody else in the household. Secondly, in order to make a profit it is necessary that new money enters the household from the world outside of it. Not only an amount of money equal to the price per unit is rechanneled within the household, but also additional money constituting the marginal profit is inserted. In this way, the domestic retailer is preventing both the cost of the product and the marginal profit from being appropriated by a non-domestic retailer. And the money so collected can be used in other monetary transactions that benefit the household.

Thirdly, and this is the focus of the subsequent discussion, the members of the same household understand this strategy as intended to reproduce the economic conditions that enable the purchase of a new stock and its consumption. It follows that the domestic commercialization of food stocks is understood as a saving strategy, rather than an attempt to extract a profit from the members of the household.

Members of the same household understand that, according to kinship values, food stocks should not be given to relatives in exchange of money. They very clearly articulate the principle by which relatives are expected to share, that is to give to each other without receiving anything in return. This is indeed the basis of reciprocal family care. However, they do not believe that this domestic commercialization of food stocks contradicts such principle. The reason is that they understand that the store would simply not work without a constant injection of marginal profit. They understand that the motives of the exchange cannot be explained with reference to market rule, or at least not exclusively. The rationale is that treating each other as merchant and customer is functional to a saving strategy that benefits the household as a whole, rather than the person who receives the money.

They do not see this strategy as the complete alienation of a personal property by the part of a possessive individual (Mosko, 2013). They rather see it as the redistribution of domestic resources through a form of demand-sharing that locks the circulation of money within the household. In contrast, the market is regarded as the source of all scarcity precisely because the money they insert into it will never transit in their hands again. By taking part in this commercialization of food stocks, they are resisting the centrifugal forces by which the market impoverishes them and keep that money within their network of circulation.

Undoubtedly, the concretion of market values such as the marginal profit, the immediacy of the exchange and the arithmetical formulation of debt is a problematic issue in a family context. For example, if the co-resident customer does not have the money to pay, he will buy on credit, but only as long as his credit history suggests that he will be able to repay. Should that not be the case, the only way for the concerned person to appropriate the item of food would be for another member of the household to purchase it for him. That happens regularly, and the most common example is the case of a mother who buys from her husband in order to feed their children. The fact that this is not considered as morally compromising can only be explained as long as one considers the household as a membership of shared calculative agencies threatened by scarcity and confronted with the prospect of economic failure.

This strategy could be interpreted as a hybrid between two extreme sets of principles. On the one hand, giving money in exchange for food constitutes a concretion of the principles of commodity exchange, most specifically the contractual character of the reciprocal obligation, the fact that such obligation is regulated and enforced by the law of the state, and the fact that the exchange takes place, virtually, in the marketplace. On the other hand, co-resident relatives taking food in exchange for money do so according to traditional kinship principles that ensure their reciprocal care and nurturance, thanks to an implicit, tacit and deeply embedded understanding of each other as mutually dependent. While it seems difficult to formulate such a contradictory set of values in the form of a coherent theory, the growth of domestic tradestores constitutes a trending mechanism that combines such incompatible values into a coherent system.

This trend demonstrates that the people of Gilbert Camp are constructing the *maket haus* as a space for the manipulation of market and kinship logics in conditions of scarcity. Rather than in terms of penetration of capitalism and/or neoliberalism intended as the responsabililization of the individual on matters of resource allocation, this strategy suggests that the Gilbert Camp residents are actively concretizing a sort of moral critique. On the one hand, it is a critique against the aggressive requests from relatives who do not take into consideration the risk of financial failure for these small businesses. On the other hand, it is a reaction to the corrosive power of market values on social cohesion. Relatives who become accountable and loyal to the cause of these indoor stores concretize the value of money as a constitutive element of household subsistence. In conditions of scarcity, such accountability corresponds to a much stronger statement of kinship unity than the demand-sharing of *wantoks*.

OUTDOOR TRADESTORES: TURNING CUSTOMERS INTO RELATIVES

People who run an outdoor tradestore in Gilbert Camp and wish to generate a profit with it have to negotiate their relationships with relatives, neighbours, friends or just unrelated customers. The economic value of money and the moral value of social relationships are negotiated on a daily basis, and selling on credit (*kaon*) is possibly the most common situation in which this negotiation happens. In Solomon Islands, the word *kaon* is most frequently used to describe the practice of buying on credit. According to Jourdan and Maebiru (2002, p. 94) the term comes from the English noun 'account' (at a supplier). *Sensim kaon* means to pay a debt or a loan, and *askem kaon* means to buy on credit. It can also mean 'to borrow' as in *kaon lo bank* (borrow money from the bank), and to owe, as in *mi kaon lo iu* (I owe you).

Kaon is a very important element in Solomon Islands economy, but it also has rather negative connotations. The negative effect of failing to pay debts is a current subject of debate. When people speak about the breakdown of small businesses, they always mention that the main cause is *wantoks* who buy on credit and fail to pay.

Kaon, however, is also an important part of society and economy in a more positive way. It is at the basis of innumerable social interactions: *kaon* is paid when a bride price contribution is given (Burt & Kwa'ioloa, 2012, p. 87), while at the same time another *kaon* is created with that very same transaction. When a man pays the school fees for his younger brothers, that is *kaon* that will be repaid when the boys have a job, and so on and so forth. In these cases, the emphasis on delayed repayment points to the trust that people have in each other, and the importance of such chain of trust and transactions for the reproduction of households.

Formulated in this way, the meaning of *kaon* seems to be found in a dichotomy that opposes *nogud kaon* (bad credit) and *gud kaon* (good credit). *Nogud kaon* is not simply *kaon* that is not paid. It is also *kaon* that threatens the financial stability of a business. Indeed, it suffices that someone demands to pay on credit to create worry in the person who is requested to concede it. In Gilbert Camp, many among those who manage a small business do not concede *kaon* because they are afraid that this will make their business fragile. Indeed, as opposed to life-time obligations, *kaon* that is paid to businesses in the long term is perceived almost as bad as one that is not paid at all.

On the other hand, *gud kaon* is not simply one that is paid. If a man is not given back some money he lent, he might see this as a condition that allows him to consider his debtors as an asset. He can demand that his debtors do things for him, and his debtors must obey without demanding anything in exchange. Their reputation is at stake, and they are supposed to be generous with the man who trusted them enough to sell on credit to them. Ultimately, that *kaon* might never be paid, and yet this will not threaten the relationship between them, as long some other form of reciprocity is concretized. This, however, is a situation that is likely to take place only if the lender has enough money to sustain his own living, while at the same time helping his relatives or friends.

So, the dichotomy between a good and a bad *kaon* is not as clear-cut as it might seem. Similarly, understanding who is suitable to pay on credit is not an easy task, because each shopkeeper has his own strategies and rules, which can be very different from each other. In general, shopkeepers think that *kaon* is not a good thing in itself, because it 'disturbs' the business. However, being totally unwilling to sell on credit can threaten the business too. People talk, and they would stigmatize the unwilling shopkeeper as a selfish man who forgets about his duties as a member of the community (cf. Graeber, 2014, p. 102). As a consequence, a delicate balance has to be found. This is why shopkeepers, while displaying the '*no kaon*' sign (see Fig. 4), still sell on credit sometimes.

Most shopkeepers find it very hard to say 'no'. Refusing *kaon*, like refusing food, is tantamount to refusing the relationship with the person who demands.[7] Instead of refusing forthrightly, they often make a facial expression that reminds you of someone who has a stomach ache. That is ironic, in a way, because it is the customer demanding *kaon* who is supposedly starving. Anyway, if the shopkeeper decides to sell on credit, he will then write down the name of the creditor on a *kaon buk* (sort of debt record) that he keeps under the counter. As a matter of fact, many shopkeepers, while displaying the '*no kaon*' sign, still keep a *kaon buk*.

Fig. 4. The *No Kaon* Notice.

There are elements that make a customer more likely to be conceded *kaon*. Tom said he would be willing to concede *kaon* only to those he can 'control'. He knows his creditors, he knows who is employed and would not waste all their money on beer, areca nuts, and cigarettes. He meets them regularly, but does not remind them of their debt every time. Often, people who are given *kaon* are people who live in the same household with the shopkeeper, or in the immediate neighbourhood. If they buy food on credit from him, they might offer him part of the meal they prepared with that food. But it would not be well regarded if they do not pay their debt with money, and in full. Such obligation is generally not deemed as wrong. People seem to understand that it is necessary for their business-minded neighbour to make a profit. They think that, if they were not willing to pay, they would do something *nogud* to him.

Those who are given *kaon* will not be given it again if they do not pay. Those who pay, in turn, can climb up a sort of ladder of trust. Geoffrey, for example, first conceded credit to his neighbour when the man arrived in Gilbert Camp from the Choiseul province. His name is Excel. Since the beginning of their relationship, Excel always paid his debts on time, each fortnight, with no exception. He was proving to be so trustworthy that Geoffrey started to treat him differently. Later, their debtor–creditor relationship progressively shifted to a relationship of fictive kinship. When Geoffrey, a Kwara'ae man, introduced me to the Choiseulese, he exclaimed:

> Geoffrey: This is my brother! Meet him!
>
> Rodolfo: Your brother?? You do not look alike at all!
>
> Geoffrey: You see how dark his skin is? And yet he is my brother, do you know why?

He told me why, and that is how I collected this story.

A relationship of economic debt can generate, alter, compromise and annihilate a social relationship. That is why *kaon* can be looked at as one of the transactional forms that the people of Gilbert Camp utilize to manage their sociality. Kwara'ae and Choiseulese come from different islands, have different customs and conceive of each other as different. That is why it is all the more surprising that a Choiseulese and a Kwara'ae man might wish to become closer to each other by addressing each other as siblings. Fictive kinship relations of this kind do happen, but they are usually limited to the church space and expressed in explicitly religious terms (i.e. 'brothers in God' or 'sisters in Christ'). That such a degree of intimacy can be pursued and attained on the basis of a debt/credit relation is unexpected and requires a dedicated discussion.

THE COMPATIBLE LOGICS OF KINSHIP AND MARKET VALUES

The logic that underpins the house and the store might seem antithetical from an analytical point of view. But the structure of the values of both indoor and outdoor *maket haus* might not be as contradictory as it might look. Of course in the household relatives are expected to take food from the stocks without having to pay, and of course in the store everyone should be treated as a customer. However, just like a relative who enters the store can be regarded as a customer only as long as such social identity is constructed in a mutual relationship with the shopkeeper, so is the identity of the relative within the household in conditions of scarcity. It is important to emphasize that scarcity is a necessary condition to determine the social construction of relatives as fictive customers, as much as of customers as fictive kins.

The fundamental difference between real and fictive customers is that real customers have to pay, whereas fictive customers choose to in order to contribute to the business venture of their kin while simultaneously maintaining their relationship. Symmetrically, scarcity can also be regarded as a cause, if not a necessary condition, for the social construction of customers as fictive relatives of shop owners. Lack of money, just like scarcity of material resources, puts pressure on these businesses as much as it does on social relationships. People in Gilbert Camp find it particularly difficult to defend one value without neglecting the other, the reason being that satisfying the pressing demands of their relatives and *wantok* is as much detrimental to the 'good' life as cutting the link with these very relatives.

Confronted with the necessity of maintaining 'good' social relationships while at the same time keeping their business in good financial health, store owners must find a strategy to cope with the tension resulting from this incompatible dyad of objectives. The solution that many of them find, as illustrated above, is to change the meaning of 'good', thereby changing the essential conditions that make that basic incompatibility possible.

It might be argued that a crucial difference lies between stores that are located inside the *haos* (house), the Solomon Islands Pidgin term used to indicate migrant dwellings away from *hom*, and those located outside. That might be true, because these stores often display different features and indeed people interact with them in different ways. Usually, stores located within the house are only imagined, meaning that they are constituted as a separated space by means of a mere set of boxes stored under a piece of furniture. In contrast, stores that are physically separated from the house have their own structure, usually the size of a small room and sometimes backed by a very small backroom. Indoor tradestores mostly serve relatives, whereas outdoor stores mostly serve unrelated customers. The former mostly sell food and are more inclined to concede credit, whereas the latter sell a wider range of products and are less inclined to accept debt. These differences, however, do not affect the underlying similarities that outdoor and indoor stores feature. The fundamental similarity lies in the ways in which social relationships are managed, that is in a creative way and to solve a specific set of problems. By means of a sophisticate manipulation of the logics underpinning the commodity exchange between customers and shop owners and the meaning of kinship between relatives, the people of Gilbert Camp avoid the disruption of their social relations and the bankruptcy of their businesses.

Gregory's position that the motivations of transactors are determined by the social context of the exchange (Gregory, 1982, p. 100) supports this argument. In both indoor and outdoor stores the motivations of transactors are strongly influenced by a general condition of scarcity: indoor stores are set up as a saving strategy and outdoor stores as an income-generating activity intended to bring the household above the level of mere subsistence. Consequently, selling to one's own relatives requires a negotiation of the meaning of kinship relation in conditions of scarcity, with a particular focus on the meaning of giving. Symmetrically, turning a customer who repeatedly buys on credit and regularly pays his debts into a relative requires a negotiation of the meaning of debt and credit relations, again, in conditions of scarcity.

In both cases, it is the attempt to take without immediate return that is being criticized. Taking, just like giving, receiving, and reciprocating, is determined by the context in which the transaction takes place. Notably, taking is motivated and encouraged by a general condition of scarcity whereby the demands of *wantok* become heavy and frequent, and the response of shop owners is informed by the ability of the individual customer to repay. When shop owners refuse to give to their *wantok*, they are concretizing a fundamental judgement about their relationship, one that threatens the very existence of that relationship. However, at the same time they are creating the possibility of a new kind of fictive kinship relation to be established, one that is based on the recognition of the value of money within the household. Virtually, they are creating a whole new array of possible relationships with accountable customers in order to compensate for those relationships that are threatened at the business interface.

CONCLUSION

It is at once ironic and revealing to note that the term *maket haus* unites the Solomon Islands Pidgin terms for 'market' and for 'house', i.e. two spaces where two seemingly incompatible sets of values are socially constructed and concretized in social action (Graeber, 2001). The market is the context where short-term balanced reciprocity regulates resource allocation between aliens, whereas in the house people maintain stable relationships on the basis of long-term generalized reciprocity. Short-term balanced reciprocity in the house would engender the denial of a moral relationship, whereas the generalized character of reciprocity in the house depends precisely from the long term of the reciprocation. It's the persistence of a long-term commitment (Bloch, 1973) between exchange partners to live a good life that enables the *maket haus* to neutralize the contradiction between incompatible values.

Perhaps, this argument underemphasizes the repressive power of market economy. Indeed, a structural perspective would possibly see these creative efforts as nothing more than an exceptional occurrence within the highly regimented system of resource allocation exclusively regulated by laws of supply and demand. However, the manipulation of market and kinship logics should not be understood as an insignificant stage along the unidirectional penetration of capitalism and/or neoliberalism. Just like religious affiliations split families and unite individuals as brothers and sisters in Christ, market values can disrupt relationships and create new ones that were not there before, and the same can be said about political or ethical positions. Hence, the development of innovative ways of circulating money and food both inside and outside households in Melanesia should be understood as a fundamental critique against both socially corrosive market values and aggressive forms of demand-sharing, with a particular focus on the notion of taking.

Taking is considered inappropriate because it does not take into consideration the likelihood of bankruptcy and its negative repercussions for migrant households. In contrast, understanding the risk of financial failure is regarded as a value. In becoming accountable, customers are *sharing* the negative consequences of scarcity with the store owners. Sharing this difficult condition, I argue, is the cause of both the acceptability of market logics between kins and the possibility of turning strangers into fictive relatives (cf. Sahlins, 2013, p. 29). Going through the experience of financial scarcity together is a fundamental experience for many contemporary Melanesians. Shifting the focus from demand-sharing to taking, in conclusion, is not only an analytical move to understand their point of view. Also, it is a way to give value to their struggle to live a 'good' life.

NOTES

1. Suffices to say that the price of rice was 2.5 times higher in 2011 than it was in 2002; the price of noodles doubled during the same time span. The cost of 500 gallons of water supply almost tripled, and that of 40 units of electricity was 5 times higher in 2011 than it was in 2002 (Solomon Islands National Statistics Office, 2011).

2. "Solomons Population, Second Fastest Growth Rate in Pacific" – *Solomon Times Online*, 05/06/2008.

3. Population growth (annual %) in Solomon Islands, World Bank; http://data.worldbank.org/country/solomon-islands. Accessed on Maarch 25, 2014, 11:18 AM.

4. The events that took place in Solomon Islands between 1998 and 2003 are commonly labeled 'Ethnic tensions', when more than 35,000 non-Guadalcanese inhabitants

of Guadalcanal escaped under the threat of paramilitary groups such as the Guadalcanal Revolutionary Army. The majority of displaced settlers were from Malaita, as were the members of the Malaita Eagle Force paramilitary group, which was formed in response to the eviction (Moore, 2004).

5. Australian Government Department of Foreign Affairs and Trade (2004). *Solomon Islands: Rebuilding an Island Economy*. Retrieved from http://www.dfat.gov.au/publications/rebuilding_solomon/. Accessed on March 25, 2014, 11:19 AM.

6. This opposition between autonomy and relatedness resonates with the work of Myers (1991, p. 22).

7. Not saying 'no' is a characteristic of Kwara'ae communicative style that Kwara'ae people share with, among others, such as Aboriginal Australians (for example, see Myers, 1976, p. 391; Liberman, 1985, pp. 13–14; Von Sturmer & Fletcher, 1981, p. 17).

REFERENCES

Allen, M. G. (2012). Land, identity and conflict on Guadalcanal, Solomon Islands. *Australian Geographer*, *43*(2), 163–180.

Annis, S. (2010). *God and production in a Guatemalan town*. Austin, TX: University of Texas Press.

Bloch, M. (1973). The long term and the short term: The economic and political significance of the morality of kinship. In J. Goody (Ed.), *The character of kinship* (pp. 75–87). Cambridge: Cambridge University Press.

Blunt, A., & Dowling, R. (2006). *Home (Key ideas in geography)*. Abingdon: Routledge.

Bohannan, P. (1959). The impact of money on an African subsistence economy. *The Journal of Economic History*, *19*(04), 491–503.

Bratman, M. E. (2013). *Shared agency: A planning theory of acting together*. Oxford: Oxford University Press.

Browne, K. E., & Milgram, B. L. (Eds.). (2008). *Economics and morality: Anthropological approaches*. Lanham, MD: Rowman Altamira.

Burt, B., & Kwa'ioloa, M. (2012). *The Chiefs' country: Leadership and politics in Honiara, Solomon Islands*. Brisbane, Australia: University of Queensland Press..

Calestani, M. (2012). Wellbeing in El Alto, Bolivia. In S. Atkinson, J. Painter, & S. Fuller (Eds.), *Wellbeing and place* (pp. 171–184). London: Ashgate Publishing, Ltd.

Carrier, J. G. (1992). The gift in theory and practice in Melanesia: A note on the centrality of gift exchange. *Ethnology*, *31*(2), 185–193.

Chapman, M. (1978). On the cross-cultural study of circulation. *The International Migration Review*, *12*(4), 559–569.

Connell, J. (1978). *Taim Bilong Mani: The evolution of agriculture in a Solomon Island Society* (No. 12). Australian National University, Canberra.

Curry, G. (1999). Markets, social embeddedness and precapitalist societies: The case of village tradestores in Papua New Guinea. *Geoforum*, *30*(3), 285–298.

Eby, M., & Thomas, V. (2016). Haus Piksa: The informal economy of film distribution in Papua New Guinea. *Information Technologies and International Development*, *12*(4), 23–33.

Fischer, E. (2014). *The good life: Aspiration, dignity, and the anthropology of wellbeing*. Stanford, CA: Stanford University Press.

Foster, R. (2005). Afterword: Frustrating modernity in Melanesia. In J. Robbins & H. Wardlow (Eds.), *The making of global and local modernities in Melanesia: Humiliation, transformation and the nature of cultural change* (pp. 207–216). London: Ashgate.

Foukona, J. (2015). Urban land in Honiara: Strategies and rights to the city. *The Journal of Pacific History*, *50*(4), 504–518.

Genova, C., Kriesemer, S. K., Neave, S., Jaw-Fen, W., & Weinberger, K. (2010). *Market analysis of fresh vegetables in Solomon Islands*. Shanhua: AVRDC-World Vegetable Centre.

Graeber, D. (2001). *Toward an anthropological theory of value: The false coin of our own dreams*. New York, NY: Springer.

Graeber, D. (2014). *Debt-updated and expanded: The first 5,000 years*. Brooklyn, NY: Melville House.

Gregory, C. (1982). *Gifts and commodities*. London: Academic Press.

Grossman, L. S. (1986). Consumer behavior and the village trade store: A Papua New Guinea example. Geografiska Annaler. Series B. Human Geography, 41–49.

Jourdan, C., & Maebiru, E. (2002). *Pijin: A Trilingual Cultural Dictionary: Pijin-Inglis-Franis, Pijin-English-French, Pijin-Anglais-Français* (Vol. 526), Canberra: Pacific Linguistics, Research School of Pacific and Asian Studies, Australian National University.

Kastom Gaden Association (2005). *People on the edge*. Honiara: Kastom Gaden Association.

Kauhue, E. (2011). Cost of living in Honiara, unbearable. *Solomon Star*, February 9.

Liberman, K. (1985). *Understanding interaction in central Australia: An ethnomethodological study of Australian Aboriginal people*. Boston, MA: Routledge & Kegan Paul.

Maggio, R. (2016a). 'My wife converted me': Gendered values and gendered conversion in Pentecostal households in Honiara, Solomon Islands. *The Australian Journal of Anthropology*, *27*(1), 1–17.

Maggio, R. (2017b). "Big Confusion": The land question in Honiara and the history of land policy in Solomon Islands. *People and Culture in Oceania*, *32*, 1–28.

Maggio, R. (forthcoming). According to Kastom and according to law: "Good Life" and 'Good Death' in Gilbert Camp, Solomon Islands. In C. Gregory & J. Altman (Eds.), *The quest for the good life in precarious times: Ethnographic perspectives from the Asia-Pacific region*. Canberra: ANU Press.

Malinowski, B. (1922). *Argonauts of the Western Pacific: An account of native enterprise and adventure in the archipelagoes of Melanesian New Guinea*. London: Routledge.

Malinowski, B. (2002). *Argonauts of the Western Pacific: An account of native enterprise and adventure in the archipelagoes of Melanesian New Guinea*. London: Routledge.

Mariz, C. L. (1994). *Coping with poverty: Pentecostals and Christian base communities in Brazil*. Philadelphia, PA: Temple University Press.

Martin, K. (2013). *The death of the big men and the rise of the big shots: Custom and conflict in East New Britain* (Vol. 3). New York, NY: Berghahn Books.

Mathews, G., & Izquierdo, C. (Eds.) (2008). *Pursuits of happiness: Well-being in anthropological perspective*. New York, NY: Berghahn Books.

McCormack, F., & Barclay, K. (Eds.) (2013). *Engaging with capitalism: Cases from Oceania*. Emerald Group Publishing Limited.

Moore, C. (2004). *Happy isles in crisis: The historical causes for a failing state in the Solomon Islands, 1998–2004*. Canberra, Australia: Asia Pacific Press.

Moore, C. (2015). Honiara: Arrival city and pacific hybrid living space. *The Journal of Pacific History*, *50*(4), 419–436.

Mosko, M. S. (2013). Dividuals, individuals, or possessive individuals?: Recent transformations of North Mekeo commoditization, personhood, and sociality. In *Engaging with capitalism: Cases from Oceania* (pp. 167–198). Bingley: Emerald Group Publishing Limited.

Myers, F. R. (1976). *To have and to hold: A study of persistence and change in Pintupi social life*. Ph. D. thesis, Bryn Mawr College.

Myers, F. R. (1991). *Pintupi country, Pintupi self: Sentiment, place, and politics among Western Desert Aborigines*. University of California Press.

Nanau, G. L. (2011). The wantok system as a socio-economic and political network in Melanesia. *OMNES: The Journal of Multicultural Society*, *2*(1), 31–55.

Peterson, A. L. (2001). *Being human: Ethics, environment, and our place in the world*. Los Angeles: University of California Press.

Peterson, N. (1993). Demand sharing: Reciprocity and the pressure for generosity among foragers. *American Anthropologist*, *95*(4), 860–874.

Peterson, N., & Taylor, J. (2003). The modernising of the Indigenous domestic moral economy: Kinship, accumulation and household composition. *The Asia Pacific Journal of Anthropology*, *4*(1–2), 105–122.

Polanyi, K. (1957). *Trade and market in the early empires: Economies in history and theory*. Free Press.

Rapport, N., & Dawson, A. (1998). *Migrants of Identity. Perceptions of Home in a World of Movement*. Oxford: Berg.

Sahlins, M. (1972). *Stone age economics*. New Brunswick, NJ: Transaction Publishers.

Sahlins, M. (1985). *Islands of History*. Chicago, IL: University of Chicago Press.

Sahlins, M. (1992). The economics of develop-man in the pacific. *RES: Anthropology and Aesthetics*, *21*(April), 12–25.

Sahlins, M. (2013). *What kinship is-and is not*. Chicago, IL: University of Chicago Press.

Saxe, G. B., & Esmonde, I. (2004). Making change in Oksapmin tradestores: A study of shifting practices of quantification under conditions of rapid shift towards a cash economy. *South Pacific Journal of Psychology*, *15*, 11–28.

Sharp, T. L. (2016). Trade's value: Relational transactions in the Papua New Guinea Betel Nut Trade. *Oceania*, *86*(1), 75–91.

Sjørup, L. (2002). Pentecostals: The power of the powerless. *Dialog*, *41*(1), 16–25.

Solomon Islands National Statistics Office (2011, April). *Honiara consumer price index*. Ministry of Finance & Treasury, Honiara, Solomon Islands.

Strathern, M. (1985). Attitudes of Hagen Migrants towards 'Home'. In M. Chapman & M. Prothero (Eds.), *Circulation in population movement: Substance and concepts from the Melanesian case*. London: Routledge & Kegan Paul.

Sykes, K. (Ed.) (2008). *Ethnographies of moral reasoning: Living paradoxes of a global age*. Basingstoke: Palgrave MacMillan..

Von Sturmer, J. R., & Fletcher, A. (1981). *Talking with aborigines* (Vol. 15, pp. 13–31). Canberra, Australia: Australian Institute of Aboriginal and Torres Strait Islander Studies.

Weinberger, M. F., & Wallendorf, M. (2012). Intracommunity gifting at the intersection of contemporary moral and market economies. *Journal of Consumer Research*, *39*(1), 74–92.

PART III
VENDING

STRUGGLES WITH CHANGING POLITICS: STREET VENDOR LIVELIHOODS IN CONTEMPORARY CHINA

Shuru Zhong and Hongyang Di

ABSTRACT

Purpose – *Today's China has striven to exclude street vendors through political campaigns such as "National Sanitary City" and "National Civilized City." Such campaigns pursue modernity and beautiful urban spaces by deeming street vendors to be disorderly, unsanitary, and obsolete. Taking a single Chinese city as a case study, this research analyzes why and how local bureaucratic apparatuses apply rapidly-changing and ambiguous political treatment to street vendors. This research also examines street vendors' struggles and coping strategies with these ever-changing politics.*

Methodology/approach – *The data for this study were obtained during a total of ten months of fieldwork, beginning in 2013 and ending in 2016. In-depth interviews were conducted with fifty-one street vendors and six government officials; additionally, the researcher consulted newspaper reports, archives, and relevant official publications.*

Findings – *First, regarding the governance of street vendors, the local administration has shifted their stance between two distinct patterns – suppression and tolerance – depending on the timing of certain political campaigns. Second, the corruption and laziness of government officials has*

Anthropological Considerations of Production, Exchange, Vending and Tourism
Research in Economic Anthropology, Volume 37, 179–204

ISSN: 0190-1281/doi:10.1108/S0190-128120170000037009

provided niches for the revival of street vending after campaigns are over, though with limitations. Third, street vendors in China tend to be passive recipients of government suppression, unable to forge effective resistance because of a lack of strong leadership and general organization.

Originality/value – *This research will add to the general understanding of the government-vendor relationship by revealing the complexity, uncertainty, and flexibility inherent in interactions between these two groups.*

Keywords: Street vendors; China; urban politics

INTRODUCTION

As a significant component of informal economy, street vending encompasses street-based and small-scale mobile enterprises that use labor-intensive technologies and little financial capital. In many developing countries, street vending provides a livelihood for millions of urban poor and a convenience for residents. The survival of street vendors, however, is inevitably linked with the wider political system in which they operate (Crossa, 2016; Hsu, 2010; McGee & Yeung, 1977; Smart, 1989). In a review of street vendors in Asia, for example, Bhowmik (2005) emphasized two facts: first, that the number of street vendors is growing rapidly, and second, that street vendors face constant harassment.

With a focus on the governance of street vendors in developing countries, recent studies have explored why local authorities tend to suppress this type of informal commerce. One mainstream explanation is that the local government tends to view street vendors as disorderly, inefficient, and unsanitary, and thus in opposition to the desired national image; they instead urge the construction of organized, privatized, and sanitized urban spaces that exclude street vendors (Anjaria, 2006; Crossa, 2009). This process is called "urban revanchism" (Smith, 1996, p. xix) or "accumulation by dispossession" (Endres, 2014, p. 97). Furthermore, the existing literature has argued that rather than remain silent in response to this punitive treatment, street vendors have both individually and collectively engaged in the "politics of redress" (Bayat, 2004, p. 79) through everyday resistance, as well as more organized tactics (Milgram, 2014, 2015). These studies have suggested that punitive policies have negatively impacted street vendors. As an alternative, they have advocated for the construction of a more transparent and humane political environment that balances the needs of both the government and street vendors (Hansen, 2004; Musoni, 2010; Swanson, 2007; Timalsina, 2011).

Though punitive governance currently prevails in developing countries, it is necessary to emphasize that a variety of policies are possible in specific political and cultural contexts. In different cases, local authorities' attitudes toward street vendors have been violent and predatory, liberal and tolerant, or somewhere in between (Anjaria, 2006; Chiu, 2013; Hansen, 2004). However, it is insufficient to simply recognize that the urban political response to street vendors tends to be "multifaceted and ambivalent rather than only punitive/revanchist" (Huang, Xue, & Li, 2014, p. 170). Merely labeling government attitudes provides limited assistance with understanding how and why certain patterns of governance are constructed. Taking one city in China as a case study, this research focuses on the complexity, uncertainty, and flexibility inherent in the government-vendor relationship. This work examines how political campaigns, as underlying factors, motivate a city government to shift back and forth from a stance of tolerance to one of repression. Furthermore, this study explores how street vendors interact with urban politics and employ diverse strategies in their struggle to survive.

Similar to many other developing countries, China has identified street vendors as a major target of governance in their state-led pursuit of modernity (Solinger, 2013). The country's rapid economic development and urbanization impressed the world in the 1990s. At that time, the central government advocated for "spiritual civilization," and launched ongoing political campaigns such as the "National Sanitary City" and "National Civilized City," the framework of which identified street vending is an obstacle. This research analyzes how state-led campaigns were understood and implemented by city governments and individual officials, radically affecting street vendors' livelihoods.

This study was conducted in Sanya city, in the Hainan province of China. With an urban population of 250,000, Sanya is a relatively small Chinese municipality. A famous tourism destination, Sanya has cultivated a prosperous commercial culture and street vending industry. Moreover, the city has become deeply involved in the national political campaigns of "National Sanitary City" and "National Civilized City," during which it has striven to eliminate street vendors. I conducted one month of fieldwork in this city in 2013, three months in 2014, and six months in 2016; during these times, I closely observed vending activities and the interactions among policeman and vendors on the street, and interviewed 51 street vendors and six government officials. I selected ten locations in downtown Sanya where street vendors were known to gather, and targeted appropriate interviewees through observation and subsequent conversations. Other sources accessed to support this research included newspaper reports, archives, and relevant official publications.

HISTORICAL BACKGROUND

The governance of street vending has regularly changed since the foundation of the People's Republic of China in 1949. During the socialist era (1949–1979), urban residents obtained their daily goods mainly through two different channels. The first one was the formal channel, as a part of the state-planned purchase and supply program that included a variety of state-owned retail outlets. The other was the informal channel, which included street markets and commercial activities that were under-supervised and not incorporated into the state-planned economy (Contemporary Chinese Commerce, 1990, pp. 67–144). Dispersed throughout urban areas, these informal street markets provided a marketing niche for independent vendors outside of the formal sector, and peasants from neighboring rural areas (Feng, 2011). Street markets were also called "free markets" because of their essentially capitalistic characteristics (*People's Daily*, 1954). Peasants were permitted to sell their surplus poultry, vegetables, and animal byproducts in the free markets after they fulfilled their state procurement quotas. In these street markets, commodity prices were not settled by the state, but instead were negotiable (Fang, 1955).

During this period, there was considerable disagreement in the Communist leadership on the issue of street vending. The marketeers' camp was led by a Party leader named Chen Yun who emphasized the necessity and merits of the street markets. Chen (1956) recognized that the formal sector was far from perfect; state-owned stores were minimally effective, and failed accurately to estimate supply and demand. The rigid rationing system was not able to provide all of the commodities needed by the masses, especially during urgent times. The marketeers also believed that because of the low level of technological infrastructure dedicated to marketing, China's locally-based street vendors were essential to reducing the losses inherent in long-distance food transportation; they served to adjust circulation and address the complex and fluctuating circumstances that attended urban consumption (Solinger, 1987). The opposite camp, the radicals, led by Mao Zedong, insisted that independent street vendors were moments of "spontaneous capitalism" that would lead to inflation, hamper state purchases, unfairly increase participants' incomes, and aggravate the class polarization that directly contradicted Mao's romantic communist ideology (Sun, 1957; Zhou, 1957).

This disagreement within the communist leadership led to a cycle in policy-making. Initially, radical ideas dominated; this led to a crisis phase, which was followed by a liberal phase and marketeer dominance. Subsequently, the liberal phase was brought to an end by a new radicalization (Skinner, 1984). From 1955 to 1956, radical policies seemed to be working, as illustrated by the state launching a policy of socialist transformations that incorporated millions of independent traders into the formal sector to be employees or dealers of state-owned stores (Liu & Quan, 1955; *People's Daily*, 1955). However, these radical policies caused serious market disorder because they destroyed the original, smoothly-functioning commercial webs of small shops distributed throughout the various communities. The emerging "formal" stores were not able to stabilize supply in the short term. In a moment, urban food retail sales could be chaotically disrupted, thus adversely affecting urban residents' everyday lives (Feng, 2011; *People's Daily*, 1956a).

Following a series of such moments, Mao made concessions to Chen's plan and allowed the street markets to reopen (only briefly, from 1956 to 1957). Soon after this liberal policy was made official, the market stabilized (*People's Daily*, 1956b; Xi, 1956). However, Mao (1957) then determined that the flourishing street markets were indeed a significant signal of "spontaneous capitalism." Radical politicians took over the discourse, which was accompanied by a quick and coercive re-closing of the street markets (Wang, Chu, & Tao, 1957). The radicals initiated the Peoples' Commune Movement and the Great Leap Forward Movement, during which even more independent businesses were eliminated and a serious economic crisis emerged (*People's Daily*, 1958a, 1958b). Consequently, the street markets were reopened from mid-1959 through 1965, the eve of the Cultural Revolution. This reopening of the street markets was more heavily restricted than ever before, evidenced especially by the control exerted over hours of operation and price ranges for commodities (Guan, 1962). During the Cultural Revolution (1966–1976), private commerce was once again strictly banned (Ministry of Commerce, 1970).

Since the 1980s, the central government has launched a series of economic reforms; the socialist system has gradually collapsed, resulting in millions of workers being laid off from state-owned enterprises. Additionally, several million educated urban youth who were sent to the countryside during the Cultural Revolution (1966–1976) were allowed to return to the cities (Dutton, 1998; Whyte & Parish, 1985). To solve the resulting unemployment issues, the central government began allowing private businesses (Vogel, 1989). Many people chose to be street vendors because there was a very low barrier to entry. Street vending has flourished since then, and continued to grow as more workers were laid off in the 1990s (Meisner, 1999). The state left room for street vendors, but hesitated to provide any official support. Under Deng Xiaoping's leadership, both the central and local governments concentrated all of their resources on attracting massive capital investment from both inside and outside the nation (Huang, 2008). Grassroots moneymakers (such as street vendors) were neglected in the national economic plan (Solinger, 2013).

The importance of street vending to vendors' livelihoods and that of urban consumers has been ignored by mainstream political discourse since 1949. As Solinger (1987) has argued, it is ironic how street vendors have been sacrificed on the altar of political correctness, and forced to struggle for a living in a state ostensibly designed to better serve the poor. In actuality, the marginalization of street vendors intensified when the central government launched its most defining political campaigns.

STREET VENDING IN SANYA CITY: LIVELIHOODS FOR THE POOR

Following the national trend in the 1980s of reopening the streets to private vendors, Sanya also began to embrace them into its vivid city life. At that time, all of Hainan Island remained agriculturally focused and relatively isolated from mainland China. Thus, Sanya locals formed the majority of street vendors. Moreover, many of Sanya's people had already left the island for more economically developed areas on the mainland to seek job opportunities. However, building upon its prosperous seashore tourism industry, Sanya's economy has flourished since the early 2000s, making Sanya attractive to small businesses. Once the central government began allowing nationwide rural-to-urban migration, a substantial number of rural migrants from peripheral areas on the island and mainland China flowed into Sanya City (Brødsgaard, 2009). As a result, street vendors are presently a mix of locals and peasant migrants. Among the 51 cases in the 2014 record, 27 of them were Hainan residents and the other 24 were migrants from the mainland.

Vendors from less-developed areas on Hainan Island are hardly distinguishable from Sanya locals, because they all tend to speak Hainan dialects. These Hainan islanders identify themselves as natives (*bendi ren*) and tend to be isolated from mainland migrant vendors who are called outlanders (*waidi ren*). When asked why they chose Sanya rather than other cities, most outlanders claimed that they were introduced to the area by hometown acquaintances. These personal contacts assisted them in initially settling in the city. As Crossa (2016) determined, differences within the street vendor group may lead to different political treatment and the ways in which these vendors resist regulation. To a certain extent, natives enjoy more tolerance from the local government and occupy better business locations than outlanders. I was told by a vendor that natives would join together to seize locations with the most visitors and physically remove outlanders who attempting to challenge them.

Despite the native-outlander difference, street vendors in Sanya City share many commonalities. For instance, generally they are not well-educated. Among the fifty-one cases in the 2014 record, only three had college-level educations, with a majority barely graduating from middle school and a significant portion being completely illiterate. Before becoming involved in street businesses, they were primarily workers in sweatshops; their low levels of education kept them from the higher-paid professional jobs. When I met Zheng[1] and her husband, they had been running their watermelon business for two months. Hoping for better lives, the peasant couple moved to Sanya from a peripheral town near Sanya. Initially, Zheng was a housewife and her husband drove a motorcycle to deliver goods; this was the only economic support for the family of four. They were embarrassed to tell me that they were forced to ask their relatives to adopt their youngest child (in total, they had three) because of their economic distress. Zheng attributed her failure in the job market to her illiteracy. "I have no education to find a job. When I applied [for] a position of waitress in a hotel, the manager turned me down because I do not speak good Mandarin." The Zheng couple is not alone. Many vendors rely on street businesses not because it is the best option among many; rather, their career choices are confined. The most common reason is: "I do not know what else I can do. I just want to make some money."

Evidence suggests that street vending provides livelihoods to the urban poor (Lincoln, 2008; Reid, Fram, & Guotai, 2010). Street vendors' incomes vary based on their merchandise, vending position, and sales tactics. The available commodities range from cooked food to fresh vegetables, tropical fruits, fresh meats, fish, apparel, artwork, toys, and other articles of daily use. A small portion of these vendors are craftsman who provide services including repairing watches, shining shoes, providing facial massages, designing signatures, fortune-telling, and more. Street vendors use mobile facilities to run their business because no fixed stall on street is permitted by the city government. Their normal monthly profits range from 2,000 to 4,000 RMB,[2] significantly lower than 4, 553 RMB, the average monthly income of Sanya City in 2014 (Sanya City Statistics Office, 2016). Earnings are also influenced by tourism; business is much better in winter, Sanya's high tourist season. These numbers are based on rough estimates. A vendor may count how much he or she earns in a day, but very few have detailed accountings of their monthly income. Low incomes keep these vendors from expensive housing; based on the interviews conducted for this research, their monthly housing expenditure ranges from 500 to 1,200 RMB. To save money and time, they often choose low-rent housing near their vending location. These rooms tend to be small, humid, and dark. Without air conditioning, inhabitants have to endure the exceptionally hot summer weather of tropical Sanya.

Similar to Tamar Wilson's (2014) findings on beach vendors in Acapulco, Mexico, some of my informants reported that they continued their street vending because it afforded them both freedom and flexibility, even though it did not allow them to make a decent living. They claimed that they were able to take breaks or close their businesses any time they needed to; office jobs would cost them their liberty. Nevertheless, few vendors were in a position to actually take advantage of this freedom. In order to survive, many peddlers were forced to work long hours. Wu, a 23-year-old man who sold cellphone cases for 12 hours a day, had not enjoyed a single day of rest, even during the Chinese New Year, since he engaged in street vending three years prior. He said, "I think the key of success is bearing hardship and standing hard work. I am spending money every day, so I have to work every day." Street vending often requires arduous physical labor. For Jin, a 40-year-old female fruit vendor, every day began at 5 a.m., with a half-hour walk to the wholesale market to replenish her stocks. Using a shoulder pole, she carried up to 80 pounds of fresh mangos, guava, or grapes, in two separated baskets, on foot, back to her vending location, a hospital gate where several vendors collected, and then sell to her customers throughout the day. When I visited her, she kept working after a meal was delivered by her husband at noon, and did not return home until 11 p.m., when passersby became few. Because the fruit afforded only a small margin of profit, it was common to see vendors price their wares cheaply, but trick customers when weighing the product. The margin for profit on other common merchandise, as well, was quite low, due to abundant supply and fierce competition among vendors.

POLITICAL CAMPAIGNS AND GOVERNMENT INSTITUTIONS

The Chinese state's indifference towards street vendors in the 1980s allowed vending to multiply in urban areas. Soon after, however, the central government began regulating the work schedules of street-based entrepreneurs. In 1989, the Ministry of Health began promoting an ongoing political campaign entitled the "National Sanitary City" (The State Council of PRC, 1989). In 2003, the Propaganda Department of the Central Committee of the Communist Party of China launched a campaign named "National Civilized City," which was designed to be the highest honor a city could achieve (*People's Daily*, 2003). The official description underscored the ambition of the leadership; their goal was to create a strong, civilized, modern China:

> The title of National Civilized City is a comprehensive title that reflects the overall level of civilization of the city during this significant period of building a moderately prosperous society and advancing socialist moderation. It refers to a city which has made remarkable achievement of material, political, and spiritual civilization, with citizens of a high degree of civilization. (*People's Daily*, 2003)

Cities are not compelled to compete in these political contests, but earning one of these honorary titles is understood as the best evidence of successful governance and is beneficial to local officials' careers. The total number of cities participating in these two campaigns is difficult to estimate; according to the published data, as of 2009, 118 cities, approximately one-sixth of all municipalities in the country, were successfully awarded the title of "National Sanitary City," while eighty-four cities were awarded "National Civilized City" (The State Council, 2015). To a large extent, the lists of winners of these two awards overlap.

The processes of competing in the two contests are very similar, and are both complicated and lengthy. Taking "National Sanitary City" as an example, the selection cycle lasts for three years. In each cycle, the participating city governments first submit materials of application to their provincial governments, who then evaluate those materials and recommend candidate cities to the

Ministry of Health. Second, the Ministry of Health organizes a panel of experts to conduct onsite investigations in the candidate cities. There are two rounds of investigation; the first is secret, and the second public. The panel then makes final decisions regarding the awardees. Importantly, the Ministry of Health reexamines the selected cities every three years and withdraws the honorary title if the city no longer meets the criteria (Patriotic Health Committee, 2015).

Assessment of the candidate cities is based on a set of rigid criteria, which includes the education of public health, city appearance and sanitation, environmental protection, water and food safety, infectious diseases control, and so on. The evaluation criteria of "National Civilized City" are even stricter and more comprehensive, including indicators of economic development. These two political campaigns are not designed to exclusively target street vending; they actually focus on the more ambitious goal of establishing organized and clean public spaces. However, the evaluation criteria for both contests explicitly require that there be "no mobile vending stalls on [the] street" (Patriotic Health Committee, 2015). Street vending is seen as directly contradicting the discourse of city beautification. In the cities participating in these campaigns, street vendors have become a primary target of governance. The Sanya city government applied to join the "National Sanitary City" contest in 1993, but was not successfully awarded the title until 2009 (Hu, 2009b).

These two campaigns aside, street vending is also discouraged because of other political propaganda in Sanya. In 2005, the city government coined a "name card" for the city, "Beautiful Sanya, Romantic Tianya,"[3] which illustrates the authorities' pursuit of a stylish and elegant city image. The city government believed that such an image would help the tourist industry. Recently, they determined the development orientation of Sanya to be that of an "International Boutique City" and "World Famous Tourist Destination," in which activities such as street vending would be considered "low-end" and incompatible with the desired image. Street vendors in Sanya have been accused of "forcibly occupying public space" and "damaging [to the] city appearance;" the government has argued that the practice inhibits the flow of traffic, generates noise, and pollutes the environment by producing dirty water, rubbish, and cooking fumes (Chen, 2001; Hu, 2007a, 2007b, 2007c; Wu, 2015).

Cities in China have specialized government institutions to regulate street vending. In Sanya, this organization is called the Sanya City Administrative Law Executing Bureau (SCALEB); it employs affiliated officials called urban inspectors (*Chengguan*). Urban inspectors are portrayed by the media in China as the natural enemy of street vendors, and there have been countless reports of their hostile relationship toward vendors (Caron, 2013). Established in 1988, SCALEB aimed to improve the city's appearance specifically by fighting against traffic-blocking parking, illegal construction, and informal street vending. The bureaucratic hierarchy in Sanya City has three levels; from top to bottom, these are the city government, district government, and neighborhood committees.[4] SCALEB has established offices in each district and neighborhood, and each sub-office leads different teams of urban inspectors. Urban inspectors at the neighborhood, district, and city levels cooperate and connect with one another through the clear assignment of responsibility areas; from main streets to forgotten alleys, the rigorous web of urban inspectors is able to surveil every corner of the city. During their daily inspections, hundreds of urban inspectors patrol the city, driving vendors away, confiscating their goods, and fining them. Street vending in Sanya has become a business on the run, with peddlers now always needing a mode of escape (Asiedu & Agyei-Mensah, 2008).

Urban inspectors act as agents of the local bureaucratic apparatuses; it is their job to put official policies and ideology into effect on the streets (Caron, 2013; Hanser, 2016). They are perceived by vendors as powerful, heartless, rude, and mindless puppets of the government. However, in reality the group is not this homogenous. According to interviews with an official working at SCALEB, there are two types of urban inspectors. The first are formal government officials registered in the national civil service system. They have college educations and have passed strict national examinations and training programs before assuming their posts. These official urban inspectors represent only a small portion of the group as a whole, and usually work at city-level SCALEB offices and lead important inspection projects. They do not usually participate in regular street patrols. Rather, unofficial urban inspectors, the other main category, take on this responsibility. Since daily street surveillance requires a substantial labor force, SCALEB offices at the city, district, and neighborhood levels hire numerous temporary workers who function as unofficial urban inspectors. In this way, SCALEB is able to reduce its fiscal burden, because these unofficial urban inspectors receive salaries and benefits inferior to those of their official counterparts. I have observed that they harass street vendors, sometimes confiscate their equipment, impose fines, destroy their commodities, and even inflict injuries. Since patrolling the street and expelling vendors is a straightforward task, the training and education requirements are minimal. Most are young men in their twenties or thirties, and are Hainan locals with little education. Unlike official urban inspectors, unofficial inspectors are not legally authorized to use force, impose fines, or confiscate goods; they often do, however. Street vendors cannot tell the difference between official and unofficial urban inspectors because they wear the same uniforms. Unofficial inspectors reported that their salaries are normally no more than 3,000 RMB monthly, which is only slightly better than the street vendors. Some have part-time jobs to supplement their income. It is widely reported that unofficial urban inspectors are quick to take bribes or other gifts from vendors. Many unofficial urban inspectors complained to me that this job is labor-intensive, boring, and offers no future; they would leave without hesitation if a better option was available. Though there are some who willingly abuse their power and become violent, most are modest, and try their best to avoid physical conflicts with street vendors.

SUPPRESSION DURING POLITICAL CAMPAIGNS

The governance of street vending in Sanya city is ultimately decided by the political goals of the local bureaucratic apparatus. Historically, during each important political campaign, the city government has endeavored to eliminate street vending by mobilizing its citizens and concentrating all its administrative resources. Once the planned political mission is accomplished, however, the city government loosens the established exclusionary policies and the suppressed commerce is able to recover, at least until the next political campaign. In other words, depending on the timing of the political campaign, the city government's response to street vending has ranged from exclusion and suppression, to tolerance. Thus, street vendors must constantly struggle to adapt to the city's ever-changing political climate.

Aggressive Governance

After years of preparation, in July of 2007, the Sanya government announced that they had received the Hainan provincial government's recommendation that they officially join the "National Sanitary City" campaign. The Sanya government responded that it would devote the entire energy of the city to guaranteeing its success (Hu, 2007a, 2007b, 2007c). Succeeding in this endeavor would be of great benefit to the careers of local leaders. For two years, an expert panel of nine judges from Beijing conducted onsite examinations in Sanya to determine if it qualified for the title. During their investigation, the judges visited government departments, community organizations, individual neighborhoods, and the city's main streets, in order to comprehensively compare the city's condition to a long list of appraisal criteria (Hu, 2008, 2009a).

The criteria clearly indicated that street vending should be prohibited. In order to satisfy this requirement, SCALEB offices at the district and neighborhood levels ceded some of their power and followed a unified plan assigned by the city-level SACLEB office; the goal was to concentrate all human resources on thoroughly eradicating the street vendors. Teams of urban inspectors patrolled twenty-four hours a day, seven days a week, in the regions the expert panels were most likely to visit. In other areas, surveillance was stricter than ever before. SCALEB organized "special actions" to conduct surprise examinations (Sanya City Government, 2008; Sun, 2009). According to interviews with an official urban inspector, in one such special action, approximately 200 urban inspectors were sent out and over 400 vending stalls removed. Moreover, residents said that materials such as posters, wall boards, and banners with slogans such as "Strictly Prohibit Street Vending, Strive for National Sanitary City" appeared everywhere. One community hung up a banner claiming they would force "all vendors … occupying public space out of business."

Sanya was finally awarded "National Sanitary City" in September of 2009. While the urban inspectors did not maintain round-the-clock patrols throughout the preceding two years, the most suppressive actions were concentrated during the weeks the expert panels visited. In other cities, such as Guangzhou, these national campaigns provided a similar framework of exclusion (Huang et al., 2014). The Ministry of Health of the central government claimed the expert panels' first visit to any city would be kept secret from the local government; however, one SCALEB official admitted that they knew the general schedule. It is difficult to estimate how many migrant vendors gave up their businesses and moved to other locations during this two-year period, given that the regulation of their livelihood had become more violent and strict, according to the reports of all vendors with whom we spoke. Soon after Sanya city received the award in 2009, SCALEB eased its intense policing of the vendors; as a result, many quietly restored their businesses. The official policy was once again a mixture of exclusion and inclusion (Chen & Yu, 2010). One SCALEB official indicated that they understood the entire process to be a political show, and many "unsanitary" features were intentionally hidden until the expert panel left and the city obtained its prize.

In November of 2016, the city government began a project named "Consolidating National Civilized City." At the timing of writing the city was waiting to be reassessed by the Ministry of Health in early 2017. If it fails this reassessment, the city will lose the honorary title it received in 2009. I personally witnessed the city striving to meet the contest's requirements, resulting in a number of small restaurants along several main streets being temporary closed because their decorations were determined to be unattractive and their tables occupied street space. One restaurant owner said that it was the urban inspector's decision, and he could only resume his business once he received official notification. Some open-air food markets experienced the same treatment as urban inspectors strengthened their control of the streets.

I observed many surprise inspections. During one such inspection, approximately ten urban inspectors split into two teams; they were dressed in plain clothes so the street vendors would not realize they were approaching. One team began at one end of the street, and the other team blocked the exit at the other end to stop any street vendors who tried to flee. There were about twenty vendors there in total, most of whom were fined and had their goods confiscated; several lucky vendors escaped punishment by hiding in stores. Urban inspectors conducted similar surprise inspections in the days following. Consequently, only a few brave vendors risked attempting to continue their business there. One female fruit vendor reported that she stayed home for the entire month of November in 2016.

The drama created by the pursuit of "National Sanitary City" is not unique. Similar phenomena have occurred in Sanya as a result of other political campaigns, such as during the competition for "National Excellent Tourism City" in 1998 (Su & Chen, 1998). In March of 2015, the city government declared a new plan to achieve "National Civilized City" status by 2018. It is predicted that efforts at exclusion will again be seen on Sanya's streets. Besides national political campaigns, the city government also arranges projects for political propaganda, such as largescale special actions during main annual festivals, when massive numbers of tourists pour into this small city. Therefore, within any given year, there are a number of special periods devoted to diverse campaigns; as regulations are kept secret from the street vendors, they feel that the government's attitude towards them is both capricious and unpredictable.

Expected Victims

Under these exclusionary policies, the strategies used by street vendors to avoid the urban inspectors' harassment are no longer sufficient. Street vendors continue to be the passive recipients of the repercussions of rapidly change policies. Conflicts between street vendors and urban inspectors occasionally occur, but the frequency significantly increases when these types of exclusionary policies are enacted. The image of urban inspectors is negative from the perspective of many vendors. Frequent comments included: "they are cold-blooded bandits" and "they are dogs of the Communist Party of China." Some vendors, however, stated that they understood the urban inspectors' behavior, because "ejecting us is their job." Vendors' attitudes varied widely. One fruit vendor expressed her outrage:

> Usually they show up as a group, sometimes with sharp knives in hand. Once their patrol cars stopped, they immediately ran to us. They did not say a single word but tossed my fruits onto the ground and smashed them. One time they used their knives to stab [the] tires of my freight tricycle. They are so bad. Not all vendors would keep silence under such suppression.

I have also heard stories of fierce conflicts between the two groups. For examples, a strawberry vendor hit one urban inspector over the head with an electronic scale. Two pancake vendors attacked inspectors with a gas tank. The nationwide media has also reported some extreme cases involving the deaths of street vendors or urban inspectors, which has led to a heated national discussion of how to ease the tension between the two groups, and how to balance the needs of the urban poor with the pursuit of modern urban management (*People's Daily*, 2013; *Procuratorial Daily*, 2013). Indeed, in cities such as Guangzhou and Hangzhou, the authorities have become much more tolerant towards street vending. On the premise of protecting city beautification, these cities have begun exploring new ways to govern street vending, for instance by formalizing it through a registration system and permitting it during specified times and in particular areas. Even so, many vendors continue to engage in "cat-and-mouse" games with urban inspectors, as many areas of tolerance are too remote to attract business (Liang & Wu, 2014).

Musoni (2010) found street vendors to be sophisticated political thinkers when faced with suppression. Because resistance on the individual level generally has limited effectiveness, some street vendors have pursued survival through collective action (Hou, 2010; Milgram, 2014). In 2014, the Sanya government passed legislation to clean up public spaces, in preparation for the Boao Forum for Asia's annual conference;[5] as a result, a night market with over 100 food vendors was forcefully removed by urban inspectors. Mr. Zhao, one of the victims, organized a number of vendors to appeal to the SCALEB office. They represented the collective wish of all vendors on the street, and hoped to formalize their businesses and attain permanent permission. This collective action, unsurprisingly, failed. SCALEB rejected their request and the night market remained closed. Zhao dejectedly admitted his failure: "we are actually a disorderly mob. We came to consensus because of our common interests, but everyone wanted to be a free rider. I am so alone in the negotiation with the government." In contrast to successful collective resistance in other cultural settings (Cross, 1998; Crossa, 2009; Milgram, 2014), street vendors in Sanya and elsewhere have lacked the ability to come together to prevent control by the local administrative powers.

However, it is both surprising and impressive that despite the rapidly-changing political backdrop, street vending continues to exist. Crowds of peddlers immediately reemerge once the urban inspectors loosen their grip. Yet, their survival has been severely impaired by these all-too-frequent political shifts. Sanya has made considerable progress in modernizing and beautifying the city through the permanent ban of street vending on an increasing number of main streets. I conducted field studies in Sanya in 2013, 2014, and 2016; each time, I observed fewer and fewer vending stalls. In May of 2016, I revisited the vending locations of my 2014 interviewees (fifty-one in total), and found that only two remained in business at the same location. The rest had either given up or hid elsewhere in the city.

DAILY REGULATION

Exclusionary policies during political campaigns reflect one mode of control. During ordinary times, the actions of the local government regarding vendors tend to be much more mild and tolerant. Since the central government has not actually formulated a national law or regulation regrading street vending, local governments are able to design policies that fit their distinct local context. Currently, the only regional legislation regarding street vending is the Hainan Rural and Urban Appearance and Environmental Sanitation Regulations, which prohibit businesses from operating in main public spaces. The Regulations, however, also urge local governments to assign certain areas to vending stalls so as to assist vendor livelihoods and provide convenience for residents. The Regulations have created a gray zone of ambivalence in Sanya. The city government has not clarified the specific geographical areas in which street vending should be permitted; instead, it has delegated this power to the districts and neighborhoods. Though street vending is officially prohibited in the daytime on main streets, in some cases, neighborhood committees have acquiesced to street vending at night. They have tolerated street vending by canceling urban inspectors' onsite surveillance in particular areas and at certain times. However, this also means that without expressly stipulating the terms, neighborhood committees can arbitrarily recall their toleration. One watermelon vendor with ten years of experience used to trade on a street where urban inspectors stopped patrolling after 9 p.m. However, sometimes this would be later, and inspectors would linger until 10 p.m or 11 p.m. Street vendors are not notified about the neighborhood committees' plans or the urban inspectors' schedules. They must surmise, confirm, and then adjust to the "permission" granted to them, meaning their days are full of risk, careful watch, and frequent escape.

Sluggish Urban Inspectors

Based his observations in Beijing, Caron (2013) called urban inspectors' attitudes regarding street vending "revocable and unpredictable." However the control exercised by urban inspectors can actually be predicted by the intensity of the political climate. During campaign time, as government officials visit communities and streets, unofficial urban inspectors risk termination if they fail to remove the mobile peddlers. Walking the streets en masse, they often adopt a harsh attitude and fierce means, destroying vendors' tools and products if vendors do not flee. When punitive policies are being emphasized by the authorities, urban inspectors appear to be the sincerest followers of the official ideology, seriously suppressing street vendors' livelihoods.

However, this does not necessarily mean that they actually identify with the official ideology. According to interviews with Sanya urban inspectors in 2014, when the city government claimed that the "National Sanitary City" campaign would bring a high-quality living environment and long-term benefits to every common citizen, urban inspectors, especially unofficial ones, knew little – and had no intention of learning – about the details of such political propaganda. To them, such campaigns mean heavy workloads rather than political conviction. The city government invested the least amount of effort possible in educating the unofficial urban inspectors, even though they held many conferences for other governmental officials in an effort to convey the spirit of the campaign. Unofficial urban inspectors did not attend training or meetings before executing their tasks on the streets; instead, they received oral orders form the heads of their teams regarding the plan to clean up mobile vending stalls. In their view, street vending should be banned not because it impairs the city's appearance, but because it is unwanted by the government.

In the intervals between political campaigns, when neighborhood committees, the lowest level of the administration, are empowered to regulate their own regions, urban inspectors are much more relaxed. There is less stress during their daily watches because most street vendors flee when they show up; therefore, it is common to see urban inspectors wander the streets, smoking, playing on their cellphones, chatting, and chewing areca nuts. They only need to fulfill the minimum requirement, excluding vending stalls during their tour of duty. I observed an urban inspector responsible for patrolling a footbridge walking backwards and forwards; vendors on the footbridge immediately moved to the adjacent sidewalk to continue their business when the urban inspector drew close, and moved back to the footbridge when the urban inspector was out of their sight. The urban inspector did not drive the vendors away, though he could clearly see them operating on the sidewalk only meters away, because the sidewalk was not his area of responsibility. Some urban inspectors explained to me that they understood the hardships vendors faced, so they were pleased to provide spaces of survival, so long as their supervisors and policies allowed it. Thus despite the state's pursuit of modernity, urban inspectors' attitude of tolerance facilitates the ongoing existence of street vending.

Street Vendors' Strategies

To confront the surveillance and exclusion they regularly face, street vendors in Sanya have developed various strategies of resistance. The most prevalent is everyday nonviolent resistance. According to my observation, when urban inspectors approach, street vendors react immediately and retreat to safe areas such as alleys, backstreets, and underground parking lots; they restore their businesses as soon as the inspectors leave. Such a scene of "cat and mouse" occurs on Sanya's streets every day. Moreover, vendors often adopt simple facilities that allow them to pack up and leave in seconds. For instance, fruit vendors use shoulder poles to lift their baskets, and apparel vendors lay out their merchandise on a cloth on the ground, so that they can quickly wrap their goods and flee. Some use minivans or moto-tricycles as stalls. Experienced vendors who are familiar with the patrol schedules of urban inspectors can keep ahead of them and recognize them when they appear, avoiding direct encounters.

Street vendors have a tendency to gather in crowded places, and they cooperate with one another. The first person to notice an approaching inspector will yell out "they are coming" to alert the other vendors. It was observed that some vendors placed their commodities inside stores along the street, then walked out, pretending to be passersby. In response, the urban inspectors did not expose the vendors' ruse, and instead stopped chasing them. Drawing from Chiu's (2013) study on street vendor/policeman interaction in a Taiwan night market, it is appropriate to apply Ervin Goffman's performance theory to this behavior in Sanya. In this scenario, the urban inspectors served as the audience to the street vendors' performance; they had no intention of expelling the vendors, but did expect them to demonstrate their respect for authority by temporarily moving away.

Some individuals enjoy special benefits through their close relations with local officials. Studies on China have revealed that as state power became more commercialized, patron-client relationships, or "guanxi," came to replace the "comradeship" encouraged in Mao's era; this has spread widely to the nation's various entrepreneurs and government officials at the different levels of China's current bureaucratic capitalist government (Osburg, 2013; Vogel, 1989; Wank, 2001; Zhang, 2001). Not necessarily a form of corruption or resistance, such relations are instead a subordination of state power (Yang, 1994). One of my informants, Li, was a middle-aged woman running a mobile vending stall selling fried shrimp. Once Li's sister, a key official on the local community committee, discussed Li's situation with the urban inspectors, Li no longer ran the risk of being expelled. The inspectors ignored Li's business and focused instead on other vendors. Moreover, they also notified Li in advance of surprise inspections.

Vendors also use bribes to form client relationships with urban inspectors. Zhang, a 24-year old watermelon vendor, said: "They will not embarrass you if you are courteous and know the rules. When they are moving forward to me, I know it is time to buy cigarettes." Zhang also bribed the head of the local urban inspectors' team with several hundred RMB to reduce her overall number of interactions with the inspectors. Client relationships based on bribes, however, are not as strong as familial ones such as Li's. When circumstances become intense, such as during the "National Sanitary City" campaign, businesses such as Zhang's will likely be eliminated despite his close relationship with the inspectors; enterprises such as Li's, though, are likely to survive even if they need to temporarily close. Zhang's collusion with the urban inspectors can only be sustained during periods between political campaigns when urban inspectors are empowered to temporarily take a tolerant stance.

Differences in levels of connection may also lead to street vendors being treated differently by political authorities; in Hanoi, Vietnam, for instance, resident vendors are much more tenacious and resourceful than migrant vendors (Turner & Schoenberger, 2012). Compared with migrant vendors (outlanders), Hainan locals and the Hui people (Muslim Chinese) enjoy greater advantages when they deal with urban inspectors. As the state focuses on the construction of harmonious relations among the Han people, the major ethnic group in China, and other minorities, local governments strive to avoid ethnic conflicts (Gladney, 2003). Sanya's government provides comprehensive support to the Hui people, hoping to ensure social stability. I observed Hui women wearing hijabs and selling areca nuts sitting at their stalls while urban inspectors harassed other vendors in regular patrols. The advantages enjoyed by Hainan locals can be attributed to their warm personal relationships with local officials and urban inspectors. However, this priority can be retreated when exclusionary policies are enacted during campaign time.

CONCLUSIONS

In the socialist era (1949–1979), street vending was discouraged as "the tails of capitalist economies." In today's market economy, street vending is still under enormous political pressure because it has been stigmatized as unsanitary and uncivilized, and in contradiction to the state's ambition of constructing a modernized, strong, and developed China. Such a state ideology has been clearly manifested in campaigns such as "National Sanitary City" and "National Civilized City." During and subsequent to these political campaigns, the governance of street vending served to highlight two distinct patterns: exclusion and tolerance. Sanya's city government shifted its stance from exclusion to tolerance and back again, depending on the immediate political goal. As a result, street vendors have used coping strategies to survive the shifting tides.

There is a political basis for the exclusionary mode. According to John Cross (1998, p. 238), state integration refers to "the degree to which the interests of state agents are integrated with the interests of the state itself," that is, the loyalty of agents to the state's objectives. In the context of low-level state integration, state officials tend to corrupt state policies during implementation in order to pursue their own interests; accordingly, street vendors have survived and even flourished because they relied on their client relationships with state officials. During national campaigns, even though there may be a substantial gap between the state's goal and local officials' interests, *de facto* state integration has been achieved, as evidenced by the local government's contribution of energy and resources to enforcing the state's ideology. As many researchers have remarked, the overwhelming power held by the state has not been reduced by the current free market force in China (Farquhar, 2002; Huang, 2008; Zhang, 2001). In todays' China, the state's political propaganda must be put into practice by local bureaucratic apparatuses, no matter what the form.

Why does tolerance exist? At the city level, the official intention of the campaigns has mutated. From the perspective of local leaders, these campaigns offer excellent opportunities to accumulate personal political capital for future promotion, rather than bring benefits to the people. Consequently, the campaigns have been distorted into illusory political shows, during which street vending has been forcefully abolished. Urban inspectors, as the actual actors in these policies, do not universally identify with the state's ideology. In their understanding, the inspection of street vendors is a responsibility inherent to their job, and not at all associated with the dream of modernity. Moreover, beyond the state's political movements, when local governments and lower-level political organizations are able to design flexible policies to regulate street vendors, tolerance and ambivalence exist; additionally, the corruption and laziness of urban inspectors provides niches for the revival of street vendors after campaigns are over, though with limitations.

In Sanya, the presence of street vendors continues to be threatened by political campaigns, as well as by the ever-quickening pace of constructed modernity. This is not a unique phenomenon; a number of cities in China have gone through or are replicating Sanya's experience, which seems to indicate a gloomy future for street vending. The current dilemma, however, should be attributed not only to unsupportive politics, but also to the intrinsic political weakness of street vendor groups. Though street vendors use a variety of strategies to resist the authorities, their effectiveness is restricted, especially when exclusionary policies are enacted. As of now, collective resistance, as evidenced by the night market story, is still in its infancy; loose street vendor organizations are not strong enough to fight powerful government forces. If street vendors cannot develop vigorous associations in the near future, they may have to anchor their hopes in changes in the authority's attitude.

Could street vending be totally eliminated in a contemporary China? Many studies have commented upon the complexity of the relationship between the state and street vendors. Smith (1988), for example, argued that though the state lost tax income from street vendors, their relationship is not necessarily conflictive, considering that street vendors are able to provide services and resources that supplement state-owned channels. As early as the 1970s, McGee and Yeung (1977, p. 116), forerunners in the formal study of street hawkers, advocated that vendors must be accepted as a face of urban life and integrated into the retailing system, as they had numerous links (e.g., personnel, goods, information) with the formal sector. For example, the hawker centers located in Singapore bring vitality to the city, and represent a successful mode of governance of street vending (Ghani, 2011). Many recent studies also argued that street vending remains embedded in an increasingly modernized and developed setting (Cross, 2000; Gaber, 1994; Turner & Schoenberger, 2012).

In my opinion, street vending will remain a substantial and long-term livelihood in today's China. First, growing urbanization will not only increase the rural-urban gap, but also force a massive number of peasant migrants to the cities; street vending provides one of the most vital livelihoods for this particular group. In other words, it is unlikely to disappear so long as rural-to-urban migration continues. Second, as distinguished from residential areas in other developed countries that feature suburbanization, cities in China – including Sanya – tend to have concentrated populations in their downtown cores. Factors such as the locations of residential spaces and the low rate of private vehicle ownership force urban dwellers to seek their entertainment, services, and material provisions on the street. It is, more than anything else, urban residents' practical needs that ensure the vitality of street vending in China. As Bromley (2000, p. 22) says, "Only the most authoritarian regimes have tried to eliminate it, and they have generally failed." The Sanya case demonstrates the improbability of completely excluding street vending. Nevertheless, given the current state-mandated punitive ideology, it is also valid to argue that street vendors in China will continue to face arduous struggles.

NOTES

1. All vendor names presented in this paper are pseudonyms.
2. According to the international exchange rate in June of 2017, 1 RMB was approximately equal to $0.15 USD.
3. Sanya was called Tianya in ancient China.
4. Currently, Sanya is divided into four districts, with a varying number of neighborhoods in each district.
5. The Boao Forum for Asia, also known as the Asian Davos, is a non-profit organization that hosts high-level forums for government leaders and officials in other areas to promote regional economic integration. Its conference is held annually in Bo'ao in Hainan Province, a town 180 kilometers away from Sanya City.

ACKNOWLEDGMENTS

The fieldwork was funded by the Department of Anthropology at Texas A&M University and the Melbern G. Glasscock Center for Humanities Research. I sincerely thank the two institutions for their generous support. I am deeply indebted to Jingjing Xie of Sanya University, who worked as my research assistant in 2014 and helped me to conduct interviews. I would also like to express my profound gratitude to Dr. Norbert Dannhaeuser and Dr. Cynthia Werner for their valuable comments on earlier drafts. Some of the findings were presented at the 2015 annual conference of the American Anthropological Association in Washington, D.C. and the Thirteenth Graduate Seminar on China held at the Chinese University of Hong Kong in 2017. Many thanks to the audience members and colleagues who offered me useful suggestions after these presentations.

REFERENCES

Anjaria, J. S. (2006). Street hawkers and public space in Mumbai. *Economic and Political Weekly*, May 27, pp. 2140–2146.

Asiedu, A. B., & Agyei-Mensah, S. (2008). Traders on the run: Activities of street vendors in the Accra Metropolitan Area, Ghana. *Norsk Geografisk Tidsskrift* [Norwegian Journal of Geography], *62*(3), 191–202.

Bayat, A. (2004). Globalization and the politics of the informal in the Global South. In A. Roy & N. AlSayyad (Eds.), *Urban informality: Transnational perspectives from the Middle East, Latin America, and South Asia* (pp. 79–104). Lanham, MD: Lexington Books.

Bhowmik, S. K. (2005). Street vendors in Asia: A review. *Economic and Political Weekly*, May 28–June 4, pp. 2256–2264.

Brødsgaard, K. E. (2009). *Hainan: State, society, and business in a Chinese Province*. Abingdon: Routledge.

Bromley, R. (2000). Street vending and public policy: A global review. *International Journal of Sociology and Social Policy*, *20*(1/2), 1–28.

Caron, E. (2013). Interactions between *chengguan* and street vendors in Beijing: How the unpopularity of an administration affects relations with the public. China. Perspectives, *1*, 17–28.

Chen, L., & Yu, J. (2010). Street business should be strictly managed. *Sanya Daily*, January 14, p. 3.

Chen, R. (2001). Street markets need regulation. *Sanya Daily*, July 23, p. 2.

Chen, Y. (1956). Problems regarding Socialist transformation of private commerce. *People's Daily*, June 19, p. 3.

Chiu, C. (2013). Informal management, interactive performance: Street vendors and police in a Taipei night market. *International Development Planning Review*, *35*(4), 335–352.

Contemporary Chinese Commerce Editorial Office (1990). *Chronicle of events: China's Commerce 1958-1978*. Beijing: China Commercial Publishing House.

Cross, J. (1998). *Informal politics: Street vendors and the state in Mexico City*. Stanford, CA: Stanford University Press.

Cross, J. (2000). Street vendors, and postmodernity: Conflict and compromise in the global economy. *International Journal of Sociology and Social Policy*, *20*(1/2), 29–51.

Crossa, V. (2009). Resisting the entrepreneurial city: Street vendor's struggle in Mexico City's historic center. *International Journal of Urban and Regional Research*, *33*(1), 43–63.

Crossa, V. (2016). Reading for difference on the street: De-homogenizing street vending in Mexico City. *Urban Studies*, 1–15. doi:10.1177/0042098014563471

Dutton, M. R. (1998). *Streetlife China*. Cambridge: Cambridge University Press.

Endres, K. W. (2014). Downgraded by upgrading: Small-scale traders, urban transformation and spatial reconfiguration in post-reform Vietnam. *Cambridge Anthropology*, *32*(2), 97–111.

Fang, T. (1955). The change of rural markets. *People's Daily*, February 8, p. 2.

Farquhar, J. (2002). *Appetites: Food and sex in post-socialist China*. Durham: Duke University Press.

Feng, X. (2011). The marginal men in Socialism: Petty traders around 1956. In H. Gang (Ed.), *Studies of Contemporary Chinese History* (pp. 3–45). Beijing: Jiuzhou Press.

Gaber, J. (1994). Manhattan's 14th Street vendors' market: Informal street peddlers' complementary relationship with New York City's economy. *Urban Anthropology and Studies of Cultural Systems and World Economic Development*, *23*(4), 373–408.

Ghani, A. (2011). A recipe for success: How Singapore Hawker Centres came to be. *IPS Update*. Retrieved from https://lkyspp.nus.edu.sg/ips/wp-content/uploads/sites/2/2013/08/AG_history-of-hawkers_010511.pdf. Accessed on January 9, 2017.

Gladney, D. C. (2003). Islam in China: Accommodation or separatism? *The China Quarterly*, *174*, 451–467.

Guan, D. (1962). Commercial work needs to better serve production and consumption. *People's Daily*, October 23, p. 5.

Hansen, K. T. (2004). Who rules the streets? The politics of vending space in Lusaka. In K. T. Hansen & M. Vaa (Eds.), *Reconsidering informality: Perspective from urban Africa* (pp. 62–80). Spain: Grafilur Artes Graficas.

Hanser, A. (2016). Street politics: Street vendors and urban Governance in China. *The China Quarterly*, 1–20. doi:10.1017/S0305741016000278

Hou, J. (2010). Not your everyday public space. In J. Hou (Ed.), *Insurgent public space: Guerrilla urbanism and the remaking of contemporary cities* (pp. 1–17). London: Routledge.

Hsu, C. (2010). "Making streets": Planned space and unplanned business in New Kujiang, Taiwan. *City & Society*, *22*(2), 286–308.

Hu, Y. (2007a). When street business will be ended? *Sanya Daily*, June 25, p. 2.

Hu, Y. (2007b). Sanya officially announced to apply "National Sanitary City". *Sanya Daily*, July 20, p. 1.

Hu, Y. (2007c). Sanya passed the expert panel's secret examination for "National Sanitary City". *Sanya Daily*, December 19, p. 1.

Hu, Y. (2008). Sanya passed the state's second examination for "National Sanitary City". *Sanya Daily*, March 28, p. 1.

Hu, Y. (2009a). Confronting the final state examination for "National Sanitary City": Sanya strives to improve city appearance. *Sanya Daily*, March 17, p. 1.

Hu, Y. (2009b). Chronicle of events: Sanya constructing "National Sanitary City". *Sanya Daily*, October 16, 2.

Huang, G., Xue, D., & Li, Z. (2014). From revanchism to ambivalence: The changing politics of street vending in Guangzhou. *Antipode.*, *46*(1), 170–189.

Huang, Y. (2008). *Capitalism with Chinese characteristics: Entrepreneurship and the state*. Cambridge: Cambridge University Press.

Liang, Y., & Wu, G. (2014). Guangzhou tried to construct tolerance areas for mobile vendors. *Yangcheng Evening News*, July 28. Retrieved from http://news.ycwb.com/2014-07/28/content_7314601.htm. Accessed on May 29, 2016.

Lincoln, M. (2008). Report from the field: Street vendors and the informal sector in Hanoi. *Dialectical Anthropology*, *32*(3), 261–265.

Liu, X., & Quan, M. (1955). How street vendors organized themselves in Daguan. *People's Daily*, April 26, p. 2.

Mao, Z. (1957). On the correct handling of contradiction among the people. *People's Daily*, June 19, p. 1.

McGee, T. G., & Yeung, Y. M. (1977). *Hawkers in Southeast Asian cities: Planning for the bazaar economy*. Ottawa: International Development Research Centre.

Meisner, M. (1999). *Mao's China and after: A history of the People's Republic*. New York, NY: Simon and Schuster.

Milgram, L. B. (2014). Remapping the edge: Informality and legality in the Harrison Road Night Market, Baguio City, Philippines. *City & Society*, *26*(2), 153–174.

Milgram, L. B. (2015). Unsettling urban marketplace redevelopment in Baguio City, Philippines. *Economic Anthropology*, *2*(1), 22–41.

Ministry of Commerce, P.R.C. (1970). The direction of the Socialist commerce. *People's Daily*, October 19, p. 2.

Musoni, F. (2010). Operation Murambatsvina and the politics of street vendors in Zimbabwe. *Journal of Southern African Studies*, *36*(2), 301–317.

Osburg, J. (2013). *Anxious wealth: Money and morality among China's new rich*. Stanford, CA: Stanford University Press.

Patriotic health Committee. (2015, September 16). *The assessment and regulation of National Sanitary City*. Retrieved from http://www.nhfpc.gov.cn/jkj/s5898/201509/a758669061fd469aa3a754c8781acae4.shtml. Accessed on January 10, 2017.

People's Daily. (1954). Enhancing the material exchange between cities and countryside. *People's Daily*, April 11, p.1.

People's Daily. (1955). Transforming small vendors through mutual cooperation. *People's Daily*, February 4, p. 1.

People's Daily. (1956a). The State Council's notification regarding the Socialist transformation of private commerce. *People's Daily*, July 30, p. 1.

People's Daily. (1956b). Shanxi province prepared to reopen the free market. *People's Daily*, December 24, p. 3.

People's Daily. (1958a). The rapid growth of commodity in markets of Jilin City. *People's Daily*, December 11, p. 1.

People's Daily. (1958b). Focusing on the production of provision of food. *People's Daily*, December 28, p. 1.

People's Daily. (2003). National civilized city award: Questions and answers. *People's Daily*, September 9. Retrieved from http://politics.people.com.cn/BIG5/1026/3683208.html. Accessed on May 26, 2016.

People's Daily, (2013). Out of "chenguan" dilemma. *People's Daily*, August 27. Retrieved from http://www.gov.cn/jrzg/2013-08/27/content_2474496.htm. Accessed on May 28, 2016.

Procuratorial Daily. (2013). Chengguan: What course to follow? *Procuratorial Daily*, July 31. Retrieved from http://news.xinhuanet.com/politics/2013-07/31/c_125092895.htm. Accessed on May 28, 2016.

Reid, D. M., Fram, E. H., & Guotai, C. (2010). A study of Chinese street vendors: How they operate. *Journal of Asia-Pacific Business*, *11*(4), 244–257.

Sanya City Government. (2008, October 25). *The special project of creating National Sanitary City*. Retrieved from http://www.fae.cn/fg/detail321499.html. Accessed on April 26, 2016.

Sanya City Statistics Office. (2016, March 30). *The average income*. Retrieved from http://www.systats.gov.cn/tjsj/tjnj/2015/14/201603/t20160330_1823256.html. Accessed on January 10, 2017.

Skinner, W. G. (1984). Rural marketing in China: Revival and reappraisal. In S. Plattner (Ed.), *Markets and marketing* (pp. 7–48). Lanham: University Press of America.

Smart, J. (1989). *The political economy of street hawkers in Hong Kong*. Hong Kong: University of Hong Kong Press.

Smith, M. E. (1988). Overview: The informal economy and the state. In G. Clark (Ed.), *Traders versus the state: Anthropological approaches to unofficial economies* (pp. 189–199). London: Westview Press.

Smith, N. (1996). *The new urban frontier: Gentrification and the revanchist city*. London: Routledge.

Solinger, D. J. (1987). *Chinese business under socialism: The politics of domestic commerce, 1949–1980*. Berkeley, CA: University of California Press.

Solinger, D. J. (2013). Streets as suspect: State skepticism and the current losers in urban China. *Critical Asian Studies*, *45*(1), 3–26.

Su, Y., & Chen, W. (1998). Model streets become beautiful after banning mobile vendors. *Sanya Daily*, May 28, p. 1.

Sun, J. (1957). Problems on opening the free market of vegetables. *People's Daily*, February 21, p. 3.

Sun, Q. (2009). Banning street business. *Sanya Daily*, July 4, p. 2.

Swanson, K. (2007). Revanchist urbanism heads South: The regulation of indigenous beggars and street vendors in Ecuador. *Antipode*, 708–728.

The State Council of PRC. (1989, March 7). *The State Council's decision on strengthening the patriotic health work*. Retrieved from http://www.nnws.gov.cn/CL0076/171.html. Accessed on May 26, 2016.

The State Council of PRC. (2015, December 8). *The winner list of "National Sanitary City" in 2015*. Retrieved from http://www.gov.cn/xinwen/2015-12/08/content_5021061.htm?from=androidqq. Accessed on January 10, 2017.

Timalsina, K. P. (2011). An urban informal economy: Livelihood opportunity to poor or challenges for urban governance, study of street vending activities of Kathmandu metropolitan city. *International Journal of Politics and Good Governance*, *2*(2), 1–13.

Turner, S., & Schoenberger, L. (2012). Street vendor livelihoods and everyday politics in Hanoi, Vietnam the seeds of a diverse economy? *Urban Studies*, *49*(5), 1027–1044.

Vogel, E. F. (1989). *One step ahead in China: Guangdong under reform*. Cambridge, MA: Harvard University Press.

Wang, H., Chu, Y., & Tao, X. (1957). Need to greatly transform the ideology of small vendors. *People's Daily*, May 24, p. 3.

Wank, D. L. (2001). *Commodifying communism: Business, trust, and politics in a Chinese city*. Cambridge: Cambridge University Press.

Whyte, M. K., & Parish, W. L. (1985). *Urban life in contemporary China*. Chicago, IL: University of Chicago Press.

Wilson, T. (2014). Self-employed women in the informal economy: Beach vendors in Acapulco. In D. C. Wood (Ed.), *Production, consumption, business and the economy: Structural ideals and moral realities* (Vol. 34, pp. 269–292). Research in Economic Anthropology. Bingley: Emerald Group Publishing Limited.

Wu, Q. (2015). Street markets push pedestrians away. Sanya Daily, December 28, p. 4.

Xi, P. (1956). Shanghai City reopen the state-led free market. People's Daily, November 15, p. 3.

Yang, M. (1994). *Gifts, favors, and banquets: The art of social relationships in China*. Ithaca, NY: Cornell University Press.

Zhang, L. (2001). *Strangers in the city: Reconfigurations of space, power, and social networks within China's floating population*. Stanford, CA: Stanford University Press.

Zhou, E. (1957). Strengthening the Socialist transformation of individual farmers. *People's Daily*, December 22, p. 1.

APPENDIX: BACKGROUND CHARACTERISTICS OF INTERVIEWED VENDORS

Case	Gender	Age	Place of Birth	Education	Years of Business	Goods Sold
1	Male	66	Hainan	High school	30	Watches
2	Male	25	Hainan	High school		Mobile phone cases
3	Male	31	Hainan	Middle school	2	Watches
4	Female	36	Mainland	College	0.3	Hats
5	Female	58	Hainan		10	Fruit
6	Female	33	Hainan	Illiterate	13	Fruit
7	Female	20	Mainland	Middle school	0.2	Cooked food
8	Male	32	Mainland	Middle school	5	Belts
9	Female	60	Mainland	Middle school	1.5	Cooked food
10	Male	39	Mainland	Middle school	7	Fortune teller
11	Male	38	Mainland	Primary school	10	Flowers
12	Male	21	Hainan	Middle school	4	Umbrellas
13	Male	50	Hainan	Primary school		Milk tea
14	Couple	32/33	Hainan	Middle school	10	Cooked food
15	Male	38	Mainland	High school	5	Photos
16	Female	57	Hainan	Illiterate	30	Vegetables
17	Female	40	Hainan	Illiterate		Fruit
18	Couple	60/62	Hainan			Fruit
19	Male	23	Mainland	Primary school	0.5	Balloons
20	Male	30	Mainland	College	5	Socks
21	Male	33	Mainland	Middle school	10	Accessories
22	Female	30	Hainan	Middle school	0.1	Apparel
23	Male	33	Mainland	Middle school	0.5	Balloons
24	Male	70	Mainland	Illiterate	10	Fruit
25	Couple	40/47	Mainland	Primary school	20	Apparel
26	Male	26	Mainland	Primary school	0.9	Fruit
27	Couple	29/33	Hainan	Illiterate	0.2	Fruit
28	Male	35	Mainland	Illiterate	0.4	Fruit
29	Female	40	Hainan	Primary school	3	Fruit
30	Male	42	Hainan	Primary school	4	Cooked food
31	Male	32	Hainan	Middle school	8	Video tapes
32	Female	31	Hainan		0.3	Fruit
33	Couple	21/21	Hainan	Middle school	0.3	Snacks
34	Male	25	Hainan	High school	0.1	Drinks
35	Female	23	Mainland	High school	1	Hats

(Continued)

Case	Gender	Age	Place of Birth	Education	Years of Business	Goods Sold
36	Male	33	Mainland	Middle school	4	Apparel
37	Male	50	Mainland	Primary school	1	Cooked food
38	Male	36	Mainland	College	0.5	Milk tea
39	Male	46	Mainland	High school	1	Cooked food
40	Male	62	Mainland	Primary school	18	Artwork
41	Female	43	Hainan	Middle school	10	Fruit
42	Female	50	Mainland	Middle school	4	Fruit
43	Male	23	Hainan	Middle school	5	Mobile phone cases
44	Female	27	Hainan	Primary school	2	Fruit
45	Female	44	Hainan	Illiterate	0.5	Fruit
46	Female	19	Hainan	Middle school		Hats
47	Female	62	Hainan	Primary school	30	Fruit
48	Female	46	Mainland	Primary school	10	Fruit
49	Female	35	Hainan	Middle school	0.5	Cooked food
50	Couple	54/55	Mainland		1	Cooked food
51	Female	34	Hainan	Middle school	0.5	Accessories

SONS OF PEASANTS ON THE BEACH: VENDORS IN CABO SAN LUCAS, MEXICO

Tamar Diana Wilson

ABSTRACT

Purpose – *To summarize the shocks and stresses that peasants in Mexico have been subjected to since the 1940s and to examine the responses of sons of peasants working as semi-informal beach vendors in Cabo San Lucas as to what they define as the worst problems of the peasantry in their hometowns.*

Methodology/approach – *This chapter offers an analysis of the responses of 32 sons of peasants interviewed on Medano Beach in Cabo San Lucas in October of 2012 partially as concerns whether they would like to be peasants themselves and as to what they define as the worst problems of the peasantry in their hometowns.*

Findings – *Twenty-five of the thirty-two vendors interviewed would be happy to be peasants. According to all of the vendors, the overwhelming problems facing the peasantry were primarily droughts or floods (related to climate change) and lack of government aid (related to neoliberalization).*

Social implications – *The peasantry in Mexico is being and has been marginalized both by a number of stresses and shocks, currently identified*

Anthropological Considerations of Production, Exchange, Vending and Tourism
Research in Economic Anthropology, Volume 37, 205–229

ISSN: 0190-1281/doi:10.1108/S0190-128120170000037010

by some of those at risk as factors related to climate change and neoliberalization.

Keywords: Peasants; climate change; neoliberalization; migration; informal economy; beach vendors

INTRODUCTION

Since World War II, peasants in Mexico have been subjected to a number of stresses and shocks, often taking the form of transnational corporate invasions, that have marginalized ever greater numbers of them. While in the wake of these shocks, some became capitalist farmers as the middle-peasantry differentiated, for many of them this was only a temporary status until another shock drove them or their progeny off the land or into off-farm income-generating activities. Many peasants and small farmers – both of whom consider themselves *campesinos* as do all who work the land – rely and have relied on an off-farm income to subsidize their farms, whether in the form of migrant remittances, salaried work or petty entrepreneurial activities in the formal, semi-informal, or informal economies, or as a rural proletariat for larger farmers and agribusiness.

Among the many shocks the Mexican peasantry has been subjected to were the post World War II Green Revolution and the neoliberal structural adjustment policies of the 1980s – which eventually led to the entry of Mexico into the General Agreement on Tariffs and Trade in 1986, the 1992 reform of the Article 27 of the Mexican Constitution concerning *ejido*[1] and indigenous *comunidad agraria*[2] rights and the initiation of North American Free Trade Agreement (NAFTA), the free trade agreement between Mexico, Canada, and the United States in 1994. More recently, the second green revolution, spearheaded by large biotechnology corporations and sometimes accompanied by land-grabbing, has impacted the peasantry, as has climate change which provokes more droughts and/or flooding.

In this chapter, I will first summarize some of the before mentioned shocks that have marginalized much of the Mexican peasantry, though these are not the only shocks they have been subjected to. Second, I will look at the results of interviews with 32 beach vendors in the semi-informal economy who hawk their wares to tourists in Cabo San Lucas,[3] one of the most vibrant tourist centers in Mexico. All those interviewed were sons of *campesinos* – which can be translated as "peasants" but in their view included anyone who works in the agricultural fields, whether as a small capitalist farmer, a subsistence farmer, or as a field hand. Most offered the information that they had worked on their father's fields, and it is to be expected that they were exposed to family and community lore about farming. These beach vendors can be considered petty entrepreneurs, and most of them would like to be *campesinos* if they were given the opportunity. They are not completely informal, but rather semi-informal, since they must acquire licenses from the municipal government in order to operate, renew them every year, and show that they have paid taxes as part of the process of renewal. They also belong to one of the five unions concerned with organizing beach vendors. As will be seen below, many of those who were driven from the countryside would be happy to return if conditions were favorable. Many mentioned the lack of money or lack of government aid, both referring to the current lack of credits, loans, or other supports for small-scale agriculture.

Notably, although there were daughters of campesinos among the beach vendors, I concentrated on male beach vendors because passing the land to a son is the preferred inheritance practice in Mexico. The normal practice is to leave the land to the youngest son, or, alternatively, the son most willing to farm the family plot. This is especially true of communally held but often individually tenured *ejido* plots. Two of the few exceptions are the passing of land to widows in the case of the existence of only minor children, or to a daughter in the rare case of the family's not having a son. In the case of large private property owners, the land may sometimes be split up and bequeathed to all offspring, however.

It is important to note that the decades from the late 1930s until 1980 were the period of the "Mexican Miracle," when import substitutions policies led to a strong growth of the economy. Although in this chapter, I will be looking at the "push" factors that have marginalized the peasantry and led to their out-migration from rural regions, the dynamics of import substitution policies must be mentioned as constituting a "pull" factor. Import substitution policies pulled people into manufacturing activities primarily in a few large cities, such as Mexico City, Guadalajara, and Monterrey and led to massive urbanization (Garza, 2002, pp. 9–11; Portes & Roberts, 2005, pp. 44–45). Many of the rural-to-urban migrants could not find employment in these capital-intensive industries, however, and were forced to find work in the informal economy – characterized as work situations not covered by labor laws (Portes & Roberts, 2005, p. 44) – whether as waged workers or as self-employed entrepreneurs.

The growth of secondary cities centered on manufacturing was also important, as Garza (2002) underscores. Furthermore, beginning in the 1960s, Mexico began developing its sun and beach tourist centers, such as Cancún and Los Cabos, as well, which led to migration from their rural hinterlands as well as other rural regions to these cities (Castellanos, 2010; Clancy, 2001; Wilson, 2008; Wilson, 2012a, pp. 6–8). Mexican immigration to the United States, spurred on by the Bracero Program of 1942–1964, also constituted a cross border pull factor that affected many rural regions and fomented undocumented immigration as well (Massey, Alarcón, Durand, & González, 1987). After the close of the Bracero Program, the Border Industrialization Program was begun, under which foreign owned *maquiladoras* (assembly plants) were located initially and primarily in U.S.–Mexico border cities such as Ciudad

Júarez, Tijuana, and Mexicali. These border cities grew rapidly, pulling in many migrants from other parts of Mexico (Sklair, 1993). In the following section, I will emphasize the shocks and stresses that uprooted peasants from the land, thus concentrating on push rather than pull factors.

THE CONTEXT: SHOCKS TO PEASANTS/SMALL FARMERS IN MEXICO

Since the 1940s, the Mexican peasantry has been hit by a succession of shocks. These include the effects of the Green Revolution and newer biotechnological invasions; of neoliberalization leading to the reform of the 1917 agrarian reform law; and of the entry of Mexico into the NAFTA (which was accompanied by the elimination of many governmental subsidies for peasant–farmers); and climate change leading to drought. Many peasants were forced to migrate to Mexican cities or internationally, whether temporarily or permanently. Although many became wage laborers, others took up semi-informal or informal income-generating activities.

The Green Revolution

In many instances, peasant dispossession and marginalization have been due to corporate invasions. The first corporate invasion of Mexican agriculture occurred in the early 1940s with the introduction of the Green Revolution package of hybrid seeds and chemical fertilizers, herbicides, and pesticides. This agricultural revolution was initiated, financed, and publicized by the Rockerfeller and Ford Foundations and the World Bank. These are institutions that – as Segrelles (2013, pp. 95–96) points out – represented the interests of those transnational corporations that supplied the various items in the package. As Ross (2003, p. 440) underscores:

> Whatever the public discourse, behind the scenes the Green Revolution had never been regarded by those who managed it as primarily about helping peasants to produce more food but rather about creating a global food system in which peasant agriculture, widely regarded as backward and unproductive in the context of a modern market economy was subordinated to a more commercial and capital-intensive mode of production.

Predicated on large-scale monocropping on irrigated land and on the utilization of hybridized seeds, pesticides, herbicides, and fertilizers as well as tractors and other farm machinery, the Green Revolution package was of value to large-scale farmers, especially those in the northern regions of Mexico, but ignored the needs of the capital-poor small peasants who lived primarily in the central and southern states (Hewitt de Alcántara, 1978; see also Chrispeels, 2000, pp. 3–4).

Many critical commentators agree that although the imported technological package led to higher yields, it nonetheless reinforced and led to even greater inequalities in the countryside (Otero, 1999, p. 66; Otero & Pechlaner, 2008; Segrelles, 2013, pp. 98–99; Sonnenfeld, 1992, p. 34). The results of the introduction and ongoing use of the Green Revolution package took several decades to evolve. Between 1960 and 1970, the following pattern became clear:

> [T]he middle units appear to be going bankrupt, thus reinforcing the polarization of agriculture; both the semiproletarian and bourgeoise sectors are increasing, while there is a disappearing middle group. Moreover, a large proportion of the former peasants or semiproletarians simply fell out of the analysis: They are ex-peasants who cannot hold onto at least a semiproletarian position and have become day laborers or have moved to the cities (Otero, 1999, p. 66).

Semi-proletarianization, or the recurrent migration of peasants into off-farm income-generating activities for a portion of the year or for several years at a time, was for some the first step in full proletarianization. Not only were differences between large and small farmers sharpened in a Leninist model of predicting the differentiation of the peasantry, but throughout Latin America even more problems emerged in rural areas, which were accentuated by the export of biotechnology – with its promotion of genetically modified, not just hybrid, seeds – more recently (Segrelles, 2013). Among them were greater land concentration, impoverishment of the countryside, the dispossession of the peasantry leading to their forced exodus, technological dependence on agroindustry and transnational capital flows which increased national debt, and destruction of the ecosystem as monocropping replaced a diverse system of intercropping (Segrelles, 2013, pp. 97–99) under both the regimes of Green Revolutions and the more recent biotechnological revolution.

The transnational capital accumulation that the Green Revolution effected impacted the offspring of small farmers and peasants – whether *ejidatarios* or small property owners or beneficiaries of communal lands, and whether indigenous or mestizo. These agriculturalists are also being affected in a similar manner by present developments in biotechnology, pushed to an even greater extent by the same transnational corporations that profited from Green Revolution packages, and causing an accentuation of the socioeconomic changes that were propelled by the Green Revolution (Otero, 2013, pp. 56, 60; Otero & Pechlaner, 2008).

Under both the Green Revolution and the newer biotechnology revolution that began in the 1990s, many peasants and their offspring were forced into a recurrent, temporary, or permanent migration stream, whether to the United States or to Mexican primary and secondary cities (Otero, 2013, p. 62). Although most attention has been paid to migration steams to the United States, it is notable that between 1960 and 1980, the urban population rose from 50.75% to 66.34% (IndexMundi, 2012, pp. b4–b5). This trend toward rural–urban migration would continue under further shocks to the agricultural economy and constituted push factors.

Rural-to-urban migration within Mexico increased over the course of the century. In 1990, eight years after neoliberal structural adjustment policies were instituted, the urban population rose to 71.42% and in 2000, six years after the initiation of NAFTA and eight years after the reform to Article 27 of the Mexican Constitution, to 74.72%. By 2010, 77.83% of the population was urban. This is despite the fact that even with rapid decreases in the birthrate over the last decades, rural women have always had, and continue to have, more children per capita than urban women, so that natural increase is higher in the countryside (Romo Viramontes & Sánchez Castillo, 2012; Zavala de Cosio, 2014).

The Green Revolution was a shock that led to further differentiation of the peasantry, with only capitalist and semi-proletarian peasant families able to continue on the land. Meanwhile, the middle farmers, often dependent on remittances from circular migration, were differentiating into capitalist and semi-proletarianized and proletarianized segments. Left without sufficient government subsidies, small- and medium-sized farmers, especially ejidatarios, took part as contracted labor in the U.S. agricultural fields under the Bracero Program of 1942–1964 in order to earn capital to invest in farming (Massey et al., 1987, pp. 55, 74). Between 1960 and 1970 the middle peasantry was disappearing and many peasants were converted from semi-proletarians to full-time laborers (Otero, 1999, p. 66). Many landless peasants joined the migration stream to the United States (Massey et al., 1987, pp. 61–62) – among, whom, it can be conjectured, were the offspring of small farmers and semi-proletarianized peasants or were non-inheriting sons of ejidatarios. Furthermore, permanent rural-to-urban migration within Mexico increased, with almost 9% more people living in Mexican cities in 1970 than had done so in 1960 (IndexMundi, 2012, p. 4). This tendency was reinforced more recently by climate changes that augments the periodic droughts and periodic flooding that has been the bane of the Mexican countryside historically (Appendini & Liverman, 1994, p. 149), and destroy crops, thereby making small farming less viable as a subsistence strategy. Furthermore, pesticide and fertilizer run offs have led to environmental degradation in the form of water pollution and, in the case of the monocropping of some grains, common in northern Mexico, to methane emissions, one of the greenhouse gases fueling climate change (Altieri & Nicholls, 2001, p. 126; Jorgenson, 2006).

Neoliberalism and Its Discontents

In the 1970s, boosted by high oil prices, "petro dollars" fueled loans to developing countries at low interest rates. Partially because of the steep rise in interest rates at the beginning of the 1980s, and partially because of the fall in oil prices (Mexico's number one export being petroleum products) Mexico declared in 1982 that the country could no longer service its debt (Vázquez Castillo, 2004, p. 79). The reaction of the International Monetary Fund, the World Bank, and the U.S. Treasury was to impose structural adjustment policies with the stated aim of making the Mexican economy more competitive. These policies, informed by neoliberalism, included the liberalizing trade, the undercutting of organized labor and the erosion of labor rights, the privatization of national industries, cutbacks in subsides and welfare programs and, in general, minimizing the role of the state in the market except for a role in facilitating competition and capital mobility (Brenner & Theodore, 2002).

The "neoliberalization" (Brenner and Theodore's term) of Mexico took place over several decades. In the beginning, the imposed structural adjustment policies included pressuring Mexico to enter GATT in 1986, and thus open its economy to liberalized commerce through lowering tariffs and elimination subsidies for exported goods (Ortiz Wadgymar, 1986) – including agricultural exports.

By 1992, under President Salinas de Gortari (1988–1994), a reform of Article 27 of the Mexican Constitution was put into effect. As Vázquez Castillo (2004, p. 76) comments:

> ... the transformation of Article 27 of the 1917 Constitution, and consequently of land policy in Mexico ... was one of the various requirements established in the structural adjustment programs designed by financial global institutions – the World Bank, the IMF, and private banks – in order to transform Mexico's economy and enable it to pay and renegotiate its debt, and to continue to be eligible for loans.

Article 27 had bestowed communally held agricultural lands, often individually tenured, to landless peasants with the proviso that they could not sell, rent, or mortgage them, or leave them uncultivated for more than two years. These lands were known as ejidos and their possessors as *ejidatarios*. The article also recognized the *comunidades agrarias* – indigenous agrarian communities – that had held land in common prior to the 1910–1917 Revolution. Among the changes that the reform of Article 27 encompassed were that ejidatarios could now rent, mortgage, or sell (this latter with the permission of the ejido assembly) their lands; they could enter into joint ventures with individuals and private companies; they could sign production contracts with outsiders; and they could form associations to maximize economies of scale (Cornelius & Myhre, 1998, pp. 3–4; see also Foley, 1995, pp. 65–66). Furthermore, foreign direct investment became permissible as well as the "formation of production associations between foreign private investors and ejidatarios" would be permitted, with the proviso that foreign investors would "be limited to 49 percent of equity capital" (Cornelius & Myhre, 1998, p. 4). Meanwhile, support prices for crops were removed, subsidized credit for small and medium peasants was eliminated, and fertilizers and seeds, once supplied through government sources, were privatized (Appendini & Liverman, 1994, p. 161).

The government fostered privatization of both the ejidos and communidades agrarias, with special attention given to the ejidos. In 1993 PROCEDE (Program for Certification of Ejidal Rights) was introduced to certify the boundaries of ejido and indigenous agrarian communities (comunidades agrarias), and of individually tenured plots that may have existed within them. The ejidatarios voted on whether their ejido lands would be certified or not. The program ran until 2003 when PROCEDE had mapped and certified 91.3 percent of the land in both types of communities, with lesser participation by indigenous agrarian nuclei (Kelly, Herlihy, Viera, Smith, & Hernández Cendejas, 2010, pp. 165, 171). Only a minority of the communities moved on to full private ownership (*domino pleno*) (Kelly et al., 2010, p. 165) – an option they could chose after certification and a move that entails the payment of property taxes (Cornelius, 1998, p. 237). This meant that property taxes would be paid for the first time since the establishment of the ejido. Private titling also means that the land can be taken over by a bank in case of a loan default (Smith, Herlihy, Kelly, & Viera, 2009, p. 197). Notably, in the highly indigenous states of Chiapas, Oaxaca, and Guerrero, lower than average percentages of communities followed through with land certification (de Ita, 2006, p. 156). Conversion to private property was also resisted among indigenous peoples in San Luís Potosí and Oaxaca. This limited conversion "is due in part to the fact that for indigenous peoples ... communal lands are not merely an economic asset and a commodity that can be sold, but rather a core element of their identity, social organization, and way of life" (Smith et al., 2009, p. 191). Smith et al. (2009, p. 198) also note, that "Amid the many forces of change and assimilation, *ejidos* and *communidades agrarias* have played a key role in the cultural survival of smaller, more vulnerable indigenous populaitons."

Although many critics of the reform of Article 27 predicted that ejidatarios would sell or be dispossessed of their lands, except in peri-urban areas this has not usually happened (Jones & Ward, 1998, p. 259; Vázquez Castillo, 2004).[4] Contract farming, on the other hand, has become quite common since it is now allowed, with large Mexican merchandisers leading the way as contractors (Echánove Huacuja, 2009). Under the old ejido regime, contract farming was not allowed. Contract farming may lead to the phenomenon of farmers and peasants becoming proletarianized on their own land. Land certification has also led to greater rates of migration from the ejidos, especially among offspring of the ejidatario (de Janvry, Emerick, González-Navarro, & Sadoulet, 2013; p. 18), since guarantees of holding on to the farmland are undermined by shocks experienced in the countryside. This was not the case when ejido land was inalienable.

Several major shocks occurred in the wake and as a result of the institutionalization of the NAFTA in 1994, aimed at liberalizing trade between Mexico, Canada, and the United States. Furthering the cause of neoliberalization the treaty was aimed at the (sometimes gradual) lowering of tariffs on imports. It reversed Mexico's import substitution industrialization and emphasized exportation, including the exportation of agricultural products for which each country had comparative advantage.

Connecting the reform of Article 27 to the facilitation of NAFTA policies, Harvey (2005, pp. 101–102) holds:

> The ... lowering of import barriers delivered yet another blow, as cheap imports from the efficient but also highly subsidized agribusinesses in the United States drove down the price of corn and other products to the point where only the most efficient and affluent Mexican farmers could compete. Close to starvation, many peasants were forced off the land, only to augment the pool of unemployed in already overcrowded cities, where the so-called informal economy (for example street vendors) grew by leaps and bounds.[5]

While neoliberal policies framed in the 1980s forced Mexico to cut back subsidies to small farmers, including a guaranteed price for corn,[6] the United States continually increased subsidies for agribusiness, with an average input of 18 billion dollars annually beginning in 2002 and 2012 (Amat, Fried, Daniels, Ticeburst, & Maia, 2003, p. 5). This has led to what is known as "dumping." As Amat et al. (2003, p. 7) claim:

> One of the most important causes for the collapse of rural livelihoods in Latin America and the Caribbean is dumping by transnationals from the US, i.e. the export of products below production costs that compete unfairly with local products and force global prices down in an artificial manner. For example, the US exports wheat at 46% below the production cost and corn at 20% below production cost.

It is notable that tariffs on imported corn were phased out in 2008, opening the competition between undercapitalized small farmers and transnational agribusiness (Richard, 2008, p. 396). According to Otero (2011, p. 392), since NAFTA, "Agricultural liberalization ... has provoked the greatest population exodus that Mexico's countryside has experienced in its history." It is estimated that between the signing of NAFTA and the year 2011, almost 2 million farmers have been "forced off their land" (Carlsen, 2011, p. 2).

As a result of NAFTA's facilitating of dumping (and its concurrent lowering of prices), more Mexican farmers were induced to enter the formal or informal economies to sustain their families. Some did so as recurrent migrants (often called the semi-proletarianized though they might be independently self-employed) though many of their non-inheriting offspring, or those who just gave up in the face of overwhelming odds, became permanent migrants to the United States or elsewhere in Mexico. Among them are the informal and semi-informal beach vendors in Mexican tourist centers.

Throughout the South, food has continually been commoditized, leading to new forms of contemporary land-grabbing as land is taken over in a number of ways in the interests of producing food and biofuels for (often foreign) investors (Magdoff, 2012, pp. 20–21). Among the many types of land-grabbing outlined by Borras and Franco (2012) the negative consequences of the shift from domestic food crops to export agriculture and the production of biofuels are notable. These land grabs may be through purchase, long-term leasing or contracting with farmers (Borras & Franco, 2012, p. 40). Outright rentals with or without long-term leasing contracts are also common (Whiteford, Bernal, Díaz Cisneros, & Valtierra-Pacheco, 1998, p. 395). The provisions in the reform of Article 27 facilitate all of these methods, and may perpetuate forms of what Harvey (2003, p. 54 *et passim*) has identified as "accumulation by dispossession."

It is notable that although some forms of land-grabbing (e.g., outright purchase) lead to a dispossession of small farmers and the peasantry,

> ... not all land grabbing requires the expulsion of the "rural poor" from their land. In cases where capitalism does need both land and labour, it is in the interests of capital to retain peasants on their land via contractual relationships, either as lessor-labourers or as contract growers (Borras, Jr., & Franco, 2012, p. 53).

Peasants become, under these regimes, proletarians on their own land, with decisions such as to what to grow and how to grow it made by the contractor. Though only one of the families of beach vendors interviewed had been subject to land grabbing, it can be inferred that their families were bludgeoned by some of the other shocks mentioned above. Almost all were forced into the migration stream, whether recurrently or permanently, to Mexican cities.

One ameliorative program initiated by the Mexican government in 1994, in an effort to mute the effects of trade liberalization under NAFTA, was PROCAMPO (*Programa de Apoyos Directos al Campo*, Program for Direct Assistance in Agriculture). Originally scheduled to last only 15 years, it has been renewed until the end of 2013. It was renewed under the name of PROAGRO in 2014, when the Department of Agriculture was reorganized by the Peña Nieto administration. Offering a subsidy of 1,000 pesos per hectare of land planted in specified crops, it is a regressive cash transfer program favoring larger farmers (Rodríguez Gómez, 2014, p. 186; Sadoulet, de Janvry, & Davis, 2001, pp. 1044–1045; Winters & Davis, 2009, p. 621). PROAGRO continues this trend with the mission of increasing production in the countryside. As will be seen below a common complain of the sons of campesinos, most offspring of small or subsistence farmers, is the lack of government aid, whether in the form of credits, loans, or support, for agricultural pursuits. In sum, many small farmers have not been beneficiaries of these subsidies. That this is a widespread problem is suggested by studies that show differential receipt of PROCAMPO support in states where small farmers predominate and in states containing larger-scale farms, with more benefits going to the latter (Piñera Barajas, Saldaña, Jiménez Velázques, & García Cue, 2016, p. 156) and lesser support extended to the more vulnerable – those who have only small plots of land, and those who are poorly educated and/or indigenous. (Taylor & Yúnez-Naude, 2013, p. 14).

THE BEACH VENDORS; SONS OF CAMPESINOS

All over the world, the migrants from rural to urban centers have often taken up street vending, especially when other employment was not available (Bhowmik, 2010). As I have elucidated elsewhere (Wilson, 2012a, p. 5), beach vendors are a subset of street vendors. Street vendors, whether ambulatory or selling from a fixed or semi-fixed stall, are ubiquitous throughout the developing world and found even in some core capitalist countries, including U.S. cities such as New York (Duneier, 1999; Stoller, 2002), Washington, DC (Spatler-Roth, 1988), and Los Angeles (Bhimji, 2010; Kettles, 2007). Literature on street vendors in Mexico is ample and includes studies by historians (Gordon, 1997; Mendiola García, 2008), sociologists (Cross, 1998a, 1998b; Cross & Peña, 2006; González, Torres Medina, & Jimenéz, 2008; Peña, 1999; Silva Londoño, 2010), and anthropologists (Arizpe, 1979; Martí, 1994; Martínez Nova, 2003), most of whom concentrate on street vendors in Mexico City. Other anthropologists who have done fieldwork in Mexican villages, especially in the state of Guerrero, have briefly described out-migration into beach vending (García, 2007; González et al. 2008; Good Eshelman, 1988; Good Eshelman & Barrientos López, 2004; Schryer, 2007). Only a few have interviewed beach vendors in the tourist cities where they work (González Chévez, n.d.; Wilson, 2012a, 2012b, 2014a, 2014b; Wilson & Gámez, 2010; Wilson, Gámez, & Ivanova, 2012).

Among those that approach the situation of the peasantry in Latin America there are those who argue that a partial repeasantization can occur in situations of economic crisis (Otero, 1999; van der Ploeg, 2009). Others argue that the peasantry is disappearing (Bartra, 1993; Robinson, 2008). Both of these things may occur under certain political and economic conditions and are linked to globalization and climate change, though the general trend seems to be depeasantization. As will be seen below, many of those displaced from the countryside would be happy to return if conditions were favorable.

An earlier study I conducted in 2010 of 166 beach vendors in Acapulco, Puerto Vallarta, and Cabo San Lucas showed that of the 81 vendors whose father's occupation was asked, 45.1% of nonindigenous vendors and 61.3% of indigenous language speakers had fathers who were campesinos (2012a, p. 84). Of male vendors (56 of the 81), 46.4% had fathers who were campesinos and another 12.5% had fathers who were campesinos but recurrently migrated to vend on the beach (Wilson, 2012a; Table 3.1, p. 62). Because of these findings it was decided to do another study – limited to Cabo San Lucas – specifically aimed at interviewing sons of campesinos. Thirty-two of them were interviewed on Medano Beach in October of 2012; they were chosen by a random asking of the approximately 200–250 male beach vendors (outnumbering women beach vendors by about three to one) whether their fathers were campesinos, and whether, if so, they would agree to an interview. Most did so agree, perhaps as a means of earning the 50 pesos (about $5 at the time) offered to them in return.

Of the 32 beach vendors interviewed, 10 were born between 1950 and 1969, and thus they and their families were immediately affected by all of the shocks, leading to deepening inequality in the countryside, that were outlined above. Twenty were born between 1970 and 1989, thus they and their families would have been impacted directly by the 1982 debt crisis, and the neoliberal reforms, including NAFTA, that followed. Two were born in the 1990s (1990 and 1994), when these structural adjustment policies, including most especially liberalized trade, were deepening throughout Mexico. Many could not verbalize the results of these shocks but claimed lack of government support for their endeavors. Government support for the small farmers decreased after each of the structural shocks. All but one of the vendors had farmed the land at their father's side.

Ten of the vendors were indigenous, including eight Nahuatl-speakers from Guerrero, one Nahuatl-speaker from Puebla, and one Zapotec speaker from Oaxaca. The fathers of five of these held ejido or communal lands, one worked as a sharecropper on ejido lands, three had small private properties, and the man from Oaxaca was an agricultural day laborer. Notably, vendors identify themselves and their fathers as campesinos if they have worked the land in any capacity.

Twenty-eight of the vendors plied their wares by walking up and down the beach or approaching beach restaurants and attempting to attract the attention of tourists with their goods; four were commission sellers who worked at a stall, offering "aquatic activities" such as tickets for fishing boats, boat tours in the bay and they also rented beach equipment such as life jackets and jet skis. Although it is questionable whether all of the ambulatory vendors were "independent," since they were often dependent on merchandisers, some of whom come to the beach to sell to the hawkers, the commission sellers were most obviously not independent sellers. Nonetheless, it cannot be claimed that the ambulatory vendors were completely in the informal economy, since they had to have licenses in order to ply their trade – or otherwise risk having their goods confiscated and to be subject to a fine. Thus, they were "semi-informal." They had no social security benefits, such as medical care, attached to their jobs like workers in the formal economy do. Many sold goods that they had acquired from merchants, such as t-shirts or sunglasses, *sombreros*, dresses, serapes, or silver-plated or silver jewelry brought in from Taxco; a few sold handicrafts, such as palm-leaf handbags, hand-woven name bracelets, hand-painted ceramic or clay plates or hand-painted fish mobiles; one sold dresses made by his sister, distinguishing him from others who bought them wholesale.[7] While some vendors sold goods they bought at local stores, others bought from merchants who came to the beach to sell to them.

Table 1 summarizes the answers that the various vendors gave to the question of what lands their father's farmed, whether they would themselves like to be farmers, and what farmers they thought farmers faced. I take "lack of

Table 1. Sons of Campesinos.

Interview Code	Age	Years Schooling	Place of Origin	Indigenous Language	Years Vendor	Father's Holdings	Would Like to Be Campesino?	Problems Farmers Have
CSL-1C	41	0	Guerrero	No	2	2 ha. pp	Yes	Animals entering fields
CSL-2C	48	5	Guerrero	Nahuatl	22	5 ha. ejido	Yes	No government loans
CSL-3C	45	3	Guerrero	Nahuatl	10	8 ha. ejido, 6 ha. pp	Yes	Drought
CSL-4C	36	0	Guerrero	Nahuatl	25	2 ha. pp	Yes	Drought
CSL-5C	32	2	Guerrero	Nahuatl	20	1 ha. pp	Yes	Drought
CSL-6C	40	8	Guerrero	Nahuatl	15	1 ha. pp	Yes	Drought
CSL-7C	48	2	Guerrero	No	14	2 ha. ejido	No	Drought
CSL-8C	30	6	Guerrero	No	6	6 ha. ejido	No	No schools
CSL-9C	39	3	Guerrero	Nahuatl	25	8 ha. communal lands	No	Drought
CSL-10C	53	3	Michoacán	No	37	FaFa: 60 ha. pp	Yes	Drought
CSL-11C	32	3	Guerrero	No	15	Communal lands	Yes	No money for pesticides
CSL-12C	40	4	Guerrero	Nahuatl	17	Sharecropper on 5 ha. ejido	Yes	Drought
CSL-13C	32	3	Guerrero	Nahuatl	7	>10 ha. communal lands	Yes	Drought
CSL-14C	42	9	Jalisco Fa: Guerrero	No	20	FaFa pp (killed for land)	No	Drought; land grabbing by caciques
CSL-15C	3	6	Puebla	Nahuatl	7	½ ha. ejido	Yes	Drought
CSL-16C	47	9	Guerrero	No	36	4 ½ ha. ejido	Yes	Lack of money for fertilizers & pesticides
CSL-17C	18	12	Guerrero	No	<1	Mo: 8 ha. ejido	No	Lack of money, no government loans
CSL-18C	23	9	Durango	No	5	7 ha. ejido	Yes	No government aid

Table 1. *(Continued)*

Interview Code	Age	Years Schooling	Place of Origin	Indigenous Language	Years Vendor	Father's Holdings	Would Like to Be Campesino?	Problems Farmers Have
CSL-19C	62	6	State of Mexico	No	26	3 ha. pp	No	No government aid
CSL-20C	56	12	Guerrero Fa: State of Mexico	No	50	4 ha. ejido	Yes	Lack of money
CSL-21C	40	6	Oaxaca	Zapotec	22	None. Ag. day laborer	Yes	Lack of money
CSL-22C	23	6	Chiapas	No	<1	9 ha. ejido	Yes	Difficulty marketing crops
CSL-23C	31	6	Guerrero	No	3	3 ha. pp	Yes	Plagues > crop failure
CSL-24C	28	6	Sinaloa	No	6	None. Ag. day laborer	Yes	No government aid
CSL-25C	49	7	Guerrero	No	27	18 ha. ejido (privatized)	Yes	Drought; No government aid
CSL-26C	56	6	Guerrero Fa: Oaxaca	No	21	2 ha. ejido, 2 ha. pp	Yes	No government aid
CSL-27C	28	9	Veracruz Fa: Michoacán	No	5	32 ha. pp	Yes	No aid through PROCAMPO
CSL-28C	38	9	Baja California	No	3	12 ha. ejido	Yes	Flooding
CSL-29C	26	9	Guerrero	No	6	4 ha. ejido	No	No government aid
CSL-30C	28	6	Guerrero Fa: Oaxaca	No	<1	28 ha. pp	Yes	Lack of money
CSL-31C	36	6	Baja California Fa: Durango	No	7	5 ha. pp	Yes	Drought
CSL-32C	22	12	Acapulco, GRO Fa: Oaxaca	No	2 ½	20 ha. pp	Yes	None

money" to be equivalent to the statement that there are now lack of government loans that were available prior to the coming into being of NAFTA.

Fourteen of the vendor's fathers had access to ejido and three to communal lands, and two of them also had private property. In one case ejido lands had been converted into private property under PROCEDE (these are counted as ejido lands in the calculations). The lands in question were located outside of Acapulco and consisted of 18 hectares. Notably, ejido privatization and expropriation have been an integral part of the history of the expansion of Acapulco both prior to PROCEDE and more recently (Vázquez Castillo, 2004).

Eight of the fathers controlled between 2 and 5 hectares of ejido or communal land. One vendor's father worked on the village's common property holdings in the indigenous agrarian community of Tlamacazapa, Guerrero as did two fathers from San Juan Tetelcingo, in the Alto Balsas region of Guerrero. Twelve had fathers or grandfathers who owned private property ranging in size from 1 to 60 hectares (grandfather's land).

Seven of the 32 beach vendors, when asked if they would like to be campesinos, answered in the negative. Six were ambulatory beach vendors and one a commission seller. Four were born in Guerrero and one of them speaks Nahuatl; one was born in the Federal District but raised in a farming village outside of Acapulco; one was born in the State of Mexico; and one was born in the tourist city of Puerto Vallarta, Jalisco. Notably, all but one of the 32 vendors had worked the land along with their fathers when children and adolescents.

Fermín,[8] from Puerto Vallarta, is 42 years old, and feels farming takes much effort. He feels that the major problems that campesinos face are continual droughts and land grabbing by local casiques. His paternal grandfather had a large amount of land on which Gonzálo's father worked, but was killed in a land dispute, which led to the family moving away from their home town of Ayotac, Guerrero. Fermín would have liked to be a lawyer – and his 21-year-old daughter is studying law – but says his family was too poor to send him beyond the secondary school that he completed (making him one of the more educated beach vendors). The continual droughts underscore the effects of climate change in the Mexican countryside, and in this case, land-grabbing is also a problem in the village.

Gonzálo, from Monte Alegre, Guerrero, is 30 years old; he feels that in the town he came from there were no opportunities, not even to study, and prefers not to live there. His father has 6 hectares of ejido land in Monte Alegre on which he cultivated maíz, beans, squash, and peanuts with the help of his oldest son, aged 45. When asked what problems campesinos have, Gonzálo answered with respect to his father's situation, that he hadn't the resources to put a fence up around his fields. He also mentioned occasional plagues, including worms, that invaded the fields – Gonzálo would have liked to be a mathematics teacher, but finished only primary school, partially due to lack of family funds and partially because there was only a primary school in his home town, and he would have had to travel at least 2 hours one way each day to attend secondary school.

The father of Tobías, a 47-year-old vendor born in San Miguel, Guerrero, had 2 hectares of ejido land but migrated recurrently to Trevor, California to work in the fields, and gained amnesty under the 1986 Immigration Reform and Control Act (IRCA). His circular migration continued until 2006. Tobías also worked in the fields in Trevor, California for one year, from 1985 to 1986 but did not receive amnesty. He completed two years of secondary school and he enjoys being a vendor because he can work the days and hours he wishes. Although Tobías misses the life he had in his hometown, he would not like to be a campesino because one must make investments in the fields, but the maíz sells for such a low price that there are no earnings. This reflects the elimination guaranteed corn prices that occurred after NAFTA.

A 39-year-old Nahutal speaker from San Juan Tetelcingo, Guerrero, whose father farmed 2 hectares of communal lands, rejects farming because there is so often a lack of rain. He says that for this reason few people are planting crops anymore in his hometown. One might ask if this relatively recent trend is because of climate change, as some of the comments below also suggest, and whether it will lead to further temporary or permanent migration from the village. Notably, a number of studies have shown that climate-driven internal and international migration, whether recurrent or permanent, has increased from rural communities in drought-stricken regions of Mexico and elsewhere in the world (Bardsley & Hugo, 2010; Feng, Krueger, & Oppenheimer, 2010; Nawrotzki, Riosmena, & Hunter, 2013; Tacoli, 2009).

Sixty-two-year-old Oliviero, from the village of La Magdalena de los Reyes, State of Mexico, whose father had 3 hectares of private property, would not like to be a campesino because he feels he cannot thereby earn enough money to support his family. He states that lack of government aid – as always, he adds – is the major problem facing the campesinos. His youngest brother, aged 40 is, however, a campesino who grows maíz.

An 18-year-old whose maternal grandfather (and later, his mother) had 8 hectares of ejido land identifies alternate flooding and drought as problems on rainfed lands in the Acapulco region, showing the effects of climate change. He feels life in the countryside is too hard for him to want to be a campesino.

Commission seller Urbano, aged 26, born in the Federal District but brought up in a small town near Acapulco, has no desire to be a campesino. He says that work in the fields is very, very hard. He feels the problems that campesino's have in his home own are the heavy rains that come and destroy the crops. His father has 4 hectares of jland on which he grows maíz, jamaica, and watermelons. Although Urbano has three brothers, none of them help their father in the fields: All vend aquatic activities on the beach in Cabo San Lucas.

The other 25 beach vendors interviewed answered that they would like to be campesinos. Common reasons were because they would like to be able to live in their home villages and/or because they intrinsically liked the work of sowing crops. Sixteen vendors mentioned that they liked working the land, including sowing, cultivating or harvesting and eating their own crops and three that they liked being in their hometown or near family members. All, if they became campesinos, expected to do so in their home villages. Notably, all but one of the eight Nahuatl-speakers from the state of Guerrero would like to be campesinos, which suggests that indigenous identity includes ties to the land. While 78% of the vendors affirmed they would like to be campesinos, only six chose farming as being their preferred alternative to their vending activities. This may have been more to do with possibilities open to them while others perceived the alternative of returning to farming to be closed. Seven had previously worked in construction and contemplated this form of work as an alternative to vending.

Emetrio is a 48-year-old Nahuatl speaker from Temalac, Guerrero. He last visited Temalac 5 years ago. Emeterio's father farmed 5 ha. of ejido land in Temalac. His father cultivated corn, beans, squash, and sesame seeds. When asked what problems campesinos have, Emeterio underscored that the work is very hard. "Es eltrabajo más duro – lleva mucho trabajo." Concerning the problems campesinos have in his village, Emetrio points out that there is no aid for those who have no money to buy fertilizer – there are no loans or credits available. Thus, whatever government subsidies exist are not reaching his family's farm.

Emeterio has three brothers and three sisters. His 56-year-old brother is a beach vendor in Cabo but also farms their father's ejido lands, which now belong to him. This brother leaves his family in Temalac and one of *his* son farms the land for him while he is absent in CSL. Notably, this circular migration of peasants to vend on the beach is more common in Acapulco than in Cabo – though it does occur there – due to greater distances and the expense of travel.

If he were not a vendor, Emeterio would like to return to his village and cultivate land. He would like to be a campesino simply because he likes sowing the land (cultivating crops). He feels the greatest problems facing campesinos are the lack of access to loans or credit. It is obvious that the PROCAMPO program is not reaching his village.

A 40-year-old vendor from Tlamacazapa, Guerrero, who speaks Nahuatl, also recurrently migrated to his hometown to help his father on his hectare of private property (and perhaps to help out on a plot etched from the communal lands that make up most of the farmland in that town). He engaged in this circular migration for the first 5 of the 10 years he has lived in Cabo. Now Filimón's 35-year-old brother, who is a beach vendor in Cabo as well, does so. Their father, who grows corn, beans, and squash on his small plot, recurrently migrates to sell wares on the beach, and previously was a seasonal ambulatory vendor in Taxco, the city closest to Tlamacazapa. Filimón likes sowing maíz and thus would like to be a campesino, but sees crop failures due to over-abundant rain as the major problem facing campesinos in Tlamacazapa. This family has thus been impacted by negative climate changes.

In these families, there are thus members who could be called "semiproletarinazed," though proletarianization should be accompanied by coverage of the legislation protecting workers in the formal economy. "Semi-proletarianized" in this case is a misnomer, because the vendors are engaged in informal (in Acapulco) or semi-informal (in Cabo) income-generating activities as self-employed micro-entrepreneurs. Although licenses were not needed to vend in Acapulco during the study period, one must belong to an informal association of already present beach vendors that facilitates or hampers a vendor's entry into vending on the beach. It was not until 2009 that licenses were required for vendors in Cabo.

Orlando, a 32-year-old Nahuatl-speaker from San Juan Tetelcingo, Guerrero, mentions the lack of money hampering peasants: there is not enough available to buy seeds or pesticides. He is not very content with being a vendor because he earns so little and cannot send money to his father, who controls what he describes as a large ejido plot, (more than 10 hectares) – not a result of the redistribution of hacienda lands as traditionally ejido lands have been, but carved out of communal lands; he mentions, however, that he is getting too old to farm it by himself. Orlando is thinking of returning to his village to work his father's land. This would be the only case of possible "repeasantization" in the sample. When I ask Orlando what problems campesinos have, he answers with respect to the problems in his village of origin, as do the other vendors: first, the lack of rain, and second, the lack of money to buy fertilizers and other inputs that are needed. Thus, both climatic factors and the cutbacks in government-supplied credit are the main problems Orlando identifies. Notably, the family control of 10 hectares of land, more than that of other sons of campesinos interviewed, makes repeasantization a possible strategy.

In total, 19 vendors mentioned droughts and/or flooding (these sometimes happening alternatively) as one of the major problems facing campesinos. Eighteen vendors mentioned lack of funds to invest in farming, with seven underscoring the lack of economic aid to farmers by the government.

Cirilo, a 47-year-old vendor from San Marcos, near Acapulco, Guerrero, whose father controls 4.5 hectares of ejido land, points out the corruption involved in government loans for fertilizers. The loans are sent to the ejido commissioner who keeps back a portion of them before handing them over to the ejidatario. Isidoro, a 28-year-old vendor born in Cordoba, Veracruz where his father has 32 hectares of private property, says the PROCAMPO subsidy is not giving the promised funds to farmers. Thus, it is problematic whether the still extant programs to help campesinos are really working.

CONCLUSIONS

Although 7 of the 32 vendors have essentially abandoned the countryside, 25 would be content to return to it and work the land. The problems both groups identified have to do with climate and with finance. In some regions, there are continual droughts, in others alternative lack and superabundance of rainfall, and plagues often decimate the crops. Many of the vendors from Guerrero mentioned droughts as a problem in their hometowns. Although Guerrero is known for its periodic droughts, global warming is leading to their increased intensity, duration, and severity in all parts of the developing world (Leighton, 2011, p. 331).

Furthermore, many of the vendors underscored the lack of money in the forms of loans or credit in order to buy pesticides, fertilizers, and agricultural tools and machinery – and of these a number mentioned directly the lack of government aid. Although the PROCAMPO program was in existence for two decades, it appears that its funding did not reach all campesinos who could have benefited from it. PROCAMPO promised to subsidize fields planted in corn, and all of the campesino fathers of vendors planted corn, often along with other crops.

Continual shocks have led campesinos to seek an off-farm income through temporary or recurrent migration or are dependent on remittances, however small, from one or more of their offspring. Continual shocks have also widened and deepened the differentiation of the peasantry, with the sons of campesinos forced to find permanent or temporary employment in the informal, semi-informal, or formal sectors of the economy. Most of the approximately 600 beach vendors in the two towns composing Los Cabos seek an income through semi-informal self-employment – with no labor benefits such as those supplied to formal sector workers. There is a form of independence, including flexible hours and lack of a boss among the beach vendors – though they may have some degree of dependency on merchandisers – that is reminiscent of farming on one's own plot of land. Beach vending, like farming, also has seasonal peaks, since the former earn more during high tourist seasons. It is possible that having a peasant background thus makes such activities as vending a preferred income-generating activity – though network-mediation is also an important aspect among vendors.

Results from the interviews suggest support for two opposing views concerning the peasantry. First, there is occurring, in the face of continual and evolving economic shocks, an "agonizing death" (Robinson, 2008, p. 169) of a portion of the peasanty. The offspring of campesinos, who identify themselves as campesinos as well, are disappearing into the full-time proletarianized and informalized workforces. They are part of the rural migration to primary and secondary cities in Mexico. On the other hand, there are those who would happily return to being campesinos, and if inheriting land from their fathers, may take part in a process of "repeasantization." This latter alternative is less likely, however, since agricultural aid programs like PROCAMPO or more recently PROAGRA, besides being regressive, are not reaching many campesinos who are in dire need of government aid, especially in the face of dumping by the United States.

Notably, however, after Hurricane Odil devastated Cabo in September of 2014, destroying tourist hotels and discouraging subsequent visits by tourists, large numbers of beach vendors disappeared from Medano Beach. Local gossip holds that many of them returned to their villages of origin, where some will probably take up farming again. Others may have moved on to other beach cities to continue to ply their trade. At least a few probably moved into the (re) construction industry called forth after the damage caused by the hurricane. It is important to note that 12 of the beach vendors interviewed had previously worked in construction, 10 in Cabo San Lucas, 1 in Cabo San Lucas and Puerto Vallarta, and 1 in his hometown of San Juan Tetelcingo.

In this respect, it is notable that a study by Rodríguez-Oreggia (2013) of natural disasters and labor market outcomes in 32 Mexican municipalities showed that low-skilled workers often increased their formal sector employment, most probably because of reconstruction activities that took place in cities affected by hurricanes in the 2000–2011 period. His data probably underestimate the importance of reconstruction activities, because many are employed informally in construction and construction-related enterprises.

NOTES

1. Ejidos are communally held, but usually individually tenured, stretches of farmland, established by Article 27 of the 1917 Mexican Constitution and constitute lands that, prior to the Mexican Revolution, belonged to haciendas. Prior to the reform of Article 27 in 1992, they could not legally be sold, leased, mortgaged, or used as credit for loans. Although there were some illegal sales, they were most usually to other *ejidatarios*. The ejido plot was essentially inalienable, but upon the death of the ejidatario could be passed on to offspring or to widows. Ejido lands could not be split up, but the whole inherited by only one of the family's offspring, usually a son.

2. Comunidades agrarías (agrarian communities) usually consist of communal lands that may, as in the case of ejidos, be farmed as individual plots and even passed on to progeny. Although some agrarian communities were established – along with the ejidos – after the Mexican Revolution, many have pre-Colombian and Colonial roots. The main distinguishing feature of communidad agrarias is that "their land was technically not "given" to them by the state, but rather the state recognized what was already theirs" (Kelly et al., 2010, p. 164). Many indigenous communities did apply for ejido lands, however.

3. In October of 2012, 32 beach vendors in Cabo San Lucas who were sons of campesinos were interviewed, half by my assistant Ernestina Ibarbol Luna and half by me.

4. Nevertheless, Jones and Ward (1998, p. 259) point out that ejido lands had been taken over by the state for several decades prior to the reform of Article 27; they underscore

> ... the irony of the new legislation that allows joint ventures between the ejido and the state, when it has been the state that for the past two decades has expropriated ejido land for developments that require a leap of faith to describe as benefiting the public good: ecological parks to act as buffers between low and high-income settlements, shopping malls, private universities and golf courses, and tourist complexes, including large parts of Acapulco and Cancún.

5. It is notable that the informal economy, including micro-enterprise owners, salaried workers in informal firms, and petty entrepreneurs, but excluding informal agricultural employment was responsible for 50.3% of all employment in Mexico by 2009 and 60% of all employment in 2014 (International Labour Organization, 2012, p. 3; Instituto Nacional de Estádistica, Geografía, y Informatica, 2014).

6. In 1999, five years after NAFTA came into effect, price supports for corn and other grains provided under CONASUPO (Compañía Nacional de Subsistencias Populares) were withdrawn (Bachmann Fuentes, 2014, pp. 90, 97). PROCAMPO was an attempt to temporarily fill in the gaps as well as intending to aid the countryside in its adaptation to NAFTA policies.

7. Nahuatl-speaking vendors from the Alto Balsas region of Guerrero, where craft-making and craft-vending in a variety of Mexican cities have been common, have been in existence and have persisted for various decades (Good Eshelman, 1988; Schryer, 2014, Ch. 2). I would estimate that in Cabo San Lucas at least 50 percent of all vendors sold merchandise they or family members had made or to which they had added value. Value added activities consist of such things as sewing blouses, shirts, or dresses (often from imported cloth) or stringing semi-precious stones into necklaces.

8. All names are pseudonyms.

REFERENCES

Altieri, M. A., & Nicholls, C. I. (2001). Ecological impacts of modern agriculture in the United States and Latin America. In R. Paarlsbegg & F. de Castri (Eds.), *Globalization and the rural environment* (pp. 121–135). Cambridge, MA: Harvard University Press.

Amat, P., Fried, M., Daniels, K., Ticeburst, S., & Maia, K. (2003). Making trade fair for the Americas: Agriculture, investment, and intellectual property: The reasons to say no to the FTAA. *Oxfam Policy and Practice: Agriculture, Food and Land*, *3*(1), 1–36.

Appendini, K., & Liverman, D. (1994). Agricultural policy, climate change and food security in Mexico. *Food Policy*, *19*(2), 149–164.

Arizpe, L. (1979). *Indígenas en la Ciudad de México: El Caso de las "Marias"*. México: Secretaría de Educación Pública.

Bachmann Fuentes, R. I. (2014). La Inseguridad Alimentaria y la Tragedia del Campo en México: Consequencias de las Políticas Agrícolas Neoliberales. *Espacio Regional*, *1*(11), 89–108.

Bardsley, D. K., & Hugo, G. J. (2010). Migration and climate change: Examining thresholds of change to guide effective adaptation decision-making. *Population and Environment*, *32*(2), 238–262.

Bartra, R. (1993). *Agrarian structure and political power in Mexico*. Baltimore: Johns Hopkins University Press.

Bhimji, F. (2010). Struggles, urban citizenship and belonging: The experience of undocumented street vendors and food truck owners in Los Angeles. *Urban Anthropology*, *39*(4), 455–492.

Bhowmik, S. K. Ed. (2010). *Street vendors in the global economy*. New York, NY: Routledge.

Borras, Jr., S. M., & Franco, J. C. (2012). Global land grabbing and trajectories of agrarian change: A preliminary analysis. *Journal of Agrarian Change*, *12*(1), 34–54.

Brenner, N., & Theodore, N. (2002). Cities and the geographies of actually existing neoliberalism. *Antipode*, *34*(3), 348–379.

Carlsen, L. (2011). NAFTA is starving Mexico. *The Americas Program*, October 20. http://www.ciamericas.org/archives/5617. Accessed on May 17, 2015.

Castellanos, M. B. (2010). *A return to servitude: Maya migration and the tourist trade in Cancún*. Minneapolis, MI: University of Minnesota Press.

Chrispeels, M. J. (2000). Biotechnology and the poor. *Plant Physiology*, *124*, 1–3.

Clancy, M. J. (2001). *Exporting paradise: Tourism and development in Mexico*. New York, NY: Pergamon.

Cornelius, W. A. (1998). Ejido reform: Stimulus or alternative to migration? In W. A. Cornelius & D. Myhre (Eds.), *The transformation of rural Mexico: Reforming the Ejido Sector* (pp. 229–246). La Jolla, CA: Center for U.S.-Mexican Studies, University of California, San Diego.

Cornelius, W. A., & Myhre, D. (1998). Introduction. In W. A. Cornelius & D. Myhre (Eds.), *The transformation of rural Mexico: Reforming the Ejido Sector* (pp. 1–24). La Jolla, CA: Center for U.S.-Mexican Studies, University of California, San Diego.

Cross, J. C. (1998a). *Informal politics: Street vendors and the state in Mexico*. Stanford: Stanford University Press.

Cross, J. C. (1998b). Co-optation, competition, and resistance: State and street vendors in Mexico city. *Latin American Perspectives*, *25*(2), 41–62.

Cross, J. C., & Peña, S. (2006). Risk and regulation in the informal and illegal markets. In P. Fernández-Kelly & J. Shefner (Eds.), *Out of the shadows: Political action and the informal economy in Latin America* (pp. 49–80). University Park, PA: Pennsylvania State University Press.

de Ita, A. (2006). Land concentration in Mexico after PROCEDE. In P. Rosset, R. Patel, & M. Courville (Eds.), *Promised land: Competing visions of agrarian reform* (pp. 148–164). Oakland, CA: Food First Books.

de Janvry, A., Emerick, K., González-Navarro, M., & Sadoulet, E. (2013). Delinking land rights from land use: Impact of certification on migration and land use in rural Mexico. Paper presented at the 2014 meeting of the Society for Economic Dynamics. Retrieved from https://ideas.repec.org/p/red/sed014/138.html. Accessed on May 14, 2015.

Duneier, M. (1999). *Sidewalk*. New York, NY: Farrar, Straus, and Giroux.

Echánove Huacuja, F. (2009). Políticas Públicas y Maíz en México: el esquema de Agricultura por Contrato. *Anales de Geografía*, *29*(2), 65–82.

Feng, S., Krueger, A. B., & Oppenheimer, M. (2010). Linkages among climate change, crop yields and Mexico-US cross-border migration. *Proceedings of the National Academy of Sciences of the United States of America*, *107*(32), 14257–14262.

Foley, M. W. (1995). Privatizing the countryside: The Mexican peasant movement and neoliberal reform. *Latin American Perspectives*, *22*(1), 59–76.

García, M. (2007). Migraciones de Alto Balsas. *Regiones: Suplemento de Antropolgía*, *30*, 2–4.

Garza, G. (2002). Evolución de las Ciudades Mexicanas en el Siglo XX. *Revista de Infromación y Análisis*, *19*, 7–16.

González Chévez, L. (n.d.). *Anclajes y Transformaciones Culturales de un Pueblo Nahua en Transición: El Case de Temalac, Guerrero*. Retrieved from http://webhosting.com/%7Emigracion/modules/seinarioe/gonzalezlilian.pdf. Accessed on September 29, 2010.

González, M., Torres Medina, J., & Jimenéz, O. (2008). *La República Informal: El Ambulantaje en la Ciudad de Mexico*. México: Porrúa.

Gordon, G. I. (1997). *Peddlers, pesos, and power: The political economy of street vending in Mexico City*. Ph.D. Dissertation, Department of History, University of Chicago.

Good Eshelman, C. (1988). *Haciendo la Lucha: Arte y Comercio Nahuas de Guerrero*. México: Fondo de Cultura Económica.

Good Eshelman, C., & Barrientos López, G. (2004). *Nahuas del Alto Balsas: Pueblos Indígenas del México Contemporáneo*. Mexico: Comisión Nacional para Desarrollo de los Pueblos Indígenas. Retrieved from http://www.edi.gob.mx

Harvey, D. (2003). *The new imperialism*. New York, NY: Oxford University Press.

Harvey, D. (2005). *A brief history of neoliberalism*. New York, NY: Oxford University Press.

Hewitt de Alcántara, C. (1978). *La Modernización de la Agricultura Mexicana, 1940–1970*. Mexico: Siglo Veinteuno Editores.

IndexMundi. (2012). *Mexico—Urban Population*. Retrieved from http://www.indexmundi.com/facts/mexico/urban-population. Accessed on April 30, 2015.

Instituto Nacional de Estádistica, Geografía, y Informatica (2014, March). *INEGI Buletin de Prensa Núm 124 24 Marzo 2014*. Retrieved from http://www.inegi.gob.mx. Accessed on April 17, 2014.

International Labour Organization (2012). *Statistical Update on Employment in the Informal Economy*. ILO Department of Statistics. http://laborsta.ilo.org/applv8/data/INFORMAL_ECONOMY/2012-06-Statisticalupdate-v2.pdf. Accessed on 17 August 2015.

Jones, G. A., & Ward, P. M. (1998). Deregulating the Ejido: The impact on urban development in Mexico. In W. A. Cornelius & D. Myhre (Eds.), *The transformation of rural Mexico: Reforming the Ejido Sector* (pp. 247–276). La Jolla, CA: Center for U S.-Mexican Studies, University of California, San Diego.

Jorgenson, A. K. (2006). Global warming and the neglected greenhouse gas: A cross-national study of the social causes of methane emissions intensity, 1995. *Social Forces*, *84*(3), 1779–1798.

Kelly, J. H., Herlihy, P. H., Viera, A. R., Smith, D. A., & Hernández Cendejas, G. A. (2010). Indigenous territoriality at the end of the social property era in Mexico. *Journal of Latin American Geography*, *9*(3), 161–181.

Kettles, G. W. (2007). Legal responses to sidewalk vending: The case of Los Angeles, California. In J. Cross & A. Morales (Eds.), *Street entrepreneurs: People, place and politics in local and global perspective* (pp. 58–78). New York, NY: Routledge.

Leighton, M. (2011). Drought, desertification, and migration: Past experiences, predicted impacts and human rights issues. In É. Piguet, A. Pécoud, & P. de Guchteneire (Eds.), *Migration and climate change* (pp. 331–358). New York, NY: Cambridge University Press.

Magdoff, F. (2012). Food as commodity. *Monthly Review*, *63*(8), 15–22.

Martí, J. E. (1994). Subsistence and the state: The case of Porfirian Mexico. In E. M. Brumfield (Ed.), *The economic anthropology of the state* (pp. 316–323). Lanham, MD: University Press of America.

Martínez Nova, C. (2003). The 'Culture' of exclusion: Representations of indigenous women street vendors in Tijuana, Mexico. *Bulletin of Latin American Research*, *23*(3), 249–268.

Massey, D., Alarcón, R., Durand, J., & González, H. (1987). *Return to Aztlán: The social process of international migration from western Mexico*. Berkeley, CA: University of California Press.

Mendiola García, S. C. (2008). *Street vendors, marketeers, and politics in twentieth century Puebla*. Ph.D. dissertation. Department of History, Rutgers University.

Nawrotzki, R. J., Riosmena, F., & Hunter, L. M. (2013). Do rainfall deficits predict U.S.-bound migration from rural Mexico? Evidence from the Mexican Census. *Population Research and Policy Review*, *32*(1), 129–158.

Ortiz Wadgymar, A. (1986). El Ingreso a GATT: Nuevo Cerco de la Dependencia. *Momento Económico*, *26*, 9–10.

Otero, G. (1999). *Farewell to the peasantry? Political class formation in rural Mexico*. Boulder, CO: Westview Press.

Otero, G. (2011). Neoliberal globalization, NAFTA, and migration: Mexico's loss of food and labor sovereignty. *Journal of Poverty*, *15*, 384–402.

Otero, G. (2013). El Régimen Alimentario Neoliberal y su Crisis: Estado, Agroempresas Multinacionales y Biotechnologia. *Antipoda: Revista de Antropología y Arqueología*, *17*, 49–78.

Otero, G., & Pechlaner, G. (2008). Neoliberal globalism and the biotechnology revolution: Economic and historical contextin. G. Otero (Ed.). *Food for the few: Neoliberal globalism and biotechnology in Latin America* (pp. 2–30) Austin, TX: University of Texas Press.

Peña, S. (1999). Informal markets: Street vendors in Mexico City. *Habitat International, 23*(3), 363–372.

Piñera Barajas, A., Saldaña, T. M., Jiménez Velázques, M. A., & García Cue, J. L. (2016). Public policy for rural areas: PROCAMPO in the central region of Mexico. *Revista Mexicana de Ciencias Agrícolas, 7*(1), 147–157.

Portes, A., & Roberts, B. R. (2005). The free-market city: Latin American urbanization in the years of the neoliberal experiment. *Studies in Comparative International Development, 40*(1), 43–82.

Richard, A. (2008). Withered Milpas: Government disaster and the Mexican countryside. *Journal of Latin American and Caribbean Anthropology, 13*(2), 437–461.

Robinson, W. I. (2008). *Latin America and global capitalism: A critical globalization perspective*. Baltimore, MD: Johns Hopkins University Press.

Rodríguez Gómez, K. (2014). ¿Neo o Post-Neoliberalismo en la Política Social de México? Una Comparación entre las Estrategias de Política Seguidas Durante la Década del 2000 y la ¿Nueva? Estrategia del sexenion Priista (2012–2018). *Revista Mexicana de Análisis Político y Administración Pública, 3*(1), 179–202.

Rodríguez-Oreggia, E. (2013). Hurricane and labor market outcomes: Evidence from Mexico. *Global Environmental Change, 23*(1), 351–359.

Romo Viramontes, R., & Sánchez Castillo, M. (2012). *El descenso de la fecundidad en México, 1974-2009: A 35 años de la puesta en marcha de la nueva política de población*. Retrieved from www.cimac.org.mx/cedoc/camp_dsyr_Jovenes2012/documentos/abril/el_deceso_de_la-población_en_Mexico.pdf. Accessed on April 27, 2015.

Ross, E. B. (2003). Malthusianism, capitalist agriculture, and the fate of peasants in the making of the modern world food system. *Review of Radical Political Economics, 35*(4), 437–461.

Sadoulet, E., de Janvry, A., & Davis, B. (2001). Cash transfer programs with income multipliers: PROCAMPO in Mexico. *World Development, 29*(6), 1043–1056.

Schryer, F. J. (2007). Continuidades y discontinuidades en la communidad de Ahuehuepan: Lengua, Trabajo, y Migración. *Regiones: Suplemento de Antropología, 30*, 9–12.

Schryer, F. J. (2014). *They never came back: A story of undocumented workers from Mexico*. Ithaca, NY: Cornell University Press.

Segrelles, S. J. (2013). El problema de los cultivos transgénicos en América Latina: una "nueva" revolución verde. *Entorno Geográfico, 3*, 93–120.

Silva Londoño, D. A. (2010). Comercio Ambulante en el Centro Histórico de la Ciudad de México (1990-2007). *Revista Mexicana de Sociología, 72*(2), 195–224.

Sklair, L. (1993). *Assembling for development: The maquila industry in Mexico and the United States*. (2nd ed.). San Diego, CA: Center for U.S.-Mexican Studies, University of California.

Smith, D. A., Herlihy, P. H., Kelly, J. H., & Viera, A. R. (2009). The certification and privatization of indigenous lands in Mexico. *Journal of Latin American Geography, 8*(2), 175–207.

Sonnenfeld, D. A. (1992). Mexico's 'Green Revolution', 1940-1980: Towards an environmental history. *Environmental History Review, 66*(4), 28–52.

Spatler-Roth, R. M. (1988). The sexual political economy of street vending in Washington, D.C. In G. C. Clark (Ed.), *Traders vs. the state: Anthropological approaches to unofficial economies* (pp. 165–187). Boulder, CO: Westview Press.

Stoller, P. (2002). *Money has no smell: The Africanization of New York City*. Chicago, IL: University of Chicago Press.

Tacoli, C. (2009). Crisis or adaptation? Migration and climate change in the context of high mobility. *Environment & Urbanization, 21*(2), 513–525.

Taylor, E. J., & Yúnez Naude, A. (2013). *PROCAMPO: ¿Hay Fugas en la Tubería?* Centro de Estudios Económicos, El Colegio de México. Retrieved from cee.colmex.mx/documentos/documentos-de-trabajo/2013/dt2013.pdf. Accessed on May 13, 2016.

van der Ploeg, J. D. (2009). *The new peasantries: Struggles for autonomy and sustainability in an era of empire and globalization*. Sterling, VA: Earthscan.

Vázquez Castillo, M. T. (2004). *Land privatization in Mexico: Urbanization, formation of regions, and globalization*. New York, NY: Routledge.

Whiteford, S., Bernal, F. A., Díaz Cisneros, H., & Valtierra-Pacheco, E. (1998). Arid-Land Ejidos: Bound by the past, marginalized by the future. In W. A. Cornelius & D. Myhre (Eds.), *The transformation of rural Mexico: Reforming the Ejido Sector* (pp. 381–400). La Jolla, CA: Center for U.S.-Mexican Studies, University of California, San Diego.

Wilson, T. D. (2008). Economic and social impacts of tourism in Mexico. *Latin American Perspectives*, *35*(3), 37–52.

Wilson, T. D. (2012a). *Economic life of Mexican beach vendors: Acapulco, Puerto Vallarta, and Cabo San Lucas*. Lanham, MD: Lexington Books.

Wilson, T. D. (2012b). Indigenous beach vendors in Puerto Vallarta and Acapulco. *North American Dialogue*, *15*(2), 31–42.

Wilson, T. D. (2014a). Self-employed women in the informal economy: Beach vendors in Acapulco. *Research in Economic Anthropology*, *34*, 269–292.

Wilson, T. D. (2014b). Transnationalism within: A study of beach vendors in Cabo San Lucas (Mexico). *Canadian Journal of Latin American and Caribbean Studies*, *39*(2), 299–313.

Wilson, T. D., & Gámez, A. E. (2010). A consideration of social and human capital among beach and Marina vendors in Cabo San Lucas, Mexico. *Urban Anthropology*, *39*(4), 425–453.

Wilson, T. D., Gámez, A. E., & Ivanova, A. (2012). Women beach and Marina vendors in Cabo San Lucas, BCS, Mexico: Considerations about their marginalization. *Latin American Perspectives*, *39*(6), 83–95.

Winters, P., & Davis, B. (2009). Designing a programme to support smallholder agriculture in Mexico: Lessons from PROCAMPO. *Development Policy Review*, *27*(5), 617–642.

Zavala de Cosio, M. E. (2014). *La Transición Demográfica en México (1895–2010)*. Retrieved from https://hal.archives_ouverts.fr/file/index/docid/968364/Filename/capitulo_version_final140512.pdf. Accessed on April 28, 2015.

PART IV
TOURISM

DEBTS AND UNCERTAINTY: CIRCULATION OF ADVANCE MONEY AMONG TOURISM ENTREPRENEURS IN AGRA, INDIA

Riddhi Bhandari

ABSTRACT

Purpose – *This chapter examines how the everyday interactions that are fostered with the circulation of debt impact the socioeconomic order in which they operate. Employing the theoretical framework of "circuits of commerce," scholars have examined how social relations and economic activities intertwine, are negotiated and transformed through the circulation of debt. The focus of such studies has been on the motives of actors, such as the desire for relationship-making, and structural conditions, like the inaccessibility of formal institution, that necessitate the emergence of debt-centered circuits of commerce (Hampton, 2003; Heslop, 2016; James, 2014). However, such circuits also have broader impacts and affect socially pervasive moral evaluations and work cultures (Ho, 2009; Zelizer, 2011). Building on these findings, I examine commission-based alliances among showroom owners and tour guides in Agra's tourism market to understand how "bad debt" between them shapes Agra's local tourism economy.*

Methodology/approach – *This chapter is based on ethnographic research conducted in 2012–2013 with Agra's tourism entrepreneurs, like showroom owners, tour guides, and convincers.*

Anthropological Considerations of Production, Exchange, Vending and Tourism
Research in Economic Anthropology, Volume 37, 233–256

ISSN: 0190-1281/doi:10.1108/S0190-128120170000037011

Findings – *Entrepreneurs' everyday practices around the circulation of debt impact how tourism in Agra is perceived and conducted. Although debt is initiated to mitigate uncertainty of getting clientele, its circulation exacerbates that very uncertainty.*

Originality/value – *This chapter contributes to the theory of economic practice, highlighting how economic actors, through their everyday practices, shape the macro-structure of the economic system in which they operate.*

Keywords: Circuits of commerce; commission; debt; tourism; showroom owners; tour guides

INTRODUCTION: MARKETS IN CIRCULATION

Money, and how it is earmarked, handled, and circulated, undergirds both impersonal and intimate social relations. In the economic sphere, actors employ monetary transactions to establish work relations, assert their entrepreneurial status, and access credit or extend loans (De Neve, 1999; Heslop, 2016; Zelizer, 2011). Closer to home, money is an integral part of spousal and parental exchanges that range from joint contribution to household expenses to payment of "pocket money" to the partners and children and claims over property at the time of separation or death (Zelizer, 2011). That social relations impact monetary transactions and that monetary transactions are negotiated and transformed by social relations among actors is now a well-acknowledged, sociological fact. What remains underexplored is if, and how, the circulation of money through social relations impacts the wider socioeconomic order in which such exchange occurs. In this chapter, I pursue this question; I follow a "circuit of commerce" between Agra's tourism entrepreneurs that is predicated on the exchange of tourist clients for commission payments. Pending debt is central to this circuit and affects entrepreneurial relations. By analyzing these relations as they unfold around debt, I arrive at how Agra's tourism is impacted and shaped by the everyday functioning of circuits of commerce that it encompasses.

I begin this chapter by examining the intersections between social relations and economic activities using the framework of circuits of commerce to emphasize their intricate and multifaceted relations. My chapter looks to address the pending question of how micro-level processes affect the socioeconomic macro-system in which they occur. In the next section, I introduce readers to Agra's tourism, emphasizing why the uncertainty of getting clientele is a core concern for entrepreneurs and necessitates commission-based alliances between showroom owners and tour guides. But these alliances are only a beginning as tourist visits do not automatically translate into sales and showroom owners face risks of cheating and nonreciprocity from tour guides. In the following section, I explicate how showroom owners look to make commission alliances binding and economically productive by "engineering indebtedness." The manipulation and circulation of these debts impact relations between guides, showroom owners and tourists, causing friction and suspicion. Although these tensions play out at the level of interpersonal relations, I argue that their impact is felt in Agra's tourism economy; the result is an economic system marked by heightened uncertainty and additional costs. In conclusion, I reiterate the need to build a theory of economic practice that links micro-practices with macro-structures, assessing the impact of everyday economic exchanges on the wider socioeconomic system in which they operate.

THE SOCIAL AND THE ECONOMIC: BETWEEN EMBEDDEDNESS AND CIRCUITS OF COMMERCE

The entanglements of social relations and networks and economic activities have been a productive site for intellectual engagement. Scholars have focused on principles of exchange, like reciprocity, redistribution, and appropriation, around which social relations and economic activities unfold. In this vein, scholars have stressed how periodic and repetitive exchange is necessary to sustain social relations, to establish new ones and to stake claim to (improved) social status (Mauss, 1990). Goods and money are also circulated to "engineer indebtedness" and to elicit deferred reciprocity (Firth, 1983). Sahlins (1972) suggests negative reciprocity, like theft, where appropriation rather than reciprocity is the defining motive.

Two broad frameworks help elucidate the working relationships between social relations and economic activities: "social embeddedness" and "circuits of commerce." Granovetter (1985) invoked "social embeddedness" to point out that economic actions were entrenched in entrepreneurs' social relations and shaped by the social context in which they occurred. Entrepreneurs frequently mobilized their social ties to enhance their participation in the market and get jobs, reliable information and access to resources. While "weak ties," with limited intimacy, emotional intensity, and reciprocity between social actors, and as exemplified by brokers, help expand one's network of resources and information, "strong ties" – close-knit group of family and friends – provide "motivational" resources, assisting entrepreneurs to cope with uncertainties and to undertake risks (Granovetter, 1973, p. 1361; Strobl & Peters, 2013, p. 62).[1] Even in typically "adversarial" relations, as between buyers and sellers (Geertz, 1978), transacting parties often look to establish social familiarity to advance their economic interests. Such attempts to transform "strangers into kin" were the cornerstone of economic negotiations in the vegetable markets in Biak City,

Indonesia (Rutherford, 2001, p. 309). Here, shoppers gravitated toward sellers from their regions and villages and often found classificatory kin. Building on this familiarity, both aimed to maximize their economic interests; women sellers hoped to get a loyal clientele, while women buyers looked to get quality products and an occasional extra bundle of taro roots or spinach for a fair price.

However, critics have pointed out that this framework merely offers the social as an "additive" to the economic sphere where social ties only act to facilitate or constrain economic actions (cf. Zelizer, 2012). Such a conceptual relationship limits the scope of economic transactions to those that occur in the market, neglecting, for instance, economic exchanges that take place in the household or in romantic relationships (Zelizer, 2012).

"Circuits of commerce" conceptualize an intricate yet fluid relationship between economic transactions and social relations, and address the concerns raised with embeddedness (Zelizer, 2011, p. 304). According to Zelizer, an early proponent, circuits of commerce "emphasize the centrality of negotiated meanings and social relations in … economic transactions …." These circuits entail "… *distinctive social relations among specific individuals*; [and] … *shared economic activities* carried on by means of those social relations …" (Zelizer, 2011, p. 304, emphasis added). Conceptualized in this manner, existing social relations emerge as a critical component of economic transactions, determining the types of economic exchange that are possible or unlikely between actors. This brings intimate social relations into the purview as sites of economic exchange.

Circuits of commerce are employed in markets with an aim to make and reinforce relationships to serve economic ends. Money and the different ways in which it is used and circulated play a crucial role in this. Debt is one such form of money that elucidates the complexities of socioeconomic relations in circuits. Social familiarity is often the starting point of debt, or even its precondition. To guard against credit default, creditors prefer to extend loans to those they know through ties of kinship, friendships, and locality (Guérin, 2014; Kar, 2013). Borrowers too often seek financial assistance within their social networks, turning to kith and kin to borrow money. This is particularly true of small-scale entrepreneurs who often have uncertain credit scores and are unable to secure loans through formal banking institutions (Hampton, 2003). Studies on demand-sharing – obligations faced by wealthier kin to lend money to their poorer relatives without hopes for timely repayments and at negative interest rates – indicate the social and ethical pressures that creditors face to lend money contrary to their economic interests (Gregory, 2012). Even in formal lending practices as with microfinance, credit is preferentially given to a group of socially related women so that existing social relations can be mobilized to pressurize all participants to adhere to repayments (Guérin, 2014; Kar, 2013).

While existing social ties help access credit and to make decisions to extend loans, scholars, like Roitman (2003), have pointed out that debt often marks the beginning of prolonged social engagement. For instance, rather than spend on personal needs, women in Tamil Nadu, India, frequently used the money they borrowed through microfinance to lend it forward to fulfill their social obligations and to reinforce existing relations (Guérin, 2014). Debt's ability to generate new social and economic relations and establish circuits of commerce is evident in the market as entrepreneurs look to "engineer indebtedness" by "rolling the money" (Firth, 1983; Heslop, 2016). Commission agents in the wholesale vegetable market in Dambulla, Sri Lanka, offered loans to farmers to ensure a steady supply of fresh produce, and often deferred collecting payments from shopkeepers to extend their relationship into a future transaction (Heslop, 2016; also see, Crona, Nyström, Folke, & Jiddawi, 2010). A successful commission agent looked to "roll the money" between farmers and sellers to produce "... relationships whereby people remain indebted, and thus 'in business' with one another." (Heslop, 2016, p. 535). Both Jan Breman (2008) and Geert De Neve (1999), working in India's labor-intensive sectors, like the power-loom industry, have noted that the practice of offering advance to workers was initiated to maintain a steady and reliable workforce when the number of factories and worker mobility were both rising. Thus, debt, as Guérin (2014, p. 42) points out, quoting Charles Malamoud (1980), "organizes social life, and therefore the life of man as a social being: it makes its presence in the world of network links, a net that both traps and supports."

As these examples illustrate, debt and circuits of commerce usually reinforce one another. Debt is often extended within circuits of known associates as creditors look to ensure repayments and borrowers can secure loans easily; however, debt is often the first step toward establishing circuits of commerce as it creates obligations and reciprocal relations. The circulation of debt also affects interpersonal relations in myriad ways. As many of the examples above show, the need for trust and reliability and lack of access to formal institutions are important reasons for such debt-centered circuits to emerge (De Neve, 1999; Hampton, 2003; cf. Zelizer, 2011). However, attempts at "indebtedness engineering" sometimes yield unexpected results. In Tamil Nadu's expanding power-loom industry, factory owners initiated advance payments – *baki* – to maintain an indebted and stable supply of workers, but workers mobilized the demands for their labor to leverage for increasing amounts of *baki*. Trapped in the web that they had set out to weave, factory owners referred to *baki* as "lost capital" that was rarely recovered, could not be invested elsewhere, and that could barely control workers, who, aware that they could not be fired while they held unpaid loans, indulged in foot dragging and shirking (De Neve, 1999, p. 394).

Moral evaluations of debtors and creditors are closely intertwined with debt. Peebles (2010) has pointed out that debt is overwhelmingly marked by negative moral evaluations; because of the stigma, those unable to repay experience feelings of self-blame, inadequacy, and anger toward familial responsibilities that necessitate such debts (cf. Gregory, 2012; James, 2014). However, debt is sometimes socially approved; in post-Apartheid South Africa, taking a loan indicated an individual's desire for upward mobility and her willingness to work toward fulfilling aspirations (James, 2014). While holding a debt may not be ideal, it is the creditor who is often a morally dubious figure. In India, the neighborhood money lender who specializes in subprime loans, is commonly portrayed as shrewd, exploitative and greedy, and sometimes subject to violence (cf. Guha, 1983; Kar, 2013; Neelima, 2016). Ethical concerns are sometimes internalized by those in charge of credit; microfinance loan officers in Kolkata, India, questioned their moral conduct when lending money to and recovering debts from subprime borrowers (Kar, 2013). However, feelings of obligation, gratitude, and mutual interdependence are also common; subprime debtors are aware that neighborhood money lenders extended their credit when formal institutions, like banks, would not (Gandhi, 2013). Gratitude toward and respect for lenders are not unknown; Guérin (2014) shows how lenders are the first to be invited to social ceremonies and are treated with respect and honor. Thus, complex social relations are articulated around debt where tensions, animosity, and manipulations coexist alongside trust, gratitude, and intimacy.

With these productive and seminal insights into circuits of commerce, their functions, and impact on social relations among those who constitute them, one question remains: how do circuits of commerce impact the socioeconomic order in which they operate? That the functioning of circuits impacts the broader socioeconomic order has been suggested. Tracing the trajectory of life insurance for children in the United States, Zelizer (2011) has noted how perceptions of money and the parent–child relationship underwent moral transformations. In the early nineteenth century, when life insurance for children was first offered in the United States, parents who bought insurance were charged with profaning the lives of their "priceless" children and insurance companies were accused of having "child blood" on their hands for providing monetary motives to parents for violence against children (Zelizer, 2011, p. 45). These pervasive moral evaluations of child insurance affected governmental policies; between 1889 and 1902, Zelizer (2011, p. 44) notes "at least eighty legislative attempts across the country to prohibit or restrict the insurance of children's lives as being against public policy and the public interest." However, over time, public sentiments changed; insurance came to embody the value of children and of parents' love and affection for them, and became widely acceptable. Commonly deemed as hard and impersonal, money in child insurance was softened and made humane by the touch of intimacy, care, and love (Zelizer, 2011). To show that the "cultural biography" of an object may sometimes alter the "social history" of commodities, Appadurai (1988) refers to Gandhi's endorsement of *khadi* as locally produced cloth. This "commodity resistance" checked the desirability of British textiles in India and helped frame the political discourse of India's independence (pp. 30–34). Working with Wall Street investment banks, Ho (2009) show how their work culture of "liquid" employees that are hired and fired expeditiously has influenced America's corporate culture, where employer loyalty is increasingly considered to be expendable. This chapter draws from these provocative suggestions and offers an ethnography to show how interpersonal relations that are centered around debt in a circuit of commerce shape the economic system in which they operate.

In Agra's tourism, the uncertainty of getting tourist clientele leads to the formation of a circuit of commerce between showroom owners and tour guides that is held together by the circulation of debt that articulates intimacy and economic manipulation, need, and assistance. This chapter evaluates the overall impact that these circuits and their functioning have on Agra's tourism vis-à-vis risk, trust and uncertainty. I begin with assessing how the circulation of debt affects the relationship between showroom owners and tour guides. This offers an entry point to arrive at the bigger picture and understand the impacts of these circuits of commerce on Agra's tourism.

TOURISM IN AGRA: UNCERTAINTY AND COMMISSION

Tourism in Agra centers on the Taj Mahal, a Mughal era heritage monument that was planned in 1631 by emperor Shah Jahan as a mausoleum for his wife, Arjumand Bano, popularly known as Mumtaz Mahal. Taj Mahal has been recognized as protected heritage by India's federal government and placed under the care of the Archaeological Survey of India. It is designated as a World Heritage Site by UNESCO and is one of the seven wonders of the world. As India's premier tourism attraction, Taj Mahal draws 7–8 million visitors annually (http://www.tajmahal.gov.in/taj_visitors.html).[2]

I conducted ethnographic fieldwork in Agra's tourism markets from October 2012 to August 2013 as part of my doctoral research. Primarily, I relied on peripatetic participant observation to gather data, roaming the different market segments, catching snatches of conversations among different entrepreneurs, observing them at work, and talking to them in their free time. These constant peregrinations helped ensure that I did not obstruct entrepreneurs as they pursued tourists, hawked their wares or conducted sales. As a single, unmarried female researcher in a male-dominated market, fieldwork was sometimes challenging and I often worried if I was perceived as alone and vulnerable to harassment. To counter this, I initiated circuits of commerce that blended my familial and professional relations mediated in part, by economic activities. I frequently invited my mother and sister to visit me and on our sightseeing and shopping expeditions, I introduced them to guides, photographers, and shopkeepers; with them, I was finally locatable in a familiar patriarchal familial structure as someone's daughter and sister.[3]

One unexpected obstacle was people' concerns that I worked with the Lonely Planet or was an undercover journalist, there to report on commission alliances and cheating, facets of ill-repute and notoriety for Agra's tourism. To allay their concerns and to reassert my student status, I publically "handled" my student ID card as often as I could; India's love for bureaucratic stamp and seal was the best antidote to soothe some concerns that my research participants had about my identity (Heslop, 2016).

In this chapter, I focus on showroom owners and tour guides who work together, constituting a "circuit of commerce" in response to uncertainty and its risks. The showroom owners who are part of this study primarily sell marble merchandise, sometimes alongside other goods like jewelry and clothing. These showrooms are located at an approximate distance of 1–2 kilometers from the Taj Mahal and look to cater exclusively to foreign tourists who are widely perceived to have considerable spending power; entrepreneurs gauge this from the fact that they hire travel agencies, stay in expensive hotels, and request tour guides and travel escorts for the duration of their visit.

In keeping with the tourist niche, entrepreneurs who are part of this study, maintain some of the biggest marble showrooms in Agra that are stocked with diverse merchandise like marble table-tops, wall clocks, lamp shades, and photo frames, all adorned with intricate inlay and carving work. A handful of these showrooms are old and reputable and find mention in travel guide books where they are recommended to tourists. Most however, are new enterprises that have sprung up in the past decade as tourism in Agra has grown. Anonymous because of their lack of reputation and because there are numerous others just like them in Agra today, these establishments are a poorer but ambitious imitation of their bigger and better-off counterparts. They are smaller in size and rarely recommended in travel guidebooks or tourist blogs; entrepreneurs here look to attract middle-income foreign tourists.[4]

Uncertainty of getting clientele weighs heavily on these showroom owners, particularly the ones with new and lesser-known businesses. Agra's easy connectivity with Delhi is as much a bane as boon; because there are several short-distance fast trains from Delhi to Agra and a road expressway with a travel time of approximately 3.5 hours, tourists who visit Agra often make whistle-stop trips, arriving in the morning and leaving by evening.[5] Tourists often combine their travels to Agra with visits to Delhi and Jaipur, the "golden triangle" of India's heritage tourism. Because Agra's tourists are very mobile, their interactions with local entrepreneurs are short and few; this inhibits the formation of long-term patron–client relationships, an oft-employed strategy to mitigate the uncertainty of getting clientele. Additionally, the showrooms in this study are located away from the Taj Mahal and border vehicle-populated thoroughfares without proper sidewalks. Consequently, one never finds tourists walking around them, window-shopping on their way to the monument. In the absence of an assured tourist foot traffic, showroom owners rely on commission-based alliances with tour guides and travel agents to get tourist clientele.

COMMISSION ALLIANCES BETWEEN SHOWROOM OWNERS AND TOUR GUIDES

Commission is the practice where some economic actors pay money to others for bringing in clients and facilitating sales; it is a popular strategy among tourism establishments to attract clients although by no means restricted only to tourism.[6] In Agra, economic actors with "fixed" establishments, like the showroom owners in this study, pay commission to tour guides, drivers, and travel agencies. The direction of payment indicates that commission is paid to those who have initial or prolonged contact with tourists and subsequently, have the power to determine and facilitate their contact with the rest. Tour guides have an expanded role in taking care of tourists through the duration of their visit. As they lead tourists on their sightseeing visits, guides inhabit the role of experts; aside from getting historical information about monuments, tourists frequently ask guides for recommendations about places to eat and shop; they expect them to ensure they are not harassed and to take care of them if they get sick or need any help. Guides, on their part, convert this dependence into a strategy for economic gain; they take tourists to different establishments and in return, earn commission from the owners (also see, Crick, 1994; Edensor, 1998). Akin to commodity chains, commission-based alliances seek to establish consumer chains through which a tourist client passes, moving from those entrepreneurs who have first contact and prolonged interaction with tourists to those who, by the nature of their work, spend the least amount of time with them and cannot chase after them.

While prevalent earlier too (e.g., see Edensor, 1998), commission alliances in Agra have grown in strength, number, and importance.[7] Commission today is one of the defining principles in Agra's tourism even as alliances vary based on duration (long or short term), amount of money paid and promised (a fixed percentage on sale or a token amount for simply bringing in tourists), and manner of payment (post-sale commission or advance payments alongside commission). In this chapter, I focus on commission alliances that are long term, lasting at least for a season, with a predetermined percentage of commission, and that are accompanied by advance payments to tour guides. Such commission alliances are the norm in Agra, supplemented with short term and token amounts of payments given to all guides and drivers who bring their tourists to showrooms.

Agra's Entrepreneurs: Showroom Owners and Tour Guides

In November 2012, Mohsin began setting up his marble showroom; by May 2013, the premises had been rented and stocked with merchandise, and sales staff hired. The showroom was open yet not functional as no tourists were coming in. Mohsin explained that he was negotiating his commission alliances with tour guides and Delhi-based travel agents, who would ensure a steady supply of tourists to his showroom. For this purpose, he was in talks with Shahdab, a "convincer"[8] and hoped that by August 2013, his showroom would be functional.

Rajesh, a well-to-do man in his 50s, was the owner of a big marble and jewelry showroom. There were about 8–10 employees, most of who worked as salesmen, one managed commission payments, and another maintained account books. Rajesh's showroom has long-lasting relations with many Delhi-based travel agencies that sent tourists. In return, the showroom paid them commission and made provisions for tour guides and drivers for tourists. At the time of my fieldwork, 15 guides were working with the showroom; they were not paid a salary but kept the tips they received from tourists and earned commission on sales.

Tour guides, as noted earlier, are an important nodal member of these commission alliances because of their intimate and prolonged interactions with tourists. Increasingly, showroom owners in Agra approach tour guides with offers of work. Parvez is one such guide who works from a marble showroom. In 1987, Parvez started work from a ticket-window outside the Taj Mahal before moving to the nearby parking lot. However, he did not like the work environment there; he complained that the parking lot was overcrowded as most guides converged there to solicit tourists who arrived in cars and buses. Competition among guides was intense and physical fights over tourists and in front of them were frequent. Fed up with the daily squabbles, facing familial problems, and searching for stable income, Parvez approached his neighbor who worked as a manager in a marble showroom, and found employment there. This showroom, like others around it, had alliances with travel agencies in Delhi; when their clients visit Agra, Parvez's neighbor, the manager, assigns a guide. For his work, Parvez is not paid a salary but earns 20% commission if the tourists make a purchase at the showroom; he also keeps the tips that tourists give him. Parvez, however, is not the only guide who works from this showroom; six other guides are tied to the showroom on similar payment arrangements.[9]

Deepak is another tour guide who, during my fieldwork, worked from two different showrooms. When I met him, he worked from Rajesh's showroom, having found a job through his friend, Rajat, who was a salesman there; later, Deepak moved to another showroom. In both establishments, Deepak kept tourists' tips and earned commission on any purchase made by his clients; he was not paid a salary. Javed, another tour guide, worked from a showroom owned by a distant relative;[10] he also earned his money in tips and commission with no daily wage. Javed chose to work from his relative's showroom because he believed that as a kinsman he could ask for and would get his pick of tourist clients, primarily those who were perceived to be wealthy and more likely to make purchases. This would increase his chances of earning heftier commission.

Commission-based alliances between tour guides and showroom owners of the nature discussed above are the norm in Agra's tourism market. These alliances were crucial during the high tourism season that lasted from August to March. For this, frenzied negotiations took place in the low tourism season, between April and July. During this period, tour guides and showroom owners reached out to one another through middlemen, their managers and other employees, friends, family members, and neighbors. Both explored work opportunities and payment offers, and made their availability known. Alliances were finalized with an agreement on the percentage of commission, and tour guides came to work with showroom owners. Although such alliances were only meant to last for the duration of the tourism season, tour guides often worked with showrooms for several years.

Proliferation of Risks through Commission Alliances

Commission-based alliances were initiated to reduce uncertainty and promised stable monetary returns for showroom owners and tour guides. However, these alliances only constitute an opening, a potentiality, albeit a critical one, of transacting business. While uncertainty is mitigated as tourists are brought to showrooms, visits still need to translate into sales. Furthermore, there have been known instances of tour guides who indulge in cheating and opportunism. Motivated by better commission offers from other showrooms, guides sometimes split their clientele, sending wealthier ones to a new showroom where they wish to work or where they are promised more commission, and bring the rest to the showroom where they work; in Agra, this is referred to as "double-dealing." On a less deliberate but equally risky note, tour guides fail to persuade their tourists to return to the showroom; I refer to this as nonreciprocity. Double-dealing and nonreciprocity both entail loss of clientele and culminate in showroom owners' failure to mitigate their uncertainty of getting clientele despite commission alliances. The repercussions of an unsuccessful encounter with uncertainty are severe; showroom owners' investments in their business threaten to exceed their returns, entailing monetary loss, an unsustainable business and no income. While setting up his new showroom, Mohsin had already spent a cumulative of INR[11] 300,000 (US$4,958) on rent, workers' salary and merchandise, and had not yet sold a single item. Consequently, showroom owners are hard pressed to combat risks of cheating and nonreciprocity by tour guides as they also look to convert tourist visits into sales. For this, showroom owners attempt to make commission alliances more binding and economically productive by extending advance payments to guides to extract allegiance and reciprocity from them.

CIRCULATING DEBT

Most showroom owners extended advance payments to tour guides to work with them. Such payments were made with the understanding that they would be deducted from guides' commission till the total advance was recovered.[12] However, such recovery was rarely pursued; most showroom owners were content to let the advance remain pending. Explaining why they offered advance, some showroom owners stressed altruistic motives of helping the needy and their sense of responsibility towards those less fortunate; others spoke of reciprocating work with money. Amir, a showroom owner, said that he sometimes gave advance to *zarooratmand* guides, those in need of monetary help, while another explained that, "This [Agra's tourism] is not just business but also a small community. I know so many of these people and their families. I feel obliged to help out when I see young guides burdened with providing for their families." Anjum, another showroom owner, underscored the mutually beneficial aspect of such payments, explaining, "I use their [guides'] services to keep track of tourists so I should also extend to help them when they need it."

As per these showroom owners, advance was offered to guides they knew through community ties, familial relations, and through work. The importance of familiarity in extending credit is well-documented and backed by economic rationality; creditors prefer to offer loans to those who are traceable so that the risks of flight and credit default can be kept at bay. To minimize chances of incurring a bad and unrepayable debt, creditors often look to extend loans to those who they know will be able to repay them (Lyon, 2000; Mahmoud, 2008). Showroom owners' advance payment offers to Agra's tour guides seem to follow this logic; both sets of entrepreneurs have roots in Agra and are known to one another through extended social networks. Located in Agra with strong family ties there, tour guides are easily traceable to enforce repayments.

However, contrary to showroom owners' assertions of goodwill, recipients of these advance payments, that is, tour guides, experienced these payments as constraining. The narrative of forwarding advance to "zarooratmand" or needy guides that is propagated by showroom owners was repeated by guides as "paise jo baandh dete hain" or money that ties them up. In this vein, Shamshuddin, president of the tour guides' association in Agra, referred to guides who work for showroom owners as "bandhua mazdoor [bonded labor]." These pervasive sentiments are not merely reflective of a Maussian discontent when unable to reciprocate a gift or repay a debt. A closer look at the considerations after which guides were offered advance payments, and how these impacted the work relations between them and showroom owners, indicates that advance payments were backed by purposeful calculations to engineer debt with an eye on long-term work reciprocity.

Showroom owners generally offered advance to those tour guides who faced pressing expenses *and* were known to have limited financial liquidity to repay loans. The coexistence of these two factors meant that tour guides would not be able to repay loans easily, allowing showroom owners to "engineer indebtedness" (Appadurai, 1988; Firth, 1983). I refer to these debts as "bad debts" because showroom owners' offers were predicated on the knowledge that tour guides would not be able to repay them. Monetary dependence thus created, showroom owners mobilized it to extract work-based allegiance from tour guides beholden to them. However, to determine financial need and restricted liquidity, showroom owners needed intimate knowledge about tour guides' personal lives, living conditions, material aspirations, and financial constraints. To access this information, showroom owners searched guides' social networks and contacted them through their friends, family members, and neighbors.

Mr. Bohra, manager of Rajesh's showroom, explained how social knowledge about guides' personal lives and needs was deliberately sought and utilized by showroom owners. In his words, "We get direct orders from the owner to find those guides who are in need [of money]. This is easy, the trade is small and Agra is small. Everyone knows everyone's *haalat* [condition] and word gets around. There are so many of them here, young men who are sole earners in large families with 10–11 dependents. They always need money and, I feel bad saying it, but we especially go after them and offer money to help them." He then proceeded to tell me about some guides that he had got to the showroom talking about their domestic financial needs surrounding such moves: one guide had been given an advance at the time of his sister's wedding, another had come when his father's convenience store had caught fire and closed down, another's mother had been sick and needed prolonged treatment.

Sometimes knowledge of a person's financial condition was widely available because it could be assumed to be generally applicable to members of a social group. For example, one could zero in on a specific social group that lived in a lower-income neighborhood, like Taj Ganj, where most guides who are a part of this study lived; one could also find a group where people lived in large multi-generational families and wage work was highly gendered. The Muslims in lower-income neighborhoods of Agra were one such group where large families comprising the ego, his siblings, parents, and grandparents lived together and where female members of the household did not usually engage in wage work. Based on this social knowledge, a reasonable assumption could be made about the financial pressures faced by young male tour guides. This general knowledge about guides' financial needs and constraints could then be further corroborated by tapping into their intimate social relations. Neighbors, friends, and kinsmen often yielded information that helped showroom owners make monetary offers that guides could scarcely refuse.

Parvez recalled joining the showroom where he had been employed for three years. While working independently as a guide from the Taj Mahal parking lot, Parvez's income was supplemented by his two brothers': one a guide and another a low-level government employee. The brother with the government job subsequently got married, had a falling out with his family and moved out.

With one source of income gone and frustrated with the intense competition at the parking lot, Parvez sought steadier employment. He approached his neighbor, the showroom manager, for help. The neighbor-manager responded with a job offer and an advance payment of INR 20,000 (US$330) that Parvez still owed.

Young tour guides were particularly susceptible to advance payments and the demanding work obligations that these created. Although most young guides did not yet shoulder the complete financial burdens of their families, their parents usually controlled their expenses, often denying their desires for lifestyle goods. Many shared their aspirations and frustrations with their age peers, like cousins and friends, who often worked in showrooms as salesmen or tour guides; showroom owners incentivized the sharing of such information.

Rajat, a salesman in Rajesh's showroom, had helped his cousin, Suraj, and his friend, Deepak, find work as guides there. Suraj, Rajat's cousin in his early 20s, had recently finished college and obtained a guiding license. When I met the two cousins, Suraj expressed his gratitude toward Rajat for helping him find work that allowed him "some freedom." Suraj explained that after college, he had been desperate for a job because his father, Rajat's father's younger brother, maintained a tight fist over the household's expenses. The old man, the cousins alleged, often reprimanded Suraj for wasteful expenditure on electronic gadgets and clothes. Aware of Suraj's constraints, Rajat proposed his case to the owner, who hired Suraj and gave him an advance of INR 10,000 (US$165). Deepak, Rajat's friend, too hailed him as a "true friend and brother" for helping him find work. Deepak said that he had wanted to purchase a used car but his mother and aunt (father's sister, who was unmarried and lived with them) reprimanded him for irresponsible desires and wastefulness. Deepak's father had passed away a few years ago and the women wanted him to shoulder more financial responsibilities for the household. Deepak complained about this "*emotional atyachaar*–emotional blackmail" to his friends, including Rajat. Rajat brought Deepak's case to his employer, who offered him work and an advance. Neither of the young men had told their family members about having received advance payments. For his referrals, Rajat earned a one-time bonus from the showroom owner.

Lateral kinship relations, such as of young cousins, and friendships are important to access personal information about the aspirations and frustrations of guides. Young men in India frequently find themselves torn between familial responsibilities and control by adults, and their desire for lifestyle consumer goods like electronic gadgets, clothing, and cars that are often deemed wasteful by older household members. Burdened with unrequited desires and limited means to fulfill them, these men frequently turn to their age peers to vent their frustrations. Showroom owners look to these relationships to understand monetary needs of young guides and offer them advances to fulfill their consumption desires. However, in a bid to portray themselves as fiscally responsible adults or to avoid making monetary contributions to the household, these young men are inclined to conceal their debt from family members. Clandestine debt thus established, threats of repayment can subsequently be employed effectively to discipline guides or coerce them to not only bring tourists to the showroom but also to facilitate sales. In the following section, I will discuss how these bad debts are put to work by showroom owners.

CIRCULATION OF BAD DEBT AND ITS IMPLICATIONS

As we have seen in the previous sections, bad debts were circulated between showroom owners and tour guides through their social networks and intimate social relations. In this section, I elucidate how these debts were invoked by showroom owners to demand work-based compliance from guides and sometimes to expand the scope of their work. Interestingly, the circulation of such bad debts did not only weigh upon tour guides; showroom owners as well as tourists were affected. I will attend to this later in the section.

Paisa jo bandh deta hai: *The Obligations of Bad Debts for Tour Guides*

As noted above, tour guides made the bulk of their daily earnings from commission; consequently, they faced tremendous pressure to ensure that tourists return to the showroom for shopping. Shamshuddin, president of the guides' association in Agra, explained this, "Since these shops don't pay salary and guides only work for commission, he [guide] is always thinking about shopping rather than guiding. Nowadays, they show monument for half an hour and spend three hours in shopping." Showroom owners further exacerbate the pressures of making a living by threatening to fire guides and demanding that they repay the advance if their tourists do not visit the showrooms or visit other showrooms.

Showroom owners regularly used the debt that guides owe them as a punitive measure against those who lose clients to other showrooms or as a potential threat to deter others from reneging on their commitments. Javed, a tour guide, summed up the fallout of such "tourist dissidence." According to him, "If you lose clients a number of times, you will be sent off [fired] from that showroom. It is often hard to find new work once you have been sent off like that. It's a small trade and everyone will know that either this guide is not reliable or he is not good at his work and cannot hold on to the clients." I got the showroom owners' perspective on this from Mohsin. He explained that guides were responsible for losing tourists even if tourists themselves insisted on going to another shop, "I will warn him the first few times, then I will threaten to let him go, maybe slap him or curse him. I'll ask him to return his advance immediately. He works for me, it's his job to make sure that the client comes back here." Commission-reliant earnings and the pending debt put incredible work pressure on tour guides. In the words of Mr. Bohra, a showroom manager, "Then [after taking advance] guides are tied to this job. The owner will threaten them to persuade clients to buy things or to return the money. They obviously don't have spare cash lying around so they spend their days like this only, eyes downcast in front of the owner and tourists, and getting shouted at by both. I feel bad but I also have a family to feed. It's all business."

Sometimes, showroom owners used the pending debt to expand the roles and duties of guides. When Parvez and Deepak had joined their respective showrooms, their only job had been to ensure that tourists returned to the showroom after sightseeing; that accomplished, the guides' work ended. However, Parvez recalled that a few months into his job, his neighbor, the showroom manager, approached him and requested that he talk to tourists about different merchandise. This request, according to Parvez, was presented as a one-time favor; the manager told him that one salesman was on leave and others were occupied with clients; Parvez obliged. However, such requests began to come regularly under different pretexts; either the salesmen were busy or the manager would extol his proficiency in spoken English, lamenting that most salesmen's patchy English hindered their sales pitches. On shifting grounds, Parvez's daily work sphere expanded; now, it is part of his job to assist salesmen with the tourists he brings to the showroom. Parvez was annoyed with his neighbor-cum-manager for the sly approach he adopted to expand his work duties. He was hurt that the manager's approach had demonstrated his solidarity with the showroom owner rather than with Parvez, his neighbor for as long as he could remember, and that the expansion in duties had not been accompanied by a fixed salary that salesmen got. However, being of a nonconfrontational disposition, Parvez did not raise these issues with the manager; he reasoned that his neighbor had helped him find work and acknowledged that he still owed the advance money. However, Parvez added that he frequently pondered over arranging money to settle the debt so that he could renegotiate his duties and payments.

Deepak recalled being severely reprimanded by the showroom owner when his tourists did not buy anything, "I was told [by the showroom owner] that if I cannot sell things to tourists, there was no need for me in the shop. 'I don't run a [tour] guide agency, this is a shop,' the showroom owner told me." According to Deepak, such complaints caught him off-guard because he had not been told that facilitating sales was a part of his work. As these threats and abuses became routine and unbearable, Deepak eventually left the showroom. He was able to repay the loan by joining another showroom that paid him an advance; the new debt stands unpaid.

To employ pending debt as a technique of control, showroom owners needed to establish the guide's need for money *and* his inability to make prompt repayments. The coexistence of these two factors alone could create long-term monetary dependence and the ensuing obligations that would tie tour guides to showroom owners. The unpaid bad debt was therefore, a calculated investment by showroom owners rather than a poorly conceptualized expenditure on their part. In effect, these bad debts reversed the natural order of dependence between the two economic actors. Owing to their prolonged contact with tourists, tour guides ideally are in a position of power vis-à-vis showroom owners who have limited contact with tourists. The direction of commission payments also indicates that showroom owners are dependent on tour guides for access to tourists. However, by lending money to the financially strained guides, showroom owners created obligations that effectively reversed this power equation; tour guides, owing them money and their jobs, became subservient to the showroom owners.

Although the pressures of a bad debt are most acutely felt by tour guides, showroom owners are not free from their adverse implications. Furthermore, the effects of bad debt are not restricted to the creditor and the debtor; the implications – social and economic – are widespread and affect how tourism in Agra is perceived and conducted.

Relations between Tour Guides and Tourists

Owing to their outstanding debt, guides are under tremendous pressure to ensure that tourists visit showrooms where they have alliances and not any other. However, travel guidebooks like the Lonely Planet, draw from the experiences of tourists who have visited Agra and have had unpleasant encounters with tour guides, and routinely warn tourists about commission. Usually under the "safety tips" section, tourists are warned about touts and tour guides who work for commission and harass and cheat tourists by making them purchase merchandise at inflated prices. Consequently, many tourists are wary of guides who insist on taking them to specific showrooms.

This wariness on the part of tourists conflicts with tour guides' work who must bring tourists to showrooms if they intend to keep their jobs, earn money, and not incur the risks of job loss and debt repayments. But in a suspicious environment, deliberately taking tourists to a particular showroom and directing them away from others can be a tightrope walk for guides. To prevent tourists from going in to other showrooms, many guides adopt scare tactics. Parvez told me that he routinely warns his tourists about goods of inferior quality and the wide prevalence of fakes. To ensure that tourists are disinclined to explore the city without him, Parvez stresses the lack of safety in Agra where unsuspecting tourists without local escorts may be vulnerable to cheats and thieves, and exposed to harassment and petty or serious crimes. In his words, "I scare them a little and then tell them that they should only shop where I take them; most agree. They don't know the city anyway, so I'm helping them, helping my employer and helping myself."

However, tourists are not always accommodating and many want to venture into the city on their own; some wish to visit showrooms they see on the way or have read about in guidebooks; still others may not want to shop at all. Faced with noncomplying clients, guides resort to persuasion that borders on harassment. Many pester tourists, talking up additional attractions, like being able to see inlay work in progress, or meeting with artisans whose ancestors did inlay work on the Taj Mahal. When these fail, tour guides often take tourists to showrooms without informing them or obtaining their consent. Needless to say, this annoys many tourists and validates the warnings that they have read in travel accounts. Several tourists that I met in Agra spoke of the guides' aggression and wiliness; many narrated stories of finding themselves in showrooms despite not wanting to shop and without being informed. Annoyed, most did not buy anything and a few even complained to their travel agency. Many tourists report these experiences in guidebooks and travelogues, creating a discursive circuit about the circuit of commerce, feeding popular narratives about the nuisance of commission in Agra. The two circuits intersect, affecting the everyday economic activities of guides and showroom owners. Having read commission stories, tourists are suspicious of guides who try to direct them to specific showrooms that are not of their choosing and this often affects their consumer patterns; many entrepreneurs complained that tourists were increasingly becoming reluctant shoppers after reading travel guide books. Travel agents, upon receiving complaints from tourists, sometimes asked showroom owners to fire responsible guides. When such requests come from travel agents that have longstanding alliances with the showroom or ones that represent valuable customers, the threat of job loss is real; guides may be fired or removed from the roster of that agency. Thus, a tour guide sometimes stands to lose his job by fulfilling his responsibilities toward the showroom owner. The result is a vicious cycle of deception, suspicion, and bad press that breeds an unfriendly and uncertain consumption environment, pitting tour guides and tourists as "adversaries," who are constantly on guard against one another.

The Costs and Risks for Showroom Owners

The circulation of bad debt also strains relations between tour guides, showroom owners, and those who played a role in bringing the two together. Often, the pressures of a pending debt take a toll on the intimate social relations between guides and their friends, cousins and neighbors who got them the job. Rajat and Deepak, once close friends, stopped talking to each other altogether. Talking about the estrangement, Deepak spoke of the work and debt that he believed Rajat had knowingly gotten him entangled in without informing him about the showroom's abusive work environment. During this conversation, Deepak lamented that he had treated Rajat like his "brother" but Rajat had failed to fulfill that role. He complained that aside from not warning him about the showroom owner's bad behavior, Rajat had repeatedly chosen not to intervene on Deepak's behalf when the owner shouted at him. Rajat, on his part, was angry with Deepak for his lack of gratitude and questioned his commitment to work. "Some people think that they will get a job and just earn money without doing any hard work. People just want to make easy money without breaking a sweat," he grumbled one time, referring to Deepak. "He [Deepak] left the job abruptly and did not even tell me or think about how this would affect me. The showroom owner is angry with me for bringing unreliable guides. He [Deepak] is selfish; he only thinks about himself and not how his actions can affect others, especially those who have helped him," Rajat concluded. Similarly, Parvez too was annoyed with his neighbor-cum-manager for the increasing pressures of the job although he still felt beholden to him. Thus, social relations that were instrumental in finding jobs and facilitating debt were frequently strained when tour guides began to feel the obligations and pressures of a bad debt.

Showroom owners too faced repercussions of bad debts. Tour guides, frustrated and pressurized by the constant work demands, are always on a lookout for other and better-paying work options. Deepak was one such guide who switched to another showroom that paid better commission and offered him an advance to repay his standing debt. This is not an exception; guides routinely kept their eyes and ears open for better work offers and frequently indulged in double dealings by taking better-paying tourists to other showrooms that offered more commission and held out the inducement of a new job offer. This opportunistic behavior of guides is so well known in Agra that it has given rise to two critical market functions: to conduct monitoring and surveillance on guides to deter cheating, and to poach guides who work with other showrooms. Convincers are Agra's mediator actors who discharge these roles.

When I met him, Shahdab had been working as a convincer for the past 7–8 years and was in negotiations with Mohsin, who had set up a new showroom. Shahdab outlined his daily work routine for me. On the day of the expected tourist visit, Shahdab reports to the showroom and waits there till the guide calls to inform him that he is with the tourist party and headed for sightseeing. When the tour is supposed to be over, as per pre-decided time specifications, Shahdab heads to the Taj Mahal and keeps a lookout for the guide. Unknown to the tourists, he discretely follows the party till they head to the showroom. By tracking the guide and his tourists, Shahdab makes sure that guides are not taking tourists to other showrooms or negotiating work offers with other showrooms.

Lucky, a salesman in Rajesh's showroom, undertakes convincing in a part-time capacity; his role tends towards inducing guides that are attached with other showrooms to visit Rajesh's. In the mornings and evenings, Lucky hangs around the Taj Mahal and seeks out guides. He indiscriminately approaches all guides and drivers, without any concern for whether they have prior "setting"[13] with another showroom. Once he zeroes in on guides who appear interested, Lucky requests them to bring their tourist clients to the showroom. He quotes them a commission amount and if the tourists make a purchase, Lucky too earns commission.

There is significant room for error in deciphering guides' indiscretion. Guides' conversations with friends may be interpreted as negotiations of new job offers; guides' inability to prevent tourists from visiting another showroom can appear as double-dealings. Predictably, tour guides are resentful of such surveillance and expressed bitterness toward showroom owners as well as convincers. Many accused convincers of manufacturing instances of guides' infringement to secure their own jobs. Similarly, poaching guides often led to tensions between different showroom owners, many of who in Agra's local and intimate tourism market, are related to one another through myriad social relations.

The bad debts that showroom owners make to protect themselves against cheating, opportunism, and nonreciprocity by their tour guides intensifies an atmosphere of trust deficit. The ultimate result is ironic; by pressurizing tour guides with debts, showroom owners face those very risks – of cheating, opportunism, double-dealing – that they sought to guard against in the first place. Faced with the possibility of tour guides' disloyalty, showroom owners must bear the additional costs of hiring convincers to conduct daily monitoring, surveillance and poaching. The circulation of ill-will among all economic actors – showroom owners, tour guides, and tourists – creates an uneasy economic system with heightened uncertainty and recurring costs.

CONCLUSION: CIRCULATION OF DEBT AND ITS IMPLICATIONS

Intersections between social relations and economic transactions have been subject to much scholarly attention, and circuits of commerce provide a productive framework to think through them (cf. Zelizer, 2011). The circulation of debt is integral to many such circuits. Social familiarity within circuits allows people to access credit and extend risk-free debt but debt also helps establish relationships, build trust and assert entrepreneurial status (De Neve, 1999; Hampton, 2003; Heslop, 2016). With these seminal insights into the complex workings of debt-centered circuits of commerce, it remains to be assessed how local circuits of commerce and the interactions they foster impact the socioeconomic system in which they occur. This chapter presents an ethnographic account of one such circuit and examines how the negotiations and transformations of relationships between participants within a circuit affect the larger economic system. In Agra's tourism, considerations of risks and uncertainty of getting clientele set off a circuit of commerce into motion, comprising showroom owners, tour guides, and those with socioeconomic ties to both. As showroom owners look to make circuits productive and binding, they turn to guides' intimate social relations to engineer debt. The transformations in interpersonal relations among circuit members impact Agra's tourism as a whole.

Within the circuit, relations between showroom owners, their indebted guides, and those who brought them together are often frayed in response to the pressures and manipulations of the debt. But the effects are far reaching; in this chapter, I have noted two. One, uncertainty in Agra's tourism is accentuated owing to the circulation of bad debt, and now comes with additional costs. Tour guides, under constant pressure from showroom owners, were receptive to double-dealing and switching jobs. Faced with their disloyalty, most showroom owners had to hire convincers to monitor guides' movement and to poach new ones. Two, the circulation of bad debts impacts tourists' consumption behavior in a way that is believed to negatively affect Agra's tourism businesses, especially of guides and showroom owners. Pressurized to deliver tourists and sales, guides often resort to aggression, scare tactics and sly maneuvers to bring clients to showrooms. Understandably, tourists find such behavior offensive and reported them in travel guide books and travelogues, lending weight to prevalent narratives of wily and opportunistic guides. The result is a vitiated atmosphere of mistrust and discontent between tourism entrepreneurs and tourists that exacerbates the pressures and suspicions of both groups. Reluctant shoppers mean fewer purchases for showroom owners and less commission for tour guides, and heightened uncertainty for both sets of economic actors.

This chapter reverses the questions that are generally asked of circuits of commerce and their relations to macro-structures. Instead of interrogating the structural factors that necessitate circuits of commerce, I take heed of suggestions that micro-practices can impact the macro-system in which they operate (Appadurai, 1988; Zelizer, 2011). This ethnographic account presents one instance where the politics of interpersonal relations within a circuit of commerce have a defining influence in shaping the macro-system. I offer this as an invitation to further explore the relationship between micro-processes and macro-systems through the register of circuits of commerce.

NOTES

1. For examples on the functioning of weak and strong ties, see, Acheson, 1994; Hampton, 2003; Mahmoud, 2008; Russell, 1994; and Zhao, Ritchie, & Echtner, 2011.

2. Other important monuments and sites include Agra Fort, another World Heritage Site, and *Fatehpur Sikri*, a World Heritage Site in close proximity to Agra city. Aside from these, there are numerous other heritage monuments like *Itmad-ud-Daulah*, *Sikandra*, *Mehtab Bagh* and *Chini ka Rauza*. The World Heritage Sites in India fall under the care and supervision of the Archaeological Survey of India (ASI), a federal government agency under the Ministry of Culture.

3. I also sought to establish kinship with my research participants and referred to them by the classificatory term of "older brother," *bhai* or *bhaiyya*, irrespective of real-age considerations. I chose to carve out this relationship of "younger sister-older brother" in the hope that some of our mutual awkwardness would be mitigated if there was a normative relationship to guide our interactions.

4. Both types of entrepreneurs are disdainful of domestic tourists, who are widely perceived as budget tourists and persistent bargainers. Entrepreneurs believe that their bargaining also deterred foreign tourists from shopping; most discourage domestic tourists from their enterprises by appearing uninterested or busy. Foreign backpackers are also looked upon disdainfully for their limited purchasing power. Aside from relying on dress cues, entrepreneurs distinguish between wealthy and desirable foreign tourists and the budget backpacker foreign tourists by the company they keep. Wealthy tourists are accompanied by tour guides or a travel escort assigned by the travel agency while backpacker tourists come alone or with tour guides and drivers who are locally known to be self-employed.

5. The group of tourists that is most likely to stay for longer duration of time in Agra is typically the foreign backpackers, the group also associated with least expenditure on purchasing tourism commodities.

6. For examples of commission in tourism, see Crick (1994) on commission alliances between guest house owners and tour guides; Huberman (2010) on commission relations between tour guides and hotel and restaurant owners and shopkeepers; and Guo, Ling, Dong, and Liang (2013) for commission payments between hotels and third-party websites like expedia.com. For commission in non-tourism markets, see Heslop (2016).

7. In an oft-repeated origin story about commission, two big marble competitors, in a bid to monopolize the market, began to offer commission to guides and travel agents for bringing their tourists to the showroom. This practice was soon picked up by the new and numerous middle-range showrooms who were looking to establish a foothold in the market; from there, it spread by imitation and today, rarely does one find a showroom that does not pay commission to tour guides and drivers for bringing in tourists.

8. A convincer is a common figure in Agra's tourism economy, whose key role is to negotiate and oversee commission-based alliances with Delhi-based travel agents on behalf of their showroom owners.

9. The provision of tour guides by showrooms is both a perk and a surveillance mechanism. Travel agents, especially those based in Delhi, are the most critical alliance partners because tourists come through them. When negotiating alliances with them, Agra's showroom owners offer them the services of local tour guides so that travel agents do not have to worry about finding suitable guides and incurring costs to hire them. By assigning their guides to accompany tourists, showroom owners can ensure that they return to the showroom for shopping.

10. The showroom owner, Abdullah, was Javed's father's sister's husband's younger brother's son; a classificatory cousin.

11. INR is Indian Rupee. Approximately, US$1 = INR 60.50. Retrieved from http://www.oanda.com/currency/converter/. Accessed on April 15, 2014.

12. For example, a showroom owner gave INR 20,000 (US$330) as advance to a guide alongside the agreement for 10% commission on each purchase made by his tourists. So, if a sale of INR 10,000 (US$165) is made, the showroom owner will calculate the guide's commission as INR 1,000 (US$16). The balance is now INR 19,000 (US $314). Such calculated deductions will go on till the payment equaled INR 20,000 (US $330), the amount lent to the tour guide when he started work. After paying the advance, the tour guide would continue to receive a 10% commission on every purchase made by his tourists.

13. "Setting" is used colloquially to refer to commission-based arrangements.

ACKNOWLEDGMENTS

This chapter is based on ethnographic research, conducted as part of my doctoral fieldwork from June–August, 2011 to October 2012–August 2013 in the local tourism markets in Agra, India. Additional research for this chapter was conducted between September and October, 2015, supported by the Humane Studies Fellowship, 2015–2016. I presented a draft of this chapter at the American Anthropological Association's Annual Meeting, 2015. Feedback received there were helpful in writing this chapter. I acknowledge the support of my advisor, Dr. Dolores Koenig, and my peers for their valuable inputs. Special thanks to Sean Furmage for patiently and diligently reading several drafts of this chapter and providing critical insights and endless support.

REFERENCES

Acheson, J. (1994). Transaction costs and business strategies in a Mexican Indian pueblo. In J. Acheson (Ed.), *Anthropology and institutional economics* (pp. 143–166). Lanham, MD: University Press of America.

Appadurai, A. (1988). Introduction: Commodities and the politics of value. In A. Appadurai (Ed.), *The social life of things: Commodities in cultural perspective* (pp. 3–63). Cambridge: Cambridge University Press.

Breman, J. (2008). On labour bondage, old and new. *The Indian Journal of Labour Economics*, *51*(1), 83–90.

Crick, M. (1994). *Resplendent sites, discordant voices: Sri Lankans and international tourism*. Switzerland: Hardwood Academic Publishers.

Crona, B., Nyström, M., Folke, C., & Jiddawi, N. (2010). Middlemen: A critical socio-ecological link in coastal communities of Kenya and Zanzibar. *Marine Policy*, *34*(4), 761–771.

De Neve, G. (1999). Asking for and giving baki: Neo-bondage, or the interplay of bondage and resistance in the Tamilnadu power-loom industry. *Contributions to Indian Sociology*, *33*(1&2), 379–406.

Edensor, T. (1998). *Tourists at the Taj: Performance and meaning at a symbolic site*. London: Routledge.

Firth, R. (1983). Magnitudes and values in kula exchange. In J. W. Leach & E. Leach (Eds.), *The kula: New perspectives on massim exchange* (pp. 89–102). Cambridge: Cambridge University Press.

Gandhi, A. (2013). A superlative form: How gold mediates personhood and property in Mumbai. *Ethnofoor*, *25*(1), 91–110.

Geertz, C. (1978). The bazaar economy: Information and search in peasant marketing. *The American Economic Review*, *68*(2), 28–32.

Granovetter, M. (1973). The strength of weak ties. *American Journal of Sociology*, *78*(6), 1360–1380.

Granovetter, M. (1985). Economic action and the social structure: The problem of embeddedness. *American Journal of Sociology*, *91*(3), 481–510.

Gregory, C. A. (2012). On money debt and morality: Some reflections on the contribution of economic anthropology. *Social Anthropology*, *20*(4), 380–396.

Guérin, I. (2014). Juggling with debt, social ties, and values: The everyday use of microcredit in rural South India. *Current Anthropology*, *55*(9), 40–50.

Guha, R. (1983). *Elementary aspects of peasant insurgency in colonial India*. Delhi: Oxford University Press.

Guo, X., Ling, L., Dong, Y., & Liang, L. (2013). Cooperation contract in tourism supply chain: The optimal pricing strategy of hotels for cooperative third party strategic websites. *Annals of Tourism Research*, *41*, 20–41.

Hampton, M. P. (2003). Entry points for local tourism in developing countries: Evidence from Yogyakarta, Indonesia. *Geografiska Annaler. Series B Human Geography*, *85*(2), 85–101.

Heslop, L. (2016). Catching the pulse: Money and circulation in a Sri Lankan marketplace. *Journal of the Royal Anthropological Institute*, *22*, 534–551.

Ho, K. (2009). *Liquidated: An ethnography of wall street*. Durham, NC: Duke University Press.

Huberman, J. (2010). The dangers of Dalālī, the dangers of Dān. *South Asia: Journal of South Asian Studies*, *33*(3), 399–420.

James, D. (2014). "Deeper into a hole?" Borrowing and lending in South Africa. *Current Anthropology*, *55*(9), 7–29.

Kar, S. (2013). Recovering debts: Microfinance loan officers and the work of "proxy-creditors" in India. *American Ethnologist*, *40*(3), 480–493.

Lyon, F. (2000). Trust, network and norms: The creation of social capital in agricultural economies in Ghana. *World Development*, *28*(4), 663–681.

Malamoud, C. (1980). La dette. *Collection Purushartha, 4*. Paris: Éditions de l'École des hautes études en sciences sociales.

Mahmoud, H. A. (2008). Risky trade, resilient traders: Trust and livestock marketing in northern Kenya. *Africa: The Journal of the International African Institute*, *78*(4), 561–581.

Mauss, M. (1990). *The gift: The form and reason for exchange in archaic societies*. New York, NY: W.W. Norton.

Neelima, K. (2016). *Death of a money lender*. Delhi: Penguin Books.

Peebles, G. (2010). The anthropology of credit and debt. *Annual Review of Anthropology*, *39*, 225–240.

Roitman, J. (2003). Unsanctioned wealth; or, the productivity of debt in Northern Cameroon. *Public Culture*, *15*(2), 211–237.

Russell, S. (1994). Institutionalizing opportunism: Cheating on baby purse seiners in Batangas Bay, Philippines. In J. Acheson (Ed.), *Anthropology and institutional economics*, (pp. 87–108). Lanham, MD: University Press of America.

Rutherford, D. (2001). Intimacy and alienation: Money and the foreign in the biak. *Public Culture*, *13*(2), 299–324.

Sahlins, M. (1972). *Stone age economics*. Chicago, IL: Aldine, Atherton Inc.

Strobl, A., & Peters, M. (2013). Entrepreneurial reputation in destination networks. *Annals of Tourism Research*, *40*, 59–82.

Zelizer, V. A. (2011). *Economic lives: How culture shapes the economy*. Princeton, NJ: Princeton University Press.

Zelizer, V. A. (2012). How I became a relational economic sociologist and what does that mean? *Politics and Society*, *40*(2), 145–174.

Zhao, W., Ritchie, J. R. B., & Echtner, C. M. (2011). Social Capital and Tourism entrepreneurship. *Annals of Tourism Research*, *38*(4), 1570–1593.

MAKING "EASY" MONEY: RESILIENCE AND RISK IN JAMAICA

Lauren C. Johnson

ABSTRACT

Purpose – *Local adaptations to economic blight and overreliance on the tourism industry demonstrate significant aspects of resilience and risk among Caribbean populations. Those individuals who choose sex tourism as a way to benefit from its increasing revenue demonstrate resilience through their adaptations to shifts in the local and national economies, including national debt, expansion of the all-inclusive hotel industry, and seasonal variations in tourist arrivals. Based on ethnographic research conducted in Negril, Jamaica, I argue that the very activities of "hustling" and sex work that illustrate local men's resilience are the same practices that put their sexual health at risk.*

Methodology/approach – *This research contextualizes the practice of female sex tourism using the anthropology of tourism, gender and sexuality studies, and the anthropology of HIV/AIDS with a focus on the Caribbean region. This work is based on a project that entailed nine months of fieldwork in 2010–2011 in Negril where I conducted ethnographic observations, life history interviews with three men who sell sex, and 54 semi-structured interviews.*

Findings – *Men who sell sex to women tourists demonstrate resilience in the face of economic shifts and changing cultural norms. These men are also, however, exposed to risk through their sexual activities and health seeking behaviors.*

Anthropological Considerations of Production, Exchange, Vending and Tourism
Research in Economic Anthropology, Volume 37, 257–273

ISSN: 0190-1281/doi:10.1108/S0190-128120170000037012

Research implications – *In order for the issues of STI/HIV risk to be adequately addressed among this population, effective public health efforts must prioritize health over tourism revenue and utilize anthropological approaches to explore the health costs of the tourist dollar.*

Keywords: Sex tourism; resilience; sexual health; Jamaica

INTRODUCTION

Research on Caribbean tourist destinations demonstrates numerous ways in which local populations respond to national, regional, and global economic shifts. The tourism industry itself, having become the principal industry in the region in recent decades, provides an effective lens for viewing both large- and small-scale sociocultural and economic adaptations. This discussion focuses on the ways in which some residents of a particular Jamaican tourist town have adapted to their changing landscape by engaging in "hustling" behaviors, earning a living by engaging in illicit activities that involve tourists. Female sex tourism, a method that a substantial number of local men choose to earn, represents the resilience of men who are determined to benefit from the growing industry despite the low wages, high turnover rates, and selective employment practices within the formal tourism sector. Men who are otherwise unemployed, or those who choose to supplement their regular incomes, are able to make significant profits from involvement in sex work even as tourism communities are threatened by inflation, encroachment of the all-inclusive industry into locally owned establishments, and fluctuating numbers of stopover tourists. Sex tourism is an accepted practice for men in some resort areas where local residents seem to relate associated behaviors with their ideas of masculinity and sexuality. This resilience, however, comes at a cost. Rates of sexually transmitted infections (STIs), including HIV, are significant in Jamaican tourist destinations. Health risks due to mobility, STI/HIV education, condom accessibility, and testing are of concern in areas where a segment of the population relies on earnings from sex tourism. Utilizing ethnographic work conducted in Negril, Jamaica, this chapter explores questions related to the economic and health impact of this type of tourism. To what extent does engagement in female sex tourism endanger participants in regard to sexual health and what are the responses from state tourism and health authorities? How do these responses compare between populations of female versus male sex workers? And, considering the significant boost that tourism provides to the Jamaican economy, do tourism and public health entities prioritize the health of residents over foreign currency earnings?

BACKGROUND

Economy

The Jamaican economy has become increasingly more reliant on tourism and remittances for its gross domestic product (GDP) and less so on bauxite/alumina as it was before the global economic recession. Tourism began to boom in 1965 when it replaced the declining sugar industry in terms of foreign exchange generated (Taylor, 1993). The service industry now accounts for approximately 70% of the GDP, of which tourism revenues total approximately 30% (CIA World Factbook, 2016). This economy has been blighted with consistently high unemployment rates and considerable national debt. The current unemployment rate is approximately 13.5% with the highest rates of unemployment among youth and men (Statistical Institute of Jamaica, 2016). The debt-to-GDP ratio is a crucial concern when considering the economic climate in Jamaica, as it is one of the most indebted countries in the hemisphere. The government has borrowed heavily from the International Monetary Fund (IMF) and World Bank since Prime Minister Michael Manley was forced to sign the nation's first loan agreement with the IMF in 1977 due to the dire economic situation at the time. The country currently has an accumulated public debt of approximately 140% of its GDP (The World Bank, 2016). Reasons cited for this considerable borrowing include the significant decreases in remittances, the declining exportation of bauxite, and reductions in tourism revenues during the global economic crisis, although Jamaica's economy was not on steady ground prior to the crisis. The export of crude materials, including bauxite and alumina, declined 55% between 2008 and 2009, and remittances decreased by 11% during the same time period. Jamaica has recently returned to both the IMF and World Bank for additional loans with a support package of US$932 million from the IMF, as well as US$510 million each from World Bank Group and the Inter-American Development Bank (IDB) in order to "facilitate the [Government of Jamaica's] economic reform agenda to stabilize the economy, reduce debt and create the conditions for growth and resilience" (The World Bank, 2016). This debt and the interest payments it has incurred have led to reductions in government spending on infrastructure, health care, and education in the country over the last decade (Johnston & Montecino, 2011; Weisbrot, 2011).

Tourism in Jamaica

The development of the tourism industry in Jamaica began in the 19th century. In the late 1800s, businessmen affiliated with global trade, and particularly those involved in banana exportation with the United Fruit Company, promoted Jamaica as a health retreat for cruise passengers from the United States (Taylor, 1993). Despite the growth of a competitive hotel industry, including the enactment of the Jamaica Hotels Law in 1904, the tourism industry did not flourish on the island until after the Second World War. During the 1950s, the development of international airlines contributed to tourism along with the growth in hotel accommodations triggered by the 1944 Hotel Aid Law. This legislation, which was passed to replace previously expired laws, assisted in tourism development by granting financial concessions for the construction of resorts, including waived customs duties for imported building materials and equipment. The Jamaica Tourist Board, created in 1954, provided additional contributions to the development of the tourism industry through its advertising and promotion campaigns. Later, in 1961, hoteliers in the country formed the Jamaica Hotel and Tourist Association (JHTA) to represent their interests to the tourism board and government. The steadily increasing profits from the industry further benefited from the Hotel Incentives Act of 1968, which gave additional tax and construction incentives that encouraged the growth of accommodations on the island, yet failed to ensure that profits from tourism stayed in Jamaica (Taylor, 1993).

In his description of the link between politics and the economic history of the Caribbean, former Prime Minister Michael Manley writes,

> There never was any attempt to produce what was needed but only to produce what someone else needed. Trade did not involve a calculated exchange involving surpluses but the importation of virtually everything that was needed and the export of virtually everything that was produced. Finally, the surplus which a group normally uses to increase its production was largely explored in the form of profit to the centre of colonial power. (Manley, 1982, p. 25)

Following the model of industrialization-by-invitation, Jamaica joined other Caribbean islands in implementing the "Puerto Rican Model" of development. This included a system of diversification and import substitution through development in the manufacturing sector, mainly utilizing foreign investment. In place prior to 1962, these conservative policies were continued even after a new independent government was installed. Initially assisting with growth in employment, the bauxite industry, and the tourism industry in the 1960s to early 1970s, the model seemed to benefit the economy. However, as occurred in other developing countries, the eventual socioeconomic costs were high (Manley, 1982; Yelvington, 1995). Unemployment, low educational attainment, illiteracy, and malnutrition became serious issues in Jamaica, in addition to an increasing economic imbalance. The tourism industry that had been built on this model, an industry based on investment from abroad and the provision of tax incentives to foreign companies, grew exponentially. This growth, however, failed to ensure that Jamaican citizens were receiving the majority of the benefits of this growth. As Manley states (above), Jamaica has a history of producing for countries at the center, and Jamaican tourism has followed the same pattern.

International tourism receipts increased from approximately US$1,197 billion dollars in 2013 to over US$1,245 billion in 2014; of this amount, US$27.1 billion was generated in the Caribbean region (UN Word Tourism Organization, 2015). Jamaica received the third highest number of tourist arrivals in the Caribbean in 2013, following Cuba and the Dominican Republic, with 2,008,409 total stopover visitors, and another 1,288,184 cruise passenger visits (Caribbean Tourism Organization, 2014). According to the Jamaica Tourist Board (Jamaica Tourist Board), 80% of U.S. visitors reported travel to Jamaica for leisure purposes, with women outnumbering men from each of the main countries of origin: the United States, England, and Canada. Tourism receipts overall in Jamaica have increased over the last decade, adding up to over two billion dollars in gross foreign exchange earnings in 2012. The increasing importance of all-inclusive resorts, however, has left smaller hotel units vulnerable to declining occupancy rates. The number of hotel room sold in all-inclusive resorts in Jamaica totaled 15,539 in 2012; in contrast, the number of non all-inclusive rooms sold totaled just 5,435. All-inclusive hotel stays have remained on the rise for the last several years with the number of room nights sold increasing by nearly one million between 2006 and 2010. For those same years, there was a steady decline for non all-inclusive hotels (Jamaica Tourist Board, 2011, 2013). However, employment directly and indirectly in the tourism sector has increased in recent years. Travel and tourism directly supported 82,500 jobs (7.3% of total employment), and in total supported 277,000 jobs (24.7% of total employment) in 2014. The industry contributed 8.1% of Jamaica's GDP in that same year, with a projected increase of 4.7% in 2015 (World Travel & Tourism Council, 2015). Tourism has clearly generated significant revenue in the country; however, the costs of relying upon the industry have been considerable. The negative impact on the environment, the increasing demand for illegal drugs, and the public health concerns surrounding STIs and HIV are each evident in the small tourist town of Negril.

Setting

Located on the western coast of Jamaica, Negril is popularly known as a laid-back beach town and tourist destination with approximately 7,000 residents. The town was once a fishing village that began to draw Jamaican tourists in the 1960s, along with "hippies" from the United States seeking a natural spot for relaxation where marijuana and magic mushrooms were readily available. According to native Negrilians, tourism took off in the town in the 1980s after the road between Montego Bay, where the closest airport is located, and Negril was improved. Visitors to Negril were no longer simply young, liberal Americans, but rather began to include more affluent vacationers from abroad. The town has a relatively small resident population that is constantly outnumbered by tourist visitors. It is because of this that many Jamaicans find that the place actually feels less like a part of Jamaica than it does a tourist enclave in itself. This is an aspect of Negril that reflects the colonial and post-colonial socioeconomic conditions of the country overall; the island was inhabited by colonial powers for the purpose of serving their countries of origin. This included the export of agricultural products and, later, bauxite and alumina. Resort towns like Negril only became heavily populated once the tourism industry took off and provided another way to export what Jamaica has to offer. In this case, however, it is the "local" culture that is being presented to visitors from abroad as a purchasable commodity. This concept of "local" is produced for foreign tourist consumption, but has little meaning in the Jamaican context. As cited from a 1964 Gleaner article, "It is as if one part of Jamaica were reserved for Jamaicans, and the other part for tourists, and both are separated by a forbidding and confusing screen" (Taylor, 1993, p. 169). One aspect of this separation is the negative environmental impact of tourism in the country, and for Negril specifically with its significant beach erosion. The environmental burdens of tourism in Jamaica include the removal of coral reefs and wetlands, along with increased water usage and solid waste, and water pollution in resort areas (Dodman, 2009; National Environment and Planning Agency, 2011; Thomas-Hope & Jardine-Comrie, 2007). The National Environmental Protection Agency has indicated that tourism is one of the major strains put on natural resources in Jamaica, including energy, water, raw materials, beaches, and waste disposal facilities. According to Dodman (2009, p. 213), "Provisioning for the demands of international tourists, given the importance placed on this economic sector, has meant that providing proper environmental and sanitation services for hotels has often taken precedence over similar programmes for Jamaican citizens."

Negril was chosen for research on female sex tourism due to its reputation for attracting sex tourists and sex workers, as well as the visibility of interactions between tourists and locals within its popular touristic spaces. According to news articles, travel journals, and numerous websites, it serves as a beacon for travelers interested in sexual relationships with locals. Negril's economy relies on the flourishing tourism industry, attracting both native Jamaicans and foreigners alike to reap the perceived benefits. Negril received a 21.5% share of Jamaica's U.S. tourist visitors in 2012, following Montego Bay and Ocho Rios. The town has a third of the country's hotels and one quarter of its hotel rooms with more than 5,000 rooms (Jamaica Tourist Board, 2013). Hotels and restaurants line both sides of its one main road, Norman Manley Boulevard, from Orange Bay at the northernmost part down to the West End where Negril's famous cliffs are located. The town contains more than 130 operating hotels and guesthouses and a plethora of bars and restaurants that serve various types of cuisine. Its lively nightlife comprises a number of indoor and outdoor bars and clubs that host events every night of the week. Within Negril's purview, a fire station, police station, public clinic, and several private doctors' offices can be found. Negril has a significant number of European and North American members of its community, and a relatively small number of Chinese and Indian immigrants who operate restaurants and shops in town.

METHODS

This chapter reports on a larger research study that explored the sociocultural, economic, and health impact of female sex tourism in Negril. During nine months of fieldwork in Negril in 2010–2011, I conducted ethnographic observations, life history interviews, and semi-structured interviews. Additional data was compiled from the collection and analyses of media reports, health statistics, and documentary films focused on the topics of tourism, sex work, and sex tourism in Jamaica. Semi-structured interview guides developed prior to conducting fieldwork were modified based on the informants' specific contexts within the tourism industry, government offices, health organizations, or non-governmental organizations (NGOs). While in the field, I conducted observations of tourist-local interactions and wrote detailed fieldnotes using the work of Emerson, Fretz, and Shaw (1995) and Schensul, Schensul, and LeCompte (1999) as guides. Codes were created for the individuals included in my observations, as well as the establishments where I observed interactions. Notes from informal conversations with individual residents in Negril regarding tourism and sex tourism were also recorded in order to determine perceptions of participants on these topics. After approximately two months spent observing in specific sites in Negril, I conducted semi-structured interviews with a total of 54 local residents, tourists and foreign-born residents, government officials, and university professors selected using snowball and purposive sampling. Interviews were generally 45–60 minutes in length. I began conducting interviews with residents employed in the tourism sector of Negril and its surrounding towns. Informants involved in sex work included a former female sex worker and a female exotic dancer who have both engaged in sex tourism, multiple male and female sex tourists, as well as two men in the informal tourism sector who had previously worked in sex tourism. Interviews with the tourism police liaison, tourism board officials, health department employees, and local outreach workers provided contextual information for the study. To explore the health implications of sex tourism, this study included interviews with staff from the Westmoreland Health Department, National HIV/STI Programme, Ministry of Health, several NGOs conducting health-related work, as well as local health practitioners. Additionally, I participated in several health fairs in Negril and interviewed individuals working with the local branch of the Tourism Product Development Company (TPDCo) regarding current efforts to develop workplace policies for STI/HIV testing and education in the formal tourism sector. Thirty-six of the study participants were men and 17 women, mainly due to the higher number of men working in the informal tourism sector. I completed life history interviews with three men currently involved in sex tourism whose information was used to determine the motivations, self-concepts, health-related perceptions, and positives/negatives of sex tourism from emic perspectives. The age range of all participants was 20 to 75 years old, and the majority of these individuals were Jamaican-born; four participants were foreign-born residents from Europe.

SEX TOURISM AND RESILIENCE

Previous research on the sociocultural and economic impact of female sex tourism indicates the significance of the practice for a number of Caribbean tourist destinations (Brennan, 2004; Cabezas, 2009; Kempadoo, 2004, 1999; Mullings, 1999; Padilla, 2007; Press, 1978). Jamaica has its three main resort areas where this type of sex tourism can be observed, Negril being the smallest and most easily navigable of these towns along the Northwest coast. The town is a magnet for entrepreneurial men and women from various parts of the island seeking to earn from the exceedingly profitable tourism industry. Men in Negril are apt to self-identify as "hustlers" when their incomes are generated through jobs selling CDs, jewelry, souvenirs, and drugs, among other items, to foreign tourists. In addition, many local men take on the roles of informal tour guides and drivers for visitors in the town. The men who engage in hustling are often undereducated and lack employment opportunities in the formal tourism sector. Those without the formal educations, advantaged social status, and skills training to compete for tourism-related jobs can hustle for a living instead; selling drugs, crafts, and sex are viable options. While some men are also employed as chefs, water sports operators, and construction workers, conversations and interviews with informants indicated that self-proclaimed hustlers tend to work solely in the informal sector. As described in literature on informal tourism work, these men are cultural brokers who provide for visitors' needs in the tourist areas (Smith, 1989). During interviews with men who hustle tourists, some informants shared that in exchange for providing services to tourists, they can get money, gifts, invitations to parties and bars, paid drinks and meals, and trips around the island, among other compensation. Men who hustle a living tend to have increased social interactions with foreign tourists, putting them in positions to sell sex to these guests as well (Miller, 1991; Press & Clayton, 1978). These men, known locally as "gigolos" and "rent-a-dreads," act as companions, tour guides, and protectors of women spending their vacations on the island. In return for sex and companionship, the men receive gifts, cash, local tours, and opportunities to travel abroad. In Negril, as in other tourism destinations, men who work as water sports operators, taxi drivers, and hotel entertainers are perceived as regular participants in sex tourism. Observations and interviews with men employed in these capacities, in addition to interviews with other tourism employees, indicate that some men find work in these jobs in order to facilitate access to tourist women. While determining an accurate number of men involved in sex tourism in Negril is difficult, data analyzed for this research project indicate that this group includes at least 50 men.

Participation in sex tourism provides men and women with opportunities to access spaces and engage in the decadent activities that foreigners are privy to, in addition to providing significant earnings. These men exchange flattery, companionship, and sexual services to women with whom they form relationships during the visitors' vacation stays. Through relationships with foreign tourists, doors are opened for some individuals that may not have been otherwise. Involvement in sex tourism provides significantly more of an income than many formal tourism jobs below the managerial level, and includes perks that employees in the service sector are not privy to: lavish accommodations, paid meals and beverages, excursions around the island, and even, possibly, trips abroad. Some use their increased income to become entrepreneurs, to study a trade, or to complete their educations. The most fortunate and dedicated sex workers gain access to the most exclusive prize of all: a foreign visa. Several informants expressed that most of the men and women who utilize sex tourism as an income earner in Jamaica do so in order to better their lives. Through tourism marketing, word of mouth, and personal experiences, tourists often learn of the existence of local people who will offer sex in exchange for cash, gifts, and the occasional visa. Due to the illicit nature of relationships based on sex tourism, it is difficult to gauge the economic impact that it has in Negril, let alone Jamaica as a whole. However, interview participants are clear in stating that the revenue generated from sex tourism is significant. Hotel, bar, and restaurant owners acknowledge that sex tourism attracts clientele and therefore increases earnings. Specific guesthouses that offer various rates and bars/clubs with loose restrictions on illicit activities certainly profit from exchanges that occur between tourists and locals. Several informants suggested that the average tourism sector worker receives approximately J$67,000 per week, or between $70 and $83 in US dollars. A man involved in sex tourism can acquire between US$200 and US$250 from a tourist to spend as pocket money in one day. While few men are paid in simple sex-for-cash exchanges, the majority request money from their tourist "girlfriends" during the course of the women's vacation stays. Additional income is generated after the tourists have returned home and send wire transfers back to their "boyfriends" in Negril. These men can be observed during regular visits to the Western Union booth located in the local grocery store. Each Negril resident interviewed had either first-hand experiences or second-hand accounts to share regarding the amounts of cash and gifts that men regularly receive. During interviews, men involved in sex tourism shared stories of receiving money from foreign women that they used for construction on their homes, cars, cell phones, clothing and shoes, and spending money. One key informant, for example, discussed how bringing women home to see where he lived sometimes inspired them to send money once they returned home. One foreign woman sent him enough to renovate his bathroom after seeing the conditions of his dilapidated residence. Another informant who drove a taxi described excitedly during a conversation that he had just received US$4,000 to pay off his car loan from an older European woman he had invited to stay in his home to be romanced and "taken care of." Everyone in the town seems to know of multiple male sex workers who were provided with motorcycles, cars, land, and/or a house by at least one tourist with whom they were involved. Young Negril residents have friends and acquaintances who were sent millions of Jamaican dollars, either through one-time deals or over relatively short periods of time. Alan, a 32-year-old self-identified "hustler," claims that gigolos make a great deal of money from tourist women who enjoy spending money on them:

> Ah talk 'bout, man, up to US$5,000 a man can make off a tourist based on where she stay an' where she meet him, because you have different pockets go to different property, an' being a experienced player in de game, you will go for the highest bidder. So you know where to go an' hang out or where to go an' gig.

What is significant about these figures is that for the average salaried employee in the tourism industry in Negril, one's wages cannot compete with the potential to earn through sex work. For residents working outside the formal tourism industry, in such establishments as super markets, convenience stores, craft markets, an individual could earn more in one day engaging in sex tourism than their job would pay them in a month. This explains why some men who work in hotels supplement their incomes, and even risk their day jobs, by entering into relationships with foreign tourists. Overall, the prospective long-term benefits of "gigging," particularly for those who work strategically, outweigh the benefits of official service industry employment. Carla, a 21-year-old European-born Negril resident who worked in an all-inclusive hotel, stated,

> And dey have some nice Jamaican girl here, but some of dem don't have no money, and dey're [men who sell sex] lookin' for money, for *easy money*, because dey don't want to work. Work here is hard, an' you don't get pay, so for dem it's so easy to get like $300 dey gonna get in one month, here sometime dey gettin on one day, dey say, "Oh, my grandfadder is sick, I need money, an I don't know what to do," an' you know? After de man tell her how she's beautiful, she gonna say, "OK, well, it's fine if it's for your grandfadder."

Sex tourism provides the men a method for contending with the ups and downs of the tourism industry while adhering to their proscribed gender roles. This is one way in which the local population demonstrates the well-researched resilience of Caribbean men (Chevannes, 2002; Lewis, 2003a, 2003b; Miller, 1991; Reddock, 2004) They perform masculinity through their involvement with multiple women while simultaneously engaging in transactional sex. Regardless of the current influx of tourist visitors or fluctuation in the revenue earned from tourism in Negril, individuals involved in transactional sex with tourist visitors can maintain a relatively steady stream of income. This demonstrates resilience to the economic forces that, not accidentally, exclude certain members of the local community from formal licensed work in the tourism industry. Rather than accept exclusion, men who sell sex find alternative means to earn from this ubiquitous industry in resort towns like Negril. This resilience, however, comes at a cost: the risk of STI and HIV infection among participants in sex tourism.

RISKY BEHAVIORS

While the spread of STI and HIV infection in tourist destinations has been a topic of interest for researchers in the Caribbean, current research has not specifically linked the practice of sex tourism with rates of infection. The National HIV/STI Programme recognizes that after the most urbanized parishes of Kingston/St. Andrew and St. James, the parishes with tourism-based economies have the largest cumulative numbers of reported HIV cases on the island. These include the parishes of St. Ann, Westmoreland, Hanover, and Trelawney. The parishes in which Negril and its surrounding areas are located, Westmoreland and Hanover, have 966.7 and 957.3 reported HIV cases per 100,000 people, respectively (National HIV/STI Programme, 2011). Researchers have surmised that HIV infection rates are increasing fastest in the Jamaican parishes with the most developed tourism sectors (Kempadoo & Taitt, 2006; Mullings, 1999; Olukoga, 2004). The Ministry of Health and Tourism Product Development Company (TPDCo) have developed specific STI/HIV education and behavior change programs for employees in the direct tourism industry, yet these programs do not target tourism workers in the substantial informal sectors of popular tourist destinations. The link between sex tourism and HIV/AIDS in the Caribbean can be perceived as a confluence of issues involving transactional sex, economic reliance on the tourism industry, and mobility and migration. In Jamaica, transactional sex has been connected with STI and HIV prevalence among youth and adults. Research has indicated that as many as 20% of adult women and men have participated in transactional sex, placing individuals at risk because of inconsistent condom use in such relationships (Figueroa, 2008; Ministry of Health, 2008). According to Plummer (2013), gender constructs of Caribbean masculinity drive young men toward sexual risk-taking behaviors, including sex with multiple partners and failure to use condoms. Issues of mobility and migration have been studied as additional contributors to the spread of HIV in the Caribbean, particularly as related to tourism. Research on the sexual behaviors of tourists, particularly young and single travelers, indicates that vacation relationships involve increased risk behaviors and a lack of condom procurement (Forsythe, Hasbun, & Lister, 1998; Ragsdale, Digranseisco, & Pinkerton, 2006; Romero-Daza & Freidus, 2008; Thomas, 2005). Some tourists fail to associate their own behaviors with risk, or to consider the prevalence of

HIV in their vacation destinations (Forsythe et al., 1998; Rogstad, 2004). While sexual relationships between tourists and local people do not necessarily involve monetary transactions, extreme economic stratification between the two groups leads many men and women into the practice of sex tourism. Padilla and Castellanos (2009) find that "touristic borderlands" in the Dominican Republic are perceived by locals as jumping off points for global migration through relationships with tourists. Similarly, internal migration in Jamaica leads local women and men to popular resort areas in order to gain from the nation's most profitable industry by engaging in transactional sex with tourists (Boxill et al., 2005; Dunn & Dunn, 2002). While some HIV prevention programs target sex workers, researchers have questioned the motives of some Caribbean governments that have prioritized tourism promotion to the detriment of effective risk management (Figueroa, 2008; Grenade, 2007). The lack of qualitative and quantitative research on possible links between STI infection and HIV prevalence in resort areas points to neglect of an area of study that could have severe implications for the future of tourism and sexual health in tourist destinations in Jamaica.

At the national level, STI and HIV/AIDS programs focus on education and awareness for the overall population, with particular consideration for groups that have been identified as vulnerable. Female sex workers, men who have sex with men (MSM), and youth populations are principal targets for prevention programs due to the prevalence statistics of HIV among those groups. Multiple organizations, including Jamaica AIDS Support for Life, Caribbean Vulnerable Communities, and the Caribbean HIV/AIDS Alliance, are currently conducting work with sex worker populations in the country. Much of the prevention work done by Jamaica AIDS Support for Life (JASL) targets female and MSM sex workers, although at the time of this project there were no workshops being conducted. Past interventions have included peer educator trips to nightclubs, massage parlors, and beaches in Negril. In Negril, in addition to the two most popular tourist destinations in the country, the parish health department implements workshops on condom use, STI/HIV education, hygiene, and entrepreneurship to assist female sex workers in harm reduction. The beaches in Montego Bay are targeted for one-on-one JASL interventions with men involved in sex tourism. The same weekly visits do not occur in Negril, although one peer educator based in Negril gives out information on STIs and HIV, and provides individuals with condoms and lubricants for nominal donations. The National HIV/STI Programme conducts outreach work that include women's empowerment and men's health workshops providing information on condoms and STIs/HIV, as well as tackle some of the root causes of vulnerability, such as education and employability. The results of these workshops indicate the program effectiveness with participants maintaining negative HIV status and demonstrating improved health-seeking behaviors. Each region in Jamaica has an average of 20–30 field staff members who conduct outreach work, while certain regions are better staffed due to higher prevalence rates. The Western

Region, which includes the parish of Westmoreland where Negril is located, has approximately 40 people on the ground because of its high HIV prevalence rate with respect to population size.

While commendable efforts are taking place within Negril and other tourist areas, it is noteworthy that its population of men involved in sex tourism has not been identified and maintained as targets of health interventions. This is perhaps due to a lack of staffing and resources, as well as practical concerns related to work with men who sell sex. Interviewees from the health sector indicated that the health departments are understaffed and therefore struggle to program and advertise interventions with identified vulnerable groups. To this it can be added that Jamaican men tend toward poor health seeking behaviors and are difficult to attract with health fairs and workshops. Informants in the aforementioned health organizations cited challenges of targeting men who do not readily self-identify as sex workers, reaching populations that are mobile, and contending with stigma toward STI/HIV testing among men. While these challenges are certainly credible, this project indicates a wider avoidance of issues related to straight-identifying men involved in sex work who are identified as heterosexual. I suggest that this relates to prevailing perceptions of masculinity and risk in these areas; men engage in sexual relationships with (foreign) women are just doing what Caribbean men do. This perception is problematic, however, considering the risk to which men who sell sex are exposed. Men involved in sex tourism who participated in this study expressed risk behaviors, such as sex with multiple partners living both locally and abroad, inconsistent condom use, inconsistent HIV testing, fear of HIV testing, and incidence of STIs during our interviews. Doctors currently practicing in Negril who were interested in this study described high rates of STIs in Negril and other tourist destinations, including herpes, syphilis, and gonorrhea. One doctor expressed concern over a "herpes corridor" extending along the Northern coast of Jamaica through the tourist resort towns from Negril to Ocho Rios. Several health practitioners, including a former Ministry of Health official, also expressed a concern over having treated men who sell sex and had tested positive for HIV, yet continued earning a living through sex tourism. This study points to the vulnerability of the population of men who engage in sex tourism in terms of risk for STIs and HIV. Despite awareness in the health sector that this population exists and, for some, clearly represents significant risk in terms of the spread of STIs/HIV, heterosexual male sex workers remain neglected by prevention and education programs.

The tourism sector in Jamaica also presents challenges to health interventions in tourist destinations. One example is a Ministry of Health (MOH) initiative to encourage guests to wash their hands before entering hotel buffet lines that was quashed by hotel owners who found related signage to be invasive. Similarly, efforts from the MOH to implement the provision of condoms in hotels have been met with resistance, despite the willingness of some hotel owners to install condom vending machines in hotels. Data yielded from interviews conducted with hotel managers and owners indicate that while some hoteliers expressed a willingness to provide free condoms in their hotels, few were actively doing so. At one point several years ago, several hotel owners actually called for involuntary HIV testing of all employees, a measure that was quickly rejected by the Ministry of Health. This type of testing could have had serious implications for stigma and discrimination, as well as human rights, in the tourism sector. Insofar as issues regarding tourism and sex work, there seems to be a lack of cohesion between the interests of health organizations and tourism entities in Jamaica. There are ongoing initiatives with the Tourism Product Development Company (TPDCo) and local health department that conduct training and health education workshops in local hotels, which mainly occur in the larger all-inclusive resorts in Negril. However, a representative from the Western Regional Health Authority sited difficulties in working toward risk reduction for any disease or illness in the tourism sector, as stakeholders in the industry tend to perceive health education and prevention efforts as overly restrictive of foreign visitors. While there is no evidence of outright noncompliance within the hotel industry, or in the tourism sector overall, I have inferred that implementing changes within the industry has been problematic. Overall, a level of denial seems to exist within the tourism industry, which leads tourism stakeholders to shirk any responsibility for the promotion of safer sex practices. There may, in fact, be a disengagement on the part of the tourism industry overall to develop prevention programs targeting the sector due to fears that tourists will respond negatively to STI/HIV related messages.

CONCLUSION

These obstacles to interventions with men involved in sex tourism from both the health and tourism sectors leave an apparent gap in the attention given this vulnerable population. As a lone researcher conducting the study, my findings are limited to the men and women I was able to interview and observe with a focus on a specific tourist destination. This research, however, points to the need for further quantitative and qualitative research on the impact of sex tourism for the health of its participants in Negril and other Jamaican resort areas. The current lack of research on men who sell sex in these areas demonstrates a confluence of issues relating to masculinity, resilience, and risk. More specifically, men engaged in the practice of sex tourism hustle a living by employing their sexual prowess. They are involved in a practice that affords them opportunities for earning, for travel at home and abroad, and for engaging with women in ways that confirms their manhood. This practice, however, drives them toward sexual risk behaviors that can put themselves and their sexual partners at risk. The men involved in female sex tourism, while acknowledged by government entities, are not the targets of health interventions at the local, parish, or national levels. This is the result of challenges facing health officials, including the lack of resources and funding to address the issue of female sex tourism. Another possible justification is that it is easier to leave issues of heterosexual male sex work alone rather than problematize concerns of a tourism industry that protects its profits from the marginalization of a significant segment of the local population. Future investigation in these areas is necessary to determine the extent to which the sexual health of men involved in female sex tourism and their partners is a cost that the tourism industry is willing to pay.

REFERENCES

Boxill, I., Lewis, K.-A., Frey, R., Martin, P., Treasure, D., Bowen, W., & Joseph, T. (2005). *Tourism & HIV/AIDS in Jamaica and the Bahamas*. Kingston: Arawak Publications.

Brennan, D. (2004). *What's love got to do with it?: Transnational desires and sex tourism in the Dominican Republic*. Durham, NC: Duke University Press.

Cabezas, A. L. (2009). *Economies of desire: Sex tourism in Cuba and the Dominican Republic*. Philadelphia, PA: Temple University Press.

Caribbean Tourism Organization. (2014). *Latest statistics 2013*. Retrieved from http://www.onecaribbean.org/wp-content/uploads/Lattab2013MAY13.pdf

Chevannes, B. (2002). What you sow is what you reap: Violence and the construction of male identity in Jamaica. *Current Issues in Comparative Education*, *2*(1), 51–61.

CIA World Factbook. (2016). *The World Factbook: Jamaica*. Retrieved from https://www.cia.gov/library/publications/the-world-factbook/geos/jm.html

Dodman, D. (2009). Globalization, tourism and local living conditions on Jamaica's north coast. *Singapore Journal of Tropical Geography*, *30*, 204–219.

Dunn, H. S., & Dunn, L. L. (2002). *People and tourism: Issues and attitudes in the Jamaican hospitality industry*. Kingston: Arawak Publications.

Emerson, R. M., Fretz, R. I., & Shaw, L. L. (1995). *Writing ethnographic fieldnotes*. Chicago, IL: The University of Chicago Press.

Figueroa, J. P. (2008). The HIV epidemic in the Caribbean: Meeting the challenges of achieving universal access to prevention, treatment, and care. *West Indian Medical Journal*, *57*(3), 195–203.

Forsythe, S., Hasbun, J., & Lister, M. B. D. (1998). Protecting paradise: Tourism and AIDS in the Dominican republic. *Health Policy and Planning*, *13*(3), 277–286.

Grenade, W. C. (2007). Balancing economic development and security: The case of Tourism and HIV/AIDS in Grenada. Paper presented at the The 8th Annual SALISES Conference 2007, Trinidad & Tobago.

Jamaica Tourist Board. (2011). *Annual Travel Statistics 2010*, p. 80. Retrieved from http://www.jtbonline.org/statistics/AnnualTravel/AnnualTravelStatistics 2010.pdf

Jamaica Tourist Board. (2013). *Annual Travel Statistics 2012*, January 1, 2014. Retrieved from http://www.jtbonline.org/statistics/AnnualTravel/AnnualTravelStatistics 2012.pdf

Johnston, J., & Montecino, J. A. (2011). *Jamaica: Macroeconomic policy, debt and the IMF*. p. 24. Retrieved from http://www.cepr.net/documents/publications/jamaica-qr-2011-04.pdf

Kempadoo, K. (Ed.) (1999). *Sun, sex, and gold: Tourism and sex work in the Caribbean*. Lanham, MD: Rowman & Littlefield Publishers, Inc.

Kempadoo, K. (2004). *Sexing the Caribbean: Gender, race, and sexual labor*. New York, NY: Routledge.

Kempadoo, K., & Taitt, A. (2006). *Gender, sexuality and implications for HIV/AIDS in the Caribbean: A review of literature and programmes*. Retrieved from http://caribbean.unwomen.

org/~/media/field office caribbean/attachments/publications/gender sexuality and hiv aids in the caribbean a literature review pdf.ashx

Lewis, L. (2003a). Caribbean masculinity: Unpacking the narrative. In L. Lewis (Ed.), *The culture of gender and sexuality in the Caribbean* (pp. 94–125). Gainesville: University Press of Florida.

Lewis, L. (2003b). Exploring the intersections of gender, sexuality, and culture in the Caribbean: An introduction. In L. Lewis (Ed.), *The culture of gender and sexuality in the Caribbean* (pp. 1–21). Gainesville, FL: University Press of Florida.

Manley, M. (1982). *Jamaica: Struggle in the periphery*. London: Third World Media Limited.

Miller, E. (1991). *Men at risk*. Kingston: Jamaica Publishing House Ltd.

Ministry of Health. (2008). National HIV Program, Jamaica Country Progress Report to the Secretary General of the United Nations on the United Nations General Assembly Special Session. July 10, 2009. Retrieved from http://www.jamaica-nap.org/UNGASSCountryProgressReport.pdf

Mullings, B. (1999). Globalization, tourism, and the international sex trade. In K. Kempadoo (Ed.), *Sun, sex, and gold: Tourism and sex work in the Caribbean* (pp. 55–80). Lanham, MD: Rowman and Littlefield Publishers, Inc.

National Environment and Planning Agency. (2011). *State of the Environment Report 2010*. Retrieved from Kingston. Retrieved from http://nepa.gov.jm/publications/SOE/2010/State-of-The-Environment-Report-2010-Jamaica.pdf

National HIV/STI Programme. (2011). *HIV Epidemic Update: Facts & Figures 2011*. Retrieved from http://moh.gov.jm/wp-content/uploads/2015/03/HIV-Epidemic-Update-Facts-and-Figures-2011.pdf

Olukoga, I. A. (2004). Epidemiological Trends of HIV/AIDS in Jamaica. *Pan-American Journal of Public Health*, *15*(5), 358–363.

Padilla, M. (2007). *Caribbean pleasure industry: Tourism, sexuality, and AIDS in the Dominican republic*. Chicago, IL: The University of Chicago Press.

Padilla, M. B., & Castellanos, H. D. (2009). Touristic borderlands: Ethnographic reflections on Dominican social geographies. In F. Thomas, M. Haour-Knipe, & P. Aggleton (Eds.), *Mobility, sexuality, and AIDS* (pp. 91–107). Florence, KY: Routledge.

Plummer, D. (2013). Masculinity and risk: How gender constructs drive sexual risks in the Caribbean. *Sexuality Research and Social Policy*, *10*(3), 165–174.

Press, C. M. (1978).Reputation and respectability reconsidered: Hustling in a tourist setting. *Caribbean Issues*, *4*(1), 109–119.

Ragsdale, K., Digranseisco, W., & Pinkerton, S. D. (2006). Where the boys are: Sexual expectations and behaviour among young women on holiday. *Culture, Health & Sexuality*, *8*(2), 85–98.

Reddock, R. E. (2004). Interrogating Caribbean masculinities: An introduction. In R. E. Reddock (Ed.), *Interrogating caribbean masculinities: Theoretical and empirical analyses* (pp. xiii–xxxiv). Kingston: University of the West Indies Press.

Rogstad, K. E. (2004). Sex, sun, sea, and STIs: Sexually transmitted infections acquired on holiday. *BMJ*, *329*, 214–217.

Romero-Daza, N., & Freidus, A. (2008). Female tourists, casual sex, and HIV risk in Costa Rica. *Qualitative Sociology*, *31*(2), 169–187.

Schensul, S. L., Schensul, J. J., & LeCompte, M. D. (1999). Essential ethnographic methods: Observations, interviews, and questionnaires (Vol. 2). Lanham, MD: AltaMira Press.

Smith, V. L. (1989). *Hosts and guests: The anthropology of tourism*. Philadelphia, PA: University of Pennsylvania Press.

Statistical Institute of Jamaica. (2016, July 30, 2015). *Labour market & earnings*. Retrieved from http://statinja.gov.jm/LabourForce/NewLFS.aspx

Taylor, F. F. (1993). *To hell with paradise: A history of the Jamaican tourist industry*. Pittsburgh, PA: University of Pittsburgh Press.

The World Bank. (2016). *Overview: Jamaica*. Retrieved from http://www.worldbank.org/en/country/jamaica/overview

Thomas, M. (2005). 'What happens in Tenerife stays in Tenerife': Understanding women's sexual behaviour on holiday. *Culture, Health & Sexuality*, *7*(6), 571–584.

Thomas-Hope, E., & Jardine-Comrie, A. (2007). Valuation of environmental resources for tourism in small island developing states: Implications for planning in Jamaica. *International Development Planning Review*, *29*(1), 93–112.

UN Word Tourism Organization. (2015). *Tourism highlights, 2015 Edition*. Retrieved from http://www.e-unwto.org/doi/pdf/10.18111/9789284416899

Weisbrot, M. (2011, July 22, 2011). *Jamaica's crippling debt crisis must serve as a warning to Greece, News*. *The Guardian*, p. 3. Retrieved from http://www.guardian.co.uk/commentisfree/cifamerica/2011/jul/22/jamaica-debt-crisis

World Travel & Tourism Council. (2015). *Travel & Tourism: Economic Impact 2015, Jamaica*. Retrieved from https://www.wttc.org/-/media/files/reports/economic impact research/countries 2015/jamaica 2015.pdf

Yelvington, K. A. (1995). *Producing power: Ethnicity, gender, and class in a Caribbean workplace*. Philadelphia, PA: Temple University Press.

ABOUT THE AUTHORS

Lisa Marie Beiswenger is Ph.D. candidate in Anthropology at The Ohio State University. Her training includes advanced degrees in English, Literature, Media, and Cultural Studies, as well as a graduate interdisciplinary specialization in Folklore. She studies public markets, food culture, and commodity fetishism. For doctorate, she examines the importance of social networks among vendors and their customers as well as how vendors define success at Findlay Market in Cincinnati.

Riddhi Bhandari received her Ph.D. in anthropology from American University, Washington, DC. As an economic anthropologist, Riddhi's research explores how social networks and political systems intersect to impact economic lives in India's small towns and cities. Through her work, she emphasizes developing a theory of economic practice that studies everyday actions and interactions between social actors to understand prevalent economic formations. Currently, she is studying government policies that regulate gold loans in India to understand how ethics and jurisprudence intersect to shape an economic activity. She is also documenting the recent killing of the "Sugarcane Tigress" – a classified "man-eater" – to understand how state interventions impact human–animal relations in India.

Jeffrey H. Cohen, Ph.D. (1994, Anthropology, Indiana University), is Professor of anthropology at The Ohio State University. His research focuses on migration, economic development, and food in Oaxaca, Mexico, the Dominican Republic, Turkey and most recently China with support from the National Science Foundation, National Geographic Society, the Fulbright program, and TUBITAK (the Scientific and Technological Research Council of Turkey). His articles have appeared in *American Anthropologist*; *Anthropological Quarterly*, *Gastronomica*, *Human Organization*, *International Journal of Sociology*, *International Migration and Population*, *Space and Place*. His books include Cooperation and Community: *Economy and Society in Oaxaca* (1999), *The Culture of Migration in Southern Mexico* (2004) and with *Ibrahim Sirkeci*, *The Cultures of Migration: The Global Nature of Contemporary Movement* (2011) named an outstanding title by Choice Reviews for 2012. His most recent book is *Eating Soup without a Spoon: Anthropological Theory and Method in the Real World* (2015).

Hongyang Di <diyang@tamu.edu> is doctoral student in the Department of Agricultural Economics at Texas A&M University. She has also received a master's degree in economics from Texas A&M. Her research focus is on applied economics, especially nutrition and labor economics.

Edwins Laban Moogi Gwako is Full Professor of anthropology in the Department of Sociology and Anthropology and Chair of Curriculum Committee at Guilford College, North Carolina. He graduated from Washington University in St. Louis (M.A. and Ph.D. in Anthropology) and the University of Nairobi (M.A. in Anthropology) and has taught at Moi University (Kenya) and Washington University in St. Louis. At Guilford College, he was Chair of the Department of Sociology and Anthropology (2001–2007) and Chair of African American Studies Program (2008–2012). He is an Africanist economic anthropologist with special interest in small holder agricultural production, family and marriage and changing social norms in sub-Saharan Africa. His recent publications include "Exploring the interactions: Plot-level analysis of Maragoli women farmers' crop control and yields in Western Kenya" (*Research in Economic Anthropology*, Volume 36) and "Maragoli and Gusii farmers in Kenya: Strong collective action and high pro-social punishment" (Ensminger & Henrich (Eds.), *Experimenting with Social Norms: Fairness and Punishment in Cross-Cultural Perspective*, published by Russell Sage).

John S. Henderson is Professor of Anthropology at Cornell University. He holds an AB degree from Cornell and MPhil and PhD degrees from Yale. He has taught anthropology and archaeology at Cornell since 1971, and has served as Director of Cornell's Archaeology and Latin American Studies Programs. Henderson's interests center on early complex societies, especially how distinctions in status, wealth, and authority develop and how imagery and text are deployed to maintain and enhance them. Another set of interest revolves around identity – how the groups with which people associate themselves are reflected in archaeological remains. He has written extensively about these issues in the context of ancient Mexico and Central America. Henderson has authored or edited seven books, including *The World of the Ancient Maya*, a popular introduction to ancient Maya civilization. He has also written many articles for professional books and journals and popular magazines. Henderson's excavation experience has been mainly in Mexico and Central America, but he has also dug in the United States, Peru, Turkey, and Cyprus. His current research focuses the lower Ulúa river valley where he has directed many seasons of field research. He also participated in designing the archaeology section of the Museum of Anthropology and History in San Pedro Sula, Honduras.

Kathryn M. Hudson < khudson@buffalo.edu> is Instructor in the Department of Anthropology at the University at Buffalo and also a member of the

Department of Linguistics. Her research focuses primarily on mechanisms of identity construction and processes of visual and non-verbal communication, especially as they are reflected in the archaeological record, and on the documentation of endangered cultural and linguistic traditions. Her geographic foci include Central America, Mexico, and the southeastern United States.

Lauren C. Johnson is Assistant Professor and Coordinator of Diversity and Recruitment Initiatives in the College of Education at the University of North Georgia. She received her M.A. degree in TESOL from Teachers College, Columbia University and Ph.D. in Applied Anthropology from the University of South Florida. She currently teaches courses on the Social Foundations of Education and issues of diversity and inequality in education. Dr. Johnson has conducted anthropological research on issues of ethnicity and inequality, gender and sexuality, sex tourism, education, and diversity pedagogy. Her current research focuses on multicultural education, race/racism in teacher education, and social inequality in the Caribbean region.

Rodolfo Maggio is a social anthropologist currently working as postdoctoral researcher at the University of Oxford. He leads *Mothers: Early Intervention Ethics* (MO:EIE), an empirical research study about the social, political, and ethical dimensions of early intervention in maternal health and child development. He has conducted ethnographic research in a variety of cultural settings, including the metropolitan areas of Dublin, Rome and Prague, the suburbs of London, and the Asia-Pacific region. As part of his doctoral research, he conducted 13 months of fieldwork in an illegal settlement on the outskirts of Honiara, capital city of Solomon Islands. Residing with local families, he closely observed the concretion of ordinary ethics in their everyday dealing with moral dilemmas, confrontations, and tensions over the meaning and significance of their values. This has gained him an empirical understanding of how people construct, negotiate, and defend their sense of belonging, identity, and life trajectory.

Deborah Sick is Associate Professor of anthropology at the University of Ottawa. She received her Ph.D. from McGill University. Her research interests are in socioeconomic change, rural livelihoods, co-operatives, and resource management. She has conducted ethnographic research with small-scale farming families in Costa Rica and northern Mexico and with San Juan Southern Paiute basket weavers in Arizona. Her publications include *Farmers of the Golden Bean* (1999; updated 2008); *The Social Contexts and Consequences of Institutional Change in Common-Pool Resources Management* (2008), and *Rural Economies, Livelihoods, and Processes of Change in the 21st Century* (ed) (2014).

Serge Svizzero is Professor of economics in the Faculty of Law and Economics at the University of Reunion Island (France) since 1998. He has a Ph.D. in economics from the University of Nice Sophia-Antipolis (1994). He has published books and articles in academic outlets mainly related to economic globalization, macroeconomic analysis, and economic history. During the last five years, his research has focused on the economic analysis of prehistoric societies, and more specifically on the neolithization process. He was Vice-chancellor of the University of Reunion Island (2004–2008) and Deputy Director of International Affairs in the French National Research Institute for Development (2009–2011).

Tamar Diana Wilson is an independent researcher who has lived in Mexico since 1988. She has published articles on aspects of the informal economy in *Latin American Perspectives*, *Critique of Anthropology*, *Human Organization*, *Review of Radical Political Economics*, *North American Dialogue*, *Urban Anthropology*, and *Research in Economic Anthropology*. Several of those articles include considerations of peasants' migration into that economy. Her latest book is *Economic Life of Mexican Beach Vendors: Acapulco, Puerto Vallarta, and Cabo San Lucas* (2012, Lexington Press). Many of the 166 beach vendors interviewed for that book were either peasants themselves or sons and daughters of peasants.

Donald C. Wood <wood@med.akita-u.ac.jp> is Associate Professor in the Graduate School of Medicine, Akita University, Akita, Japan, where he has worked since completing a doctoral degree in cultural anthropology at the University of Tokyo in 2004. Prior to that, he studied anthropology under Norbert Dannhaeuser at Texas A&M University. He spent more than 15 years researching social conditions at the Hachirogata reclaimed land area in Akita Prefecture, which culminated in the publication of *Ogata-Mura: Sowing Dissent and Reclaiming Identity in a Japanese Farming Village*, by Berghahn Books in 2012 (released in paperback in October, 2015). He has also investigated tourism and the effects of depopulation in the Akita region, and was a contributor to the edited volume, *Japan's Shrinking Regions in the 21st Century* (Cambria, 2011). Recently he has been contributing articles to Kyoto Journal, and he self-published his first novel – *And if Strangers Come to Supper* – in May of 2015.

Shuru Zhong is doctoral candidate in the Department of Anthropology at Texas A&M University. As an economic anthropologist, she researches informal economies (e.g., street vendors), food production and trade, and urban everyday life. Her dissertation focus is the competition between traditional farmers' markets and modern supermarkets in China.

Laurel Zwissler is Assistant Professor of Religion at Central Michigan University, USA. She received her doctorate from the University of Toronto in the Centre for the Study of Religion and the Collaborative Program in Women and Gender Studies. Her book, *Cosmologies of Interconnection: Feminism, Religion and Activism in Toronto, Canada* (forthcoming with Anthropology of

North America Series, Lincoln: University of Nebraska Press), focuses on global justice activists and investigates contemporary interrelations between religion, gender, and politics, relating these to theoretical debates about empirical and ideal roles of religion in the public sphere. She is now building on this work with ethnographic research within the North American fair-trade movement.

INDEX

Printed and bound by CPI Group (UK) Ltd, Croydon, CR0 4YY

13/09/2026

14961058-0003